Other books in the series:

Religion in India
T.N. Madan (ed.)
(Oxford India Paperbacks)

Social Stratification
Dipankar Gupta (ed.)
(Oxford India Paperbacks)

Family, Kinship and Marriage in India
Patricia Uberoi (ed.)
(Oxford India Paperbacks)

Social Ecology
Ramachandra Guha (ed.)
(Oxford India Paperbacks)

Social Conflict
N. Jayaram and Satish Sabherwal (eds)

The Sociology of Formal Organizations
Abha Chaturvedi and Anil Chaturvedi (eds)

Politics in India
Sudipta Kaviraj (ed.)
(Oxford India Paperbacks)

The Village in India
Vandana Madan (ed.)
(Oxford India Paperbacks)

Methodology and Fieldwork
Vinay Kumar Srivastava (ed.)
(Oxford India Paperbacks)

SOCIOLOGY OF LAW

Oxford in India Readings in
Sociology and Social Anthropology

GENERAL EDITOR
T.N. MADAN

SOCIOLOGY OF LAW

Edited by
INDRA DEVA

OXFORD
UNIVERSITY PRESS

OXFORD
UNIVERSITY PRESS

YMCA Library Building, Jai Singh Road, New Delhi 110 001

Oxford University Press is a department of the University of Oxford. It furthers the
University's objective of excellence in research, scholarship, and education
by publishing worldwide in

Oxford New York

Auckland Cape Town Dar es Salaam Hong Kong Karachi Kuala Lumpur
Madrid Melbourne Mexico City Nairobi New Delhi Shanghai Taipei Toronto

With offices in

Argentina Austria Brazil Chile Czech Republic France Greece Guatemala
Hungary Italy Japan Poland Portugal Singapore South Korea Switzerland
Thailand Turkey Ukraine Vietnam

Oxford is a registered trade mark of Oxford University Press
in the UK and in certain other countries

Published in India
By Oxford University Press, New Delhi

© Oxford University Press, 2005

The moral rights of the author have been asserted
Database right Oxford University Press (maker)

First published 2005

ISBN 13: 978-0-19-567236-7
ISBN 10: 0-19-567236-4

Typeset in Agaramond 10.6/12.1 by Guru Typograph Technology,
Dwarka, New Delhi 110 075
Printed by De Unique, New Delhi 110018
Published by Manzar Khan, Oxford University Press
YMCA Library Building, Jai Singh Road, New Delhi 110 001

To

MY FATHER LATE DR JAGDAMBA PRASAD

a busy medical practioner who introduced me to
all round academic explorations through his masterly grip
over Sanskrit, Urdu, Persian, and Arabic literature;

MY MOTHER LATE PRIYAMVADA DEVI

who never went to school but was an inexhaustible treasure
of wise Sanskrit, Hindi, Urdu, and Persian verses that made
an indelible impression on my mind; and

MY ELDEST BROTHER DR PURNA DEVA

who is an eminent physician but in fact a teacher at heart;
he laid the foundations of my education.

Contents

Acknowledgements

The publishers wish to thank the following for permission to include excerpts in this volume:

Upendra Baxi for 'The Colonial Nature of the Indian Legal System', originally published in *The Crisis of the Indian Legal System*, New Delhi: Vikas Publishing House Pvt. Ltd, 1982.

J. Duncan M. Derrett for 'Administration of Hindu Law by the British', originally published in *Religion, Law and the State in India*, London: Oxford University Press, 1968.

V.R. Krishna Iyer for 'Law and the People', originally published in *Law and the People*, New Delhi: People's Publishing House, 1972; and 'Towards a Burgeoning Indian Jurisprudence of Social Action and Public Interest Litigation', originally published in *Indian Bar Review*, vol. 16, no. 2, 1989.

Krishna Kumar for 'Patterns for Criminal Justice amongst Some Tribes', originally published in *Journal of the Indian Law Institute*, vol. 12, no. 2, 1970.

J.S. Gandhi for 'Law as an Instrument of Change in India', originally published as 'Potentials and Parameters of Social Change through Law in Contemporary Indian Society', in A. Podgorecki, C. Whelan, and D. Khosla (eds), *Legal Systems and Social Systems*, London: Croom Helm, 1985.

Samuel Schmitthener for 'Development of the Legal Profession in India', originally published in *Indian Bar Review* vol. 13, nos 3 and 4, 1986.

K.L. Sharma for 'Legal Profession and Society: A Study of Lawyers and their Clients', originally published in S. K. Lal et al. (eds), *Readings in the Sociology of the Professions*, New Delhi: Gyan Publishing House, 1984.

Charles Morrison for 'Social Organization at the District Courts: Colleague Relationship among Indian Lawyers', originally published in

N. Jayaram and Satish Saberwal (eds), *Social Conflict*, New Delhi: Oxford University Press, 1996.

Donald Eugene Smith for 'Religion, Law, and Secularism', originally published in *India as a Secular State*, Princeton: Princeton University Press, 1967.

John H. Mansfield for 'Personal Laws or a Uniform Civil Code?' originally published in Robert D. Baird (ed.), *Religion and Law in Independent India*, New Delhi: Manohar Publishers, 1993.

Kavita Khory, 'The Shah Bano Case: Some Political Implications', originally published in Robert D. Baird (ed.), *Religion and Law in Independent India*, New Delhi: Manohar Publishers, 1993.

Marc Galanter, 'Pursuing Equality in a Land of Hierarchy', originally published in *Law and Society in Modern India*, New Delhi: Oxford University Press, 1989.

M.P. Singh for 'Jurisprudential Foundation of Reservations', originally published in *Indian Bar Review*, vol. 17, nos 3 and 4 and vol. 18, no. 1, 1990–1.

Ram Jethmalani for 'Mandal Revisited', originally published in *Indian Bar Review*, vols 17 and 18, 1990–1.

S.P. Sathe for 'Empowerment of Women: Legal Strategies', originally published in *Towards Gender Justice*, Mumbai: SNDT University, 1993.

Mahabaleshwar N. Morje for 'Public Interest Litigation', originally published in *Indian Bar Review*, vol. 15, no. 142, 1988.

Indra Deva and Shrirama for 'Growth of Traditional Legal System: The Perspective of Change Through the Ages', originally published as 'Judicial Values and Institutions in Indian Tradition', *ICSSR Research Abstracts Quarterly*, vol. 18, no. 1, 1979.

Yogendra Singh for 'Law and Social Change in India', originally published as 'Law and Social Change in India: A Sociological Perspective', *Relevant Sociology*, vol. 3, nos 1 and 2, 1986.

Peter G. Sack for 'Constitutions and Revolutions', originally published in *Constitutions and Revolutions*, Thiruvananthapuram: The Academy of Legal Publications, 1990.

Introduction

INDRA DEVA

In this introduction to the sociology of law in India we shall first consider the concept of law; then we shall briefly delineate the nature of sociology of law; its development in the West, and the state of this branch of sociology in India. After this we shall discuss the nature of the traditional Indian system of law and critically examine some of the current notions about it on the basis of the evidence of traditional Indian juridical texts. We shall then have a brief discussion on the impact of the British rule on the legal system in India. We shall not only deal with the direct consequences of the policies and measures adopted by British administrators but also have the occasion to consider the new indigenous forces that arose as a result of the catalytic effect of the British rule. This will be followed by a discussion of the state of the Indian legal system after independence and the problems that beset it. Finally, we shall briefly introduce the readings which are included in this book.

THE CONCEPT OF LAW

It is very difficult, if not impossible, to give a clear-cut definition of law. Mature thinkers like Max Radin have been compelled to come to the conclusion that 'those of us who have learned humility have given up the attempt to define law'.[1]

Hart too, in his book *The Concept of Law*, concedes that 'nothing concise enough to be recognized as a definition could provide a satisfactory answer'[2] to the question, 'What is Law?'. Instead of trying to answer this question, Hart goes on to analyse the resemblances and differences between law, coercion, morality as types of social phenomena.

One of the major difficulties in defining the concept of law arises from the fact that the Western conception tends to think of law in terms of its own institutions. It is inclined to conceptualize law in the framework of the modern centralized state and its instrumentalities. Such a conception is an impediment to the understanding of legal processes in non-modern social systems such as those of peasant civilizations and tribes. It tends to narrow down the vision to such an extent that even the need to enforce law in some societies is denied. As Malinowski puts it: 'By defining the forces of law in terms of central authority, courts, codes, and constables, we must come to the conclusion that law needs no enforcement in primitive community and is followed spontaneously.'[3]

Obviously, we should have a conception of law which has a wider and more comprehensive frame of reference. It seems that the concept of law provided by Cardozo sums up well the chief characteristics of law. Cardozo's definition of law,[4] contains four essential elements: (i) the normative element, (ii) the regularity element, (iii) courts, and (iv) enforcement. In this delineation also the terms 'courts' and 'enforcement' have to be interpreted so broadly as to cover the diverse kinds of institutional arrangements in different types of societies.

Sociologists consider law to be one of the several social codes. The primary function of social codes is to sustain the social order by upholding the basic values and norms of society. Besides law, social codes include religious codes, institutions, customs and rules of etiquette and manners. Each kind of social code is backed by its own type of sanctions. Any violation of religious codes is believed to result in supernatural sanctions. Social institutions, like the institution of marriage, are so established that they become a condition of behaviour in society. Violation of customs is punished by social disapproval and censor. Flouting of rules of etiquette of the group invites ridicule. Similarly, violation of laws is expected to lead to penalization or punishment by the state. Since the state alone has the legitimate power of violent punishment, the breaking of laws invites the ultimate sanctions which the society can inflict. In an extreme case, this can even be the sentence of death.

However, in order to have a concept of law comprehensive enough to be applicable to all kinds of social systems, including those of peasant and tribal cultures, the state too has to be defined in a broad sense. We need not think of the state only in its centralized form but as constituted by various institutions which have the authority to settle disputes and enforce their decisions.

SOCIOLOGY OF LAW

Sociology of law is the study of the relationship which the legal system of a society has with its other subsystems. The bonds of relationship between sociology and law are indeed deep and organic. Sociology deals with the study of social relationships, values, norms, and attitudes. All of these form the foundation of law. The mutual dependence of law and sociology has therefore to be given due recognition. As the established patterns of social relationships together with values and norms undergo a change, the law must also change. Otherwise a lag will be created which would generate tensions in the entire social system.

Law is the structured and crystallized form of norms and values. Its study can, therefore, provide a clue to the social values that are really enforced but remain hidden from the public eye. However, it cannot be taken for granted that there is always a real consensus on the basic values underlying the legal system among all sections of society. Though the legal system that prevails is binding on everyone, ingenious ways are found to circumvent it. Quite often the system is employed for functions which are far from those originally intended. The study of all such processes and mechanisms falls in the domain of sociology of law.

Sumner[5] has asserted that laws can never shape mores, and that the correspondence between the two is due to the fact that law is shaped by mores. However, in India today law is sought to be employed as a lever of basic social change, which implies that changes are sought to be brought about in some of the norms and values through such measures as enactment of social legislation and introducing modifications in personal laws. But this endeavour can hardly succeed without requisite sociological spadework. The prevailing attitudes among various sections of the people have to be objectively assessed and the possible points of resistance have to be identified as clearly as possible. Ways have to be devised for reducing or overcoming the obstacles. All this calls for systematic sociological research. Otherwise such pieces of legislation, although conceived with the best of intentions, tend to remain only on the statute book.

Sociology of law is still a growing branch, so its contours cannot be sharply demarcated. As Gurvitch puts it, 'the sociology of law still has no clearly defined boundaries. Its various exponents are not in agreement as to its subject, or the problems requiring solution, or its relations with the other branches of the study of law.'[6]

However, because of its importance both for the study of society and for a proper understanding of legal institutions and processes, it has come to stay and it is bound to develop further.

Initially there was some resistance to the development of sociology of law as a distinct field, both from the jurists and some sections of sociologists. The jurists of the 'analytical' school, who followed John Austin's view that law was the command of the sovereign, were in favour of confining their attention only to the laws put in place by the state. The jurists of the 'juridical empiricist' school endeavoured to encompass un-written and flexible law as well, particularly case law and customary law.

The jurists of both these viewpoints did not favour the idea of the study of law as part of the social system. On the other hand, some socio-logists too were averse to the development of sociology of law as a branch of their discipline for the fear that it would lead to entangling sociology in value judgment.

However, developments both in the fields of jurisprudence and socio-logy opened up the way for the emergence of the sociology of law, and 'the pickaxes of the two crew, each hallowing out its respective gallery, have finally met'. Of course, every discipline has its distinct focus, and it looks at the same phenomenon from its appropriate standpoint, but the interface between them yields fruit which neither of them can deliver alone. Sociology of law, being a branch of sociology, looks upon law as a subsystem of the sociocultural system as a whole.

Through the study of the prescriptions and prohibitions concretized in law, sociology is enriched by gaining insight into the operative values and attitudes. The analysis of the function of law adds to the understand-ing of the processes of social control.

Developments in juridical thinking have led to a growing concern for social relations in law. This concern in juridical thought has given birth to sociological jurisprudence, taking it out of the stifling confines of 'normative logicism'. Recognition of such dimensions in jurisprudence, as well as sociology, has brought to the fore the importance of sociology of law.

To sum up, it would be the best to quote Ehrlich's conclusion: 'At the present as well as at any other time, the centre of legal development lies not in legislation, nor in juristic science, nor in judicial decision, but in society itself.'[7]

There seems to be a need to build bridges between sociological and legal scholarship on the one hand and the judicial practice on the other. It is perhaps true that judges and eminent lawyers are so busy in day-to-day work that they do not have much time left for keeping abreast of the research and thinking in the social sciences and law. However, some way has to be found to remedy this situation. One possible avenue of pro-moting better interaction between scholarship and practice may be to appoint an eminent and perceptive law teacher to the position of a judge in the Supreme Court, or at least in a high court.

However, even among the researchers and scholars of various fields the interaction is not rich enough. It has been noted by sociologists of law that even in the USA the links between the faculties of law and sociology are rather weak. This seems to be all the more true in India. Such insulation impedes cross-fertilization of ideas, and is a big stumbling block in the growth of sociology of law.

Development of Sociology of Law in the West

Like sociology itself, sociology of law grew up in the West. Among the pioneers was Sir Henry Sumner Maine, who made a pathbreaking contribution through his *Ancient Law: Its Connection with the Early History of Society and its Relation to Modern Ideas*, which was published in 1861. Through this work Maine laid the foundations of comparative laws. He brought out certain similarities between Hindu and Irish laws. He compared the 'village communities' in various civilizations. Such communities were based on collective landed property and diffused sovereignty, and he regarded them as 'germs' of all juridical development. Maine thought that he could build a general law of juridical evolution through his studies in comparative history: 'We may say that the movement of progressive societies has hitherto been a movement from status to contract.'

W.G. Summer's emphasis on 'folkways and mores' as the basic concern of sociology can be considered to be the first step towards the issues in sociology of law in Anglo-American sociology. According to Sumner mores are those folkways in which the regulative and imperative element is concentrated. He says: 'Institutions and laws are produced out of mores.' His major work, *Folkways: A Study of the Sociological Importance of Usages, Manners, Customs and Morals*, was first published in 1906.

The American sociologist, E.A. Ross, made a remarkable contribution towards the growth of sociology of law through his series of articles on the theory of social control, which were published in the *American Journal of Sociology* from 1896 to 1898.

The great French sociologist, Emile Durkheim, was one of the founders of sociology of law. He made an important contribution to the development of systematic sociology of law by studying the relationship of law to the forms of sociality in his famous work, *The Division of Labour in Society*,[8] which was first published in 1893 in French as *Division du Travail Social*. In this work he relates kinds of law with forms of sociality. He says: 'The visible symbol of social solidarity (conceived as a solidarity in fact, that is, a form of sociality) is the Law,' and adds: 'Hence we can be sure of finding all the essential varieties of social solidarity reflected in the Law.'

The outstanding German sociologist, Max Weber, paved the way for the development of sociology of law through his refinement of the sociological method.[9] According to Max Weber, casual explanation in sociology

involves interpretative understanding of meanings, which make it possible
to construct frameworks of 'ideal types' within which casual explanation
is possible. Pursuing this method, Weber studies the various legitimate
systems constructed by jurists in Roman, feudal, capitalistic, and other
societies. He also deals with the question of how these systems of norms
are reflected in social behaviour.

Anthropologists like Bronislaw Malinowski facilitated the widening
of the perspective of sociology of law through their study of law in primitive cultures. Malinowski, who enriched anthropology by theoretical
formulations as well as ethnographic work, made a significant contribution to sociology of law through his famous work, *Crime and Custom
in Savage Society*, which appeared in 1926. This book is based on intensive
fieldwork among the tribals of Trobriand Islands which lie in the western
Pacific Ocean.

Malinowski argues that law should not be seen as working necessarily
through modern types of courts or police. Nor does he believe that the
use of sanctions of legitimatized physical coercion is a necessary condition
for the existence of law. He vigorously refuted the proposition that primitive man spontaneously obeyed custom, or that there was an undifferentiated cake of custom in savage society. Malinowski tries to show through
his fieldwork among the Trobriand islanders that law does exist in tribal
societies in a distinct form. It is not obeyed spontaneously. There are
many breaches too. The binding force, according to Malinowski, is reciprocity. Everyone has to render adequate services to others, lest others
may withdraw or reduce their services for him.

E. Adamson Hoebel has made a valuable contribution to sociology of
law through his book, *The Law of Primitive Man: A Study in Comparative
Legal Dynamics*.[10] Besides discussing the nature of primitive law and its
relationship with religion and magic, Hoebel gives a picture of primitive
law as it obtains among the Eskimo, the Ifugao, the Comanche, the
Kiowa and Cheyenne, the Trobriand islanders, and the Ashanti. His
reference to the four primary functions of law is particularly remarkable.
These functions are (i) defining relationships, (ii) taming naked force
and directing power to the maintenance of order, (iii) the disposal of
trouble cases as they arise, and (iv) redefining relations between individuals
and groups as conditions of life change.[11]

Sociology of Law in India

Sociology of law has not developed adequately as an organized branch
of learning in India. Most sociologists and perceptive jurists who have

endeavoured to make a headway in this field have been compelled to come to this conclusion.

Among the sociologists in India, J.S. Gandhi is one who has devoted almost his entire academic career to explorations in this area. He too comes to the conclusion that 'One needs to look at "Sociology of Law in India" in processual, elemental terms, because no such discipline has been developed or has even evolved in India formally bearing this title as it has in the West.' It is remarkable that this is the opening sentence of his 'Status Report on the Sociology of Law in India', in *Developing Sociology of Law: A Worldwide Documentary Enquiry*.[12]

Similarly, Veena Das, in her Trend Report on Sociology of Law in the ICSSR Survey of Research in Sociology and Social Anthropology concludes: 'The subject is in its infancy in India and there are no common issues that have been debated and discussed by sociologists of law working in India.'[13] Her survey of this field amply brings out the paucity of research work in India on vital aspects of sociology of law.

Perceptive writers on law have also noted the inadequacy of the study of the implications of legal processes for society in India. Upendra Baxi, in the 'Conclusion' to his book, *Towards a Sociology of Indian Law*, says: 'At almost every point in this survey, we have lamented the paucity of sociological research into legal processes and institutions.'[14]

Marc Galanter, in his excellent work *Competing Equalities*,[15] in which he incisively discusses various aspects of the policy of 'compensatory discrimination' (reservations) in India, laments on more than a dozen occasions the dearth of varifiable facts based on empirical research on the real effect of this policy.

There have, however, been quite a few studies on the legal profession and social relationships in the courts by sociologists and anthropologists. Similarly, there has been discussion about the reservation policy and the issue of having a common civil code. Judicial activism too has drawn attention recently. The relationship between law and social change has also been studied. Representative writings on all the above aspects, as well as incisive articles on the functioning of Indian judicial system and its implications for society, will be found in this six-part book.

Like the discipline of sociology of which it is a branch, sociology of law developed originally in the West. Its development in India does not correspond in all respects to the shape that it took in the West. One of the most prominent instances of this is the singularly stunted growth of its branch known as 'judicial behaviour'. This branch of sociology of law was among the first to engage the attention of sociologists in the West, particularly in America.

In their study of the behaviour of the judges the sociologists in the USA were not prepared to confine themselves only to that part of behaviour which is regarded as respectable or legitimate. The sociologists of law tried to proble into the extralegal sources of the courts' own conceptions of fair play. They also investigated such factors as the social background of the judges, their socialization, and the values and attitudes imparted through their training in the profession.

This line of research in the field of sociology of law does not seem to have flourished in India. There is a conspicuous dearth of material concerning this aspect. One reason for this may be the pronounced sensitivity of the judges in India for any imputation of extrajudicial influence on their judgments. There are instances when even the general denunciations of the system were taken to constitute contempt. Recently, a luminary like Arundhati Roy, the renowned writer and social activist, was charged with contempt of court and punished for criticizing a judgment. Such instances could discourage the sociologists of law in India from trying to relate judgments with the social and personal propensities of the judges.

The general feeling all over the world has been that the judiciary is usually conservative. Of course, there are many honourable exceptions to this sweeping observation. In India there are some glittering examples of progressive judges like Justice P.N. Bhagwati and Justice V.R. Krishna Iyer. Many sociological factors seem to have contributed to the frequently observed conservative inclinations of the judges. Judges, particularly at the higher levels of the judiciary, come mostly from the upper-middle class. The successful lawyers earn huge incomes, and come in day-to-day contact with well-to-do clients, such as big businessmen and industrialists, who alone can pay their high fees. Lawyers who are elevated to the position of judges of the higher courts generally belong to this category. Even those lawyers who do not come from affluent classes but have high ambition, tend to identify and interact with successful and rich members of their profession. Thus their anticipatory socialization and reference group behaviour make them prone to think and act in the same way as the well-to-do people.

Persons who suffer injustice or injury would turn to the courts for redressal only if they have sufficient faith in the prevailing system of law. It seems that in India the level of confidence in the judicial system, and the esteem in which lower levels of courts are held (where most cases have to be filed in the first instance) is not very high. It appears that most people are scared of going to the court. What is worse, some mischievous and dishonest persons make use of the complicated, expensive, and dilatory nature of the current judicial system to perpetuate injustice on innocent people. It is commonly held that in rural as well as urban areas the judicial system is often used by those who have a strong foothold in the courts for harassing their opponents, or anyone else who dares to protest against their misuse of power.

But to assess the veracity of such perceptions, systematic research in the area of sociology of law is required. This kind of research may also provide some clue to the factors which are responsible for lack of faith in the judicial system, and bring out facts which can help to remove or reduce them. Unfortunately, it appears that adequate research in this respect has so far not been undertaken in India.

Since the courts, especially the Supreme Court, have the right to quash any enactment or any executive order, which in its judgment violates the Constitution, the fundamental rights, or human rights, the judiciary works as a check on unbridled moves of the legislature and the mobocracy, and on the executive. Courts can therefore find ways to provide succour to the deprived, the underprivileged, and the disabled, when the legislative and executive arms of the state fail to do this.

Fortunately, the Supreme Court of India has started taking steps in this direction. For example, recently the Supreme Court ruled that there is no reason why so many people should go without food when government godowns are overflowing with food grains. This is indeed a laudable move. However, it may be suggested that such praiseworthy intentions of the honourable Supreme Court would have better chances of successful fulfilment if they were aided by those who have systematic knowledge of social conditions and the know-how of social science research techniques.

The degree of success in the implementation of laws and efficiency of the functioning of the legal system in India do not seem to have been studied systematically and adequately by the sociologists so far. Nor has the impact of social legislation been studied empirically. One does not know for sure how much use has been made of the innovative provisions of the Hindu Marriage Act 1955 or those of the Special Marriage Act 1954. We do not either have reliable facts about the degree of achievement of the objective of the Hindu Succession Act 1956, which was primarily meant to provide an equal share to the daughter in the property of the father. It is well known that the father often executes a will so as to deprive daughters of any share in his property. The actual impact of the Untouchability Offences Act 1955 has also not been adequately assessed in urban or rural areas on an empirical basis.

In a sociological perspective not only is the degree of achievement of the objectives of an enactment to be assessed, but also its non-intended consequences, including possible dysfunctions. For instance, it is sometimes alleged by officials that their subordinates belonging to the Scheduled Castes often shirk work and do not carry out their orders; and when they are reprimanded for this, they threaten them with filing a complaint in a police station under the Untouchability Offences Act, levelling the charge that they have been abused and harassed because of belonging to a depressed caste. The officials allege that because of such threats of facing dire consequences under the provisions of this law they cannot get work done or enforce discipline in their offices. But this is hearsay. How far such things are really happening can be reliably known only through sociological investigation. It is also a possibility that such charges emanate from upper-caste prejudice. What is the efficacy and what are the consequences of this and other such enactments can be revealed only by serious sociological research. Without such study, mere enactment of laws with pious intentions may remain meaningless, and at times may even be detrimental.

Establishing a meaningful and efficient communication network which connects the legislature, the judiciary, and the public is also an essential task in which work in the field of sociology of law can contribute a great deal. One often finds the legislative, the executive, and the judicial wings of the state working at cross-purposes. Sometimes such things happen because of genuine differences of opinion. These differences in the perspectives of the three wings of the state in the formulation of laws, in their enforcement, and in judging the fairness involved in their execution, are also areas which are important and to which sociological research can make some contribution. The perspectives of those who man the three wings of the state are bound to differ because they represent varying interests and tasks. The legislators are worried about the political implications of the law that they frame, those in administrative positions have to run the government, and the judiciary is concerned about the questions of justice and legitimacy.

However, there are some vital gaps in the communication process also. This is true not only of communication between the legislature and the judiciary, but more importantly between law making and judicial action on the one hand, and the public on the other. Neither are the people adequately aware of the laws and legal procedures, nor are the legislature and judiciary sensitive to the perceptions and sentiments of the common people. The level of knowledge of the public regarding the basic laws of the land is very low. Unfortunately, this is true not only of the rural folk but also of a large number of the so-called 'educated' people. When such are the social facts the oft-repeated admonition that ignorance of law is no excuse sounds meaningless. The real need is to have some effective institutional arrangement for communicating basic information about the prevailing laws and legal procedures. It would also be desirable to give some information to the public regarding the essential portions of the laws that are still on the anvil; and to have their feedback so that the laws may be shaped in accordance with the wishes and requirements of the people.

Such a two-way process of communication between the public and the decision makers is indispensable both for the health of the legal system and for the proper functioning of democracy. The decision makers in this context include members of the judiciary, legislators, and officials who execute the laws. All the three have to be adequately aware of the inclinations and feelings of various sections of society. It is a moot point in what sense and how far the legislators represent the people.

The real opinion of various segments of society can be found out only with the help of systematic sociological research. To mention one example, it was widely believed not only in the political circles but also by knowledgeable legal commentators that the 'Muslim opinion' was strongly opposed to the verdict of the Supreme Court allowing the right of maintenance to a divorced Muslim woman, Shah Bano, from her former husband.[16] However, empirical research work which was carried out among Muslim women in Agra soon after the enactment of the law reversing this judgment revealed that the vast majority of the Muslim women, who were predominantly uneducated and non-working, were of the view that Shah Bano should have got maintenance from her former husband.

Obviously, no systematic attempt was made to assess the opinion of common Muslim women on a matter that primarily concerned this section of society. The views of those who claimed to be the representatives of the Muslims were accepted on their face value as expressing Muslim opinion as a whole. Such distortions are bound to occur unless proper attention is given to systematic sociological research while enacting laws, implementing them, and deciding matters related with them.

It may also be pointed out that those who vociferously claim to represent the entire community, either Hindu or Muslim, are usually extremists. And often they have a political axe to grind. If their claims of having the monopoly of representing the views of all the people of their community are accepted without empirical verification, this can pose a serious threat to national integration and social progress.

Similarly, the level of success of the constitutional provisions and enactments for the amelioration of the lot of the depressed classes and tribal communities has to be evaluated on an empirical basis through sociological research. The non-intended consequences and possible dys-functions of such measures have to be systematically investigated and analysed. The uproar among the urban middle classes against the re-commendations of the Mandal Commission envisaging reservations in services and educational institutions for the members of the Other Back-ward Classes (OBCs) may be recalled in this context.

The study of the attitudes of various sections of society have great importance. In addition to this, certain socio-economic realities which have vital linkages with enactments and measures deserve sociological investigation. It is well known, for instance, that certain castes included among the OBCs in various parts of the country possess substantial land-holdings. They are usually industrious and upwardly mobile. Some em-pirical studies have shown that as compared to the traditional upper castes their landholdings have appreciably increased after India's inde-pendence. It is these castes which take to commercial agriculture more readily and employ people belonging to the Scheduled Castes (SCs) as farm labourers on a large scale. Not unexpectedly, many of the atrocities against the people of the depressed castes are caused by the clash of inte-rest between the landless labourers who usually belong to the SCs, and the enterprising landowners belonging to the OBC category.

It may appear that in post-independence India blatant cases of atrocities against the SCs have been committed largely by persons be-longing to the middle castes, and not so much by those of traditional uppermost caste, the Brahmins. It needs sociological research to reveal whether providing additional administrative and political clout to these castes, through measures like reservations in government services for the OBCs, would have the effect of accentuating such clashes and atrocities.

The people belonging to the depressed castes have suffered injustice, humiliation, and exploitation for thousands of years. The bulk of the people of these castes cannot, therefore, be legitimately expected to com-pete on an equal footing with the upper-caste persons. It seems proper and just to have initially some reservations in educational institutions and government services for them, so as to raise their educational level and capability to bring them eventually at par with the upper- and middle-caste people. Provisions for such reservation have been made in the Indian Constitution and through various enactments. Marc Galanter uses the appropriate term 'compensatory discrimination' for this policy.[17]

However, for the success of these laws and the measures emanating from them, systematic sociological research is indispensable. It has to be assessed empirically how far the really deprived, exploited, and dis-abled sections of these depressed castes are getting the benefit of these enactments and measures, and what portion of the benefits envisaged for them is being cornered by those small sections of these castes which have already achieved educational and economic upliftment comparable to the people belonging to the upper castes.

It seems that those SCs who had the means and were in a position to derive benefits from reservations have already gained sufficiently. They have been enjoying such benefits through more than one generation. They have shed their age-old handicap and have succeeded in entering the middle classes. Their educational level and standard of living are not appreciably different from those of the other middle-class people who may belong to the upper castes. Yet they continue to derive the same benefits which were meant for the really downtrodden. From the socio-logical viewpoint, the basic objection to this situation is not that they have an unfair advantage over the upper caste people with whom they compete, but that they deprive the truly deserving depressed and exploited SCs of the benefits which were actually meant for them. This is why the Supreme Court has ruled that the 'creamy layer' among the castes which come under the purview of reservations should be excluded from such benefits. This entire issue is an appropriate subject for deep and systematic study by the sociologists of law. Among female agricultural labourers the overwhelming majority are SC women. Their life is hard and their wages are very low. Such conditions prevail in the country even now.

Sociology of law has a part to play also with regard to planning of re-forms in the legal system. This is a vexed but pressing problem. Although the reports of the successive Law Commissions and the writings of judicial luminaries throw up a number of worthwhile ideas, extensive sociological research in the field seems necessary for the successful implementation of the suggestions that are made.

For example, Justice V.R. Krishna Iyer, who has been a member of the Law Commission besides being a judge of the Supreme Court and a great champion of radical reform in the present judicial system, has vigorously advocated the necessity of giving legal aid to the poor and real power to village panchayats. The objectives of both these proposals are indeed laudable. But if the intended goals are to be truly reached, a good deal of sociological investigation of ground realities will have to be undertaken. Some pilot projects may also have to be undertaken to find out the efficacy of various models. Without such research some unforeseen dysfunctions may emerge.

For instance, it has been reported that in some places the schemes of legal aid to the poor have served only to provide a captive clientele of poor people to the worthless lawyers who could not otherwise find any clients. One can easily imagine how the cases of the poor are being pleaded by such lawyers. Similarly, giving real power to the village panchayats can have many pitfalls. As the study of Oscar Lewis brought out a long time ago, villages are rife with contending factions.[18] Since then faction fights have become much more bitter due to factors like frequent elections. If the power of the village panchayat goes to the hands of one faction, the plight of those in the other can be easily imagined.

It is also a reality that because of the overall failure of worthwhile land reforms in most parts of the country, distribution of landownership is still far from equitable. This combines with some other factors like caste to make one section dominant over all others in the village. It is not unlikely that most of the power of the village panchayats is grabbed by this dominant section directly or indirectly for its own benefit and to the detriment of the majority of the people.

This is not to say that such proposals should not be taken in hand. All that is means is that research in the field of sociology of law should be made an integral part of legal reform. Empirical sociological research is required for making available to the decision makers reliable data on the basis of which possible bottlenecks may be avoided and obstacles to legal reform surmounted.

In May 2003, the Delhi High Court made the observation that the anti-dowry law is being misused and that 'It is hitting the foundation of marriage itself and has not proved so good for the health of the society at large'. Such conclusions can hardly be based on the evidence of a few isolated cases that have apparently not been selected on the basis of sound sampling methods. The extent of veracity in this and similar observations can be reliably known only by carrying out systematic sociological research through the case study and social survey methods.

Traditional Indian Law

Traditional Indian law and legal system have not remained the same through the ages.[19] It is true that the Indian cultural tradition has maintained a remarkable continuity. But despite this continuity it has undergone tremendous changes through the three thousand years and more of its existence. Insofar as the legal system is a part of the sociocultural system, this applies to law and the legal system as well. Unfortunately, this dynamics of Indian society and culture has not received the attention that it deserves.[20] The shastras or the Sanskrit texts are usually treated as the source of the classical Hindu tradition, but their content is presented in such a manner that an impression is created that all of them refer to the same sociocultural system. This is far from true. The *Ṛgveda* was composed around 1500 BC, if not earlier. And the later *Smṛtis* of Nārada, Bṛhaspati, and Kātyayāna, which are known as the grand trio of Indian jurisprudence and mark its zenith, were composed from the fourth to the sixth century AD. This makes a good 2000 years of Indian civilization. The fact is that Indian jurisprudence continued to grow for centuries even after the later *Smṛtis* were composed, through numerous commentaries and digests which were not mere explanations of earlier texts but embodied substantial development of traditional law. How effective these commentaries have been can be easily seen from the way that the commentaries of Vijnyāneśvara (*Mitākṣara*) and Jimūtavāhana (*Dāyubhāga*) have held till recent times for Hindu succession law.

The contents of traditional Sanskrit texts are often presented without reference to the times in which they were composed, the ideological and economic forces that shaped them, and the segment of the society that brought them into being. In this way the picture that is presented is artificial. It is made up of different, and often discordant bits. It does not represent any real sociocultural era. Serious attempts towards a truly sociological interpretation which relate the text with the social context, have rarely been made. The monumental six-volume *History of Dharmaśāstra* which is the product of the sustained hard work of the towering scholar, P.V. Kane, does meticulously put together the content of various *Dharmaśāstras*,[21] but it does not relate their content to the social forces at work in those times, nor to the sociocultural background.

The traditional Sanskrit texts which expound the classical Hindu law are the *Dharmaśāstras*. They include the *Dharmasutras*, which are believed to have been composed during the sixth century BC, and the *Smṛtis*. The *Manusmṛti* is the first among the line of the *Smṛti* texts. This work is appropriately attributed to Manu, the primeval father, for it was the *Manusmṛti* which laid the foundation of the Hindu social system as we know it today. Before that the formidable impact of Buddhism had shattered the ancient Vedic tradition. The *Smṛtis* are attributed to Vedic seers, which seems to be a device to relate that emerging ideology to the Vedas, though in fact a lot in religion and society had changed since the Vedic times.[22]

Designating the texts expounding law as *Dharmaśāstras* clearly indicates that traditional Indian law is closely related with dharma. As many great scholars have shown, dharma is a very comprehensive concept. It is applicable to nature as well as people. For instance, it is the dharma (physical property) of fire to burn things; and learning and performance of rituals are the dharma (duty) of the Brahmins. Naturally, the term dharma is employed in different contexts in a variety of meanings. One of the meanings of dharma is law. The most sophisticated texts of Hindu jurisprudence like the *Nāradasmṛti* and *Kātyāyanasmṛti* term the court of law as *dharmāsna* or *dharmādhikaraṇa*. Law is one of the aspects of dharma.

Robert Lingat's highly admired work, *The Classical Law of India*,[23] is undoubtedly scholarly. But some of his views are debatable and seem to require further thought. For instance, he says that *Dharmaśāstra*s obviously are not codes, 'there never was in India . . . a power to pass legislation, in our sense of the word, at least on matters of private law'. Lingat says that the *Dharmaśāstra*s 'offered some framework for judicial reasoning'[24] and it was only through their interpretation that a true judicial science began in India.[25] Similarly he says in the conclusion of his book: 'The precepts of *smṛti*s are not an authority because in them was seen the expression of law in the sense in which that word is used in natural sciences, a law which rules human activity. . . . But it has no constraining power by itself. It puts itself forward, it shows the way one should follow, but it does not impose that way.'[26]

Such statements do not appear to be in conformity with the real content of various *Dharmaśāstra*s and *Smṛti*s. For example, the *Smṛti*s of Nārada, Bṛhaspati, and Kātyāyana lay down meticulously and in great detail the law concerning a wide variety of matters, the procedure to be followed by the courts, and specify precisely the quantum of punishment for different types of offences.[27] In the *Nāradasmṛti* and *Bṛhaspatismṛti* lawsuits are termed as *vyavahāra*.

It would suffice here to mention just the names of the eighteen titles of disputes (*vyavahārapada*s) described by Nārada: (i) *Ṛṇadān* (recovery of debt); (ii) *Nikṣepa* (deposits); (iii) *Sambūyasamutthāna* (partnership); (iv) *Dattapradānika* (resumption of gift); (v) *Abhuyupetyaśuruṣā* (breach of contract of service); (vi) *Vetanasyānapākarma* (non-payment of wages); (vii) *Asvāmivikraya* (sales effected by another than the rightful owner); (viii) *Vikriyasampradāna* (non-delivery of sold chattel); (ix) *Kritānuśaya* (rescission of purchase); (x) *Samayasyānapākarma* (transgression of compact); (xi) *Kṣetrajavivāda* (boundary dispute); (xii) *Strīpuṅsayoga* (duties of the husband and the wife towards each other); (xiii) *Dāyabhāga* (law of inheritance); (xiv) *Sāhasa* (heinous offence); (xv) *Vākpāruṣya* (abuse); (xvi) *Daṇḍapāruṣya* (assaults); (xvii) *Dyūtasamāhavaya* (gambling); (xviii) *Prakirṇaka* (miscellaneous).[28]

The *Smṛti* texts discuss elaborately all aspects of each of these wide variety of disputes and the grounds on which each should be decided.

The procedure which has to be followed in lawsuits has also been described elaborately in the *Smṛti*. Nārada declares that every trial has four stages: in the first stage the facts of the dispute are received; in the second the appropriate title of law in which the dispute falls should be ascertained; in the third the pleadings and evidence should be examined; and only after that a decision should be given. The details of the procedure in all the four major stages of trial are discussed meticulously in the *Smṛtis*. Plaint and its defects, issuing of summons, the reply in defence and its defects, adducing of proof, documents and their types, possession, witnesses, and circumstantial evidence are treated in great detail.[29] The quantum of punishment for each offence is clearly laid down. Similarly, the composition of the court and the duties of the judge (*prādvivāk*) and the members of the court (*sabhya*s) are carefully discussed. Kātyāyana describes the hall of justice as 'the place where the lawsuits are tried in accordance with the rules of Dharmaśāstras.'[30]

It is, therefore, difficult to agree with Lingat's observation that the *Dharmaśāstras* only 'offered some framework for judicial reasoning' or that 'the precept of *Smṛti* only puts itself forwarded, it shows the way one should follow, but it does not impose that way'. What the *Smṛti*s ordain does not seem to be essentially different from what the law does today. The *Bṛhaspatismṛti*[31] and the *Kātyāyanasmṛti*[32] state that lawsuits originate over disputes on wealth or injury. This is quite close to the modern distinction between civil and criminal cases.

It is true that in the Indian tradition the king could not lay down the law; nor did the legislative bodies for enacting laws exist. But the *Dharmaśāstras*, particularly the *Smṛti*s, laid down the law, and the king and the court of justice had to conform to it.

In fact the king is enjoined not even to decide himself single-handedly. Kātyāyana states that the king should dispense justice with the help of the judges, ministers, learned Brāhmaṇas, the *purohita* and sabhyas.[33] Nārada also says that the king should take into account the views of his chief judge as well as the rules of *Dharmaśāstras* while trying the lawsuits.[34] In certain matters, where texts are not available, the customs of the country should be depended upon. But in any case the king should not take the responsibility of deciding suits on his single self. Kātyāyana points out the evil results of deciding suits by the king according to his own will.

It is often said that the precepts of *Dharmaśāstras* were not really operative in the settling of disputes. However, there is evidence to show that courts did follow the rules laid down by the *Smṛti*s. In the famous play, the *Mṛcchakaṭikam* written by Śūdraka, the case of the thief follows, in almost every detail, the same legal procedure as laid down in the *Nāradasmṛti*.

Of course, all the disputes were not decided in the king's court or in the court of the judge designated by the king in accordance with the rules of *Dharmaśāstras*. This was neither practicable nor desirable. The *Dharmaśāstras* too do not ordain this. Nārada, Bṛhaspati, and Kātyāyana describe many other institutions which decide the disputes. These are *kulāni* or family gatherings of agnatic and cognatic relatives, *pūga* or councils, *śreṇi* or corporations of traders or artisans, *gaṇa* or assemblies of Brāhmaṇās. Two more courts have been mentioned: one headed by the judge who has been appointed by the king and another headed by the king himself. These courts are arranged in the descending order of importance, with each court being superior to the one preceding it. The first three forms of private arbitration are quite close to the modem panchayats.[35] Kātyāyana also mentions pūga, śreṇi, and gaṇa. Pūga refers to one village or city consisting of different caste and professions; śreṇi to guilds of artisans or association of persons having the same trade though they may belong to different castes; and gaṇa to groups of Brāhmaṇās.[36] Kātyāyana also quotes Bṛhaspati saying that these and other types of groups have been called by Bṛhaspati as *varagas*.[37] Bṛhaspati says that *kulas*, śreṇis and gaṇas which function in the kings' knowledge can decide disputes, excepting criminal (sāhasa) lawsuits.

The *Smṛti* writers have given great importance to local usage. Kātyāyana explicitly says that the disputes of residents of the same country or the same capital or the same hamlet of cowherds and of the same town and village should be decided by their own conventional usage. But when disputes arise between others, the decision must be in accordance with the sacred texts.[38] Bṛhaspati ordains that the disputes of husbandmen, craftsmen such as carpenters, artisans such as painters, moneylenders, guilds, dancers, sects, such as *paśupatas*, and criminal tribes should be decided by their own conventions and usages. The trials of foresters should be conducted in forests, soldiers should be tried in military courts and *sarthas* or members of caravans and traders should be tried in their own courts.[39]

The overall evidence of the *Smṛti* texts shows an admirably practical approach of balancing the demands of the custom and the requirements of various professional, ethnic, territorial groups on the one hand, and the dicta of the *Dharmaśāstras* on the other. There also is a palpable endeavour to creatively harmonize the diverse sets of norms.

IMPACT OF BRITISH RULE

Many writers[40] on the influence of British rule on the legal system in India have rightly concluded that it has brought into being the Anglo-Hindu and Anglo-Muslim laws. It has also been noted that this change is marked by a decline in the authority of customary laws and the traditional decentralized institutions that dealt with such laws. It led to an ascendancy of the elite (high-culture) laws over the laws prevalent among the common folk; codification of laws, and the requirement of Western type of proof even for the customs. It resulted in stagnation of customary laws as well as those contained in the shastras. The emphasis shifted from the group to the individual in all matters related with law and justice; and the mobility of property increased radically, so that land became a marketable commodity bringing about unforeseen changes in the life of the village community. Most writers tend to explain all this transform ation primarily on the basis of the direct influence of various measures taken by the British rulers.

From a sociological angle, however, it seems that these changes were a product of two different, but related, sets of social forces. One set of these forces was undoubtedly constituted by the policies and measures adopted by the British administrators; but there was another indigenous set of forces as well. This latter set of social forces was constituted by the various sociocultural and religious movements which were led by the urban middle class that had emerged with the impact of the British rule in India. This set of forces too may be considered to have come into being because of British rule but it was not a consequence of the will of the British rulers. There was a sort of catalytic effect. Indeed some of such movements openly opposed the British rule and played an important part in mobilizing public opinion against it. We shall discuss briefly the influence of both these sets of social forces.

We shall first see how the attitudes, policies, and measures adopted by the British rulers led to the development of the Anglo- Hindu and Anglo-Muslim law. The early British rulers included some persons who had a genuine curiosity regarding the indigenous law. At the same time they did not consider it expedient to impose their own law in full on the natives. This is brought out clearly in Section 23 of Warren Hastings's Judicial Plan of 1772:

> In suits regarding inheritance, marriage, caste and other religious usages and institutions, the laws those of the Shashter with regard to the Gentoos will be

invariably adhered to; and on all such occasions, Maulivis or Brahmins shall
respectively attend the Courts to expound the law and they shall sign the
report and assist in passing the decrees.

Besides associating Pandits and Maulivis in decision making by the courts,
the British administrators commissioned Pandits to compile and prepare
digests of shastric laws. The most well known among these is *Colebrooke's
Digest*. It is an English version of the enunciation of Hindu law by a
Pandit of that time.

It is not surprising that the Hindu and Muslim laws that were formulated and enforced by the British rulers did not really conform to the
genuine content of the texts. To a certain extent the Englishmen could
not understand fully these traditions and introduced their own conceptions into them. But many of the changes were the products of deliberate
readaptation.

The British rulers did yield some space to usages and customs. But
their transformation into some sort of laws to be enforced by courts di-
vested them of their flexibility and amenability to evolve according to
circumstances. Obviously, the British administrators did not find it convenient to take into account the myriad diverse customs that prevailed
among the innumerable castes and localities. They, therefore, gave primacy to the laws supposed to be propounded by the *Dharmaśāstra*s and
the Shariat. This gave the elite or high-culture laws an upper hand over
the customs and usages that the common folk followed.

But in addition to the measures taken by the British administrators,
British rule had the catalytic effect of giving rise to a modern urban
middle class in India. The concentrated impact of modern forces which
had developed in the West over centuries gave a strong momentum to
this class for breaking away from medieval ideas and practices. Like the
fourteenth- and the fifteenth-century Renaissance in Europe which marked the rejection of the styles and thought of the Middle Ages and the
desire to return to the glories of classical Greece and Rome, indigenous
cultural movements which developed among Hindus and Muslims in
India looked down upon medieval attitudes and customs and rejected
them in the name of classical texts. British rule first came to Bengal after
the Battle of Plassey in 1757, and later it spread its wings to other parts
of India as well. The Indian Renaissance and Reformation movements
too first took shape in Bengal and then in other parts of India. Thus, the
Brahmo Samaj in Bengal harked back to the Upanishads and led the
revolt against medieval beliefs and customs; and the Arya Samaj which

built considerable influence in other parts of northern India sought to reject the caste system based on birth (in other words, rejecting the ascriptive principle in favour of the achievement principle) and many prevailing customs on the supposed authority of the most ancient Vedas.

Among the Muslims too the middle classes led the Renaissance and Reformation movements that made all effort to suppress the popular customs prevalent among the Muslims in various parts of India and made a strong appeal for returning scrupulously to the dicta of the Koran. Before the advent of British rule and in its earlier phase, among Indian Muslims too custom functioned as a source of law. From the beginning of the twentieth century a movement developed for complete suppression of non-Islamic customary law among all groups of Muslims, and for the compulsory enforcement of the Shariat legal system. This movement culminated in the Shariat Act of 1935. This law listed all areas where the Muslim personal law (Shariat) was to apply 'notwithstanding any custom or usage to the contrary'.

From a sociological angle it appears that when a society seeks to break away from medievalism, in the beginning this can only be done in the name of something which is much older. This seems to happen because in traditional societies the old ipso facto enjoys a positive value—the older a custom, the more binding it is. (Just as in modern societies there is a tendency to attach positive value to the new—the latest fashion is preferred, even though it may be ugly or uncomfortable.)

Whether this hypothesis is correct or not, it is clear that the influential modern middle class that emerged in India played an important role in the suppression of customary law among various territorial and ethnic groups. The leaders of opinion belonging to this class led movements for the enactment of laws for the abolition of certain customs and practices that were considered undesirable. Long ago, Raja Ram Mohan Roy built public opinion against the practice of sati (the burning of the widow on the funeral pyre of her dead husband) and later in 1829, it was prohibited by law through Regulation XVII which declared sati illegal and punishable by courts.

This English-educated urban middle class was imbued with post-medieval ideas of individualism, private property, and competitiveness. This class led the movement for turning India into a nation state, and for its independence. This movement culminated in India's independence and the birth of the Constitution of India. This Constitution reflects many of the values inherent in the Western legal system as against the values of the traditional Indian system of dispute settlement. Indeed some people have said that it is a lawyers' paradise. It seeks to establish a nation state and shuns parochial loyalties.

Thus the modern Indian middle class seems to have strengthened what may be called 'the steam-roller effect' of British rule in India; and it is carrying it forward.

The Legal System after India's Independence

Even after the Constitution of India came into being the basic structure of the Indian legal system does not seem to have changed appreciably from what it was during British rule. The foundations of this legal system were laid around 1860 when such basic laws as the Civil Procedure Code, the Criminal Procedure Code, and the Law of Evidence were put in place.

Quite sometime ago the famous Fourteenth Report of the Law Commission[41] vividly brought out the deficiencies of the prevailing legal system. But these have hardly been remedied. We may briefly describe the serious shortcomings of the present legal system as follows: (i) the vast majority of the people in India do not have even an elementary knowledge about the laws and legal procedures, nor do they have adequate access to the legal system; (ii) the language used in courts, especially the higher courts, is not understood by litigants and witnesses; (iii) the arguments in lawsuits are not so much about the substantive issues of the dispute as on far-fetched technicalities; (iv) the lawyers and their touts are interested in protracting litigation rather than in the settlement of the dispute; (v) many unscrupulous persons entrenched in the court system harass innocent people and subject them to injustice with the confidence that they would not dare to go to the court against them; (vi) going to court of law costs so much money because of the high fees of the lawyers and the court fees, and it is so time consuming, that most people cannot afford to take advantage of the legal system; (vii) there is excessive litigation and there is a huge backlog of pending cases in the courts at all levels; and (viii) perjury and forgery are quite common in law courts and most often these remain undetected.

A pernicious feature that has come to the fore in the post-independence era is that of enacting too many laws and subjecting them to numerous amendments from time to time. This has created such a thick jungle of laws that it is difficult for anyone to find his way. This proliferation of legislation, with too many provisos and amendments, makes it impossible even for the jurists specializing in an area of law to be sure about the exact legal position on various points in that field. This too has become an important factor in prolonging litigation and in adding to the backlog of cases in courts.

Some idea of the magnitude of this problem can be had from the fact that according to one estimate, during the period from 1955 to May 1970 the Parliament passed 959 statutes and the legislatures of seventeen states enacted at least 6,358 laws.[42] But even these figures do not tell the whole story because every piece of legislation confers the power of making various rules under it to administrative authorities.

In the post-independence period a large number of laws have been passed to ameliorate the lot of weaker sections of the society and to remedy the inequalities to which various handicapped groups such as the scheduled castes and tribes, and backward classes have been subjected. Laws have also been enacted to protect women from various kinds of atrocities and to do away with social injustice from which they have suffered for a long time.

However, much of this social legislation seems to remain primarily symbolic or ritualistic. It is doubtful whether it has been successful in reaching its objectives.[43] The laws have generally been framed without the requisite support of research on ground realities. Nor has there been adequate scientific investigation to assess the degree of success in attaining their objectives and their non-intended consequences.

As an example of the ineffectiveness of the Indian legal system, we are discussing below the failure of land reform legislation. Land reform has been chosen as an example because it concerns the bulk of the Indian people.

Land Reforms

There has also been a lot of legislation to bring about land reforms. But as many studies show it has hardly achieved its objectives.[44] The factors responsible for failure of land reform laws have been summed up well by Upendra Baxi.[45] These factors are being briefly mentioned below.

Among the legal factors the 'most universally stressed group of factors comprises flexibilities, "loopholes" and exemptions in land reform laws'.[46] In addition, the deleterious and complex nature of the Indian legal system has been noted as an important factor by many experts in the field.

As regards the administrative factors, an important reason is that the revenue administration has neither the capability nor the will to implement land reforms.

Further, the preparation necessary for proper implementation of land reforms has not been made and the personnel needed has not been made available. The revenue administration remains busy in its routine work and has little time for paying heed to land reforms. The rich landowners and moneylenders often influence administrators through illegal gratification.

The sociocultural and political factors which impede land reforms are no less important. Gunnar Myrdal has drawn attention to the heterogeneity of interests of the village population as an obstacle. Myrdal rightly says that for the landless labourers land reforms have no meaning unless there is redistribution of land to the workers.[47]

Obviously the interests of landowners lie elsewhere, and those in authority tend to be on their side. A Planning Commission report says that in case of 'conflicting evidence, there is a greater tendency to believe the landlord than the tenant'.

Many expert committees appointed by the government have underlined the importance of the lack of 'political will' for the failure of land reforms. For example, the Task Force on Agrarian Relations sharply highlighted the lack of political will for the failure of land reform in India.[48]

This lack of political will is reflected both in land legislation and in the implementation of land reform measures. In fact the Planning Commission of India has candidly said that such political will cannot be expected in the present political power structure of the country.[49] In the circumstances, Myrdal's conclusion that very little reform 'will be actually accomplished and even greater inequality may result . . .'[50] seems inescapable.

PROBLEMS BESETTING THE LEGAL SYSTEM IN INDIA

We shall discuss briefly the problems that beset the Indian legal system and try to see what factors impede its functioning as a mechanism for maintaining social harmony and dispute settlement, and as a lever of social change. This exploration is based not only on the study of literature on the judicial system in India and Indian society, but also on my empiric studies over the last thirty-five years and on my own observation and interaction both with persons connected with the legal system and the common people. Some references to these are inevitably there in what follows.

It seems that the present legal system is far too inadequate for the needs of the Indian society. As Justice V.R. Krishna Iyer has said, it is a question not only of tightening the nuts and bolts but that of redesigning the entire ramshackle machine. It is worth quoting him:

> Rather, we must not only tighten nuts and bolts and press the accelerator but redesign the project to replace a ramshackle machine.
>
> The renovation and re-organisation of the judicial set-up involves the sophistication of the machine incorporating modern advances in technical knowledge so that delay killing devices may harmonise with better functional performance, and humanisation of the system may find application in judicial process (Iyer 1972, pp. 136–7)

Apart from forcefully bringing out the need for thorough restructuring of the whole legal system, Justice V.R. Krishna Iyer has drawn attention to another important aspect—the undue dependence of our legal system on an outmoded set of evidence required to prove a case.

Our procedures of investigation and judgment do not take the help of modern forensic means which can settle cases speedily and decisively without leaning solely on evidence that can easily be bended, derailed, or destroyed by influential parties. Key witnesses are often bought off or intimidated so as to contradict or change their own statements made earlier. Not unoften, even the victims of cases such as those of rape, and the surviving relatives of persons murdered, are forced or lured to change their stand. Crucial witnesses are known to have been eliminated to weaken the prosecution. In many such cases simple forensic methods can be used with telling effect, and may greatly reduce the chances of acquittal by influencing the witnesses or the victims themselves, through lack of evidence.

This brings us face to face with another gap in our legal system through which the mighty offenders frequently escape. While the judiciary is comparatively impartial, and its independence is considered to be sanctimonious, the prosecuting agencies such as the police are not immune to influences of diverse kinds, and their functioning is not free from outside interference. It can be subjected to all sorts of pressures. The political rulers and high officers control such matters as the promotion and transfer of police personnel. As ordinary human beings they cannot be expected to resist the influence of those who control them in various ways. Furthermore, our police personnel do not have high salaries comparable to the income of such sections as businessmen, politicians, and successful lawyers. Many of them fall prey to the power that money wields, especially in an increasingly consumerist society. And it is the police and similar prosecuting agencies that are responsible for making the cases against those accused of offences. If sufficiently influenced, the police can easily leave such lacunae in the evidence which they gather, or the case which they make, that the judge cannot punish the culprit even if in his heart he knows that the accused is the real culprit. In many a judgment the judge laments that the case had not been made properly, but he can hardly do anything about it.

This is one of the reasons why the high and mighty are seldom prosecuted even after committing heinous offences. The famous dictum that 'law is like a spider's web; small worms are caught into it and the big ones pass through', seems to have the full approval of the bulk of the people in India. They have little faith in the legal system or the rule of law. This was clearly brought out through an empirical research project which I carried out for the Indian Law Institute in 1967–8. This project involved extensive study over two states and covered all sections of the people both in urban and rural areas. The respondents included both common folk and those connected with the legal system in various ways, such as lawyers, judges at different levels, and law teachers. Since then many more instances have come to light for everyone to see.

Apart from persons belonging to the influential sections of society, even the overall rate of punishment for crime in our system is lamentably low. Only in 4 per cent of the cases in which the First Information Report (FIR) is made to the police, the culprit is punished.[51] And the FIR is not recorded in all the cases either because of the reluctance of the police or due to the victim's lack of means. K.R. Narayanan, when he was the president of India, while inaugurating a seminar on Judicial Reforms rightly remarked: 'A reform that can be undertaken is to simplify the legal procedures involving litigation and the disposal of cases. Law's delays are proverbial and it is in this field that reforms are urgently needed not only to reduce the mounting cost of litigation but to see that justice is not denied to people.'[52]

A combination of factors has conspired to make law an unduly lengthy process: the intricacies of procedure, the ingenuity of lawyers in prolonging cases, the indifference of the judges, and the unending process of appeals that is available. It has been calculated that the judgment for an average case in our country takes more than four years, and that in 96 per cent of the cases in which FIRs are filed with the police the accused goes unpunished. The growing population, the rapidly growing volume of cases and the work connected with them, and the low ratio of judges to the population are often cited as reasons for the intolerable delay in the disposal of cases. However, one of the chief reasons for such a situation seems to be the unfathomable complexity of the legal system, and the acumen of many lawyers in taking advantage of this for their own advantage. It has been estimated that a mind-boggling number of around thirty million cases are in arrears in various courts of the country. The government and the judiciary itself must apply their minds more seriously than hitherto in order to tackle this enormous backlog of un-disposed cases. Each of the thirty million cases in arrears represents delay and denial of justice to people.

There is such a plethora of laws, sometimes more or less contradictory, that it is almost impossible for anyone to say for sure what the legal position is on a certain point.[53] Even among the judges of a Supreme Court bench, there are often sharp differences of opinion. This is one of the reasons why judgment in a case is generally unpredictable. This is well brought out by an incident which the eminent former Chief Justice of India, Justice Gajendragadkar narrated, in response to my query regarding the predictability of judgments, at a meeting of the Committee on Law and Social Change set up by the Indian Council of Social Science Research in New Delhi in 1970. He said: Once a senior lawyer had concluded his arguments in a case and sent his junior to hear the judgment. The junior lawyer had been told that it was certain that they would win that case. But when the judge began reading out his judgment it was going entirely against the senior's definite prediction. The junior was surprised and he said to the judge, 'My Lord, you are giving the judgment against us, but at least do not order us to pay the costs of the case.' The judge angrily asked, 'Why?' The junior lawyer said: 'But this is a very surprising judgment.' The judge was offended and issued a notice of contempt of court against the lawyer. When his senior, who was in the court of another judge, was told that a notice of contempt had been issued against his junior, he rushed to the court of the concerned judge and pleaded that a lenient view may kindly be taken against his junior as this was his first case. However, the judge asserted: 'But he said that this was a very surprising judgment.' The senior lawyer replied: 'This is what I say My Lord, he will not be surprised when he gets experienced.' Coming as it does from an eminent Chief Justice of India, this is indeed revealing.

Legal procedure, like sociology and indeed all science, insists that no inferences can be drawn which are not verified by evidence. But when the mandatory evidence required is of such a nature that it can just not be made available in a good many cases, and fabricating of evidence to prove even a genuine case tends to become necessary; one begins to suspect that all is not well. Whenever impossible tasks are set, corrupt compromises tend to arise.

In addition to the complexity of laws themselves there is an endless body of precedents by which the judge has to abide. The lawyer is free to choose the precedent which suits his case best, and he puts it forth before the court. It has rightly been pointed out that too much dependence on the precedent leads inevitably to adherence to status quo. When law is sought to be employed as an instrument of social change, too much dependence on precedents is surely an impediment.

There is so much dependence on precedents that even when new laws are framed it is not unoften that old laws which prevailed during the British rule and have become clearly obsolete are copied out for the most part. A ridiculous, or pathetic, example of such practice was brought to light when a couple of years ago a law was framed and even passed by the Lower House of the Parliament, the Lok Sabha, which provided, inter alia, that a certain percentage of the revenue concerned was to go to the British treasury. This was reported by the BBC and a few Indian newspapers (but was ignored by the bulk of Indian media). This incident brings out not only the extent of the propensity of those who are at the helm of our governance for their slavish adherence to what had been going on before, but also the stark lethargy and carelessness involved in the framing of our laws. That draft bill must have passed through a number of ministries of the Government of India, whose officials were supposed to have gone through the draft meticulously. It should also have received attention from the honourable members of the Lok Sabha, both of the treasury benches and of the Opposition. But obviously, none of these worthies considered it necessary to give it even a cursory reading. If this had been done such an atrocious provision could not have sneaked into the bill.

Law has been used as an instrument of subjugation and exploitation of vast lands by the colonial powers. Even within a country the legal system can serve as a tool for the oppression of certain sections of society by the privileged strata. It is an open question whether the present legal system in India is being put to this use against such sections as the tribals.

As has already been shown in the subsection on land reforms, most studies bring out the fact that lack of political will and the presence of too many flexibilites, loopholes, and exemptions in land reform laws are responsible for the failure of land reforms. This is acknowledged even in the reports of the Planning Commission of India. Obviously, in the making of laws, big landowners play an important part. Otherwise, such loopholes would not have been built into the laws.[54]

The common people are not involved in the process of law making on the plea that they would not understand. This is the same plea on which ordinary people were earlier denied the right to vote. It is not really true that ordinary people cannot think or are devoid of reasoning or critical faculty. I have argued elsewhere that even the unlettered folk criticize and poke fun at their own age-old customs and institutions. Their cultural level is in no way low and they are not deficient in the power to think (Indra Deva 1977).

The delays in courts of law are proverbial. Even simple cases take decades to come to a conclusion. Such unacceptable delays have many serious consequences. Many undertrials have already served longer years in jail than the maximum duration of sentence, even if they were to be found guilty of the offence of which they had been accused. And if, eventually, after years in jail they are found to be not guilty, a grave injustice is perpetrated against them because of the excessive rectitude, complexity, manipulation, and lethargy embedded in the existing legal system. The number of such cases is enormous.

Another serious consequence of this dilatory legal system is that the deterrent function of punishment is almost entirely lost. When a known criminal remains unpunished for years after committing murder and other such offences, even though it is clear to everyone that he is the person responsible for perpetrating it, the purpose of deterrence is hardly served. In most such cases the criminal escapes punishment, but even if the punishment is given after too long a time, it does not serve the purpose, because by that time most people forget the whole gruesome episode.

A legal system cannot be beneficial unless the people who are affected by it have a minimum awareness of the laws and the legal procedures. However, the level of this awareness is lamentably low not only among the common people but also among those who are actively involved in the legal processes. This was evident from an extensive empirical survey which I carried out in 1967–8. In both the rural and urban areas in the two states which we studied, the level of awareness about law was found to be extremely poor, among almost all sections of the people. What is surprising is that knowledge about certain aspects of law, such as social legislation was found to be astonishingly deficient even among the higher sections of those actively involved in the legal system.[55]

Besides lack of awareness regarding social legislation, several instances can be cited of the ignorance of leading district-level lawyers about basic procedures of higher courts, and of senior high court advocates about those of the Supreme Court.

Indeed, our entire system of law has to undergo a lot of change if it is to be really useful for our society and to the people at large.

THE READINGS

The readings contained in the six parts that follow cover all the major aspects of sociology of law in India on which significant work has been carried out by noted scholars in the fields belonging both to the discipline of sociology and to that of law. There are essays not only by sociologists but also the writings of perceptive law teachers, eminent judges, and lawyers. A multidisciplinary approach is necessary at this stage of development of sociology of law in India. It is in its infancy and it requires nutrition from diverse sources for its proper growth.

The inclusion of representative writings both of sociologists and of jurists is necessary to lay the groundwork for building up a systematic sociology of law relevant to India. It is intended also to promote a more vigorous interaction between professional sociologists, practising jurists, and law teachers. Without sustained interaction among all these three categories of thinking people a really worthwhile discipline of sociology of law cannot develop in India.

Despite wide and deep dissatisfaction with the functioning of the legal system it has not received adequate attention. Ordinary people are afraid to go to court for getting justice as litigation is very expensive and it involves untold humiliation. This is common knowledge and yet it has not been given the systematic thought and investigation that it deserves. Part I of this book attempts to focus on this whole problem in a broad historical and sociological perspective. Upendra Baxi, who is an eminent law teacher, brings out in a forceful manner, in the opening reading, how the present legal system retains its colonial character, and how under this system the vast mass of Indian people are treated as if they were still under colonial subjugation. J. Duncan M. Derret, who is regarded an authority on the subject, tells us how the anxiety of the British administrators not to offend those whom they wished to rule, led to distortions in the traditional Hindu law. In his essay, Justice V.R. Krishna Iyer, a former judge of the Supreme Court and a member of the Law Commission, unravels the combative culture embedded in the legal system and shows how it prolongs and complicates disputes instead of settling them. Justice Krishna Iyer emphasizes the need to redesign the entire legal system. 'Otherwise,' he says, 'it will remain a happy hunting ground of crafty lawyers.' The essay by Krishna Kumar et al. is based on collaborative research among the tribals in the north-east. It suggests that an alternative legal system is not impossible. Gandhi's piece presents a vivid view of the changes brought about by British rule in the traditional Indian system of law.

For a very long time outstanding British administrators and other thinking people have considered lawyers to be the worst part of the legal system. Their social characteristics and their relationship with their touts and clients have received a good deal of attention from sociologists and anthropologists. Part II presents some of their writings.

The general public opinion about lawyers is that they are crafty and interested mainly in enhancing their personal gain by complicating and prolonging cases. Such eminent people as Metcalfe and Elphinstone said long ago that they constituted the worst part of the legal system. The general level of competence of the lawyers and perhaps even the magistrates at the lower level of judiciary does not seem to be high. Yet some lawyers earn huge incomes and this seems to have raised the status of lawyers as a class in public eye.

In the opening paper of this part, Schmitthener gives an interesting and illuminating account of the development of the legal profession in India for more than two centuries. This well-documented piece brings out clearly that since the time of early British rule the lawyers have shown astonishing unity in guarding their pecuniary interests. K.L. Sharma, who is a reputed sociologist, has made a systematic empirical study of the lawyers and their clients in Jaipur. The major findings of this study are presented here. Charles Morrison has made an anthropological field study of the relationship among lawyers at district level. His essay presents a lively picture of the atmosphere in a typical district court. Dieter Conrad traces the course that the question of personal law has taken from the time when Warren Hastings promulgated his famous 'Judicial Plan' in 1772. He brings out how the rise of Hindu nationalism is related with this issue.

Though the Directive Principles of State Policy in the Constitution of India enjoin the state to strive for a common civil code for all citizens of India, this is not a simple matter. Those who framed the Constitution were inspired by the idea of making India a modern nation state. But the fact that India comprises numerous religions and ethnic groups cannot be disregarded. As we have seen earlier[56] the *Dharmaśāstras* gave full recognition to this diversity, and the *Smṛti*s of Nārada, Bṛhaspati, and Kāt-yāyana have explicitly provided that matters concerning personal laws will be decided by the councils of various ethnic groups; and disputes arising among members of various professions will be dealt with by the appropriate council of that profession.

As D.E. Smith whose essay is included in Part III points out, Hinduism and Islam are not mere religions. They represent ways of life and it is not surprising that by the imposition of an uniform civil code a community is afraid of losing its identity.

John Mansfield's piece in this part presents well both the sides of the issue. And the essay by Kavita Khory traces the entire course of the Shah Bano case, which made the question of uniform civil code a central issue in the politics of India.

There are certain sections in the Indian society which have suffered from social and economic disadvantages for centuries. These sections include the SCs, the Scheduled Tribes, and the OBCs. Women, who constitute about one half of the total population, have also been suffering from various social, cultural, and economic disadvantages. A number of laws have been enacted, especially after India's independence, to end the injustice to which they have been subjected. But how far has such legislation been successful in achieving its objectives is a moot point. Some such pieces of legislation are alleged to have unforeseen detrimental consequences. Systematic sociological investigation is indispensable to give a correct picture of the ground reality on such matters.

Part IV contains readings regarding the disadvantaged groups. In the opening essay Marc Galanter, who has done outstanding work in the study of the reservation policy, presents various aspects of this whole problem in an incisive manner. M.P. Singh attempts to present a strong case in favour of the reservations on the basis of constitutional provisions and the spirit underlying them. Ram Jethmalani, with his characteristic brilliance, argues the case for reservations for the OBCs. It appears, however, that arguments or discussion alone is not sufficient for deciding such social issues. Scientific investigation of the ground realities is also necessary.

A keen realization of the inadequacy of the present legal system has prompted some thoughtful judges of the Supreme Court to bypass certain hackneyed procedural requirements which are impracticable for a large part of India's suffering people who are subjected to injustice. This urge has led to the development of judicial activism, and public interest litigation (PIL). This development opened up the way for, what Justice Krishna Iyer has called, 'broader access to justice', and marks a departure from the 'combatant culture' inherent in the Western and modern Indian judicial systems. According to this new trend, it is no more necessary that a person who takes a case of injustice to a court of law should himself or herself be a victim of that injustice. Any public-spirited person can approach the court for redressal of an injustice done to the people who have no means to present their own case. Such helpless people include, for example, *Bandhua Mazdoors* (bonded labourers) and the poor under-trials who languish in jails for years without their case being brought to a court of law. Part V includes writings on these issues.

Understandably, the first essay in this part is by Justice V.R. Krishna Iyer, who himself is a pioneer of this shift in judicial practice. This essay too is marked by the power of his style. Morje's article underscores the need of judicial activism by showing that a variety of groups would remain in a miserable plight without it. However, it would be unrealistic to think that the legal system alone can remedy all injustice that exists in society.

In countries like India which endeavour to bring about social trans-formation at a fast pace, law is being employed not only as a means of social control but also as lever of social change. But when old institutional patterns and attitudes are sought to be radically transformed it is indis-pensable to understand the circumstances in which they have emerged and the social forces that shaped them. Some of the patterns of rela-tionship and thought that exist in Indian society owe their present form to forces that have been working for centuries or even millennia. They may be regarded as tenacious obstacles to social change today, but trying to remove them without understanding the basic structures and processes would be like performing a major surgical operation without knowing the basics of anatomy and physiology. These are the topics discussed in Part VI.

The opening reading in this part on social change therefore attempts to reveal the roots of some of these sociocultural structures that are being sought to be changed. The reading that follows presents a sociological analysis of the relationship between law and social change. The next essay seeks to show that the Constitution of India does not provide a sound foundation for radical social transformation. Thus, various aspects of law and social change are brought out in this concluding part.

NOTES

1. Max Radin, 'A Restatement of Hohfeld', *Harvard Law Review*, 51, 1938, p. 1145.
2. H.L.A. Hart, *The Concept of Law*, Oxford: Clarendon Press, 1961, p. 16.

3. Bronislaw Malinowski, *Crime and Custom in Savage Society*, New York: Harcourt, Brace, 1926, p. 24.

4. B.N. Cardozo, *The Growth of the Law*, New Haven: Yale University Press, 1924, p. 52.

5. William Graham Sumner, *Folkways*, New York: Blackwell, 1940.

6. George Gurvitch, *Sociology of Law*, London: Routledge & Kegan Paul, 1973, p. 1.

7. E. Ehrlich, *Fundamental Principles of Sociology of Law*, W.L. Moll (tr.), Cambridge: Harvard University Press, 1936.

8. Emile Durkheim, *The Division of Labour in Society*, George Simpson (tr.), New York: Macmillan, 1933.

9. Max Weber, *Law in Economy and Society*, M. Rheinstein and E. Shils (tr.), Cambridge: Harvard University Press, 1954.

10. E.A. Hoebel, *The Law of Primitive Man: A Study in Comparative Legal Dynamics*, Cambridge: Harvard University Press, 1964.

11. Ibid., p. 175.

12. V. Ferrari (ed.), *Developing Sociology of Law: A Worldwide Documentary Enquiry*, Milano: International Sociological Association, Research Committee on Sociology of Law, 1990, p. 387.

13. ICSSR, *A Survey of Research in Sociology and Social Anthropology*, vol. II, Bombay: Popular Prakashan, 1974, p. 392.

14. Upendra Baxi, *Towards a Sociology of Indian Law*, Delhi: Satvahan, 1984, p. 118.

15. Marc Galanter, *Competing Equalities: Law and the Backward Classes in India*, Berkeley: University of California Press and New Delhi: Oxford University Press, 1984.

16. For a detailed discussion of the events relating to the Shah Bano case, see the article on the Shah Bano case in Part III of this volume.

17. *See* Marc Galanter's article in Part IV of this volume.

18. Oscar Lewis, *Group Dynamics in a North Indian Village*, Delhi: Government of India Press, 1954 and *Village Life in Northern India*, Urbana: University of Illinois Press, 1958.

19. A detailed analysis of the development of judicial values and institutions since the Vedic times supported by references to the chapter and verse of various traditional texts can be found in Indra Deva and Shrirama, *Growth of the Indian Legal System*, New Delhi: ICSSR/Allied, 1980.

20. For an exposition of the dynamics of various aspects of the traditional Indian socio-cultural system, *see* Indra Deva and Shrirama, *Society and Culture in India: Their Dynamics through the Ages*, Jaipur, Rawat, 1989.

21. P.V. Kane, *History of Dharmaśāstras*, Poona: Bhandarkar Oriental Research Institute, 1930–62.

22. *See* Shrirama Indradeva, 'Reassertion of Subjugated Cultures: The Case of Religion in India', *Diogenes*, Paris: UNESCO, 1990.

23. Robert Lingat, *The Classical Law of India* (translated from French with additions by J. Duncan Derrett), New Delhi: Oxford University Press, 1998.
24. Ibid., p. 141.
25. Ibid., p. 143.
26. Ibid., p. 258.
27. For an elaborate discussion of legal precepts and procedure expounded in the later *Smṛtis, see* Shrirama, *Social Structure and Values in Later Smṛtis,* Calcutta: Indian Publications, 1972. *See* especially Chapter IX (Concept of Justice and Judicial Procedure, pp. 187–269) and Chapter X (Titles of Law, pp. 270–344).
28. *Nāradasmṛti, ṛṇa,* 34; *Kātyāyanasmṛti,* 497.
29. *Bṛhaspatismṛti,* I, 63; *Nāradasmṛti, Sabhālakṣaṇa,* 4–5; and *Kātyāyanasmṛti,* 72, etc.
30. *Kātyāyanasmṛti,* 52.
31. *Bṛhaspatismṛti,* I, 3.
32. *Kātyāyanasmṛti,* 25, 26, 30.
33. *Kātyāyanasmṛti,* 55–6.
34. *Nāradasmṛti,* I, 35, 37.
35. *Nāradasmṛti,* I, 7; *Kātyāyanasmṛti,* 82.
36. *Kātyāyanasmṛti,* 225.
37. *Kātyāyanasmṛti,* 682.
38. *Kātyāyanasmṛti,* 47.
39. *Bṛhaspatismṛti,* I, 74.
40. J.D.M. Derrett, *Religion, Law and State in India,* London: Faber and Faber, 1968; Rajeev Dhavan, 'Introduction' to Marc Galanter, *Law and Society in Modern India,* Delhi: Oxford University Press, 1989; Upendra Baxi, *Towards a Sociology of Law in India,* New Delhi: Satvahan Publications, 1986.
41. The Fourteenth Report of the Law Commission, 2 vols, published with the title *Reform of Judicial Administration,* Delhi, 1958.
42. Upendra Baxi, *The Crisis of the Indian Legal System,* New Delhi: Vikas Publishing House, 1982, p. 79.
43. For a more detailed discussion of these policies and measures, see Part IV of this book (Law and the Disadvantaged Groups). This part consists of the writings of eminent scholars and jurists on the subject.
44. *See,* for example, M.L. Dantwala and C.H. Shah, *Evaluation of Land Reforms with Special Reference to the Western Region of India,* Bombay: Bombay University, 1971; P.C. Joshi, *Land Reforms in India: Trends and Perspectives,* New Delhi: Allied, 1975.
45. Upendra Baxi, *Sociology of Law in India,* New Delhi: Satvahan, 1986, pp. 45–59.
46. Ibid., p. 48.
47. Gunnar Myrdal, *The Asian Drama: An Enquiry into the Poverty of Nations,* New York: Pantheon, 1968, pp. 1052–64, 1331.

48. *Planning Commission of India*, 1959.
49. *Planning Commission of India*, 1973.
50. Myrdal, *The Asian Drama*, p. 1834.
51. President K.R. Narayanan's Inaugural Address to the Seminar on Judicial Reforms, organized by Supreme Court Advocates on Record Association, 1998, p. 2.
52. Ibid.
53. In fact the magnitude of multiplicity and complexities in law is such that even the eminent lawyer, Nani Palkhivala, who was considered to be the top authority on Income Tax laws had to admit that the Income Tax laws had become so complicated because of the innumerable amendments and provisos that it was just not possible for anyone to say for sure what the exact legal position was. This complexity of the law makes it a happy hunting ground for the crafty lawyers and an area of darkness for the innocent clients.
54. To give one instance, at a meeting of the ICSSR Committee set up in 1970, to which I have referred earlier also, I asked both former Chief Justice Gangendragadkar and Justice V.R. Krishna Iyer, why land reform legislation in most parts of India remained ineffective. Both of them said that a large number of legislators belonged to the landed class and they see to it that sufficient loopholes are left in the enacted laws so that they may not have to lose any substantial part of their land. The fact that these eminent judges were constrained to say this shows how some judges feel helpless in the face of the phraseology of tendentious laws. In later times the big business and industrialists started playing a more important part in ensuring that laws are so framed that they do not go against them but further their interests.
55. To give only one example, one of the senior judges of the Rajasthan High Court came in the stratified sample of our study. The interview schedule that was to be used for all the respondents, whether they be common folk or judicial professionals, therefore contained some elementary questions about various kinds of laws to assess the level of awareness about the legal system. I was rather worried that the senior high court judge may feel offended if such simple questions about law were to be put to him for answering. I implored a senior colleague to go for interviewing him and requested my colleague to be very polite to the respondent who happened to be a senior judge. My colleague began by apologizing and pleading that he had to ask him these questions which were too simple for him. The judge was generous. He said, 'I understand, go on.' My colleague put to him a question which was meant to assess awareness about the provisions of the Hindu Marriage Act, 1955, an important piece of social legislation. He asked, 'If a Hindu male marries again when his wife by earlier marriage is alive, is it an offence under law?' The judge replied, 'Well, this is perfectly legal and legitimate. Even King Dasharatha, the father of Lord Rama, had more than one wife.' But when my colleague pleaded again and again that this may not be considered legal now, he reluctantly

picked up a book from his rack, and after glancing over a few pages, agreed: 'Yes, my boy,' he said, '*now* there is a law which says that when a spouse is alive one cannot marry again.' About twelve good years had passed when he could be persuaded to become aware that such a law did exist. When this is the level of awareness of a senior high court judge, doubts begin to arise about the claimed educative function of social legislation.

56. *See* the section on Traditional Indian Law earlier in this Introduction.

REFERENCES

Ambedkar, B.R., *What Congress and Gandhi have done to the Untouchables*, Bombay: Thacker, 1945.

Austin, G., *The Indian Constitution: A Cornerstone of the Nation*, Oxford: Clarendon Press, 1966.

Aziz, K.K., *A History of the Idea of Pakistan*, Lahore: Vanguard Books, 1987.

Baird, Robert D. (ed.), *Religion and Law in Independent India*, New Delhi: Manohar, 1993.

Baxi, Upendra, 'The Little Done, The Vast Undone: Some Reflections on Reading Granville Austin's The Indian Constitution', *Journal of the Indian Law Institute*, 9, 1967, pp. 339–48.

————, 'Legal Assistance to the Poor: A Critique of the Expert Committee Report', *Economic and Political Weekly*, 27, 1975, pp. 1105, 1009–11.

————, *The Crisis of the Indian Legal System*, New Delhi: Vikas, 1982.

————, *Towards a Sociology of Indian Law*, New Delhi: Satvahan, 1986.

Bhagwati Committee, *Report on National Juridicare—Equal Justice, Social Justice*, Ministry of Law, Justice, and Company Affair, 1978.

Cohn, B.S., 'Law and Change in North India', *Economic Development and Cultural Change*, 8, 1959, pp. 79–93.

————, 'From Indian Status to British Contract', *Journal of Economic History*, 21, 1961, pp. 613–18.

Deva, *see* Indra Deva.

Desai, A.R., 'Sociology of the Under-Privileged', *Fifth U.P. Sociological Conference*, Kanpur, 1983.

Dhagamwar, Vasudha, *Towards the Uniform Civil Code for All*, New Delhi: Indian Law Institute, 1989.

Diwan, Paras, *Muslim Law in India*, Allahabad: Allahabad Law Agency, 1987.

Embree, Ainslie T., *Utopias in Conflict: Religion and Nationalism in Modern India*, Berkeley: University of California Press, 1990.

Gajendragadkar, P.B., *Lawyers and Social Change*, New Delhi: National Forum of Lawyers and Legal Aid, 1976.

Galanter, M., 'The Modernization of Law', in M. Weiner (ed.), *Modernization: The Dynamics of Growth*, London: Basic Books, 1969.

————, 'The Aborted Restoration of Indigenous Law in India', *Comparative Studies in Sociology and History*, 14, 1972, p. 53.

————, *Competing Equalities*, Berkeley: University of California Press, 1984.

Gandhi, J.S., Jonathan M., *Lawyers and Touts*, Delhi: Hindustan Publishing Corporation, 1982.

Gordon, and Richard K., Jr Lindsay, 'Law and the Poor in India: The Prospects for Legal Aid', *American University Journal of International Law and Policy*, 5, 1990, pp. 655–772.

Gupte, K.V., *Hindu Law in British India*, Bombay: N.M. Tripathi, 1947.

Gurvitch, Georges, *Sociology of Law*, London: Routledge & Kegan Paul, 1973.

Haksar, Nandita, 'Justice for the Common Man', the *Hindustan Times*, New Delhi, 1983.

Heimsath, Charles H., *Indian Nationalism and Hindu Social Reform*, Princeton: Princeton University Press, 1964.

Hellwege, A., 'Underdevelopment, Dependence and Modernizaton Theory', *Law and State*, 17, 1978, p. 45.

Hussain, Wahed, *Administration of Justice during the Muslim Rule in India*, Calcutta, 1934.

Indra Deva, 'The Cultural Level of Unlettered Folk', *Diogenes*, Paris: UNESCO, 100, 1977, pp. 26–47.

Indradeva, *see* Shrirama Indradeva.

Indra Deva and Shrirama, *Growth of Legal System in India*, New Delhi: ICSSR/ Allied Publishers, 1980.

————, *Society and Culture in India: Their Dynamics through the Ages*, Jaipur: Rawat, 1999.

Jain, M.P., *Outlines of Indian Legal History*, Bombay: Tripathi, 1981.

Joshi, B., 'Whose Law, Whose Order: Untouchables, Social Violence and State in India', *Asian Survey*, 22, 1982, p. 678.

Joshi, P.C., *Land Reforms in India: Trends and Perspectives*, Bombay: 1975.

Kane, P.V., *History of Dharmashastra*, 5 vols., Poona: Bhandarker Oriental Research Institute, 1930–46.

Khosla, D., 'Untouchability—A Case Study of Law in Life', in Adam Podgorecki, Christopher J. Whelan, and Dinesh Khosla (eds), *Legal Systems and Social Systems*, London: Croom Helm, 1985.

Kolenda, P., 'Micro-Ideology and Micro-Utopia in Khalapur: Changes in the Discourse on Caste in 30 years', *Economic and Political Weekly*, XXIV, 1989, p. 1831.

Krishna Iyer Committee, *Processual Justice to People*, 1975.

Macauley, S., 'Law and Behavioural Sciences: Is There Any There There?', *Law and Policy*, 6, 1984, p. 148.

Madan, T.N., 'Coping with Ethnic Diversity: A South Asian Perspective', in Stuart Plattner (ed.), *Prospects for Plural Societies*, Washington, Amer. Ethnological Society, 1984.

————, 'Secularism in Its Place', *Journal of Asian Studies*, 46, 1987, pp. 747–59.

Mahmood, Tahir, *Muslim Personal Law: Role of State in Indian Society*, Nagpur: All India Reports, 1983.

————, *Personal Laws in Crisis*, New Delhi: Metropolitan, 1986.

Mendelsohn, Oliver, 'The Pathology of the Indian Legal System', *Modern Asian Studies*, 15 (4), 1981.

Menski, Werner F., 'The Reform of Islamic Family Law', in Chibli Mallat and Jane Connors (eds), *Islamic Family Law*, London: Boston: Graham & Trotman, 1990.

Natarajan, S., *A Century of Social Reform in India*, Bombay: Asia Publishing House, 1962.

Nehru, Jawaharlal, *The Discovery of India*, Bombay: Asia Publishing House, 1961.

Oommen, T.K., *State and Society in India*, New Delhi: Sage, 1990.

Pollock, Selton, *The English Legal System*, Orient Longman, 1974.

Rudolph, Lloyd and Rudolph, Susanne H., *The Modernity of Tradition*, Chicago: University of Chicago Press, 1967.

Saberwal Satish and Heiko Sievers (eds), *Rules, Laws, Constitution*, New Delhi: Sage, 1998.

Sack, Peter G., *Constitutions and Revolution*, Thiruvananthapuram: The Academy of Legal Publications, 1990.

Seervai, H.M., *Constitutional Law of India*, Bombay: N.M. Tripathi Pvt. Ltd, 1983.

Sharma, K.L., *Sociology of Law and Legal Profession*, Jaipur: Rawat, 1984.

Sharma, M., *The Politics of Inequality: Competition and Control in an Indian Village*, Honolulu: University Press of Hawaii, 1978.

Shrirama, Indradeva, 'Correspondence between Woman and Nature in Indian Thought', *Philosophy East and West*, 16, 1966, pp. 161–8.

————, 'Status of Woman in Ancient India: Compulsives of the Patriarchal Order', *Diogenes*, Paris: Unesco, 93, 1976, pp. 67–80.

————, 'Evolution des Formes Traditionnelles de Stratification Sociale en Inde'. *Diogenes*, Paris: Unesco, 130, 1985, 15–40.

————, 'Untouchability and Stratification in Indian Civilization', in S.M. Michael (ed., *Dalits in Modern India*, New Delhi: Vistaar Publication, 1999.

Singh, Yogendra, 'Legal System, Leginiation and Social Change', *Essays on Modernization in India*, Delhi: Manohar, 1978.

Smith, D.E., *India as a Secular State*, Princeton: Princeton University Press, 1963.

Sontheimer, G.D., and P. Aithal (eds), *Indology and Law*, Wiesbaden: Franz Steiner, 1982.

Sowell, T., *Civil Rights: Rhetoric or Reality?*, New York: Quill William Morrow, 1984.

Stokes, Eric, *The English Utilitarians and India*, Oxford: Clarendon Press, 1959.

Vilhelm, Aubert (ed.), *Sociology of Law*, Harmondsworth: Penguin Books, 1969.

von Mehren, A.T., 'Law and Legal Education in India: Some Observations', *Harvard Law Review*, 78, 1965, 1180–89.

Vyas, V.S., 'Changes in Land Ownership Pattern: Structural Change in Indian Agriculture', E.J. Hobsbawm, Witold Kula, and Ashok Mitra (eds), *Peasants in History: Essays in Honour of Daniel Thorner*, Calcutta: Oxford University Press, 1980.

Weiner, Myron, *The Indian Paradox: Essays in Indian Politics*, New Delhi: Sage, 1989.

I

Functioning of the Legal System

Even though there is widespread disappointment with the functioning of the legal system, both among the people at large and the knowledgeable, commensurate systematic thought has not been given to this vital problem. The laws, the legal procedures, and those who ply the trade of law—all three are of such a character that ordinary people are scared of going to a court of law. And those who venture to enter into litigation for the redressal of any injustice done to them do so at the risk of incurring unimaginable expenses, a huge waste of time over a number of years, and killing humiliation.

Of course, this nature of the system is immensely useful for those entrenched in the litigation processes. They perpetrate injustice on ordinary people in the firm belief, confirmed by long experience, that no one would dare to go to court against them, and if anyone does, he or she will be put to untold misery. The laws are complicated and have many loop holes; the legal process is costly, lengthy, and tiring; and being a litigant amounts to losing self-respect in unforeseen ways.

Cases are dragged into a quagmire of technical details for years and even decades, while the victims of injustice continue to suffer. Their suffering is aggravated by the severe rigours of pursuing complicated and expensive legal procedures. There is no attempt to arrive at an amicable settlement. The whole system is embedded in a harsh combative culture.

The lawyers are known to be the toughest part of the judicial system in all parts of the civilized world. This seems to be all the more true of India. For instance it is said that the fees of Indian lawyers, right from the eighteenth and nineteenth centuries, have been five to seven times those of their counterparts in England. The reports of the Law Commissions set up by the British in those times give the comparative figures.

While the high, mighty, and rich have all the resources to bend laws and the legal processes to their own advantage, the common people hardly have even workable access to the legal system. The lobbies of influentials get laws framed in a manner so that they would stand to gain. One common method is to ensure that enough loopholes are left in the laws so that they can escape through them without much difficulty. They hire the best and the most expensive lawyers so that they go scot-free even after committing serious offences.

Common people, on the other hand, do not have the resources to seek legal redressal even for the major wrongs done to them. They cannot engage competent lawyers and do not have even the elementary knowledge about the laws that govern them.

Our empirical studies and observation over the past thirty-five years show that there is an appalling ignorance about the law that prevails, and the basic procedures of the legal system. When no effort is made to disseminate necessary knowledge about laws and legal procedures, it is hardly justifiable to assert that 'ignorance of law is no excuse'. Had dissemination of information about a product or an activity been unimportant, business houses would not have spent so much money on advertisement. Nor would they have paid the highest to those who are in marketing—higher even than to those who are engaged in production. Serious consideration needs to be given to the building and maintenance of an adequate system of communication for disseminating basic knowledge about existing laws and legal procedures. Elementary knowledge about laws and legal processes should be included in courses of study in schools and colleges. If the students are expected to know about the flow of winds and the movement of clouds over the continents, why should they not have basic knowledge about the laws that prevail in their society? Concerted effort should also be made through the electronic media to make the people aware of the laws and the legal procedures.

There is no doubt that the prevailing legal system is colonial in nature. Its structure remains basically the same as that created around the 1860s. At that time the colonial power resided overseas. Today it seems that certain sections in India who have similar colonial attitudes look at with disdain and exploit the deprived masses, especially in the rural and tribal areas. They employ the old colonial practices and bring into being laws which have the same colonial tenor and intent.

However, a good deal of thought and investigation is called for before large-scale implementation of programmes of reform such as those of decentralization of the legal system and legal aid to the poor. While taking up programmes of decentralization and those of giving real power to the panchayats we have to take into account the nature of social stratification and of differential distribution of power in the community. This would require not only fresh thinking but also comprehensive empirical research work. If we decentralize decision making for disputes to the panchayats the danger is that the dominant sections may have another weapon in their hand to perpetuate and strengthen their hegemony. This has actually been reported in the case of several village panchayats. The landed sections have captured the village panchayats and the *nyāya* panchayats and their decisions have acquired a new binding power. The scheme of legal aid to the poor also requires a lot of empirical study. If such schemes are to function effectively, and for the purpose for which they are brought into being, a lot of research work is needed on the nature of society and on matters of organization.

These are a couple of examples of the need for more explorations in the field of sociology of law. Law functions in society and it is a part of the larger social system. Therefore, without adequate headway in the sociology of law for Indian society it does not seem likely that an efficient and adequate legal system can be built for India.

However, it does not mean that we should wait indefinitely and put a stop to all measures for the reform of the current legal system. This is not being suggested here. We should urgently take up well-thought-out programmes and at the same time try to study systematically how these are functioning in society, and what non-intended consequences they are leading to. We cannot leave the present legal system as it is for long. It is a system of delayed responses. It cannot take care of human rights or timely settlement of disputes. It does not even serve as a deterrent because the verdict is arrived at too long after a heinous offence had been committed. By that time people tend to forget what had happened.

The readings which follow in this part elaborate in various ways and substantiate the ideas briefly presented above. Of course, some counterviews too find a place.

In the opening essay of this section, Upendra Baxi incisively unravels the colonial birthmarks of the prevailing legal system. Much of the structure of the juridical system that was built by the British colonial power remains intact in its spirit, style, and content. No real effort seems to have been made after India's independence to make it people-friendly.

Baxi rightly points out that in fact not even a serious debate has taken place about the character and shape that the juridical system should take in future. Baxi shows that even after the British departed, large sections of people tend to be dealt with in the same way as they were under colonial subjugation. Common people are not involved in the framing of laws on the plea that they would not understand. There is appalling inequality in access to legal redressal, and not even information is available to common folk.

The British sought to avoid disapproval and resistance from the large population of Hindus over whom they ruled by trying to apply the laws propounded in the Dharmashastras. Derret describes vividly, how this effort led to many serious distortions in the Hindu law that was enforced by the British.

In his inimitable style, Justice V.R. Krishna Iyer in his essay demonstrates the pressing need for a thorough restructuring of existing legal system: 'Otherwise it will remain a happy hunting ground for crafty lawyers.' This system promotes quibbling over technicalities rather than seeking to dispense justice. Instead of solving disputes, it tends to further them. Its slow motion makes it ineffective in protecting human rights. Justice Iyer emphasizes the need to replace the combative culture by an effort towards redressal and reconciliation. Since the state is a party in a large number of cases, it should take the lead in this direction.

The piece on criminal justice amongst tribes in this part is a product of a group effort. An attempt has been made to outline the structure and functioning of the legal system in some tribes of India's north-east, particularly the Khasis. This may serve as an example to bring out the fact that alternatives are not impossible.

J.S. Gandhi's essay brings out how the imposition of the British legal system changed the entire judicial ethos that existed under the traditional system of law. This essay also deals with the inadequacy of the legal system of post-independence India in bringing about basic social change.

1

Colonial Nature of the Indian Legal System*

UPENDRA BAXI

The Indian legal system (ILS), in its cultural, normative, and institutional aspects offers a vignette of Indian development. Although the constitutionally desired social order makes radical, and indeed in some respects revolutionary, normative departures from its pre-colonial moorings, it is, in its operations, still very much burdened with its colonial past.

It is astonishing, but true, that there has been no real debate in independent India on the nature and the future of the ILS. The only impulse towards sustained discussion has arisen in terms of 'revivalists' and 'modernists', between neo-Gandhians and neo-liberals, on the eve of the Constitution-making (see e.g., Austin 1966; 26–46; Baxi 1967; 339–44; Galanter 1972: 53). Large, and unproductive, questions have been raised concerning the suitability of the Western legal system for a peasant Asian society and these too have mainly focused on the restoration of some supposed aspect of the 'genius of the Indian (mostly Hindu) society and people'. The genius, it has been argued, required a wholesale transformation of the ILS going back to some kind of communitarianism which prevailed in ancient (Hindu) India. Naturally, it has been possible for the 'modernists' to give a short shrift to all this by saying that history has, if anything, Indianized and socialized colonial legal system, indeed to a point that it suits the genius of the Indian people (Law Commission 1958). It would perplex, if not shock, a future historian of India to find that there was comparatively a far more sophisticated and solicitious debate concerning the introduction of the Western legal system in India in

*Excerpted from Upendra Baxi, 'The Colonial Nature of the Indian Legal System', in *The Crisis of the Indian Legal System*, New Delhi: Vikas, 1982, pp. 41–83.

colonial times among the British administrators than the state of debate of India, on and since independence, concerning its retention. The fact that in many of its normative, institutional and cultural aspects, the ILS remains burdened with its colonial past, even after more than fifty years of independence, constitutes an indictment not of our past colonial masters but of the elite of independent India, who have over the years been content with the colonial mould and mode of law.

The word 'colonial' is a somewhat treacherous one and a fairly useful one for polemical purposes. We endeavour to use it here with a degree of clarity as regards its meaning. Historical continuities with the past are perhaps ineluctable; we should, therefore, expect to find certain features which were predominant in the British Indian Legal System (BILS) to be so in the legal system of independent India. Institutional, normative, and cultural continuities may, however, be of three types. The first type is where the norms, ideology (or values), and institutions of the BILS were consciously examined, accepted, and adapted to the needs of independent India (e.g., the structure of adjudication, adversary mode, laissez-faire structure of legal profession, and vast bodies of legal norms). The second type of continuity arises out of sheer inertia. The third type is one where change away from the BILS is frequently demanded but the change is opposed, and the status quo defended, by political and professional elites of independent India through arguments and justifications which are either reminiscent or very much the same as were advanced by the operators of the BILS. The rhetoric and 'logic' of justifications for the status quo (or continuities between the BILS and the ILS) which almost regards the attainment of political independence as *immaterial* or *irrelevant*, deserves to be characterized as distinctively colonial rhetoric and logic. If this third type of continuity is substantially manifested, perpetuating the same element of colonial governance through the law, one should have no hesitation even in characterizing the entire legal system as colonial. We highlight here some marked continuities between the BILS and the ILS.

Of course, the notion 'colonial' can be used more extensively to signify a number of wider states of affairs. For example, one might wish to use the epithet 'colonial' to denote a state of dependency on the 'mother' country, even long after the liquidation of the historical phase of actual colonization. Continuous reliance on Western legal systems (particularly the common law culture of England and America) by judges, legislators, administrators, and jurists could be tellingly documented in support of the view that the ILS in this sense is colonial. Thoughtless transplants of legislative models, inapposite borrowings of Western institutional blueprints and the underlying ideologies, excessive judicial dependence on

Anglo-American legal materials, and many other similar factors are easy enough to document. All this manifests the juridical counterpart of what Latin American theorists of development and underdevelopment have identified as *dependencia*, as a 'situation in which the economy of a certain group of countries is conditioned by development and expansion of another economy which is subordinate to the first' and involves a ' "historical condition" which affects a given structure of economy in such a way that few countries can derive advantages to the detriment of other countries' and thereby restrict 'the subordinate economy's opportunities for development'. For the word 'economy' we have only to substitute the words 'law' or 'legal systems and cultures' to arrive at the situation of juristic *dependencia*.

The phenomenon of juristic *dependencia* manifests itself most strikingly in planning or initiating through legislative or judicial processes, evident in copycat drafting of laws or reliance on obsolescent Anglo-American decisional law (or legislative models) *which have undergone drastic changes even in the countries of their origin*. In 90 per cent of the cases, the legislative draftsmen follow the model and language of English laws: judicial interpretation continues to rely heavily on Anglo-American decisional materials. The point is that through these processes legislative and judicial development remain conditioned by development and expansion of 'overseas' models (mainly Anglo-American) and the ILS became a subordinate, almost a *vassal* legal system, thereby only *occasionally* serving the needs of Indian society.

We do not further elaborate or use the notion of *dependencia*, or cognate forms of new colonialism in the wide-ranging contemporary sense. The main reason for this denial in intellectual self-indulgence is that the Indian reality is far too complex to be captured by a mere invocation of the notion of *dependencia* which is itself not entirely unproblematic conceptually. For example, the demarcating line between 'copycatism' and cross-cultural diffusion is susceptible to confusion as well as to clever manipulation for specific ideological or political purposes. This is *not* to deny that the operators of the ILS (judges, legislators, administrators, or jurists) *are* excessively oriented to an Anglo-American legal culture. They *are*. But to call this situation colonial is, in the present opinion, unproductive of scientific understanding of the problems and processes which give rise to this phenomenon, which deserves to be studied on its own terms. As a general maxim, we have to remember that Indocentrism by itself is no answer to Eurocentrism.

Nor do we use the term colonial in a wider sociological sense to signify the relationship of domination and subjugation between the rulers, whether alien or indigenous, and the ruled. This state of affairs was clearly the core of colonialism as a historical phenomenon but it is doubtful whether denial of freedom to large masses of people by indigenous rulers after decolonization can be fruitfully looked upon simply as a colonial process, though in the literature on self-determination as an aspect of contemporary international order this is precisely how the term is used (e.g., in the case of Bangladesh or Biafra). Once again, we do not deny the possibility of the use (or abuse) of the legal system as an instrument of denial of freedom and subjugation of vast masses of people. Undoubtedly, it is possible to design and use a legal system to sustain favoured constellations of power distribution in such a way as to ensure the hegemony of certain ethnic or caste groups over others, or that of the proprietariat over the proletariat, or of the privileged few over the grossly deprived masses. Undoubtedly, too, the legal histories of colonial regimes do actually supply the normative and the institutional models which are 'apt' for such uses of the law. It is certainly possible, and some would say even desirable, to accentuate such features of the ILS in its critique from a 'radical' standpoint. But it remains doubtful whether the already overworked label, helps much, except providing polemical wealth, in a sharp formulation and clear handling of the problems.

The ILS follows broadly the normative and the institutional features of the BILS. Let us look at some of the persistent colonial features (in the sense defined by us) of the ILS.

The Non-Participative, 'Top-Down' Models of ILS

During the British Indian period, participation by broad masses of people, or even by the interests immediately affected by it, in the process of the making and implementation of laws was virtually unknown; unless, of course, we regard protest and disobedience as forms of group participation in law-making. The British Indian model of law-making was a top-down model: it was a paradigm of Austinian type. There was a group of determinate human superiors which issued commands; the political inferiors had the option either to comply or to risk the application of sanction.

The model of law-making adopted in free India is not much different, unless again you wish to regard periodic participation in the electoral processes by masses and collective protest as forms of participation. By and large, only the bureaucrats and legislators participate in law-making; the former predominate in any case as a large man of rule making is in

effect delegated to the executive. Occasionally, other elite groups participate. The Law Commissions at the centre (and in some states) attempt to
offer guidance and elicit informed public opinion. These and other
specialist law reform bodies tour sometimes throughout India (that is, *the
capital cities of various states*) and collect opinions and views. The Select
Committees of the legislatures also receive the evidence of interested
groups and citizens. In the sphere of delegated legislation, there is no insistence, either in law or in policy, on prior consultation with the affected
groups, a procedure considered to be both just and efficient. We do not
as yet know whether and how far, Indian legislatures function in response
to 'lobbies' converting policy into law; nor do we know as yet as to the
interests which such groups represent, although it would be relatively safe
to say that they would represent the resourceful and not the vulnerable
and underprivileged groups of society.

Thus, law-making remains, more or less, the exclusive prorogative of
a small cross-section of elites. This necessarily affects both the quality of
the law enacted and its social communication, diffusion, acceptance, and
effectivity. It also reinforces the highly centralized system of power. It is
time that we considered the desirability and feasibility of building into the
law-making processes a substantial amount of public participation. For
example, there is no reason why the state may not require that major
changes or new legislative proposals be discussed and debated in all dominant institutions of society and that the substance of deliberations be
reported to the legislative bodies There is no reason why the *Gaon Sabha*
(in so far as these exist) under the panchayati raj system may not be asked
to discuss at their meetings the proposed legislation affecting agricultural
credit or investment, ameliorative legislation concerning agrarian reforms proposed from time to time in relation to the general body of law
such as changes in the family law, penal code, procedure, etc. The panchayati raj institutions as well as other dominant social institutions (universities, bar, media groups, voluntary bodies, etc.) should be given the fullest
scope for structured participation in important legislative proposals. As
regards delegated legislation, the requirement of consultation with the
affected groups should be mandatory. The argument that this will take
time and consume resources is misconceived; passage of legislation is in
any case costly and time consuming. And the overall gains—in terms of
mobilization of mass consciousness, accessibility of legal information,
social acceptability—will far outweigh the costs. But so strong is the hold
of the colonial model of law-making that such ideas have never been
articulated with any degree of vigour. Even the neo-Gandhian thought,

including *Sarvodaya* 'school' has not moved beyond the inspiring but programmatically sterile grandiose conceptions of *lokshakti* (people's power) or *lokniti* (people-oriented polities). (That is why the proposed method of amendment of certain parts of the Constitution through referendum at which at least 51 per cent of people should vote, constitutes an important innovation; after all people should vote, constitutes an important innovation; after all, people should have a say in such a vital matter. The opposition by intellectuals and other elite groups takes on a subtle form. It is argued that in a vast country like India this is not just feasible. People, 80 per cent of them living in villages, would not understand the complexities of amendment. The Constitution will then remain ultimately inflexible. This kind of argument betrays a non-egalitarian and even authoritarian approach: 'people' are not to be associated or involved in changes of the basic rules of the game of power. Only the 'enlightened' groups should have a say in the process. This is colonial logic.)

People's participation in the enforcement and implementation of the law is also not actively sought, sponsored, or structured by the state. Once again it is assumed that such tasks are, more or less, the exclusive prerogative of the state. There are occasional sermons that people should help the state make the laws effective, that they should not withhold active cooperation from the law enforcement agencies, that they should develop a civic competence, a stake in the maintenance of social control and promotion of social change. All this rhetoric is no doubt nobly inspired but the legal systems as structured provide little or no effective scope for public participation in the implementation of legislation. The idea that the beneficiaries of ameliorative legislation should have a role in the implementation of laws favouring them is still a new one: it was only at the stage of the formulation of the Fifth Five-Year Plan that the proposal was seriously made, for example, that tenants should be involved through committees in overseeing the implementation of agrarian tenancy legislations. The Sixth Plan, ushered in after the 'revolution' and the democratic 'restoration' of 1977, is equally anemic in emphasis on its beneficiary participation in the implementation of redistributive legislation. Equally new is the idea that there should be a 'social audit' of major legislations by the beneficiaries or, more generally, the consumers of legal justice.

Broadly, the ILS also follows the colonial model of reactive mobilization of the law rather than proactive mobilization. In the former, the citizen is left to initiate the legal process by filing a complaint; in the latter the state agencies initiate the legal process. Laws that attack certain segments of the social structure in the title of justice and equity obviously need proactive mobilization; this, however, is not the case in major areas of legal innovation in independent India despite the very obvious and stark fact that the vulnerable groups are in no position, by themselves, to activate the redistributive legislation (e.g., agrarian reform measures, protection of rural and urban unorganized labour, laws for socially and economically vulnerable populations). This may be due to resource constraints; but one does not know whether this is so simply because the patterns of mobilization of law have not engaged any systematic attention of the lawgivers and the lawmen generally. The resource constraints could be somewhat offset by the organization at the local levels of the beneficiary groups and consumers of law: again this important beginning can only be made if participation in implementation of law as well as in lawmaking is accepted in the first place as an important social value, and as a crucial component of human and social development in India.

ACCESS TO LEGAL INFORMATION

The colonial model is also perpetuated in terms of access to law by citizens. Access to law means not just access to courts as the lawyers generally think about it. It means, in a broader and socially more relevant sense, access to lawmakers, to dispensers of legal services (legal profession) and to normative and institutional information concerning the legal system. In all these dimensions of access value, we find that the ILS is based on rather clear violations of democratic legality. We have already seen how non-participation, which is a *preferred value*, renders the actual operation of the ILS, for a whole variety of situations, almost identical with that of the BILS. We now briefly turn to some other aspects of the problem.

One major way in which the Indian legal system violates the principles of democratic legality is that information concerning the norms of law is not accessible easily even to those who are affected by the law. The notorious axiom that 'ignorance of the law is no excuse' casts a *duty* upon the citizen to know the law on the pain of sanction; however, there is no *right* conferred upon the citizen to have access to legal information. Even the most generally formulated directive principle of state policy will not easily yield the proposition that the state is under a duty to make law accessible, even in bare terms of normative information, to the citizen. It would require several generations of juristic effort similarly to produce by sheer exegesis the proposition that the chapter on fundamental rights *necessarily* imparts a fundamental right of the citizen to have access to legal information.

The requirement that acts of legislatures be notified through the official gazettes ensures, theoretically at least, that the laws made by Parliament and state legislatures and in force from time to time are easily accessible. This is just not the case, although the situation is relatively (and that is really not saying much) better as regards the union legislation. There is no all-India collection of laws in force throughout the territory of India; there is not even an index. An Indian citizen in Delhi wishing to have, or affected by a need for, some information on relevant laws prevalent, say, in the state of Karnataka, may find this an uphill task even with the intervention of the professional intermediaries. The situation in regard to delegated legislation, the volume of which is immensely larger than that of usual legislation, is even more alarming. The Indian Parliament enacted from the period 1973 to 1977 a total of 302 laws; against this the total number of statutory orders and rules (on the rough count) passed in the same period was approximately 25,414. The corresponding figures for states and union territories are just not available; but the number of rules issued under the delegated legislative powers may well be astronomical. While the Supreme Court of India has, in a handful of decisions, required publication of delegated legislation as a precondition of its validity, and the legislature usually requires some form of publication, mostly through the gazette, the situation is that information concerning the rules is very hard to come by. Even well-endowed companies, some of them multinationals, are known to have difficulties in gathering up-to-date information concerning subordinate legislation passed from time to time by the central government. The government of India has been unable to agree with the Lok Sabha Committee of Subordinate Legislation which recommended that there should be an annual publication, as in Britain, of statutory instruments and rules. The government advanced as reasons that the 'government press cannot undertake such voluminous work', that rapid changes would in any case make such publications obsolete, and that the costs involved would be too high. In the circumstances, the question of each state and union territory bringing out such a publication simply does not arise. Obviously, publication of laws of this kind by private entrepreneurs through government contracts or otherwise is also not encouraged, perhaps on the ground that this would intrude on the natural monopoly of the governments in this regard.

We have so far been referring only to a special strata of people in industry or business in urban India. If consumers, beneficiaries, and victims of law in urban India have such problem of accessibility to normative law, one might well despair of communication of law to the rural masses, even in situations where the law is ostensibly meant to protect their interests and rights. Normative law is virtually inaccessible to the most underprivileged and vulnerable groups in Indian society. Legal illiteracy of the beneficiaries of the law thus contributes to its ineffectiveness, e.g., prisoners may not even get to see the jail manuals when distinguished criminologists find it extremely hard to get a copy. Neither the bonded labour nor the contract labour nor the landless labour have much idea of the law and the uses that can be made of it.

Access to normative information concerning one's legal status—rights and duties— is impeded not just by the legislatures and the executive but also by the judiciary. There is no comprehensive law reporting in India and the official reports of decisions of the high courts are both inadequate and even irregular. The highest court in the land, whose declarations of law are binding through all courts in the territory of India (Article 141 of the Constitution), retains and also exercises the power to classify certain of its decisions as 'unreportable' or 'non-reportable'. Similar discretion is reserved by high courts which are also courts of record. A leading law publisher who has unsuccessfully tried to get the judgments of the Supreme Court declassified found that during the 1950–5 period as many as 250 decisions were classified by the court as 'non-reportable'. The number must have increased since the Supreme Court often cites in its reported judgments the very decisions it classifies as non-reportable, thus causing considerable distortions in the development of the law. There might have been perfectly proper reasons from the court's managerial standpoint for the retention and exercise of this, perhaps 'inherent', power. But the question is whether such power ought to exist in the first place in a democratic society. One may ask: does not such power violate what the Supreme Court has so seminally developed as the doctrine of the 'basic structure' of the Constitution?

Access to institutional information concerning the law is as problematic as access to normative information. Reports of the state governments on administration of justice, as and when published, are almost impossible to obtain; so are the reports of the state departments of law and justice. The union government brings out the valuable *Crime in India*, giving immensely useful information, but for some reason this is a non-priced publication, not easily available in most parts of India. Sometimes valuable reports are published; but they are regarded as confidential and are given restricted circulation. A classic example is that of the Justice J.C. Shah Committee Report on arrears in high courts, published in 1972. But for the courtesy of a high government official who was kind enough to loan a copy of this report to me, with some anxiety whether its contents could be properly used even in scholarly work, I would never have been able to obtain and use that invaluable report. In this democratic republic of ours, there may, in effect, exist not merely a regime of secret *laws* (clearly antithetical to civilized legal system) but of secret *reports* as well.

ACCESS TO LEGAL SERVICES

If the citizen has difficulties in reaching the legislator with his advice and opinion on the laws which are enacted for his own benefit or detriment, these difficulties are compounded when he actually has to encounter the operations of the law enacted without any substantial participation and without even minimal awareness of his legal status. Clearly the value of access to legal services has not been taken seriously at all in India, although from time to time there has been a spurt of very genuine concern with the state of legal services.

The Constitution, both in its fundamental rights and in the directive principles of state policy, was construed to be silent concerning the provision of legal aid in deserving cases; it was only in 1976, and during the national emergency, when paradoxically even minimal human rights were totally denied to a large section of Indian masses, that the duty of the state to endeavour to provide legal services was according the status of the directive principle of state policy. Although the Law Commission in its famous Fourteenth Report (1958) suggested the provision of counsel at state expense in all cases triable by the sessions courts as an 'immediate step', it was only in 1973 that the Criminal Procedure Code was amended so to provide. A more callous attitude towards the rights of the indigent citizens—in a subcontinent of harrowing poverty—is hard to imagine. It was understandable, in these circumstances, that Madhu Limaye's bill (1960), to provide legal aid in all criminal cases to needy people, was consigned to dignified oblivion. However, the argument that there are not enough resources to operate legal services in criminal law contexts does not fit well when the state and its agencies are the most prominent litigants and when the state levies court fees which have been demonstrated to result in considerable profits to the state for expenditure as general revenue. This is not to say that the resource constraint is entirely imaginary; surely the Indian state cannot meet all the legal needs of all its underprivileged and vulnerable sections. This would require a mind-boggling outlay of human and financial resources. The point is that it should not take a democratic nation twenty-three years to decide on priorities of legal services, in the most minimal sense of providing counsel to indigent accused at the sessions level. If this is the measure of urgency, one would wonder whether another quarter-century would pass before action on any of the recommendations made in the deeply humanistic and luminous reports by the Krishna Iyer and Bhagwati Committees (1974 and 1978). To characterize the state's underlying attitudes towards the legal needs of the large masses of poor people as 'colonial' would be stating the matter in the mildest possible terms.

Provisions for adequate legal services to meet the litigation-oriented legal needs of the poor have not caused as much excitement and commitment at the Bar as have the high 'superstructure' issues such as the 'supersession of judges' or constitutional amendments narrowing the scope of the writ jurisdiction of the high courts. Although there is now a degree of responsiveness at the Bar to the claims of legal services, the legal profession is so organized as to discourage, rather than foster, any worthwhile institutionalization of legal services programme. The fact remains, as pointed out so bluntly (and rightly) by the Krishna Iyer Committee, that the 'legal profession in India . . . enjoys a near monopolistic power' permitting no equalization of the 'bargaining power between the consumers of legal services and the closed group of legal profession' and that the 'legal services market is essentially a seller's market' where the demand for services is backed by purchasing power. The Committee noted, by way of mild exoneration, that the legal profession is merely an aspect of 'the capitalistic society' which is an 'acquisitive society' where the 'greatness of a lawyer is measured by the amount of the fees he charges and not by the quantum of social service which he renders as lawyer'. Interestingly the Committee saw a nexus between the legal profession and the state agencies: it found that it was 'the Central and State governments, corporations managed and/or controlled by (these) . . ., governments and Private and Public Companies which are really responsible for inflating the standard of fees'. It recommended that the government adopt a policy on maximum fees payable by its own agencies and thus dry up the 'major feedstock of the senior lawyers'. The committee also suggested the creation of legal services in the 'public sector'. Even these modest recommendations have not been accepted. The recommendations are here characterized as 'modest' simply because the Committee shares the liberal assumption that the 'autonomy of legal profession' is as 'invaluable' and 'inalienable' a guarantee of 'free society' as is the 'independence of the judiciary'. Not a single subgroup of the Indian Bar has, understandably, championed this specific recommendation although the Bar as a whole may be quick to denounce the very idea of a 'public sector' in the delivery of legal services as fatal to the 'rule of law' values.

Access to legal services transcends, of course, litigation-oriented legal aid. The programming of legal services should include non-litigative services as the two recent Committees (the Iyer and Bhagwati Committees) have stressed. Non-litigative legal aid will include a whole range of functions—skilled counselling, mediation, arbitration, conciliation, and continual monitoring—in resolving potentially litigious situations. Legal services strategies would have to extend as well to a re-examination of the normative and institutional aspects of the ILS. Massive reform of substantive and procedural laws and of the administration of justice institutions may also be needed, as stressed by the Iyer Committee.

It is a strange paradox that while the Indian government both at the national and state levels has been prolific in enacting a very large number of laws making a determined attack on the inequities of the social structure, it should have been so quiescent on the need for different types of mobilization of law for effective implementation of these very measures. In any case, the experience has now clearly shown that such laws require not just bureaucratic and legal mobilization; what is needed is not just the spruce palliative of random provision of legal services. What is needed is a thoroughgoing attempt at increasing civil participation in the making and implementation of laws: the colonial idea that one can promote social change by normative proclamations of objectives and random bureaucratic enforcement of legal provisions needs to be given a timely, and unceremonious, farewell.

ACCESS TO COURTS: THE 'MISAPPROPRIATED' COURT FEES

Lord Macaulay condemned the preamble to the Bengal Regulation, which imposed in 1795 high court fees with the avowed objective of inhibiting litigation, as 'the most eminently absurd preamble that was ever drawn'. In 1835, Macaulay launched a vigorous, though futile, attack on the justification of the continuation of court fees. In words still cogent today, he said:

> If what the Courts administer be justice, is justice a thing which the Government ought to grudge to the people? . . . It is undoubtedly a great evil that frivolous and vexations suits should be instituted. But it is an evil for which the Government has only itself and its agents to blame, and for which it has the power of proving a most efficient remedy. The real way to prevent unjust suits is to take care that there shall be just decision. No man goes to law except in the hope of succeeding. No man hopes to succeed in a bad cause unless he has reason to believe that it will be determined according to bad laws or by bad

Judges. Dishonest suits will never be common unless the public entertains an unfavourable opinion of the administration of justice. And the public will never long entertain such an opinion without good reason . . . [The imposition of court fees] neither makes the pleadings clearer nor the law plainer, nor the corrupt judge purer, nor the stupid judge wiser. It will no doubt drive away dishonest plaintiffs who cannot pay the fee. But it will also drive away the honest plaintiffs who are in the same situation.

A case against this eminently absurd tax on litigation cannot be more cogently made. The colonial government duly ignored Macaulay's rather inconvenient analysis. Although this analysis has been reiterated times without number by law reformers, including the Law Commission of India since independence, the Indian state has retained the colonial system of imposition of court fees and indeed made the fees nearly exorbitant over the course of the last fifty years. The Fourteenth Report of the Law Commission did not merely invoke Macaulay's memorable observations; it went further (and by a thorough analysis of budgets on administration of justice) to show that the amount raised by court fees was not merely adequate for meeting the administration of justice but resulted in surpluses which were appropriated to the general revenues of the states concerned. The Fifty-fourth Report of the Law Commission went out of the way to reiterate the unhonoured recommendations made in the Fourteenth Report. The Krishna Iyer Committee on Legal Aid was 'cold and blunt' concerning state inaction:

> Something must be done, we venture to state, to arrest the escalating vice of burdensome scales of court fee. That the state should not sell justice is an obvious proposition but the high rate of court fee now levied leaves no valid alibi is also obvious. The Fourteenth Report of the Law Commission, the practice of 2 per cent in the socialist countries, and the small standard filing fee prevalent in many Western countries make the Indian position indefensible and perilously near unconstitutional. If the legal system is not to be undemocratically expensive, there is a strong case for reducing court fees and instituting suitors fund to meet the cost directed to be paid by a party because he is the loser but in the circumstances cannot bear the burden (p. 35).

Interestingly, even the Bar has missed the hint that the levy of court fees could be challenged on the ground that it is 'perilously near unconstitutional'. And such is the state of arrears, that eight years after the Gujarat High Court invalidated levy of court fees, we still await a final pronouncement by the Supreme Court in this matter! That aside, the democratic governments of the states in India have just not bothered to respond to these stirring observations. *How else* can one characterize the attitude and approach to this question except as distinctly, and pejoratively, 'colonial'?

What is worse, by any standards, is the fact that despite the huge collections by way of court fees, the amount thus realized (as in British India) is not put to service of administration of justice. Physical and administrative 'facilities' provided to the subordinate judiciary are, by and large, scandalous. The requirements—for office space, for adequate maintenance of buildings, for furniture and office staff for subordinate judiciary—are ignored with undemocratic nonchalance. Whenever pressed for reasons, the stock answer of the governments is: 'lack of resources' ('where have all the court fees gone?. . .'). For example, the report on the administration of justice in Uttar Pradesh for 1969 contains revealing exposures. Out of thirty-one proposals for courtroom buildings (and some residential quarters for judges) made in 1969–70 only four were sanctioned. Three such sanctioned proposals included electrification of the munsif's court at Bansi in district Basti (Rs 5,900), extension of record room at Mirzapur (Rs30,200), and construction of munsif's courtroom at Kashipur, Naini Tal (Rs13,300). Of course, the sanction did not arrive till the end of 1981 and the work had yet to begin on any of these projects (one hopes that by now it has been completed!). Original allocations placed at the disposal of the high courts for the expansion of physical facilities are abruptly curtailed in the middle of the period, causing great confusion and demoralization all round. Even the biannual whitewashing of court buildings has not been possible, according to the report; and 'the condition of the furniture of civil courts is in general very deplorable'. The existing items are 'rickety and have outlived their utility'. The report humbly reiterates the need for providing fan coolers to civil courts in Uttar Pradesh as the *khas tattis* are more expensive to operate. The courts do not have enough typewriters and typists: 'from time to time the Court has been requesting Government in the interest of work to accord permission to the District Judges to take English typewriter wherever necessary on hire, but that request too has been unheeded'. (Three cheers for the independence of the judiciary!) It is pointless to multiply examples.

Of course, our immediate purpose in referring to some details of the Uttar Pradesh report is to show that, even assuming that there is some kind of justification for the retention of court fees, there cannot be any justification whatsoever for what must be called 'misappropriation' of the proceeds for purposes other than administration of justice. Surely, the minimum needs of the justice institutions should met; neither equity nor expedition, nor even excellence, can be expected when judicial institutions are denied the bare physical and functional facilities. If this state of affairs continues, it is both conceivable and likely that judicial offices at the level of the subordinate judiciary may cease to be attractive to young and talented people, who might opt for other careers. Perhaps, this is already happening. To this extent, urgent attention needs to be given to more financial outlays being provided to coordinate courts, and the court system generally, lest the integrity of the legal process suffer.

The Uttar Pradesh report reveals another, and more insidious, aspect concerning the autonomy of the judiciary in its relations with the executive. The administration of subordinate judiciary is the responsibility of the high court, which is at the apex of the state judicial system. If the high court's carefully formulated demands for budgetary appropriation are treated callously by the executive, the legitimacy, dignity, and prestige of the high court concerned are likely to be adversely affected. More fundamental is the further point: is it not the height of centralization of power in our country that district judges, who have substantial discretionary power for the administration of justice, should have to await permission from some faceless bureaucrat even to hire typewriters for the expeditious handling of matters before the courts or to provide fan coolers instead of *khas tattis*? Some structural device has to be found to make administration of justice by the courts independent of stringent financial and bureaucratic controls. The crisis facing the Indian court system in terms of crushing arrears of work may be attributed partly to the inadequate infrastructural facilities compounded by the lack of adequate and timely funding and above all the lack of autonomy characterizing the present system.

2

Administration of Hindu Law by the British*

J. DUNCAN M. DERRETT

The knowledge that the British were bound to administer a 'new' shastra, the traditional book-law in a new guise, and would introduce deliberately or accidentally concepts drawn from their own legal background, had several effects on the Hindu scholarly public. We have tentatively concluded that they, for all their remarkable adaptability, were not fit to supply the newcomers with an Indian law which could be applied without difficulty or doubt. Between 1772 and 1947, when India became independent, attitudes towards the indigenous laws developed and acquired their present peculiar form. It is not English, and it is not the attitude of the *sāstris*. How it came about requires a recognition of the status of the legal decision as a maker of ideals. When this has been grasped we shall be half-way to understanding the colour of the subject, though its content can only be made out from a detailed examination, which should certainly be attempted. We should look once again at the picture of custom and law, of usage and jurisprudence, of legal endeavour and rough-and-ready 'palm-tree' justice, and ask whether the British administration made a difference, and if so what and how. We know that English administrators were sincerely anxious to find out what native laws were. Now we must see what success they made of applying them.

THE HISTORICAL BACKGROUND

Europeans acquiring territories in India were obliged by the constitutional law of the kingdom or empires within which their zamindāris lay,

*Excerpted from J. Duncan M. Derrett, *Religion, Law and the State in India*, London: Oxford University Press, 1968, pp. 274–320.

to administer justice to the natives within their jurisdictions in a fashion generally agreeable to the natives themselves. The East India Company in fact appointed one of their servants to be zamindar in Calcutta and to preside over the 'Court of Cutchery' which decided suits between natives. J.Z. Holwell, who held the post between 1752 and 1757, claims to have had much success (as the Company admitted) without introducing violent innovations. The Portuguese, though recognizing no Indian territorial sovereign in Goa, seem not to have differed in their attitude markedly from that of the British in Bombay and Madras. The newcomers took advantage of existing rights in revenue matters. In criminal matters they were torn between a desire to leave the natives to solve their own problems and a fear that unredressed complaints might endanger the peace, and so the trade and other activities which explained the Europeans' presence in Asia.

It was recognized early that Muslims claimed to be governed by rules derivable from the Koran and textbooks written by the 'doctors' of the Shariat, while the Hindus recognized, at the least, the general claims of the shastra. But it was evident that these sources of law were consulted to extents varying with the topic, the locality, the efficiency of the court, the notoriety or otherwise of a custom prima facie applicable, and with the caste of the party or parties concerned. The integrity of the official judges varied enormously, from the type of the Unjust Judge of the parable (Luke xviii. 2–6) to even less satisfactory types. The Europeans themselves were, at this period, less scandalized by this state of affairs than were their successors of the mid-nineteenth century, for conditions in India and in Europe were then more comparable than later. There was a natural reluctance to assume the position and responsibilities of the persons who in fact resolved disputes between natives, and a consequent lack of interest in the formal sources of law which these functionaries might consult in their discretion. Natives might be ousted from their traditional methods of settling disputes by the intrigues of individuals whom the Company trusted—as happened at Madras, where misinformed British legislators cut off the jurisdiction of the Company's court and the natives were driven to various shifts to enable their causes to be decided there indirectly. On the other hand, native princes might differ as to the advisability of administering English law in India; in 1642 the Nayak requested the Madras Council to execute native murderers after the English fashion, but in 1770 the Nawab of Arcot resented his servants being tried by English law.

When Britain, in the person of the East India Company, accepted the *divāni* of the eastern provinces that reluctance had to be abandoned.

The result of an attempt at the former method led to chaos. The actual power had to 'stand forth' and displace the nominal authorities behind whom they had hoped to hide, and administer justice directly. By British statute the Company's courts became subject to the appellate jurisdiction of the Privy Council in London (at first not effective), and the Company steadily appointed better qualified men to judicial posts. By the time the Company's courts were merged with the Queen's courts the standard of Company's justice was little inferior to that administered by the courts set up under the Royal Charter, staffed by appointees of the Crown, and served largely by members of the English Bar.

The structure of the judicial system by 1861 may briefly be described as a group of mutually independent superior appellate courts, viz., the high courts of Calcutta, Bombay, and Madras, subject only to the Privy Council, each at the top of a pyramid of inferior courts in the districts, themselves hearing appeals from courts of first instance which were situated in some of the towns, apart from such limited original jurisdictions as they themselves might have. While the most humble of these series of courts were staffed by Indians, the higher ones were presided over by junior British officials, until one reached the seniormost of the latter, who remained in the district courts if unable to attain a seat in high court. Outside the high courts the practitioners were Indians, none of whom learnt the English legal system in England, and, what is more significant, none of whom could have become professionally qualified in the Islamic or Hindu classical systems, for the careers are incompatible. They started their careers as mere 'pleaders', and acquired proficiency in the somewhat rough-and-ready atmosphere of the junior courts which preceded the British system in some areas. The best practitioners were soon siphoned off into the higher courts, for litigation was always remunerative and brains found their own level at the high court Bar as soon as native practitioners could cope with its procedure. The intellectual gap between judgments delivered in the high courts, where some judges were English barristers of standing, and the country vakils who were supposed to advise their clients according to them was, and to a large extent remains, marked.

While this judicial hierarchy was developing, a striking dichotomy emerged between the court law and the popular law, the interacting components we have already observed for a somewhat earlier period. It is not clear whether a precise counterpart has developed elsewhere. Its emergence is an important part of this story.

The situation prevailing when foreign rulers assumed their respective judicial responsibilities was, for all its faults, empirical. In no case did theory impose some juridical technique which had not emerged from the needs and history of the relevant group. In a relatively small area might be found several native types of decision making and decision enforcement, all satisfactory within the given limits, none suitable for sudden transference into other spheres, and hardly any conformable to British presuppositions about judicial administration. The types may be roughly categorized as (1) tribal government, where the circle of pressures would be narrow and influence from outside slight, as in cases resembling that of Santals today; (2) amongst agriculturalists a hierarchy of political governors, who could take administrative action to solve problems which family, sub-caste, village, or district leaders could not solve—a situation in which approaches to litigation would occur chiefly where pressures were nearly equal, and delinquents could not be controlled, unanimity being more important than abstract justice; (3) in better organized societies, in towns particularly, the panchayat, or ad hoc committee of castes, functioned, staffed by members identified by a kind of natural selection: the higher the standing of the parties the greater likelihood that the shastra would consulted and applied; while (4) Brahmin sub-castes would be directly served in their disputes by śāstris, and the shastra would more frequently be consulted. Throughout, however, the principle was the same: no litigation until social pressures had been tried and exhausted. Excommunication was available and operated well in some areas and for some offences. The state was called in to cope with robbery and killing and serious mayhem. Powerful groups could defy the law, and public indignation against them found no machinery wherewith to express itself. The 'king' was at all times necessary to keep the social balance, and one who could manage to achieve this by force of personality, wealth, or arms, had a good claim to be, in the locality, 'king'.

The Hindu system gave everyone his place in every possible contingency; individuality was not prized, disobedience was anathema; functions were fixed by the caste system; and sources of pressure (outside the wild and barely Hinduized tribes) were many. Where the Muslims had succeeded to Hindu rulers they took over a going concern; they authorized the natural leaders to continue their previous functions; they respected fundamental customs; they even admitted Brahmins to be the proper authorities to determine certain disputes; and they tolerated the indigenous system so long as it did not conflict with their own. The Islamic law of crimes, and their law of evidence in the criminal and possibly also in other courts, were in force where Muslims ruled, but otherwise there was no question of administering Islamic law as such to non-Muslims. In Bengal and Madras the Hindus were used to living under two systems simultaneously, both administered under the authority or with the sufferance of the ruler, and this must have gone a long way towards preparing them to accept a third.

BRITISH PRESUPPOSITIONS

British administration attracted Indian litigants early. The Portuguese, Dutch, French, and Danish, so far as we know, did not have quite the same experience. The 'success' of the British was misunderstood and led to puzzling decisions on the part of the relevant authorities. The secret of the flood of Indian cases to the early British courts, such as the Mayors' Courts, lay in the immediacy and violence of the remedies offered: needless to say the Supreme Court at Calcutta gave an even more dramatic impression of this sort. The chances of losing a good case were high, but if one won, the prizes were larger than would be available under the native system. Following the commercial class, others were attracted to enlist the aid of this new instrument of applying pressure. The British supposed that Indian litigants would elsewhere suffer from corruption or prejudice. It did not strike them at once that the Indian could take advantage within the British jurisdiction of rules of law which did not exist outside it. He could not only get his decrees executed, without relative delay or appeal, to the great discomfiture of the opposite party, but he would be able to gain legal advantages of which the native legal system knew nothing. In those very early days the English law was enforced in 'country' disputes provided the parties submitted to the jurisdiction, and since only English attorneys then knew the English law the party who submitted to the summons must frequently have been shocked at the system which he had obliged himself to obey. But as the communities in question found the gains greater than the losses a speedy adjustment to the situation took place. Where what was virtually an English court, set up under an English charter, dealt with a case between natives, English remedies and English law were inevitable. It was feared that the English law must rule even in Company's courts which existed purely for native use: this could be avoided by extensive recourse to 'arbitration', which might, it was fortunately believed, let in the native laws indirectly. In spite of themselves the Company were found administering justice along lines acceptable to the natives but under the cloak of the English legal system.

The acquisition of Bengal, Bihar, and Orissa posed the problem in an acute form. Indians who might never wish to submit to a British jurisdiction were forced to do so because the British Company was diwan of the Emperor. The questions were what form the jurisdiction should take, and what law or laws should be administered.

We have already noticed that other European powers had possessions in India. The choice which lay before the Company and later before Parliament was between following the system in use in the Portuguese possessions, or that in use in the Dutch and French possessions, on the one hand, or striking out for an improvement on both. The problem was complicated by the fact that the litigating public in the presidency towns differed from that in the *mufassil* (the 'balance', i.e., the greater part of the area). Its dealings with the European traders were regulated by English law and in certain of its private affairs it was accustomed to utilize the facilities of the British courts.

The sanction of excommunication there relied upon was early identified with the right of castes to excommunicate their members. Panchayats might have been left entirely alone to continue their functions alongside the foreign courts, which could have confined themselves to disputes between natives and foreigners, and to constitutional and criminal matters. The superstitious fear which the caste Hindus had of excommunication (especially in Bengal) or of anathema at the hands of tribunals including a Brahmin, and the helplessness of a defeated litigant or delinquent who would not accept the decision of a tribunal entitled to apply a complete boycott, impressed Europeans with the notion that this system hardly required civil or criminal penalties in the Western sense, and that it was grounded in immemorial usage and unalterable custom, interpreted in the last resort by 'priests' (as they thought) learned in the shastra. It seemed as if a system of 'Roman' law were alive in a system of 'Canon' law, in which the public believed, and which had long since won a position at the expense of the secular power. The question whether the shastra was really in use at the beginning of the British period is conclusively settled by the publication of various documents which are *jayapatras* ('certificates of victory') issued in the eighteenth and nineteenth centuries in circumstances suggesting scrupulous adherence to the shastra on the part of the courts that issued them.

INDIAN REACTIONS

Litigation soon became just another weapon of policy. Merely to summon a defendant was enough to cause him expense. The vakils (agents) who soon became available to represent clients ousted the parties themselves who had formerly appeared in person or through relations or well-placed patrons. The latter acted gratuitously, but the former required to be paid and learnt how to protract litigation. Direct contact between the judge and litigant occurred in the earliest period only. The panchayats, on the other hand, were at a disadvantage. They had retained their effectiveness in Hindu states and in many Muslim-ruled states; but in Bengal, Bihar, and Orissa the attraction to the courts was so strong that eventually they emerged with only a fraction of their power. An excommunicated man could get well-paid employment with the foreign government, and he could even bring a suit against those who had excommunicated him. At the height of the agitation against the missionaries and their very qualified success in Calcutta and its environs the orthodox Hindu leaders were unable to use the weapon of excommunication effectively, although public opinion as a whole was rather on their side than that of the missionaries—for employment and trade, upon which Calcutta was based, cared nothing for this weapon.

Caste tribunals functioned in spiritual matters which the courts left alone. A Bengali who killed a cow, in the same period to which we referred above, would no doubt be forced to undergo grievous penances. Their standards were often out of tune with those presupposed in the courts. A man might be excommunicated for doing something which the courts allowed as good. In parts of India which came later under British rule the dichotomy of standards was more marked. The judicial administration became eventually, despite expert advice, more or less homogeneous throughout British India, and the natives even of western India had to respect the newfangled and the ancient system simultaneously, even when they were incompatible. We shall see, in another connexion, how the courts themselves might defer to the caste's opinion, but this was not the general pattern. The court law had its sphere; the caste law was independent of it to a very great extent. Though it could not effectively transfer land or create a status which the court alone had jurisdiction to recognize, it might still, if the caste were well knit and active, be as inhibiting and pervasive as the court law; and indeed in many spheres (disregarding the not unimportant religious sphere which was largely its own) it reached levels of obedience far more directly than any decree of the state court. Indians learnt, however, how to litigate on British lines. Dedicated men spent their entire lives mastering the art. Some specialized in handling such litigation at the district level, others at the high courts. From them developed the class of lawyers with the occasional jurist, which played a very great part in achieving independence and modifying the country's legal system. The intellectual domicile of this class provides a problem which many have attempted to solve, and which is beyond our present scope; but it may be remarked that the failure of the lawyers to stand up to the often less well-equipped political bosses of the post-independence period may not be so much the result of adult franchise as of the cessation in the public sphere of the totally fictional standards at handling which the lawyers were the only adepts prior to independence. When the Old India sought to reassert itself those who were dedicated to knowing the machinery of British India continued to assume what was not relevant to the same extent as before, and thrust aside with commendable impatience the foggy, 'oriental' principles which still adhered to the grass roots of the culture. The conversation was no longer with the British, for whom law was part of their common language, nor with others in the hearing of the British, but with the politicians whose language the lawyer class had long since taught itself not to speak.

SUPPLEMENTATION BY IMPORTED RULES

A rapid growth occurred in enterprise and extensive changes in the social outlook of the classes most likely to profit from it. The ancient ways no longer satisfied those who envied the more individualistic ways of their rulers. Questions were asked of the pandits which their sources could not answer, and their successors, authors of textbooks, were expected to suggest how new facilities could be obtained on the basis of old rules. New legal institutions, such as English-type negotiable instruments, were expected to supplant the traditional customary law, or like insolvency were expected to be engrafted upon Hindu institutions. There were doubts how far importations such as the latter penetrated into the structure of the system. Where the texts provided no explicit indication of the way in which a right was to be worked out, or how a particular disposition should be construed, English rules filled the gap. This happened frequently even without conscious reference to justice, equity, and good conscience, the residual source of law, since, to take as an example testamentary bequests or the alienation of undivided interests in coparcenary property, the judges were not aware that in applying English common law or equity they were doing anything else but expounding the Hindu law on the point. So many rules of English law seemed to be merely rules of universal law. The present judiciary are under the impression that the contribution of justice, equity, and good conscience has transformed the shastric law to such an extent that the texts as such have lost their authority. A complete list of the debts owed by the Anglo-Hindu law to English law would be extremely lengthy. Yet in hardly a single case are the judges not discovering the Hindu law through the imported rule. Sometimes doubt arises as to whether the importation has taken place, as in the topic of guardianship, which is almost entirely English in character; but normally it is assumed, rightly, that without the importation the Hindu institution could not have been applied effectively or without unjust results. Refusals to apply an English rule as such have been common.

English law is sometimes consulted under justice, equity, and good conscience, so long as it is not unsuited to Indian conditions. Since the Hindu system is said to be equipped with its own system of interpretation and since the judges attempt to fill gaps from Hindu legal sources where possible, there would appear to be no unbounded scope for English rules. But in fact the search for local rules has not been laborious, and both common law and English statute law have been resorted to. At times the general Hindu law has been used to assist with the application of customary law, and customs have even thrown light on what the personal law ought to be: but the contribution of imported law has been far more prominent than either of these indigenous sources. The resulting patchwork effect should be recognized for what it is.

'OBSOLESCENCE' AND *STARE DECISIS*

Strictly traditional and also progressive elements have been represented amongst the Indian judiciary. P.B. Gajendragadkar, formerly a judge of the Bombay High Court, then a judge and Chief Justice of the Supreme Court, later vice-chancellor of the University of Bombay, actively forwarded the codification of Hindu law both on and off the Bench. Reviewing the case law, however, a consistent pattern cannot be made out. It is dangerous to suggest that any shastric rule is obsolete. The shastra is still a source of law by statute, except where repealed. 'Advanced' groups of Hindus have procured this repeal by stages in certain sectors. After the formative period, however, embarrassing pieces of genuine shastric law, not represented in the textbooks, have on occasions been declared 'obsolete', as not confirmed by usage. 'Usage', however, might turn out to be a creation of the courts themselves without reference to practice independent of court law (which would be speculative). *Stare decisis* will support wrong precedents. Even well-known usage of former times have sometimes been declared obsolete, and their shastric representatives with them. Castes outgrowing certain practices have sometimes managed to prevent them by legislation, of which the impractical Dowry Prohibition Act, 1961, is the most striking example; and their influence can be traced in the law reports, which from time to time refer to the current spirit of the community (*sic*).

When a new rule has to be made it is questionable whether attempts to effectuate the 'spirit of the community' are more correct than strict application of principles derivable from older authorities. But where an old rule is to be applied to new facts, room for such adjustment seems desirable. The 'orthodox' who can read the shastra without an Anglo-Hindu gloss have, it need hardly be added, no use for either result. The shastra lives on in its own small sphere (amongst scholars, priests, genealogists, and the like). Some believe that it has an important moral mission yet. The reformers who carried through codification cannot accept this, for their work largely prolongs the direction taken by the Anglo-Hindu law of which they had become tired.

A need to keep the law up to date is obvious in the case of communities who cannot exclude their members from the courts by caste rules backed up by the threat of excommunication.

When statutes amended the law the courts had a choice between deciding analogous cases in conformity with the new law or refusing (and thus was obviously more correct) to extend the spirit of the statute beyond the scope given to it by the legislature. There have been instances of both approaches, and more recently the statute-reformed system has attracted to itself its unreformed predecessor, as judges are easily persuaded that the law always must have been what the legislature says it is—but this is an intellectual exercise that few judges would feel inclined openly to imitate.

Conclusion: The Place of 'Hindu Law' in India

It is confidently asserted that the British period kept a dynamic element suppressed in Hindu society, so that the personal law of the Hindus was fossilized. One could equally well say that the codification which took place in 1955–6, the culmination of the period of reform and attempted reform which started for practical purposes in 1928 or even in 1920 did even more to fossilize the system. A statute obviously pegs the law down much more firmly than case law can. Thus the public was not worried about the effects of fossilization: what had bothered people was the distance between the personal law and the system by which they wanted to live. But the psychological reasons leading up to the partial destruction of the Anglo-Hindu law in India must be treated elsewhere. It is the state of that system and its causes which concern us now.

The choices made and confirmed in 1772 and 1781 are responsible for this system. Hastings and his contemporaries cannot seriously be blamed. Other choices could hardly have been made, in view of the ignorance of the population, the apparent absence of effective means of ascertaining custom, and the grave danger that the entire administration would collapse under multiple sources of corruption.

Major changes took place on account of this start, most of them beneficial. The law became, for all its many anomalies, more certain and much more uniform. Changes in Hindu usages, for which neither shastra nor customs as usually understood could have made room, were accommodated. The massive introduction of English law or English-type law on other fronts, which excited hardly any criticism, has been harmonized with the existing personal laws. If natural growth was to be looked for, from where would it have come? The pandits were confined to reporting the rulings of long-dead authors. The shastra as an academic discipline retained some moral but little legal authority amongst the castes at large. The artificial revival of interest in India's cultural heritage from the last quarter of the nineteenth century stimulated a romantic interest in Manu; and it is from there that the continuing interest in the shastra comes which we find in some cultured classes. The interest is reflected in some legal contexts outside Hindu law. This is intriguing in its way, but beyond our present study. Public opinion had no organ of expression. If the government had backed the customary law instead of the shastra, literally hundreds of different systems of customary law would have emerged, like the scores of instances of the *riwāj-i-ām* of the Punjab. An old-fashioned method was practicable on the happy-go-lucky basis known in several 'backward' native states before 1948, but it was not the goal of the reformers in 1955–6.

In 1864 judicial knowledge of Hindu law was assumed. If this had been refused, and the system had been treated as a foreign law (to be proved in evidence), growth would have been continuous. But the apparent unreliability of the pandits indirectly obviated this possibility. Even otherwise, pandits' powers of 'text-torturing' were not boundless. To introduce divorce on Western-type grounds, and inheritance of shares by daughters along with sons was impossible for them—yet this, it is evident, was the sort of growth the reformers wanted. To find authority for such modifications they had to dig much deeper into their cultural heritage than the legal authorities operative amongst Brahminized castes in the pre-British period.

It might be argued that in the French territories, where neither *stare decisis* nor a doctrinaire reverence for texts was to be found, the position must have been healthier. The Consultative Committee could contradict itself without causing a scandal. The area of general law available to

Hindus was wider than the very small *lex loci* in matters of private law available to Indians in British India. Yet, for all the differences, Franco-Hindu law and Anglo-Hindu law were sufficiently alike for Anglo-Hindu authorities to be commonly cited in Franco-Hindu law textbooks, and for very occasional French decisions to be cited in British Indian courts. The former native states which possessed regular judiciaries likewise differed from Anglo-Hindu law in about the same measure as the French courts (though not necessarily on identical topics), but the divergencies were small, and in the direction of the traditional and 'old-fashioned'. So, far from showing how Hindu law could progress away from British influence, they have showed the reverse; and every one of these special rules has been abolished to conform to the general Anglo-Hindu pattern, and finally to the modern Hindu legal pattern.

If Hindu law 'stagnated' under the British, Islamic law died. After numerous adjustments during the formative period, and the elimination of criminal law and evidence and absorption of contract and civil wrongs, the texts were found to supply ascertainable rules to meet most situations, and case law is much less important than in the Hindu system. Enactments modifying Islamic law have, by comparison, been trifling; and since there is little impetus to reform Islamic law in India it would appear that the method adopted to ascertain and apply it was agreeable to the Muslim public—but on that topic there remains more to be said. The method accorded in fact exactly with that adopted with reference to Hindu law, except that the British could not stimulate Muslim jurists to write for them in the early days as Hindus had done.

A comparison with Ceylon (now Sri Lanka) is instructive. A desire to reform Kandyan law and Tesavalamai (Tamil customary law in Jaffna) has been manifested. The latter was administered with the aid of a code prepared under the Dutch; the former, as explained above, is basically customary law. The judges have done little to modernize or develop either system, though the residual Roman-Dutch law has filled some gaps. Amendments have proceeded through legislation. No one suggests that the British 'retarded' or 'fossilized' the laws of Ceylon. In Burma, where the texts of the so-called Buddhist law presented intractable problems of interpretation in the field of family law, the simplifications and adjustments made by British judges were accepted without resentment or even question. The court, no doubt, consulted contemporary customary behaviour, and the size and homogeneity of Burmese Buddhist society may have helped. In any case the era of the old academic jurists seems never to have been regretted.

Where a system of law, apparently confined within the margins of written texts, comes to be administered by a foreign power, people naturally expect it to be administered in the spirit of the compilers. When the relationship between textual law and non-textual customs (which are recognized as valid in the texts) is in debate, some choice has to be made and some decision taken. It is not clear what conclusion is to be drawn from the public's acquiescence in that decision. When they change, they feel that the law administered to them is antiquated and 'rigid'. It is open to them either to admit that innovation is necessary and that this may mean the importation of foreign rules, or to accuse the judiciary of failing to interpret the sources with appropriate elasticity. The latter course is attractive when one is committed to (i) proclaiming one's own advance from the position one's ancestors occupied when foreign power commenced; and (ii) asserting that the same textual system and its cultural corpus anticipated all the advances—the current social position correctly expressing the spirit of the ancient past.

If Hindu law had been forcibly codified in 1858 it appears that there would have been no objections, except from the cautious (not to say timid) and sentimental administrators who in fact refused the responsibility when the project was mooted. So long as no legislature properly represented the population, legislation must needs be rare and cautious, especially when the governing power is wedded to the notions (i) that the religions of the inhabitants must at all cost be respected, and (ii) that the personal laws were 'religious'. After 1930 Hindus became alive to their opportunity to amend their personal law at their pleasure. They moved with caution and undid none of the previous legislation. Nothing done in 1955–6 suggested that in so far as the British amended, modified, abrogated or supplemented the law their administration had been mischievous or misdirected. Some of the rules which appear in the 'Hindu Code' do not carry the law any further forward than it had gone by case law alone. As we have seen, the gap between popular standards and usages and the court law prevents our answering as we might otherwise do, namely that the law as it had developed had moulded the people themselves. In fact the portion of the law which suffered severe modification during the British period, that relating to the joint family, remains to the time of writing this essay untouched in important respects. So much for the charge that the system was fossilized: what then was codification expected to achieve? And what relation does that enterprise have to the tradition that family law is part and parcel of the religion of those whose personal law it is? These are complicated questions.

3

Law and the People*

V.R. KRISHNA IYER

JUDICIAL SLOW MOTION

Where there is a right there is a remedy, runs the legal maxim, but the law in the books is often at cynical variance with the law in action. It is notorious that in India there is considerable backlog in the civil and criminal courts, and given judicial slow motion the situation may worsen steadily. Can't we evolve a judicial technology to solve the problem of procrastinatory justice? Can't we design a streamlined and well-lubricated apparatus (operated by capable personnel) which processes forensic hearing and delivers the end product of justice with reasonable speed and finish, even if we have to break with time-honoured notions?

Our present system has been praised and denounced, some holding that it is 'foreign to our genius', others blaming the bad performance on nonsystemic factors. While the Uttar Pradesh Judicial Reforms Committee felt that 'the need of the hour is that rules and procedures and evidence should be so simplified that justice . . . may be prompt and effective', the Law Commission of India, alive to the 'wellfounded complaints against some aspects of the present judicial administration', thought that the provisions of the existing code of procedure if properly followed would expedite rather than delay the disposal of cases and that the real causes for the tardy progress of legal proceedings lay in extraneous and personal factors like 'an inefficient and inexperienced judiciary, insufficient number of judicial officers, an incompetent and corrupt ministerial and process serving agency, the diverse delaying tactics adopted by the litigants and their lawyers, the immethodical arrangement of work by the presiding judge and the heavy file of arrears'. Whoever be the villain of the piece,

*Excerpted from V.R. Krishna Iyer, *Law and the People*, New Delhi: People's Publishing House, 1972, pp. 129–41.

the case for restructuring and energizing the apparatus is strong, for, in the words of Nehru, 'the temper (of the existing system) may have suited a very leisurely time; it may not suit the time when people have to rush, hurry, tumble, fall, get up and go on . . . it is rather out of keeping with the storms and tempests of today'.

And are we ready for big changes?

First about the structure. At the lowest tier of the edifice is the trial court but it is the trial judge who is the key man of the system who handles the greatest bulk of litigated cases, whose adjudication settles the forensic fate of the majority of men who go to the law. The image of justice for the common man is projected by the trial judiciary and no judicial reform which fails to radicalize that category grapples with the problem effectively. The quantitative explosion of cases in the lowest courts, civil and criminal, and the fact that the lowliest stop with that court emphasize the central importance of trial court reform to reduce delay and expense for the common man. After all, these courts of first instance are the poor man's high court.

An Indian legal architect must naturally lay stress on a large, indigenous base of *nyāya* panchayats to haul the load of ordinary litigation locally, cutting cost and delay to the minimum. People's courts are native to our soil and now have received constitutional recognition. The Civil Justice Committee in 1924–5 and the Central Law Commission in its fourteenth report have supported this approach. According to the former, the judicial work of the panchayat is part of the village system which has flourished from the earliest times and according to the latter the importance of reorganizing and strengthening village units as organs of local self-government and for the dispensation of justice has been greatly emphasized since the advent of independence. The Constitution has recognized the importance of these village units and in Article 40, one of the Directive Principles of State Policy, it provides that the state shall take steps to organize village panchayats and endow them with such powers and authority as may be necessary to enable them to function as units of self-government. The administration of justice was in old days, as we have seen, one of the functions of the panchayats in the villages.

The plus points of these courts are many and substantial. Local trials will reduce perjury and false pleas, diminish cost and delay. Disputes requiring local knowledge or inspection can be decided better and quicker. Conciliation, in cases peculiarly suited for settlement in the interests of family peace or village harmony, may be easier arranged by these people's courts. The lack of legal training will affect only those cases which call for more than mere commonsense, and a provision for participation of 'legal members', that is professional judges (including retired judicial officers), will help here. Contentious cases, involving questions of law, may be set apart to be heard with the legal member presiding, if any party asks for it. Special short courses in basic judicial procedure and fundamental principles of law and some little training in judge-craft may equip these laymen for their judicial work.

An outstanding advantage of these panchayat courts, apart from giving a new dimension to our democratic professions, is that at little public expense we can raise a large crop of rural courts which, given adequate jurisdiction, will relieve munsifs and magistrates of the lesser class of litigation and avoid docket delays at the trial stage.

We must accept as a national legal policy that elected panchayat and municipal courts will form the base of the judicial pyramid enjoying reasonably large (not the current jejune) powers, civil and criminal. The rural and urban lay tribunals, with provision for professional assistance, must become the normal civil-cum-criminal court which will try all simple civil and criminal cases and thus become an integral and important part of the trial judiciary. Misgivings about our political ability for self-government have been expressed and yet we have dared. Why not make similar judicial experiments on a modest scale? And if these lesser halls of justice take over the bulk of civil cases, the value of which does not exceed say Rs1,000 and criminal cases entailing imprisonment not exceeding say three months, the munsifs and magistrates may not be choked by overload. Errors committed by these popular tribunals can be corrected promptly in appeal and revision.

Do we need a four-storeyed judicial mansion—the trial court, then the automatic first appeal, oftentimes a second appeal and in some cases another appeal to a division bench within the same court, and in heavier suits a voyage to the Supreme Court? The list suffers, in its deck-by-deck progress, 'at each remove a lengthening chain'. In many cases bankruptcy beckons to both the parties at the end of it all; and in any view, the pyrrhic victory of the successful suitor is not worth having after delay has done its worst for him. In criminal cases also we have a three-tier system of the first court, appellate court, revisional court, and instead, in grave cases, the Supreme Court. A disappointed or intoxicated litigant chases every remedy, wearing himself and his opponent out and oftentimes the long legal pursuit leads to the discovery that the damsel of justice has played the vanishing trick.

One automatic appeal and then a revision or cassation, in cases of illegality or serious miscarriage of justice, must suffice for all cases. A second appeal is an expensive and dilatory superfluity in a poor country.

Remember, the judgment of the high court is final not always because it is the best but because it is the last and this applies to the Supreme Court too. Under the existing three-deck system, finality to litigation involving a thousand rupees or a few cents of land or other simple and urgent reliefs, may well stretch into a deadly decade. The Law Commission of India, rarely guilty of radical views, has said: 'Viewed against the background of the low value of the subject matter and the high rate of fatality of second appeals in the high courts, as appears from the figures found in a later chapter, the proposal to give finality to litigation at the stage of the decision of the first appellate court has much to commend itself.'

A hundred years ago, Sir Barnes Peacock urged, what I repeat for serious consideration, that second appeals be abolished altogether. The eminent judge suggested, 'I hope after sufficient reflection', (I quote from the Report of the Law Commission of India) 'that it would be cheaper to government to pay the full amount of the appellant's demand with costs of both parties and to give each a bonus for terminating the litigation than to support the establishment of the high court for hearing such second appeals.'

At present there is a further, or letters patent, appeal within the high court itself from a single judge's judgment to a bench of two judges. This proliferation of appeals is twice cursed. It curseth him who wins—his patience and purse are tried to the limit—and him who loses—his financial back is broken. The Civil Justice Committee (with Sir George Rankin as chairman) gently observed about this intra-high-court phenomenon: 'The Letters Patent Appeal, that is the right to a fourth hearing, is in no degree short of absurdity.' In its opinion the system was 'so indefensible whether from the point of view of expedition or of cost to the state or of cost to the parties that it is almost a waste of words to denounce it.'

In short, learned, experienced, and eminent men in the line have frowned upon the tantalizing—and pauperizing, shall I say—system of too many appeals. One proposal, possessing the virtue of a via media (it has appealed to the Law Commission) is to restrict admission of appeals to those certified fit. In practice this is a vicious solution. Disappointed men will move in second appeal or ask for leave for further appeal regardless of merit, and the legal profession will resent too strict a security at that stage. Avoidable judicial time will anyway be consumed, and money the litigant will be tempted to spend—both of which should be inhibited by falling in line with the sensible and widely prevalent two-tier system plus a cassation to correct gross inequality and illegality. In flagrant cases of perverse or illegal verdicts there is the constitutional right to move the high court and the Supreme Court, under Articles 227 and 138 respectively of the Constitution; and where manifest injustice vitiates a judgment, a revisional remedy will give relief at the high court level.

We may adopt the same scheme in the criminal jurisdiction also. However, cases of a petty nature, civil and criminal, may be separated and allowed to be tried summarily and finally, with no appeal but a revision where injustice is writ large on the proceedings.

There is a general impression that the quality of the subordinate judiciary has deteriorated a great deal and so finality to their decisions should not be given and an appeal to the high court, at least under restricted conditions, must be permitted. This argument of fall in standards does not take us anywhere because every generation has called its successor fool and vice versa and this criticism of substandard selection is not confined to the lower judiciary. In any case, even this argument about the subordinate judiciary being of poor quality can be adequately met by providing at the district court level a bench of two judges sitting to hear the heavier appeals from munsifs and subordinate judges. If the two appellate judges agree with the trial judge, it is a safe conclusion that, nine out of ten, judgments so affirmed are correct. In case the two appellate judges disagree, maybe an appeal to the high court is permissible. In the same way, we can constitute benches to hear appeals on the criminal side. All that I wish to drive home is that litigation must be given short shrift and must not drag on.

The current procedure in our courts breeds delays in many ways. The service of summonses and notices through the process staff of the courts takes inordinate time and is often the source of corruption. The very elaborate provisions of the civil procedure code is a paradise for those who want a case to pend interminably. Indeed, one begins to wonder watching court and counsel, caught in the meshes of mere procedural controversy, whether they realize what Lord Collins, MR, observed:

> Although a court cannot conduct its business without a code of procedure, the relation of the rules of practice to take work of justice is intended to be that of handmaid rather than mistress; and the court ought not to be so far bound and tied by rules which are after all only intended as general rules of procedure, as to be compelled to do what will causes injustice in the particular case.

ARREARS EXPLOSION AND THE COURTS

Parliament, which is the grand inquest of the nation, has time and again expressed concern over the mounting arrears in high courts and subordinate courts. The home ministry has reacted by appointing committees and urging the Supreme Court to remedy the situation by suggesting ways and means of bringing down the colossal load of old cases.

Of course, when the number of dockets increases, the number of judges must also increase, notwithstanding the gibe of Parkinson. What we need is a system of relief judges, as it were, from the lowest to the highest so that whenever the carbuncle of accumulated arrears appears, the relief judges will go into action and the regular judges will handle the workload in the normal course. Mere insistence on somehow disposing of cases, particularly at the trial stage, is likely to do more harm than good; for, judging is not as simple as baking bread. It is difficult to appreciate the rather mechanical techniques prescribed for reducing delays. The conventional pattern of questionnaires issued in these contexts by high-level committees does not sufficiently disclose a proper diagnosis of the malaise.

When is a suit to be regarded as 'old'? Why should not revisions and second appeals be disposed of in six months? Should judgments be dictated from court, admissions and interim orders refused in most cases? Do advocates ask for adjournments too frequently? Is a light cause list or a heavy one better? Is it useful to divide the high court into broad but separate 'jurisdictions'? These and like interrogatories hardly plumb the depths of the problem and are like treating tuberculosis by cough syrups which will alleviate temporarily but cannot eliminate permanently. Rather, we must not only tighten up the nuts and bolts and press the accelerator but redesign the project to replace a ramshackle machine.

The renovation and reorganization of the judicial set-up involves the sophistication of the machine incorporating modern advances in technical knowledge so that delay-killing devices may harmonize with better functional performance, and the humanization of the system so that new sociological therapies may find application in the judicial process.

The judges' approach must bear the stamp of social engineering and a keener appreciation of the justice department's goals of reducing bitterness among feuding litigants and fostering friendly solutions of conflicts, incidentally saving judicial time for tougher disputes and cutting down delays directly and indirectly. Pretrial techniques of making parties and their counsel talk to each other instead of swearing and arguing at each other, of eliciting admissions on facts and creating areas of agreement—reasoning together informally with the judge as moderator as against wrangling with each other before an umpire.

Pretrial conference has been hailed by some American writers as 'the salvation of the administration of justice in the 20th century'. Such a meeting and informal discussion with the lawyers will often bring the case into shape, eliminate surprise, and promote the litigants' knowledge of each other's case. The chances are that a confrontation between the lawyers and judge in advance of trial would result in a negotiated compromise; and even if a settlement is not achieved, the scope of the controversy can be narrowed down and agreement on some points in dispute reached. Family disputes, divorce actions, minor's welfare cases should, as far as possible, be adjusted. But the negative orientation of our judiciary now views active promotion of settlement of disputes with unconcern and as even objectionable, as if even a detached persuasion of parties through their advocates to sit round a table were injurious to legal justice or likely to imperil impartiality. More liberal resort to arbitration in commercial causes and to mediatory effort, where communal conflicts, local factions, or public institutions or rights are involved, is a desirable step for a judge. I have articulated (in a judgment) my experience about the judicial role in promoting the settlement of a long-drawn-out legal duel, which, in all humility, I may quote here:

> After preliminary hearing before me, it became apparent that a serious move to settle the entire dispute was afoot and I facilitated it by postponing further steps in the case; and now a razi has been filed in court, followed by a registered partition deed. What is more soul-satisfying to a judge than to see feuding parties compose their conflicts, bury the hatchet and become friendly again, assisted in the process by the statesmanship of counsel? Justice has an aspect of relativity; and what all disputants, on fair and competent advice, accept as just is the best that human institutions can dispense. I have always regarded that the finest hour for the bar and the bench arrives when a long-drawn-out and extremely bitter litigation has been brought to a peaceful end by mild suggestions from the bench, catalytic actions by advocates and sensible response from the parties' (1969 KLR 798).

Speaking of settlement of cases, we must remember that the state and para-state bodies contribute a large volume of litigation in the high courts and even in the subordinate courts. There is no reason why the government at the state or Central level and other public bodies should contest cantankerously or fight on technical points or prolong litigation if there is a reasonable case for or chance of settlement of the dispute. If the state sets an example, not only will a huge volume of litigation get liquidated but many others like large corporations may follow the lead. It is very interesting to read excerpts from the discussion at the Law Ministers Conference held on this subject in the 1950s. But it is saddening to see that, this long lapse of time notwithstanding, no concrete steps have been taken in this behalf. In India, we discuss prolixly, resolve piously, and postpone action indefinitely.

Anyway, let me make my point by quoting the chairman of the conference (the then union law minister), Mr A.K. Sen:

> First of all we have to see that the various cases in which the government is interested and is a party may be settled. I have various complaints relating to specific cases almost all over India. There are very grave litigations and various other types of cases in which we find that if there were some machinery to find out if a particular case should be settled or not, much of the litigation might be avoided or at least it need not be fought out till the very end. I know several instances where the government has ultimately lost with costs. So, apart from the question of reducing the expense, I think government, as a litigant, should not really carry on a litigation which should be settled. For instance, there are cases where the government takes the point of jurisdiction . . . and various other technical points. Even if the government wins, I think it leaves a very bad taste. There are cases where on merits the government ought to have conceded what is due to the claimant, but yet it has taken a technical plea and has avoided payment.

The law minister generally agreed that governments should not fight frivolously but agree where they had no case and review their own orders if there were several flaws. Justice, not prestige, vigilance in reducing pending government litigation, and not expensive and indifferent accumulation of arrears where the state is a party should be the keynote of the government's policy on litigation.

It is not my purpose in this general treatment to elaborate the new patterns which will make the judicial instrument more effective and also speed up the process. The creation of conciliation tribunals to deal with disputes between neighbours, between village factions, between groups of labour, etc., will be desirable. Similarly, family and matrimonial courts can promote understanding and concord without the highly formal trials in open court. Arbitral tribunals with sufficient expertise will be able to produce more satisfactory solutions in industrial and commercial causes and we should give them a chance to prove their worth. Comradely courts are emerging in many countries with new techniques to deal with cases of men in institutions like factories and farms committing minor offences. Mobile courts have a great role to play, particularly in crimes like petty traffic offences, drunkenness in public places leading to danger to public peace, and such other kindred categories. In Kashmir, such courts work fairly well. We must give an all-India trial to itinerant justice in a big way to deal with traffic cases, railway offences, public disturbance crimes, etc. Maybe, in some cases we may have sentencing processes separated from the convicting stage and consultation with medical and psychic experts arranged before imposing punishment. The overall aim must be an up-grading of the efficiency of the system and elimination of injustice, even though in some cases it may spell a longer life for the litigation.

After all, speed-craft is not an end in itself and should not be tried at the expense of the social goal of dispensing justice between man and man and man and state. Mechanical gimmicks accelerating the assembly-line processing of litigation produce discontent in the long run, if the accent is placed on quantity regardless of quality. The biblical saying 'husband justice that ye may garner peace' has a deeper import than forensic blitz-krieg can give.

Among the great national institutions charged with the paramount duty of overseeing democratic legality in the country is the judiciary, and Article 38 of the Constitution spells out this objective when it says: 'The state shall strive to promote the welfare of the people by securing and pro-tecting as effectively as it may a social order in which justice, social, eco-nomic and political, shall inform all the institutions of the national life.' It is, therefore, of great moment that while men seek justice, the judicial process does not plunge the nation in colossal waste of time and money for millions of people and in obstruction of administrative and other pro-cesses essential to the welfare of the community. In the larger national scheme, judicial presence, while being ubiquitously vigilant and correc-tional, should sedulously eschew delays in its process, which encourage unproductive outlay of much needed resources or foster dilatory law addicts who gamble themselves and others into ruin.

Many judges have frequently said that the legal profession is to blame for the slow speed of the judicial wheels. The truth is that without dra-matic changes in the orientation and operational techniques of our foren-sic system we cannot make courts dynamic instruments. In this context, it must be recognized that the men engaged in the law—lawyers and judges alike—being trained to venerate precedents whose potency date has long expired and being professionally charged with the preservation of the prevalent socio-legal set-up, develop an instinct for anti-change in the working methods of our courts and a mental vested interest in the status quo—although new laws of motion, not rules of stagnation, must offer an exciting challenge to the engineers of justice.

4

Patterns of Criminal Justice
amongst Some Tribes*

KRISHNA KUMAR ET AL.

A section of Indian people, called aboriginals or tribals, have a pattern of living different from that of fellow Indian citizens; they have different culture, customs, and social norms. The reasons for the difference are outside the scope of this essay and may not, therefore, be discussed here. Our knowledge of tribals is limited and is derived mainly from scholarly accounts written about them. That there was a system of law and justice quite different from the one obtaining in other parts of the country, and that this system should have proved, by and large, successful and satisfying to the tribal communities, call for a closer study for more than one reason.

Most of the tribal chiefs and people interviewed in the course of the tour in Assam (the part now comprising Meghalaya) and also Manipur still thought the tribal system to be useful for the tribal community as it was simple, cheap, and expeditious. The educated young tribals,, however, wanted the tribal courts and institutions, e.g., *morungs* (i.e., youth dormitories), etc., to be further democratized so that they could find greater representation to those bodies along with their chiefs and elders. Thus they too were mostly in favour of the preservation of their own

*Excerpted from Krishna Kumar, et al., 'Patterns of Criminal Justice amongst some Tribes', *Journal of the Indian Law Institute*, vol. 12, no. 2, April–June 1970, pp. 205–35. A syndicate study conducted under the supervision of Mr R. Deb, Assistant Director (Law and Sociology), National Police Academy, Abu (Rajastan). Chairman: Mr Krishan Kumar (Punjab). Members: Mr K.K. Majumdar (West Bengal), Mr Lachman Das (Haryana), Mr R.C. Sharma (B.S.F.), Mr S.P.S. Rathore (Rajasthan).

institutions, but in a modified form. One tribal young man at Jowai, however, expressed the view that sometimes the tribal system of administration of justice leads to miscarriage of justice as the tribal chiefs commit mistakes even in following the spirit of the Criminal Procedure Code. This view received support from another lawyer of Shillong. Thus it appears that however small, there is a group of people who hold the view that the traditional pattern of tribal justice has its drawbacks and shortcomings. Viewed by the modern concept of jurisprudence, this criticism may be justified to some extent, but having regard to the requirements of a simple tribal society, particularly its conventional crimes like theft, trespass, assault and other common offences, the system not only served the people of the tribal community in the past but is still useful to them. The system of justice that obtains in the rest of the country too has not been found to be an ideal one. In fact, many eminent jurists, the Law Commission of India, and other state law review committees too have found the so-called sophisticated system of administration of justice to be far too costly, dilatory, procedure-bound, and often a convenient handle to defeat justice itself.

Each system has its merits and demerits and the purpose of this study has been, in the main, to find out what are the beneficial features of the traditional pattern of criminal justice amongst the tribals so that in integrating the tribals with the mainstream of the Indian people and system of criminal justice, we could preserve and respect their old institutions and sometimes, if need be, emulate them to our advantage.

In the absence of any background literature and adequate information about various tribes, the selection of tribes had to be limited. Our knowledge of tribes, their social and cultural norms and usages had to be acquired by an empirical study on the spot, mostly by interviewing tribals themselves and by reading whatever literature could be laid hands on. However, the tribes studied hereunder can be said to be a representative group, for in important fundamentals most tribes have a broad substratum of similarity.

This essay does not intend to build up a complete picture of the tribal system of justice. Various limitations of the study, including lack of sufficient time, inadequate literature—which has partly become obsolete—were such as to make its utility necessarily limited. Of necessity, this study had confined itself to Khasi and Jaintia Hills of Meghalaya but a visit was paid to Manipur to study the extent of impact that has been made on the tribals due to the full extension of prevalent regular laws and codes in that region.

Among the tribals, as in almost every pre-modern society, there is no clear-cut distinction between crime and tort, both of which could be paid for by way of compensation. Amongst most tribals, the idea was to settle the dispute and restore amity, rather than to inflict a punishment for a wrong done. In the context of tribal courts in North-East Frontier Agency (NEFA) Sachin Roy observed,

> Most of the fines inflicted by the kebangs are in reality compensations for damages done. The judiciary is practical and simple, inasmuch as it seeks to maintain and establish the traditional concepts of justice and equity without involving itself in lengthy legal procedures. The system aims not only at settling disputes but also to develop disciplines code of social behaviour. Justice is speedy and free from subtleties involving manipulations and intricate tortuosities of procedural technicalities. The kebang is more a board of arbitration, equally sympathetic to both the parties than a body of stern dispensers of justice which the offenders fear and try to evade. Every offence or wrong is considered in terms of concrete damage or injury caused by it and redress is given in the form of adequate compensation.

Thus by the present notion of criminal jurisprudence this study may not always conform to the modern concept of criminal justice and may, at times, be found referring to things which may more appropriately fall today within the domain of tort or civil wrong. The concept of criminal justice amongst the tribals was, and still is, to some extent, different from ours. The whole gamut of their system is discussed here but no claim is made for exhaustiveness. It is only a 'type' study which may give a feel of the traditional criminal justice amongst the tribes.

KHASI INSTITUTIONS

The Khasis, now residing mostly in the Khasi Hills district of Meghalaya, are believed by anthropologists to be the remnants of the Austro-Asiatic race, the original inhabitants of Assam, and comprise four groups, namely, the Khynsiams of the central plateau, Pnars (also called Jaintias) of the Jaintia Hills, Wars of the War area and Bhois inhabiting the Bhoi area in the north. Culturally and linguistically, the Khasis bear close affinity to the people of Indo-China and Cambodia and this has continued through the ages probably because of lesser contact with the mainstream of Indian thought and people and the tribals' love for their customs and norms.

Khasis are a matriarchal community, perhaps one of the few in the world, and trace their origin from an ancestress, each ancestress constituting a clan—*long jaid na ka kynthei* is an old Khasi saying meaning 'from the woman sprang the clan'. Naturally, therefore the females occupy a position of privilege. The inheritance is through the female line, the youngest daughter inheriting the ancestral property; the maternal uncle occupies a very important place in the family; the mother is regarded as a moral force binding the family. The youngest daughter inheriting the ancestral property is called *khadduh*, the word being a combination of *khad* (to collect) and *duh* (losses). As the word denotes, she is responsible for the maintenance of the family and discharge of its obligations and should she fail to do so, which is very rare, she will forfeit the right to inherit, because she would cease to be khadduh. However, notwithstanding the matriarchal structure, the Khasi women have no role to play in the public life of the community. They cannot hold a public office and cannot become rulers (some exceptions notwithstanding), the right being delegated to a maternal uncle, a brother or a son, who may become a *syiem* or a ruler.

The Khasis are agriculturists. Rice, potato, maize, and millets are the main crops, rice being the staple food. They are fond of meat-eating and drinking. The Khasi women, however, do not drink. Drinks are not taboo, and are served not only for entertainment but also for sacrificial purposes.

The Khasis love outdoor life and are fond of music. They are very fond of archery. Khasi religion, initially monotheistic, in which God creator (*U Blei Nong Thaw*), represented by a goddess (*Ka Blei Synshar*), was only worshipped. It believes in ancestor worship, and glorifies the dead in the belief that the dead by their good actions in life have attained supernatural status and thus acquired the power to bless the living descendants. That is why cremation rites are considered very important and are performed with due propriety. Another important aspect of their religion is divination and ordeal system which have a direct bearing on their system of criminal justice. Some attributes of theistic religion are also, however, to be found. Thanksgiving ceremonies in which the goddess and other deities (*ke phan ki kyrpad*) are appeased are performed. A large majority of Khasis have now become Christians, but despite conversion they still follow many of their tribal customs and rituals.

The institutions of *syiem* or *syiemship* is the most important in Khasi life and permeates all walks of life—social, cultural, religious, and administrative. Khasis migrated to their present abode in clans, called *kurs*, and in due course occupied and colonized the area now known after their name. On arrival, powerful and eminent families or clans were selected to administer the community and render justice. The first leader or ruler belonged to the clan called *jaid basan*, and the ruler in due course came to be called *basan*. The basan could belong only to this clan (no other clan could supply a ruler), was elected by all male adults of the clan and normally held office for life, deposition being possible in the event of misrule by him. In addition to *basanship*, the institution of *Iyngdohship* (a state ruled by a priest) also existed. A *lyngdoh* had both spiritual and temporal powers.

With the passage of time, basans, lyngdohs, and chieftains agreed to be ruled by a *syiem* (an elected king), after forming a *syiemship*. The reason for the origin and development of this institution according to scholars was a desire to protect common interest and develop common law. Probably, the time indicated a need for unity among them, thus prompting the basans, lyngdohs, and chieftains to surrender part of their authority. The syeim thus symbolized unity of the group of clans who made the community in that area.

The methods of election of a syiem's successor differed from syiemship to syiemship. In some states, he was elected by all the male residents of the state, who assembled to elect one from amongst the candidates of the syiem's family. In others, electoral councils consisting of elected village headmen, local officials, heads of units (villages), and representatives of clans elected the syiem with the approval of the people.

The syiem was the head of the state and was given both moral and military training. His income consisted of levies collected in certain markets assigned to him, and judicial fines. Thus his income was not constant and he could not act as a feudal lord or zamindar as he was never allowed to amass wealth.

The syiem's duties were specifically laid down. He was to protect his people and promote their welfare. That is why he was called *U Kmie*, which means the mother, and was duty-bound to act in relation to his subjects in the same manner as a mother acts in relation to her children. During his tour of the interior areas, he would also hear judicial cases. He acted as a police officer, a magistrate, a judge, a military general, and the chief executive councillor. In executive actions, he was constantly advised and assisted by a group of *myntris* (ministers) who formed his cabinet. The usual executive functions which devolved upon him and his council included the administration of markets, collections of judicial fees, supervision of prisons, and the keeping of prisoners.

Durbar

The syiem was not, however, the supreme authority. He had no legislative powers, which vested in *durbar*. The durbar may be described as the most ancient and important institution of the Khasis.

In ancient days, the durbar of the people transacted all political and judicial business. The syiem had to lay down his policy in conformity with the resolutions of the durbar, and the acts of the syiem could be vetoed by the durbar if they violated the usage traditions of the community. It goes to confirm the fact that the tribals attached great sanctity to their customs and usages.

Such durbars existed at three levels: (i) the village level, (ii) the district level, and (iii) the state level. The headman and the chieftain presided over the village and district durbar respectively. Both the village and the state durbars assumed the administration of forests within their respective jurisdictions, communications, markets, and laws affecting the common interests; and as a court of justice settled judicial cases within their respective jurisdictions. Needless to say, out of the subjects listed above not many fell within the purview of village durbar but whatever fell within its purview was decided by the village durbar.

The composition and function of the durbar at the state level or the grand durbar of the syiemship may now be mentioned. The entire adult male population was duty-bound to participate in the durbar. Since such durbars were difficult to arrange, only elders, heads of clans, heads of villages and local officials usually attended. Durbar was the real parliament of Khasis and also acted as the supreme court of justice. It did the legislation, enforced new taxes, and controlled the funds of the state. During war, it used to decide the general line of strategy, equipment of troops and volunteers, and issued instructions to deal with situations in a specified manner. It would take up all civil and criminal matters. In short, nothing was beyond its scope or competence. It could by its resolutions even remove the syiems. The removal of syiems by the durbar may be compared to impeachment of a king by a parliament. Such instances of removal of syiems have occurred in the past. Khasis not only believe that the supreme power rests with the people but also believe that supreme justice rests with them. With these two principles in view they believe in circumscribing the powers of the ruler and thus lay emphasis on decentralization rather than centralization. They have faith in *lam umaw* which means that there is no place for a syiem who is a tyrant or a traitor, who should then be deposed. It would thus appear that Khasis were, and still are, following democratic principles in all walks of life and the administration of the community. Democratic ideas had not been articulated but achieved and practised almost in a state of perfection. Durbar ensured full, real, and willing participation of the people in legislation and judicial decisions. The syiem could neither stop the holding of such a durbar nor could ever interfere with the procedure of its business. If an ordinary citizen desired that a durbar should be held, it would not be refused. Officials were duty-bound to execute it. The decision of the syiem's durbar on concurrent matters relating to judiciary, foreign relations, communications, and markets which had also been fixed by usage, could not be overruled by local durbars.

Judicial Durbar

A durbar, when transacting judicial business and administering justice, was called a judicial durbar. Whenever a very complicated and technical case came, whether of criminal law or of civil law, and when the local authorities failed to resolve it, the matter was invariably referred to the syiem. The syiem would then summon a judicial durbar in which the entire adult male population was enjoined upon to attend. No breaches were allowed. A crier known as *U Nong Pyria Shnong* was sent out to proclaim, at the top of his voice, the durbar which was to assemble on a notified day to decide a particular dispute. He would ask the people to stop their work and attend it at the right time. This proclamation was called *khang shnong*, which literally means 'closure of the village'. On the appointed day all persons would assemble. The syiem would preside and act as the judge and the whole body of the durbar as a jury. The durbar would start the investigation into the matter, and would appoint, soon after its assemblage a small body consisting of the headman and local officials to deal with the matter. Adjournment would be unavoidable pending the conclusion of the investigation. Then at the next durbar sitting, witnesses were summoned and parties to the dispute took oath and the proceedings commenced.

The oath was phrased as follows: 'I take an oath, if I tell a lie, the earth shall judge me, the thunder shall destroy me.' The deities were also invoked to see that the opponent's statement was true. There were two other forms of oath. One was by licking the salt placed on the blade of a sword and the other was swearing on a hollow gourd containing liquor and fixed with arrows. The latter was regarded the most sacred as the person telling a lie was supposed to suffer the agony of being pierced by those very arrows.

In Khasi trials three more persons were very important. One was *U Saiphla*—the reporter, the second was *U Sakhi*—the witness, and the third was *Riew Said*—the lawyer. Witnesses also made statements on oath. The lawyer would address the durbar and take an important part in the cross-examinations. The lawyer, it was told at Cherrapunji, used to be the maternal uncle or some other important member related to the party concerned. Sometimes, the durbar had to sit for several days. Syiem would then close the proceedings and sum up the evidence before the durbar and durbar's findings were taken into consideration by the syiem. When all this had taken place, he would pronounce his judgment. The entire procedure including announcement of judgment was to conclude within seven days. People do not remember any instance where the decision of the durbar was flouted by anybody. The acceptance of the durbar's decision shows the compelling and binding nature of the decisions. Describing the sitting of such a judicial durbar, W. Robinson said that durbar was 'something probably after the fashion of the ancient Druids or as was the custom of the Greeks when the Heralds spoke the aged judges sat on the squared stone in circle for debate'.

The system of court fees payable to courts, as is understood by us, was probably unknown. However, some kind of a present, mainly a bottle of locally brewed liquor (and at some places cowries) was presented to the syiem. The fine was payable alongwith a pig which was eaten by the syiem and members of the durbar.

Village and District Level Durbars

The judicial durbar presided over by the syiem had its counterpart at the village and district levels, a headman, a lyngdoh, or a *sirdar* presiding over a village durbar. In Jaintia Hills, a slightly different system obtained in regard to civil cases. The civil cases were tried in the first instance by a group of *dolis* to whom the matter was reported. The extent of powers of village and district durbars is not known with certainty. But it is certain that murder cases were not tried by them as they fell within the exclusive jurisdiction of the syiem's durbar.

The following extract from the report on 'Special Multipurpose Tribal Books' issued by the ministry of home affairs, Government of India, New Delhi, may be relevant:

> Every village is traditionally governed by a Durbar which consists of all the adult male members of the village. . . . the Durbar chooses its own office bearers. The Durbars have recently been recognized by Government through an Act passed by the District Council and they have powers to inflict the fines upto Rs. 50/-. There was a case in Maisang itself where a man was fined Rs. 450/- and he paid up, since otherwise he would have been excommunicated by the village community. The Durbaris see to everything, they coordinate the other aspects of Khasi life, settle disputes and have always looked after the forests, water supply and such community services as the Municipality and repairing of roads.

Modifications during British Rule and After

The institutions of syiemship and durbar have undergone changes with passage of time. The first signs of transformation can be discerned about the year 1833 following annexation of the Khasi Hills by the British. The historical changes brought about in the social, cultural, and administrative set-up of the tribals of the Khasi and Jaintia Hills from 1833 onwards do not appropriately fall within the scope of this study. Suffice it to say that the British rulers, while extending their control over these areas, retained the neuclaus of all customary institutions. Majority of the states were retained as Khasi states, the syiems enjoying most of the powers which had been exercised by them till then, except a few villages in the Khasi and the Jaintia Hills which were annexed as British area. The tribals continued to administer their states in the manner heretofore. Even in the British area, the tribal customs and social laws did not undergo any change. The British government, however, reserved to itself the right to advise the native states in regard to administration of justice and broad aspects of policy to be followed. It may be mentioned here, that most of the criminal and civil laws applicable to the rest of India were not extended by the Britishers to this area. The local leaders could try all criminal cases except of murder, accidental deaths, and such offences where punishments to be awarded might exceed five years in prison.

By and large this system continued till 1947, when India became free. The Khasi states, like others in the country, acceded to India on the basis of an Instrument of Accession. The Instrument of Accession, however, was different from similar documents concluded in respect of other states of the country. By an agreement which formed part of the Instrument of Accession, the Khasi states federation court was set up. The said court was authorized to pass sentences of death, transportation for life, and imprisonment, subject to confirmation by a divisional bench of the Assam High court. Probably, this exception in respect of these states was a historical continuation, for, in the past the deputy commissioner of Shillong had the exclusive power to pass death sentences subject to confirmation by the then lieutenant governor.

The Khasi states federation continued for a short time, i.e., from 15 August 1947 to 25 January 1950. With effect from 26 January 1950, these areas became entitled to a differential administration in accordance with the provisions of Schedule VI of the Indian Constitution. In due course, in accordance with the provisions of Schedule VI, an autonomous district council for the Khasi and Jaintia Hills was set up and it constituted the cornerstone of administration. Subsequently, with the bifurcation of districts, two separate district councils have been constituted for the separated districts of Khasi Hills and Jaintia Hills.

The district council has been empowered with vast administrative functions. It can constitute village councils and courts for trial of cases and suits between parties belonging to scheduled tribes resident in such area to the exclusion of any other court in Meghalaya. It has got original appellate jurisdiction and its powers extend to all legislative and administrative fields. It can legislate on matters relating to the management of any forest not being a reserved forest, use of canal or water course for the purpose of agriculture, regulation of shifting cultivation, the establishment of village or town committees, and other matters relating to administration, police, public health, appointment or succession of chiefs and headmen, inheritance of properties, marriage, and social customs.

Thus, the district council of today has assumed upon itself the role of a durbar of the past. The only difference is that previously there were twenty five syiemships and each syiem along with his durbar was the supreme authority in all spheres. The state system of Khasis still retains much that is old except that all these syiems have now been brought under the district council which has also laid down the rules for their appointment, succession, and removal. As far as the customary laws of Khasis go they have been preserved, and some of them are still being enforced through the legislation made by the district council by passing certain Acts and making rules and regulations under them. These are enforced by village courts whose procedure and administration of justice is in most parts the same as was found in olden days. The only difference is that the powers of village courts have now been specifically defined. These courts have been created by the district council and most of the time they are administering the customary laws which cannot be enforced by other courts of the country.

TRIBAL CUSTOMARY LAW AND COURTS: CONCEPT OF CRIME AMONG THE TRIBALS

In the absence of a clear-cut distinction between 'crime' and 'tort' in primitive societies all wrongs, whether of a civil or criminal nature according to modern parlance, were regarded as violation of customary rules and mostly punished by fine or redressed by awarding compensation. The punishment, in most cases, was aimed at compensation for the wrong done; and even in heinous offences like murder, compensation in kind like giving of a few *mithun*s or pigs absolved the guilty of the wrong done by him. Ideas of guilt indeed vary in different societies. In some it is shame rather than a sense of guilt that matters. The real sanction in a well-knit tribal society is the fear of being despised and humiliated by fellow men rather than the dread of punishment. Verrier Elwin cautions against introducing modern concepts of guilt and punishment to the tribal systems. He observes:

> Ethics in fact can have many different motivations and still remain a powerful force for the direction of human behaviour. We have, therefore, to be careful of what has been called psychiatric imperialism, which would mean imposing our own ideas of guilt and punishment on the tribal people.

A tribal society enjoins on its members rules of conduct which are based mainly on 'ethical principles that have grown out of historical and economic circumstances which have conditioned the development of the society.' United by reciprocity of relations and bound by a common culture, the members of the tribal community form an 'ingroup,' characterized by internal peace, law, order, and cooperative effort, and there develops among them a collective sentiment of group solidarity and loyalty, a sort of 'consciousness of the kind'. Simple standards and norms of behaviour are laid down and followed by the tribe and its members without any reservation. Naturally, subtle distinctions such as between crime and tort are not needed. All breaches in defiance of custom and accepted code of conduct are, therefore, considered as crime.

Criminal laws of the tribals had their origin in the code of conduct taught by parents to their children by word of mouth from generation to generation. In primitive societies, the core of legislation was a series of taboos and that almost all early codes consisted of prohibitions. The children were taught not to do any act which they would not like others to do to them. They must not steal, theft being a taboo; they must not trespass into the land of others, etc. Manik Syiem observes:

> In subjects where no convincing epithets could be given, the forebears attached religious susceptibility so that the primitive community would not dare trifle, e.g., most of the sacred groves or priestly forests in the Khasi Hills are traceable to protection and preservation of water sources which could not have been protected without a strong administrative machinery.

Similarly instances may have been in existence in other areas as well.

Tribal Customary Law

These tribals were a simple community and an ignorant one too. They did not know how different things in nature came into being. They thought that all objects of nature, be they forests or rivers, were gifts of God. Thus a great deal of religious significance was attached to these objects. Tampering with them was regarded as a violation of God's will and that was supposed to bring the wrath of God on man which would ruin him and his family. This served as an effective deterrent. Preservation and protection of such forests became a custom which later became a law. This old custom was codified by the district council in its Act No. 1 of 1959. There are some forests which are reserved for religious purposes and some for conserving water. Others have been classified as protected forests, green block, and *raid* forests. If in any of these forests the trees are felled without the sanction of the chief forest officer of the district council, the person felling the tree is punishable with imprisonment up to three months or fine upto Rs 300. The offence is cognizable and is triable by any magistrate of the first class or second class and even a magistrate of the third class when he is especially empowered by the executive committee of the district council to try forest offences.

Similarly, fish are preserved among the Khasis as a matter of custom and this custom too has been codified by the district council in the form of an Act. If any person tries to destroy fish by explosives or by poisoning the waters, it may be any water (private or otherwise), he would be liable to be punished with imprisonment up to two months and fine up to Rs 200. This too is cognizable offence.

Another customary offence of the Khasis originated from their peculiar land tenure system. A large proportion of land belongs either to a family or a clan which settled in an area before others came. The lands are absolute properties of the owners; absolute in the sense that they do not pay tax to anyone and are answerable to none. If there are community lands, the distribution is made by the chief or headman which can be either for temporary or for permanent cultivation. But then there was a custom that no land could be sold or mortgaged by a tribal to a non-tribal. If any non-tribal was found in possession of such a land he was asked to quit. The custom has now been codified and if any non-tribal is found in possession of land in contravention of the Act of district council, he is issued a notice to vacate that. If he disobeys that notice, he commits an offence under Section 6 of that Act and becomes liable to be punished with a fine of Rs 200 and in case of continued breach of the law a further fine of Rs 50 per day can be imposed as long as the breach continues.

Uncodified Customary Laws

But all the customary laws have not yet been codified even though they are in force in modern times. Thus it is a custom which has come to acquire the force of law in the Khasi community that all villages shall combine and do the prescribed social welfare work for the village on a particular day especially on the day of *khang shnong* (i.e., closure of the village). These social welfare tasks may be megalithic erections (after burial or cremation ceremonies), stone-pulling ceremonies, making provisions for water supply, construction of new houses, and harvesting the paddy in rotation from one field to another. All these are codes of conduct envisaged to regulate the behaviour of the entire community for the social good. Among other tribes too such customary offences are in existence. Amongst Lakhers of the Lushai Hills of Assam (now Mizoram), for example, even eavesdropping (*angiapatli*) is regarded as a definite offence for which a sentence of fine may be imposed under the customary law.

It was learnt from the syiem of Mylliem that as in other communities, incest was still regarded as one of the gravest offences in Khasi community. Its definition is very vast and covers a wide range of relationship. According to the tribals incest means cohabiting with a member of the same clan even if he or she is not a relative in the conventional sense. Though it is a shocking thing yet it has not been made a criminal offence in our society. This offence is tried by the village courts in their customary manner. It is punishable with exile, excommunication, or fine. The syiem of Mylliem did not or could not tell exactly the extent of the fine that could be imposed but then there is a reference to this offence in Gurdon's book *The Khasis* where he mentioned that in olden times it was punishable with exile or a fine of Rs 550 and one pig. It is believed by the Khasis that grave evils result from this type of connection and people may be struck by lightning or killed by a tiger and even deaths may occur in childbirth. These customary laws are still being enforced by the village durbars which have to be attended by all villagers. Absentees, as in the past, are heavily fined. Villagers would be asked not to have any dealing or association with such absentees. They could also be expelled from the village or be excommunicated.

Similarly, there was another custom which is now gradually dying out. In the past, whenever a durbar was summoned, it was enjoined upon all the adult male population to attend it. Messengers of the syiems were sent to detect if there were any absentees. Such persons, if detected, were fined heavily. Now that is not so in most of the villages, except in some villages termed as conservatives where they still enforce it rigorously.

Conventional Types of Offences and their Punishment

Serious criminal offences included murder, fornication and adultery, looting, stealing, illegal marriage, false charges and prejury, and violation of durbar rules. Stealing was punished with a fine or light imprisonment, if committed for the first time; but if repeated, severe penalties were inflicted. The sorcerer was called devil (*kasuid*). Before receiving his death sentence or banishment, the kasuid was shaved off. His skull was shaved in three parts which was a sign of shame and guilt in society. Cheating was punished with a small fine and a pig but it could be increased if the offence was repeated. False reports were punishable with payment of fines and pig. Conspirators who associated themselves with acts of imposed murder were a fine of Rs1100 and a pig. Assaults with bare hands was not a serious crime. (It can be compared with simple hurt under Section 323 of the Indian Penal Code.) Injuries or death occurring in course of a physical combat were not subject to judicial enquiry. Adultery was an offence and the punishment was death, imprisonment for life, or a fine of Rs1100 and a pig. Whether such a heavy fine was ever imposed on anybody is very doubtful. According to the syiem of Cherrapunji probably it was never done. If a husband found his wife with a man in *flagrante delicto* he could under the law kill both the adulterer and the adulteress. Such a husband could not be punished for murder but he could be punished with a fine of Rs 500 and a pig.

The concept of punishment among the Khasis was, therefore, somewhat different from other tribes who believed more in multiple restitution rather than on the penal nature of punishment. Khasis on the other hand were clearly cognizant of the present concept of deterrent punishment even in their olden days.

Customary Procedural Law

There was a great variety in the old customary procedural law. The first one was the 'Mass Trial'.

Mass Trial

Whenever an exceptional case occurred where the decision could not be taken correctly, the syiem ordered a mass trial in which door to door investigation was carried out. This was considered to be the most effective form of trial because it usually succeeded in discovering the main accused or the root cause of trouble or enmity.

To quote an instance from the past. Manick Raitong was found guilty of committing adultery with the syiem's wife. The syiem was absent on a trip to Nagaon and Kamrup plains for inspection of his dominions. On return, he found that his wife had given birth to a baby. He ordered the village men to appear at the mass trial. In such a trial babies were fed on bananas. Each man would bring a couple of bananas with him. If the baby would grasp them, the man holding them would be held guilty. In the instant case, all men, one by one, appeared before the baby and showed him the bananas. Manick Raitong was the last to appear. The baby seeing his father all of a sudden grasped them and jumped on his lap. Manick was convicted. He was sentenced to death by being beaten by clubs, but he begged to die by being burnt alive on the pyre to be made by himself and this was allowed. On ascending the pyre he was joined by the syiem's wife and both perished simultaneously.

Trial by Water Ordeal

Trial by ordeal and by oath were generally resorted to when there was no evidence. Yule, writing in 1844, mentioned this trial and Col Maxwell, the late superintendent of police of Manipur state, also witnessed such a trial even amongst the Manipuris in the year 1903. While talking to the syiems and other representatives from the adjoining areas, it was revealed that such a trial was very common in Cherra Syiemship. In such a trial the man who remained longer in water was adjudged victorious in law. Both the complaint and the defendant would go inside water and if the complainant came out of water later than the defendant, the latter was pronounced guilty. In ancient days sometimes the supporters of the contending parties compelled the divers to remain in water by holding them down with their spears. P.R.T. Gurdon mentions another variety of water ordeal. Four pieces of ornaments, two of gold and two of silver were wrapped in packets and immersed in shallow water in two different pots.

> The contending parties were then directed to plunge their hands in the water and take up, each of them, one of the packets. The party who brought up the gold was adjudged the victor. If both parties brought up either gold or silver, then case was amicably settled by the durbar, if it was a land case, the land was equally divided between the parties.

The people considered these ordeals as divine decisions which were infallible. In this form of trial, the syiem and the durbar would exact heavy fee from the disputants and the defeated party had to pay heavy fine in both cash and kind.

Ordeal by Oath

This was also known as ordeal by *U Klong* or by *U Klong U Khnam*. Of all the ordeals this was the most dreaded by the Khasis. They believed that if a person swore falsely in such an ordeal, he would die or if he represents his family or his clan, his family and his clan would perish. This ordeal could be resorted to only when both the parties voluntarily agreed in open durbar to it.

The ordeal by oath was rarely agreed to but the person undertaking this would win the case, as no other evidence was required in such a trial. It is doubtful whether these practices are still in vogue. In most of the places they have been given up. A few persons, however, reported that in the interior of Jaintia Hills still conservative villagers preferred this.

But the practice that has survived even to this day is that of village durbar acting as a court of justice whose procedure remains much the same as discussed earlier.

5

Law as an Instrument of Change in India*

J.S. GANDHI

The present essay is a synoptic view of the problem of *Social Change Through Law in India*, in some of its restricted dimensions only. The question to which we have tried to address ourselves is: whether or not it is possible to carry out the process of social change as per some of the socially accepted goals and objectives through the instrumentality of law? While the search for parameters on which the facilitation of change through law depends may seem interminable, our focus here will be only on some of the intra-systemic parameters, i.e., such aspects or features as relate to the legal system itself. This choice is purely heuristic and notwithstanding the fact that the ecology of change is integral and embraces the legal system and its institutions, as well as several other subsystems such as economic, cultural, political, and even symbolic. This essay is divided into three sections: career of Western law and legal system in India; institutional setting of legal profession, and its contemporary orientations. Later, we shall draw inferences from these three sections in our attempt to answer the question: what are the potentialities of social change through law in contemporary Indian society?

CAREER OF WESTERN LAW AND LEGAL SYSTEM IN INDIA:
THE HISTORICITY AND MODERNITY

The historicity of a legal system is of paramount significance. It defines the parameters of the role that it can possibly play in the process of social

*Excerpted from J.S. Gandhi, 'Potentials and Parameters of Social Change through Law in Contemporary Indian Society', in A. Podgorecki, C.Whelan, and D. Khosla (eds), *Legal Systems & Social Systems*, London: Croom Helm, 1985, pp. 174–89.

change. Accordingly, it may either facilitate or accelerate law's intended participation in the achievement of certain social goals or it may constrict or even obviate its intended objective of facilitating a change in the social reality, and instead provide a smokescreen behind which the forces of status quo continue to operate and perpetuate the pre-existent structures of inequity and deprivation.

In India, modern law and its allied institutions based upon the legitimacy of rational legality were never created with a view to achieving any explicit social goals adopted by the collective will or consensus of the Indian people. Instead, these were founded, refined, and elaborated by the British colonial masters purely with the purposes of strengthening their political—administrative hold over the colony. They sought to devise and formulate such codifications with which they could address themselves equally to ethnically diverse sets of population. Thus, as the Pax Britannica was extended to increasingly larger reaches of territory and population, law was elaborated both in its *procedural* as well as *substantive* aspects. Lindsay sums up this process of codification as follows:

> The first Indian Law Commission, under the presidency of Lord Macaulay, was set up in 1834; its most notable achievement was the production of the draft of the Indian Penal Code, which however, did not become law until 1860. Macaulay's Commission also drew up a number of reports which embodied proposals for legislation and which fell under the consideration of succession of Law Commissions, which sat in England at various times between 1853 and 1870 and whose efforts led to the enactment of the Codes of Procedure, civil and criminal, in 1859 and 1861 respectively. This judicial system in India by the amalgamation of the Supreme and Sadar Courts into High Courts. This latter fruit of the labour of these commissions were the Succession Act (1865), the Limitation Act (1871), the Evidence Act and the Contract Act (1872), and still later, under the direction of the Government of India, there came the Specific Relief Act (1882) and the Easement Act (1882). By this time, it may be said, the process of codification came to an end, though further legislation of a comprehensive character was undertaken to define the law of land tenure for the various provisions.

The process of codification continued through the Native Marriages Act in 1872, and 'in 1891 a controversial Age of Consent Act was passed. It was further modified in 1929. The Press Act came into being in 1879, Newspaper Act in 1908; the Factory Act was passed in 1881; in 1904 a Cooperative Act was legislated'. But such an administrative steamroller broke up the indigenous character of the Indian legal system, which was characterized by autonomy of the customary and the caste law at the rural level and the kingly law—mostly based upon the traditional Hindu and Muslim scriptures—at the level of towns and cities which were the seats of political authority occupied by kings and rajas. British courts now provided alternative juridical authority invokable by one who had even lost his case at the village panchayat or the caste panchayat. Thus, traditional social and caste rivalries which were earlier contained under the necessity of maintaining social harmony, consensus, or compromise, were now thrown into the open and found for themselves a new playground in the British law courts. Rural people who had earlier been used to respect the local justice, welcomed the idea of giving their luck another trial at the British courts. Thus justice was perceived as both 'capricious' and 'manipulable'. Slowly, but surely, sociologically speaking, all this inhered a basic and fundamental change in the social relations. It was a movement from *status* to *contract*, where the *individual* was abstracted from his sociocultural milieu and viewed as an entity *equal before law*, to another of the same kind. Corporate rights and responsibilities were thus replaced by individual ones (Galanter 1966). It also meant a shift from holistic perspective of justice when an issue was related to its antecedents to a partial and fragmented perspective when a single issue was focused upon and judged in abstraction from its background, purely in terms of the principle of logic and consistency.

But even though this 'impersonal' and 'alien' character of the British law was against the sociocultural genius and needs of the Indian people, it has continued to stay and thrive having once been established. Two main reasons were mainly responsible for this. Firstly, the increasing political consolidation of the British over India lent an increasing legitimacy to their *rule of law* and gave it almost an honorific character in the perception of the Indian people. Secondly, the entrenchment of the rule of law along with the Indianization of the British bureaucracy in India, created an elitist class constitutive of both lawyers and administrators, entirely dependent upon and interested in the perpetuation of the legal system. The system came to acquire further legitimacy through the entire life of the Indian freedom movement, which was spearheaded by lawyers who used with effective advantage their knowledge of *law* and *legality*. The majority of these leaders such as Mahatma Gandhi, Motilal Nehru, Jawaharlal Nehru, Tilak, Bhulabhai Desai, and others were trained lawyers and barristers who profited immensely from their grounding in law both to create a sense of political awareness among the people as well as to weaken the legitimacy of British rule in India. Subsequently, some of these law-trained people like jawaharlal Nehru, Patel, Ambedkar also played a pivotal role in the making of the Indian Constitution after independence in 1947. The entire structure of the Constitution bears ample testimony to the *legalistic–formalistic* cognition of the Indian reality, on the part of its framers. The highly idealistic and euphoric tone in which some of its provisions are cast betokens the characteristic optimism which lawyers would have in the capacity of law to change the existing social reality.

Note, for example, the provision regarding the abolition of untouchability under Article 17: ' "Untouchability" is abolished and its practice in any form is forbidden. The enforcing of any disability arising out of "untouchability" shall be an offence punishable in accordance with law'. Or, for that matter note the Preamble to the Constitution:

> The people of India, having solemnly resolved to constitute India into a SOVEREIGN DEMOCRATIC REPUBLIC and to secure to all its citizens:
>
> JUSTICE, social, economic and political;
>
> LIBERTY of thought, expression, belief, faith and worship;
>
> EQUALITY of status and of opportunity;
>
> and to promote among them all
>
> FRATERNITY assuring the dignity of the individual and the unity of the Nation; . . .

The text of the Constitution, however, does not provide the corresponding strength to the citizens in the realization of the above mentioned utopian objectives. This is obvious from the fact that whereas all the Fundamental Rights (viz., right to equality before law; right to freedom of expression, of religion, of association; right to hold property, etc.) as listed under Articles 19–35 are guaranteed through *justifiability*, the Directive Principles of State Policy (Articles 36–51) which relate to such provisions as individuals' right to adequate means of livelihood, equal pay for equal work, protection of youth and childhood against exploitation, securing of living wage to industrial and agricultural workers, etc., are *non-justiciable*. It is enjoined upon the state, however, to move in the direction that the objectives listed under the Directive Principles of State Policy are achieved, without providing any specific legal sanction against the government which does not do so. It seems indeed a patent attempt— advertant or inadvertant—at mystifying the long-established institutions and inequity and deprivation (illustrated ideally in the institution of caste). This is so because there is no leverage provided against any such political lobbying which may bend the state apparatus to its own advantage and thereby hold in perpetual abeyance the realization of these objectives. Once again, therefore, we have evidence of a *formalistic* mentality, which through inadequate appreciation of socio-political and economic complexity, reifies the mere *form* of law into a strong bulwark of peoples' protection against inequity and discrimination. The Constitution is a unique caricature of a futile hope which conveniently forgets that structurally given and traditionally legitimized inequities are potent enough to frustrate the realization of even the most clearly intended codifications. Baxi copiously illustrates with what scant regard the law and legalism are treated both by the ruler and the ruled. He says:

> Most people regard legal rules as irritating inconveniences to be followed only if other alternatives are more irritating, more costly or unavailable. This generates a demonstration effect. If people who are at the helm of affairs or are rich, resourceful or affluent, do not follow rules when these adversely affect their interests, other people who have to follow rules are likely to do so not because the rules themselves are justified or legitimate but because they are powerless. They follow rules which hurt their self-interests, because they have no choice.

In the popular perception the breach of law, rather than its adherence is legitimized: '. . . all this (i.e., the easy exploitability of law) has the effect of convincing a large segment of the Indian people that rule-following is not *merely unjustified* but counter-productive in terms of their interests'. What explains this easy exploitability, manoeuvrability of law or rather, what explains this unbounded faith that people have in the resourcefulness of law to deliver the goods?

To answer this, we have again to refer to the original, historical compulsions behind the genesis and evolution of the present legal system in India, which was more an administrative necessity than a response to the felt needs of the people. Its character of *impersonality* and *anonymity* did not fit into the *gemeinschaft* character of Indian society, where *face-to-face* ties predominated and where, to exist socially, was to harmonize and consensualize with the social environment rather than seeking the protection of one's 'isolate' interests vis-à-vis the rest of society through hiring legal muscles (advocates) in fighting adversarial court battles.

It needs restatement that the putatively unified Western law system which sought the displacement of earlier decentralized and autonomized local juridical structures and substructures, did not emerge as a response to a qualitative change in people's expectations from justice, but rather took such a change for granted. Nothing that happened as a result of the spread of colonial administration in India generated such compulsions as to make people *need* different systems of justice, i.e., *modern* as against the *traditional* one.

Another point—that can only be conjectured here for want of space—is that in most countries of the world, the growth and evolution of a *modern law* system has accompanied the growth of an independent industrial economy, one which grows in response to the needs of the indigenous society. In India, as against this, all through the nineteenth and twentieth centuries till independence in 1947, the economy had functioned primarily as a captive economy furthering the interests of colonial economic systems. All this held in check the growth of such commerce, trade, and industry as would have created automatic compulsions for a natural proliferation and acceptance of rational legal codification.

INSTITUTIONAL SETTING

In order to draw cogent inferences on the effectivity of the legal system in ushering in the process of social change, one must examine the functional health of the overall system of justice and law-making in the country. This could include examining in detail the process of law-making and law reform in the country as well as examining courts as working systems in so far as whether or not they fulfil or try to fulfil the constitutionally given goals and objectives. A thorough reading of the Constitution, as well as various policy documents relating to national planning would bring into bold relief the egalitarian–equalitarian ethos which constitutes the most strongly cherished national objective. At the present level of information and awareness, we cannot go into this critical question of compatibility between the said institutional setting and the egalitarian–equalitarian goal. A thorough examination of the structure and functioning of courts within the framework of organizational sociology and psychology is likely to yield both diagnostic as well as prescriptive insights regarding the process of law-making (i.e., through court judgments) as well as law reforms. Pending such thorough research into this area, we can evaluate in brief whatever little evidence exists at present.

Higher Judiciary and its Orientation to the Basic Social Goals

When one thinks of the important role to be played by courts in the process of social change, one expects at least due vigilance on the part of the courts which would discourage violation of the fundamental rights of the citizenry. As far as the present record of the apex courts is concerned, one finds a display of sheer pusillanimity by the higher judiciary. Some writers on the contemporary legal scene in India, such as Upendra Baxi, a Delhi Law School professor, and, Krishan Mahajan, a *Hindustan Times* law specialist and others, have cited copious illustrations in support of this contention. Baxi reports:

> In Tamil Nadu, as early as 1961, a prisoner prayed for a *writ of mandamus*, under Article 226 of the Constitution, directing the Superintendent, Central Jail, Tiruchirapally, to act in accordance with rules 38, 278, 637, 640, 641, 379, 354, 366 and 651 to 658 of the Tamil Nadu Prisons and Reformatory Manual (Vol. II). His grievance was that the jail was overcrowded, as a result of which he (while serving a sentence of rigorous imprisonment) was not merely deprived of proper accommodation but also of minimum necessities such as food, bathing facilities, scavenging facilities, etc.' in gross violation of the above mentioned rules. The High Court dismissed the petition (W.P. No. 1234 of 1961, disposed of on 20 November 1961) although it conceded that the petitioner's grievance was 'not entirely unfounded' and that it was 'not entirely imaginary or unreal'.
>
> . . . The respondent, the Court held, could not be 'blamed or be charged with having violated the jail rules because of some little inconvenience suffered by the petitioner or his comrades in distress'.

This is only one of several such cases in which the Court buckled under the weight of procedural wrangles and failed to rise in support of constitutionally granted fundamental rights. It will, therefore, be futile to hope that courts will be ready to play any protective role in the application and interpretation of state laws.

Further, there is a pronounced degree of ad hocism in the day-to-day functioning of the courts. Rises in litigation and the piling arrears have taken a heavy toll on *consistency* in the judgments given by the courts. In a poignant narration, Mahajan illustrates how, for want of internal communication and coordination between different benches of the Supreme Court of India, three persons equally convicted for the same crime of murdering a family, met different fates. In the case of one of the co-accused, a death sentence was commuted to life imprisonment; in the second case, the Supreme Court sent the mercy petition to the president for reconsideration; whereas in the third case—that of Jeeta Singh—the death sentence was carried out. Does it not amount to playing with the most fundamental right, viz., the right to life? Mahjan maintains that such lack of internal communication between the various benches of the Supreme Court does not affect the rich who can pay fat fees to a well-informed lawyer as against a poor litigant who through lack of means suffers and rots through default of the courts. He suggests a composite registry system for the judgments of the various Supreme Court benches, eventually leading to a complete computerization of the judgments. It is a measure of the lack of urge on the part of the country's apex courts to keep in step with the contemporary reality that such dynamic suggestions have been persistently ignored.

Management of Law Reforms

If the social orientation of the law courts as well as their day-to-day functioning does not inspire us with a positive hope regarding law being able to play a socially relevant role what is the position regarding the process of law reforms? This apathy which we noticed regarding the courts also to have seeped into the process of law reforms. We shall examine in brief some evidence on this, as presented by Baxi.

The process of law reforms in India is of a highly tentative nature. There is a choice array of bodies, all of them recommendatory in nature, concerned with this process. Before the Law Commission of India came into existence in 1955, one could count a minimum of thirty-nine Working Groups or Law Committees entrusted with the task of law reforming. Even now the Law Commission adheres to this role with several other bodies. There is no specific concept which either overtly or covertly seeks to coordinate the law-making recommendations of these bodies.

The Law Commission, whose function is to reform and modify the existing laws and the legal system, is a temporary body and is appointed every three years. Its functioning as well as composition is marked by a high degree of ad hocism. For example, the membership of most of the Law Commissions has varied between four and twelve and also there has been a substantial time lag between the appointment of the chairman and the other members. Among its other operative features, it is most important to note that the government enjoys absolute monopoly in the appointment of all the members, including the chairman. This leaves the ruling political powers completely free in staffing the commissions with men of their choice. That they may have substantially succeeded in this is vivid from the 'virtual absence of dissenting opinions' in the reports submitted by various commissions.

Also, the majority of the commission members have been recruited from the retired judiciary (both of high courts and the Supreme Court). The government has shown no responsiveness whatsoever to the suggestions that the commission membership be also drawn from academic and practising lawyers and from various social sciences such as psychology, social work, sociology, etc. The political elites have thus been easily able to bend an important organ of law reform to their own advantage and interests.

As to the contents of the laws recommended and law reports submitted by various commissions so far, Baxi notes that important social issues add problems such as inequitous agrarian relations, indebtedness and money-lending, tenancy and ceiling reforms, agricultural wages, etc., have virtually been untouched. Instead, they have been concerned with refinements in the procedural law, commercial law, taxation law, property law, family law, and constitutional amendments—all of which Baxi terms as the *lawyer's law*. There is a correspondence between the above bias on the part of the courts and the bias shown by the government in its treatment of the various Law Commission reports. Whereas the reports concerning proposed legislations on the procedural law, constitutional amendments, and such like matters have been implemented, those dealing with important social issues such as consumer protection, the question of *benami* transactions, married women's property, revision of the Workman's Compensation Act, etc., have so far been shelved.

Whatever little evidence we have considered under this section drives us to the conclusion that as regards some of the fundamental goals of social changes as set out in the Indian Constitution as well as the planning documents, the institutional setting—comprising both the apex courts as well as the chief law-reforming body—is inappropriately oriented. It shows no dynamism and no capacity to meet challenges of the developing society. The lacuna lies not merely in the inappropriate social orientations, but also—and more fundamentally—in its structure and composition which precludes it from retaining their functional autonomy.

LEGAL PROFESSION AND ITS CONTEMPORARY ORIENTATIONS

Social Unresponsiveness and Mystification

The most important substructure of the legal system capable of playing an effective role in the process of social change in any society comprises those who use and apply law to day-to-day situations, i.e., lawyers and judges. It is they who draw out the inherent potentials from the existing laws and thus help give rise to new laws through the process of re-interpretation and creation of precedents. They have indeed a very special role to play in a transitional society as India is at present. It is through their efforts that law is related to the newly emergent empirical situations, claims, and counterclaims, and made increasingly more relevant. What is the existing evidence on the preparedness of these two categories of personnel to use law in furthering the process of social change, i.e., to help achieve the socially accepted goals of equalitarianism–egalitarianism? However, we shall focus our attention here only on lawyers, on whom some research-based empirical evidence is possible.

Some researches done at the district court level, i.e., the lowest onganizational level of the court hierarchy in India—the other two being the high courts and the Supreme Court—demonstrate a highly mercenary attitude on the part of the lawyers. They regard their clients as expendable and mere instruments for making profit and commit all varieties of professional improprieties including bullying, deceit, and pressuring to achieve that. They obviate the very first tenet of professional practice and secure most of their business through touts and mercenaries, using even their lawyer colleagues as touts, rather than by way of their professional reputation. Anchored in their intimate familial or caste networks they progress on their way to professional careers. Although specific research evidence on lawyers practising in the high courts and the Supreme Court yet remains to be collected, one would expect similar orientations to prevail at these levels too. This is on account of the fundamental and grassroots character of district level professional practice.

The professionals engage themselves in a lot of gimmickry, posing as custodians of the poor and the defenceless, without volunteering to do any service to their cause. Numerous Legal Aid Societies and Associations including the National Legal Aid Committee are on record as having engaged themselves in a lot of rhetoric and exhortations about the necessity of providing legal aid to the poor. But they merely want their fees to come from the state instead of private clients. There is no compulsion or persuasion generated by the various professional bodies on the conduct of their members—as has been the case, for example, in the USA and some other countries—to champion the cause of the poor. This lack of any substantive concern on the part of the lawyers with the endemic problem of poverty, and instead using the '*aid the poor*' slogan only to generate more work or employment potential for their own kind, is a poor indicator of the professionals' potentiality to use and apply law in favour of the poor. Despite this poor preparedness for a socially relevant role, the lawyers have high notions about the centrality of their existence in the scheme of things in society. A study into the structure of professional cognitions reveals a complete lack of criticality or reflexivity on their part. They perceive themselves responsible even for the socio-historical causation of the Indian society, cut out to play a crucial role even in its future evolution and development. This involuntary urge at self-mystification and self-glorification on the part of lawyers, unaccompanied by any competence in terms of their social orientations, makes them singularly unfit to play any role in furthering the process of social change.

Growth of Professional Reflexivity

A very noteworthy feature is the contemporary socio-professional reflexivity through the medium of non-practising lawyers—especially those engaged in law teaching and journalism. Some highly sensitive and creative thinking has been set in motion by some law professors and law columnists (even though only a few such as Mahajan, Baxi, S. Sahay, etc.). They have touched upon a wide array of issues ranging from critical appraisal of the functioning of the modern legal system and the law courts—in the static and unhelpful nature of modern legal codifications and legal procedures—to the critical analysis of the practice of law and the needful reforms in the current system of legal education. Some of them have even listed out new roles that the lawyers should take upon themselves to cope with the newly emergent social needs such as participation in public interest litigation, free legal pleading on behalf of the poor and indigent clients, etc. It is through the efforts of such lawyers oriented toward public interest that some shocking cases of administrative–judicial neglect have been brought into the open. One such incident relates to the case of blinding of undertrials at Bhagalpur Jail by the police. Another concerns the callous neglect of the inmates of the institution for the mentally retarded at Agra. Still another relates to the usurpation of traditional earning rights of the poor Bihars—mostly Chamars (traditionally regarded as untouchables) and Muslims—over the carcasses of dead animals, through the introduction of the system of contract sales as a result of collusion between the politicians and big business. The Supreme Court was so seized with the lament of poor petitioners that it set up an Investigation Commission, consisting of Upendra Baxi and K. Mahajan, to go into the background of the entire case and report to the Court.

A relevant question that needs answering is why this beam of critical reflection on law, legal system, and the legal needs of the people has been thrown in by non-practising lawyers rather than by those who earn their livelihood defending their clients in a court of law? The most obvious reason seems to be the incapacity of the practising lawyers to detach themselves from the conditions of their practice. Legal practice in Indian society is intensely competitive where many find it difficult even to eke out the barest survival. Another telling feature of professional practice is that it is unaccomplished—at any level of practice, i.e., whether district court, high court, or Supreme Court—by any directions, constraints, or persuasions from professional bodies, goading the lawyers to engage themselves in any non-profit activities, such as the defence of the needy and socially rejected. The law academics or the law writers like the ones mentioned above, who are exposed to international developments in the sphere of law and its use in society and who find themselves far surpassed in material affluence by even the mediocre practitioners, take a plunge into the realm of 'social responsibility' and 'social relevance' with the gusto of a *crusader*. Note the following pungent comments on the inadequacy of the existing system of legal education:

> After 30 years, the Bar Council of India, which controls professional legal education in the country has woken up to the need to include a course on rural laws in the syllabi. Even now under the new five year law course the paper has been kept optional instead of being made compulsory input. This reflects rather poorly on the socio-economic understanding of the advocates and professors who are members of the Council's legal education committee which designs the syllabi.

Or, again, in the same piece, '. . . How ironic that so much promise should be barren. Can we forgive the law men on the legal education committee who do not even perceive or on perceiving do not nurture the promise. Along with the media men, they have made the law fallow.'

What is the promise of this critical reflexivity spreading among the practising lawyers, creating awareness among them of a new role that they have to play in the contemplated process of social change? The prospects for any such transformation in the professional attitudes—so vital for effective role-playing in the social change process—are remote and virtually non-existent. There is no conduit via which the intellectual lawyer's sensitivity would be transferred to the perspective of the practising lawyers who otherwise are under no professional compulsions from their professional and controlling organisations—which if effective can go to the extent of selling new professional norms for their members. *In sociological terms a new social ethos can be universalized among the members of a collectivity only if it undergoes a new, but similar socio-historical experience, or receives a similar orientation under the influence of the same socializing agency.* None of these two possibilities exists in the Indian context. Both sets of professional categories, i.e., socially *sensitive* and *insensitive*, live under two different types of economic conditions and the corresponding normative milieux. There is no possibility, no scope, no pressure whatsoever for inter-swapping of their existential parameters. Hence, the two must live compulsorily as two isolates and under two mutually exclusive preserves. The state can play a conducive role only if it puts at a premium the critical reflexivities and value orientations of the intellectual lawyers and places them appropriately in certain crucial positions within the apparatus of state planning. But this again is not a forseeable prospect if the state's handling of the Law Commission of India—from which it has excluded in a studied manner persons with reflective backgrounds such as law teachers, law writers, and social scientists—is any guide. The plain and obvious conclusion which then one has to reckon with is that there is very little correspondence between values of the political elites and the values of reflexivity, criticality, and social relevance represented contemporaneously by the lawyer-intellectual or the socially aware.

SUMMING UP

Research materials examined by us in this brief study lead us to negative conclusions as to law's effectivity to facilitate the process of social change in India. There seems little compatibility between the social goals set out by us as a nation or society and the resources and strengths of the legal system to facilitate their achievement. The historically implanted alienative law has become further divorced from the reality of people's lives; it has proliferated without any aspirational thrust from people's and its problematics. It is not only the institutional setting of law—both in its composition and functioning which is askewed—but also the orientations of its leading role players, i.e., the lawyers who are ill-prepared to play any such grandiose role as using law for facilitating the achievement of equalitarian–egalitarian goals. A small sector of the profession, viz., the intellectual lawyers, who possess the requisite social sensitivity is powerless to wield any influence on the practising lawyers who must continue to pursue their profit interests.

It is better to live in a state of *clear* despair than to have an *unreal* hope. There is no point in celebrating the *promise of law* when all evidences are to the contrary. It will only be raising the structure of self-deception to the status of a demigod. The political power functioning must leave law-making and law reforms free and autonomous, capable of absorbing the orthogenetic compulsions of society and its needs. Also, the professional bodies must re-examine and restate the professional lawyer's role in the light of new social goals and accordingly prepare their members—both for the bar and for the bench. Only when these conditions are met, would law be the unchained Prometheus which it inherently is. But as yet, such a vista is a far cry, indeed a very far cry!

II
The Legal Profession

Of the branches of sociology of law, it is the study of legal profession that has drawn the attention of Indian sociologists and social anthropologists most of all. One of the reasons for this seems to be that the study of this branch suits the research tools of the sociologist and the social anthropologist in various ways. The sociologists carry out research surveys of the lawyers practising in a particular place or at a particular level of judiciary. The social anthropologists tend to study collectivities and the interrelationships among them through their own method. Pieces representing both of these kinds have been included in the readings that follow in this part. The material on legal profession in India is so voluminous that it has been a problem to select the most representative readings and bring them to a size which would fit into the space available.

The position of lawyers as a class is quite high in society. This has been so for a long time. One of the obvious reasons is the high earnings of the successful lawyers. It has been recorded that in the closing decades of the eighteenth century the lawyers spent more than the judges earned. A century later advocates like Motilal Nehru had fabulous incomes, and stories about the lavish living of luminaries like Motilal Nehru passed into folklore, with attendant exaggerations.

It has often been noted that for a long time the lawyers have played an important part in politics. Most of the leading lights of India's freedom struggle were lawyers by training. Many reasons have been given for this. But it appears that the most important factor has been that among the English-educated middle class, which was in the vanguard of India's independence movement, it was largely the lawyers alone who were free to take up politics. Most of the other English-educated people sought government service and were absorbed into it at one level or another. They were forbidden from taking part in politics. The lawyers on the other hand could speak out their mind and participate in political activity. Usually they happen to be more articulate than others in forcefully presenting their views.

Schmittheener has observed that the role of lawyers in politics has appreciably declined after India's independence. If we count the number of members of Parliament who hold a degree in law, this may not appear to be true. However, we have to keep in mind that all those who have a law degree may not be practising lawyers. But the more important thing seems to be that the vast majority of people now do not have faith in lawyers as a class to regard them as their leaders. While the lawyers who played a prominent part in the freedom movement, by and large, supported programmes of social reform and reconstruction, some of their counterparts today not only obstruct all attempts at reform of the legal system but also oppose most of the measures of social legislation and programmes of social change.

Lawyers do not seem to help very much in arriving at just settlement of disputes. On the contrary, it is sometimes felt that they tend to endeavour for prolonging conflicts and making them more bitter. Courts are used to further, rather than solve, disputes. Many observers have pointed out that lawyers help their guileful clients to use the legal system as a weapon to be brought to bear on their opponents. Thus, even though the people in general do not usually subscribe to the values embedded in the modern judicial system, many of them use it for a purpose very different from what was intended. In this, they are sometimes actively helped by the lawyers.

The fact that lawyers in general do not want any type of disputes to be quickly settled without their intervention is well brought out by a recent happening. In December 2002 most of the lawyers at all levels of judiciary from the Supreme Court to the lower courts went on a one-day strike, despite the clear Supreme Court order declaring this strike illegal. The purpose of the strike was to protest against the proposal for establishing Lok Adalats for government departments. It may be noted that a large number of cases pending in courts of law involve government departments in which the state is a party. If this burden on the courts could be taken away, not only would that benefit the government employees but also the people in general. But the lawyers made an astonishingly united show of protest to stall this measure. This seems to bring out clearly that lawyers as a body tend to oppose any reduction in the number of disputes from which they might stand to gain.

6

Development of the Legal Profession in India*

SAMUEL SCHMITTHENER

The legal profession as it exists in India today had its beginning in the first years of British rule. The Hindu pandits, Muslim muftis, and Portuguese lawyers who served under earlier regimes had little effect upon the system of law and legal practice that developed under British administration. At first, the prestige of the legal profession was very low. From this low state and disrepute the profession developed into the most highly respected and influential one Indian society. The most talented among the Indians were attracted to the study and practice of law. The profession dominated the public life of the country and played a prominent role in the national struggle for freedom. There was no movement in any sphere of public activity—educational, cultural, or humanitarian—in which lawyers were not in the forefront. However, after independence the relative prestige and public influence of the profession declined.

The fact that none of the early attorneys had legal training did not add to the prestige of the profession. Some of those who practised were members of the clerical staff of the court and acted as agents for parties in the court. Other attorneys seem to have been businessmen. Describing the early courts Charles Lockyer wrote, '(l)awyers are plenty, and as knowing as can be expected from broken linen drapers and other cracked tradesmen who seek their fortunes here by their wits.' Probably the most competent of these untrained attorneys were company servants appointed to act as attorneys. Some of them had studied 'something both in Civil and common law.' 'Although they were no more than ordinary covenanted

*Samuel Schmitthener, The Development of Legal Profession in India, *Indian Bar Review*, vol. xiii, nos 3 & 4, July–December 1986, pp. 308–52.

servants in the beginning appointed primarily to the cases of the Company, they took up individual cases beyond the sphere of their official duty. . . .'

THE SUPREME COURT ERA OF BRITISH PRACTICE: 1774–1861

Dissatisfaction with the weaknesses of the Mayor's court led to the establishment in 1774 by royal charter of a Supreme Court of Judicature at Calcutta. The Supreme Court enjoyed a wide jurisdiction over civil and criminal matters in the city of Calcutta and a more restricted jurisdiction over cases involving inhabitants of the *mofussil*. With certain exceptions for Hindu and Muslim law in family matters, the law to be applied was the law of England. Similar Supreme Courts were established in Madras in 1801 and Bombay in 1823.

The first barristers appear in India after the opening of the Supreme Court in Calcutta in 1774. As barristers began to come into the courts and work as advocates, the attorneys gave up pleading and worked as solicitors and the two grades of legal practice gradually became distinct and separate as they were in England. Many of the first barristers came as judges, not as lawyers. The first barrister in Bombay was the Judge of the new recorder's court set up in 1798. By 1807 there were only two barristers working as advocates in Bombay. One was the first Advocate General, Stuart Thriepland. Madras had its first barrister in 1778 when Mr Benjamin Sullivan, who was on his way to practise at the Supreme Court Bar at Calcutta, stopped for a visit and was persuaded to stay on as government advocate on a salary of 250 Pagodas per month. The salary was doubled in 1780 since he was not allowed to practise privately: 6,000 pagodas annually (£2,400 or Rs19,200).

The establishment of the Supreme Court brought recognition, wealth and prestige to the legal profession and brought a steady flow of well-trained barristers and solicitors into Calcutta. The charter of the court required that the chief justice and three puisne judges be English barristers of at least five years standing. The legal profession was recognized for the first time. The charter empowered the court to approve, admit, and enrol advocates and attorneys to plead and act on behalf of suitors. It also gave the court authority to remove lawyers from the roll of the court 'on a reasonable cause and to prohibit practitioners not properly admitted and enrolled from practising in the court'.

The court itself provided employment for three full-time lawyers with good salaries:

Advocate General	£3,000 per annum	
	with allowance of	
	Rs2,500 monthly	= Rs54,000
Company counsel for suits		
and prosecutions	£4,500	= Rs36,000
Company counsel for contracts and		
conveyances	£3,000	= Rs24,000

Besides these full-time posts there were a number of offices held by attorneys who practised as solicitors, which brought substantial supplementary income. The Register of the court, who was also allowed to practise earned £7,000 (Rs56,000) a year. Each of the judges and the chief justice had a solicitor acting as his clerk. Hickey, who served as clerk for Justice Hyde, said, 'I had a fee upon every process issued . . . I never received less than Rs500 a month, frequently Rs800. The post of deputy sheriff was served by a solicitor. Hickey reported that the most he made from that post in one year was Rs25,000. The sheriffs who could not be lawyers, did much better, the record being Rs130,000 for one year. There were other paying part-time posts open to attorneys, such as: counsel for paupers, £810 or Rs7,200; attorney for paupers, £540 or Rs4,800; and examiner, £450 or Rs4,000.

The first barrister to practise as an advocate in Calcutta was Mr Ferrer, who was admitted by the Supreme Court in October 1774. He acted as advocate for the defence of Nuncomar (Nandkumar) in 1775. The counsel for the crown in that case was Mr Durham, who proved to be so weak that the judges did most of the questioning for the prosecution. However, in a short time the bar became stronger as the great volume of legal business and high fees attracted many to the city. William Hickey reported that when he returned to Calcutta in 1793 there were nine barristers including the Attorney General. In his diary for the period 1790–1809 he mentions seventeen barristers and fifteen attorneys and solicitors (including himself). In Calcutta in 1861 there were thirty-two advocates and sixty attorneys, proctors, or solicitors of whom four were Indians.

The expense of living as a gentleman attorney was often greater than the lucrative income of legal practice. William Hickey gives us a fairly clear record of what it cost him to move with the best society (the judges, councilmen, lawyers, and military officers) of Calcutta. To get established he borrowed Rs40,000 at 2 per cent interest. Carriages and horses cost him Rs6,550. Monthly rent was Rs450, salary for sixty-three servants Rs666 and other expenses averaged Rs2,000 monthly. (His average living expense of Rs36,000 a year was equal to a judge's salary.) For fifteen years he was unable to clear off his debts in spite of a very good income. His financial problems were due in part to his clever dishonest bania and his careless bookkeeping, and to the repeated misfortune of being responsible for the bad debts of others who had absconded or died. Wishing to retire with a *modest* fortune he spent his last five years in Calcutta practising alone, living less lavishly, keeping careful records, and earning much from fees and from his post as clerk of the chief justice. Upon retirement he paid all of his debts and extra gratuities to servants, procured ticket to England, and still had Rs92,000 net balance.

INDIAN LEGAL PRACTITIONERS—THE MOFUSSIL COURTS

Bengal Regulation VII of 1793 brought order and some measure of quality to pleading and endeavoured to establish it as a respectable profession:

> It is therefore indispensably necessary for enabling the courts to administer, and the suitors to obtain justice, that the pleading of causes should be made a distinct profession; and that no persons shall be admitted to plead in the courts but men of character and education, versed in the Mohammedan or Hindoo law and in the Regulations passed by the British Government, and that they should be subjected to rules and restrictions calculated to secure to their clients a diligent and faithful discharge of their trusts.

The Sudder Dewanee Adawlut (Sadar Diwani Adalat) was empowered by the Regulation to appoint as many pleaders of the Muslim or Hindu religion as necessary, specifying the court in which they were empowered to plead, and to take oaths from each pleader upon his joining the court. These pleaders were to be selected from among the students of the Mohammedan Madrasa (college) at Calcutta and the Hindu College at Benares (Varanasi) and were to be men of good character. They were required to acquaint themselves with the Regulation.

Besides providing for discipline of the profession the Regulation offered greater opportunities for lawyers by requiring the appointment of government pleaders. These government pleaders were to be paid at the same rate, and had the privilege of working as private pleaders in other suits in which government was not a party.

The new sections of the 1814 Regulation indicate the kind of problems the courts were having with this rising profession. Section VIII stipulated that pleaders must take precaution to ascertain the real names of parties giving *vakalatnama* and would be liable for dismissal if a *vakalat-*

nama under a fictitious name were accepted. Furthermore, the pleader was warned to study plaints before they were filed and make sure that groundless, irrelevant points were not included, that useless witnesses were not summoned, and that all exhibits were examined previous to being filed. If a vakil continued, after warning, to produce irrelevant exhibits or witnesses he was to be fined Rs20 or made to forfeit his fee. Other provinces passed regulations almost identical to those of Bengal.

Regulations provided that all pleadings were first to be completely written and then read out. Then the court could make inquiries to clarify issues and call witnesses if necessary. Richard Temple, who served as a district judge before the Mutiny, described court procedure: 'The vernacular proceedings covered reams of country-made paper. These documents were read out by native clerks with a distinctiveness and fluency which I had never known in any European language. I dictated my orders to the clerks which were read out before being initiated by me.'

Professional respectability was hard to come by in spite of continuous legislation to control procedure and practice. *Leaders such as Metcalfe and Elphinstone regarded lawyers as being the most undesirable aspect of a legal system which they believed was as a whole quite unfit for India.* Elphinstone refers to 'this institution, that mystery that enables litigious people to employ courts of justice as engines of intimidation and which renders necessary a class of lawyers who among the natives are great fomenters of disputes.' Macaulay described the lawyers of Bengal as 'ravenous pettifoggers who fattened on the misery and terror of an immense community.' These attitudes were shared by many: 'The . . . whole public looked down upon (pleaders) as pests, but they were constantly employed because they were the only available guides in the new legal labyrinth.'

In 1882, Malabari described the mofussil vakil as 'a column of vapor issuing from an Ocean of Emptiness . . . He is brought alive by the Chief Justice, passes the day in the company of *chuprasis*, and . . . vegetates.' 'His chemical composition is butter, brass and asafoetida.' He describes the successful vakil as one who is in the hands of a Marwari broker, who does his business in whispers in the corridors of the courthouse earning fees of Rs3 to Rs30. However, we shall see that some of these humble pleaders rose to be great and highly respected men, and that many of their sons and grandsons became the great barristers, judges, and political leaders of India.

Besides the pleaders there were other legal agents, 'employed . . .[as] inferior advisors or agents called *mukhtars* to advise them more or less as solicitors.' These men, though not licensed or recognized by the courts, did most of the attorney work. In his report to the Select Committee of the House of Commons in 1832 McKenzie stated that though they were not included on the fees schedule, many of the *mukhtars* acted as professional men.

William Hickey gives a graphic description of one opulent Memychuru Mulliah, a bania who worked in close association with a number of solicitors for many years. He may be regarded as the prototype of the Indian non-licensed solicitor:

> This man had acquired an extraordinary efficiency in our laws so much so that he had for many years been the advisor of all those who had anything to do with courts of justice and was competent to tell them whether they had sufficient merits in their cases to justify the commencement of or defence of a suit. He was also perfectly conversant with the distinction between an equitable and a legal title, and was in the practice of sitting every evening in his own house for a certain number of hours to hear the statements of the various persons that attended for the purpose of accompanying him, for which it was said . . . that he made those suitors whose causes he espoused and patronized amply repay him for his trouble and his time by exacting a very high percentage upon whatever the amount recovered or saved might be.

Although pleading before the civil courts was limited to admitted practitioners, the *mukhtars* reaped a rich harvest by practising in the criminal courts as well as acting as solicitors for the pleaders. The *mukhtars* had enough persistence to survive the many regulations intended by Cornwallis to make them unnecessary: the Legal Practitioners Act of 1846, and the formation of the high courts with the accompanying rules. The *mukhtars* were recognized and brought under the control of the courts for the first time by Act XX of 1865, called the Pleader, Mukhtar, and Revenue Agents Act. Revenue agents who worked in the revenue offices and courts were also given status as legal practitioners by this Act. They were deemed to be the lowest in grade and did not play a significant part in the development of the legal profession.

Act I of 1846 enabled the barristers to increase their influence and income by extending practice to the *sudder* courts. 'That every Barrister in any of Her Majesty's Courts of Justice in India shall be entitled as such to plead in any of the Sudder Courts of the E. Indian Company subject to all the rules in force in the said Sudder Courts applicable to Pleaders, whether relating to the language in which the Court is to be addressed or to any other matter' (S5). The barrister could also practise alongside the pleaders in the small cause court.

THE FOUNDING OF THE HIGH COURTS AND THEIR EFFECT

After the British government assumed direct control of the territories of the East India Company (1858), the separate systems of the Company's courts in the mofussil and the royal courts in the presidency towns were consolidated into a unified judicial system in each of the three presidencies. At the apex of the new system were high courts, chartered by the Crown, established at Calcutta, Bombay, and Madras in 1862.

The commissioners appointed to arrange the *sudder* court–high court merger had advocated that the high court bench be exclusively British and the bar open only to barristers. Judge Trevelyan, opposing such restrictions, argued that exclusion of Indians from the bench would 'nourish . . . class antipathies, and injure . . . at once the state and the individual by depriving the public of the service of the ablest men, preventing wholesome competitions, and unduly exalting some without reference to their personal merits and depressing others.' His statement of policy in regard to the bar shows the spirit and intention of the merger as an attempt to make possible the full development of the profession:

> At present barristers, attorneys and vakils plead before the Sadr Court while barristers have exclusive audience before the Supreme Court. It would be hard to deprive the natives of the privilege they have long enjoyed of employing a cheap and rapidly improving, though still generally less efficient description of the agency; and I am confident that English barristers do not require exclusive privileges to enable them to maintain their position. They are employed now by all who can afford it and will continue to be so. The same objections exist to this limitation as to that proposed in reference to the eligibility for the bench. We cannot afford the weakness consequent upon social heart burnings. We want, for the improvement of all, the wholesome influence of competition. A native Bar will gradually be formed, but it will be following the lead and imitating the example of our English barristers.

Practising side by side with British lawyers, the Indian vakils learned much of law, professional ethics, and standards of practice. Gopalratnam shows that this learning of the best British traditions by Indian vakils began a sort of guru-disciple tradition:

> Men like Sir V. Bashyam Ayyangar, Sir T. Muthuswami Ayyar and Sir S. Subramania Ayyar were quick to learn and absorb the traditions of the English Bar from their English friends and colleagues in the Madras Bar and they in their turn as the originators of a long line of disciples in the Bar passed on those traditions to their disciples who continued to do the good work.

Additional high courts were established in Allahabad (1886), Patna (1916), and Lahore (1919), creating a demand for many more lawyers and stimulating the rapid growth of the profession. The high courts 'affected the legal unity of the country and brought into being a class of legal practitioners patterned alike on a national scale.' The high courts had an upgrading effect upon the district and mofussil courts and bars. Many of the high court judges encouraged leading members of the 'High Court bar to practice in the mofussil courts and aided them by giving adjournments'. This served a double purpose. It not only helped the pleader in promoting his own prestige and practice; but more important, the effect of the presence and the methods of conducting cases of experienced High Court lawyers, in the subordinate courts, would be to improve the standards of practice in these courts.'

There were six grades of legal practice in India after the founding of the high courts: advocates, attorneys (solicitors), and vakils in the high courts; and pleaders, *mukhtars* and revenue agents in the lower courts. The high courts set up standards of admission for vakils which were much higher than requirements for the old vakil–pleader of the zilla courts. Vakil became a distinct grade above the pleader.

The Legal Practitioners Act of 1879 brought all six grades of the profession into one system under the jurisdiction of the high courts. Together with the letters patent of the high courts the Act formed the chief legislative governance of legal practitioners in the subordinate courts of the country until the Advocates Act of 1961.

To be a vakil, the prospective lawyer had to study at a college or university, master the use of English, and pass the high court vakils' examination. Admission requirements were gradually raised so that by 1940 a vakil was required to be a graduate with an LLB from a university in India in addition to presenting a certificate saying that he had passed in the examinations, read in the chamber of a qualified lawyer, and was of good character.

Though vakils were the lowest rank of the high court practitioners, their position was a most honorable one, and opened the way for promotion and wider practice. After ten years of service in the high court many vakils were raised to the rank of the advocate (e.g., Sir Sunderlal, Jogendranath Chaudri, Ram Prasad, and Motilal Nehru of the Allahabad High Court).

In addition to their extensive appellate jurisdiction, the high courts of the three presidency towns also had an oriental side, whose jurisdiction included the major civil and criminal matters that would earlier have been heard by the predecessor supreme courts. On the original side in these high courts, the grades of solicitor (attorney) and advocate (barrister) remained distinct. On the appellate side and in the other high courts, 'every lawyer practices as his own attorney'. Attorneys and solicitors, therefore, practised almost exclusively in the three presidency high courts. Practice on the original side was both lucrative and prestigious.

In Madras vakils began to practise on the original side as early as 1866. However, the barristers were 'handicapped' by this success of the vakils and in 1874 challenged their right to do original side work. The issue was brought up many times and finally in 1916 this right was firmly established for the vakils. Vaikls in Bombay and Calcutta could be promoted as advocates and become qualified to work on the original side. By attending the appellate side and original side courts each for one year a vakil of ten years service in the court was permitted to sit for the advocates examination. Mr Setalvad did this and began a successful career on the original side in 1906.

EDUCATION

The standard of law courses taught in the government schools was not severe: A high school education was enough for those who wished to practise in the lower courts as pleaders or *mukhtars*. Mahajan, who later became Chief Justice of India, was licensed as a *mukhtar* after he finished high school. Sardar Patel took the district pleaders' examination after he had finished high school. His brother, Vithalbhai, finished high school and studied for a time at Gokhale Law Class in Bombay 'which coached students for the District Pleaders' examination'. The stress was on passing the examination; the institution where one studied was not very important.

Teachers were poorly paid. A full professor received Rs400 a month and a lecturer Rs150. The teacher–pupil ratio was 3:400 when Setalvad attended law school. He noted that teachers were appointed 'not always on merits but for making provision for young barristers struggling at the Bar.'

The number of law students as well as practitioners was much greater in Calcutta than in the other presidencies as the following table of Bachelor of Law graduates shows:

	Calcutta	Madras	Bombay
1864–73	704	78	33
1874–82	924	232	156

Though large numbers (nearly 3,000 a year by 1910) were graduating from the poorly equipped and staffed law colleges, a law degree did not signify a sound preparation in law or professional competence. These assets were more often gained as the young lawyer worked as an apprentice or junior to some well-known, experienced lawyer.

In England where social life and 'eating of dinners' were an important part of legal training at the Inns of Court, standards of legal education were not much better. For a time the exams for the barristers were actually easier than the LLB and high court pleaders' exams in India. This fact and the higher prestige and advantages open to the barristers induced many young men to study for the bar in England.

INDIAN BARRISTERS

Few Indians could afford the long expensive training programme for barristers that could be had only in England. The earliest candidates were predominantly sons of rich Parsi merchants. One forward-looking Parsi leader recognized the potential that barristers would have for leading Indian society and provided funds for this training:

> For some years before this (1864), it was being realized more and more in India that a barrister's profession was a natural avenue for the advancement of India not only culturally, socially and educationally, but as a means of getting her legitimate claims advanced and grievances redressed. The profession which sought justice protected and fought for the rights of a subject in court, was the profession most suited to seek justice, claim protection and fight for the rights of the people as against the government. In appreciation of this fact and from a sense of patriotism. Mr Rustomji Jamshedjee Jijeebhoy, who was a highly enlightened and philanthropic man . . . made a trust of Rs1,50,000 for the selection of five Indians to proceed to Europe to be called to the Bar. The scholarship was Rs 30,000 to each of them. The proposal was made for a Parsi, a Hindu, and a Portuguese from Bombay and a Mahomedan and Hindu from East India or Calcutta or Madras.

Sir Jijeebhoy's hopes were amply fulfilled. One of these five students was Womesh Chunder Bonnerji, who had been one of the four Indian lawyers practising as a solicitor at the Supreme Court in Calcutta. He joined the Calcutta High Court as a barrister in 1868, became president of the Law Faculty at Calcutta in 1880, served as a member of the Bengal Legislative Council, and as the first president of the Indian National Congress in 1885. From 1901 he practised before the Privy Council in England.

Pherozshah Mehta was another of these first five scholarship students. After practising for a few years as a barrister of the Bombay High Court he devoted his time fully to politics and reform. He became the most influential member of the Bombay Legislative Council, a member of the university, and a 'pillar' in the Indian National Congress and served as the sixth Congress president.

A study of the list of admissions into Lincoln's Inn (one of the four Inns of Court) reveals that from 1861 to 1893 one hundred Indian students studied there to become barristers, increasing from one or two a year at first to five or six annually towards the close of this period. Of these, four already had law degrees from Indian universities, and twenty-two were the sons of pleaders or magistrates.

The biographer of Justice Badruddin Tyabji (the first Muslim to become a barrister) describes the work required by the student at an Inn of Court:

> He now resumed his terms reading in the chambers of the barristers. Here he devoted himself to learning the routine of legal proceedings, the work of a common law barrister, then an equity lawyer and a conveyancer. He attended also the offices of Mr John Morris the solicitor . . . and drew pleadings, wills, conveyances, mortgages, deeds of trust, petitions. . . . He attended the law courts and studied the conduct of cases by eminent lawyers. When thus equipped a friendly solicitor entrusted him with some briefs and reported that he conducted the cases creditably.

The first Indian barristers to practise in the high courts were disappointed to find that they could not make a success of practising on the original side, where the lucrative commercial cases were. Work on the original side could only come to a barrister through a solicitor. The solicitors' firms were all British, and they did all of the work for the government departments and the great shipping and industrial firms. They did not want to patronize an untried Indian barrister. Nor did the few individual Indian solicitors who were struggling to expand their practice wish to risk the blame that would come upon them if some inexperienced Indian barrister mishandled a case. Tyabji, who joined the Bombay High Court in 1867, was the first to win success on the original side:

> He had one advantage over the others. He had the support of his own brother who was an eminent solicitor. Immediately on Badruddin being admitted an advocate, he received from his brother Camruddin a brief of two gold mohors, for drawing a written statement. . . . In the very first year of his practice in 1868, he received a good deal of drafting work, mostly from his brother but also

from four Hindu solicitors and an English firm Manisty and Fletcher. His work was skillfully done. He was then tried with a ten mohors case, and he justified their expectations. Henceforth, it was only a question of time and experience.

Even after Tyabji's success a number of other prominent Indian advocates failed to establish themselves on the original side. Not only British firms, but also Indians preferred to be represented by British solicitors and advocates—perhaps because it was believed they would have more influence with the English judges. The preference for English practitioners was widespread. Vachha reports that due to confidence in their impartiality and inaccessibility to extend pressures 'throughout the 19th century the inhabitants of Bombay preferred to trust their legal business, including the administration of estates, to the British solicitors, and to refer their disputes to the arbitration of English barristers.' After Tyabji, Telang was the first barrister to overcome these prejudices against Indian lawyers and to work successfully on the original side.

After 1900 vakils who had been promoted as advocates were enabled to work on the original side. After attending the appellate side courts for one year and the original side for another year a vakil could be permitted to sit for the advocates' examination, a most difficult one. Setalvad was one of the first to accomplish this, but experienced the usual prejudice that made establishing original side practice difficult. However, these attitudes changed:

When the evening in 1908 Craigie of Craigie, Lynch & Owen, a leading firm of solicitors, walked into my chamber and delivered to me a heavy brief in a case that lasted two months before Justice Beaman and marked the fees I mentioned, I realized that the ghost of racial prejudice had been buried once for all at least as far as the legal profession was concerned.

The bench gave much more encouragement to the barristers and helped them gain equality with the British practitioners. Many Indian lawyers in their memoirs or autobiographies mention some British judge who gave encouragement, help, and honour to new, inexperienced lawyers. Lawyers such as Telang showed the whole country that Indians could achieve the same eminence in the profession as could Englishmen. He was 'head and shoulders above all of his Indian contemporaries' and one of the foremost practitioners, including the many experienced Englishmen, at the bar. He was promoted to the bench at the age of thirty-two in 1889 but died less than three years after this appointment.

Professional equality was achieved by Indian advocates asserting their rights in court and by able demonstration of professional competence. Indian lawyers learned to defend their positions as assertively as did their British colleagues. Barrister Kali Mohan of Calcutta once had charges framed against him for arguing with Judge Jackson: 'I am surprised, my Lord, that though you have been a District judge for so many years I cannot make you understand what even a student of law can very easily follow.' The full bench of the Calcutta High Court dismissed the charges against Mohan as they judged that the principle he had been maintaining was correct. When Indian barristers won cases against famous English lawyers (as C.R. Das successfully defended Aurobindo against Mr Eardly Norton) they proved that the English barristers no longer had an insuperable advantage. The bringing together of the talent, learning, and tradition of Indians and Englishmen on the bench as well as the bar of the high courts gave legal practice a colour and scope that it had never had before.

The only profession preferred to that of barrister was the civil service. As it was extremely difficult for Indians to pass the examinations and be accepted into the civil service, the great majority of the young Indians trained in England were called to the bar and returned to India 'transformed into English gentlemen'.

INCOME AND PRESTIGE

The great volume of legal business, high fees, and the prestige conferred by the high courts combined to make the practice of law the most important of the professions in late nineteenth-century India. In 1881 there were 1.6 million civil suits valued at 16.54 crore of rupees. By 1901 there were 2.2 million suits. Some areas, notably where the zamindari system was in force, had an extremely high incidence of litigation. This volume spurred the growth of the profession.

The charging of high fees, which had been part of the pattern of Supreme Court practice, continued in spite of attempts at control. In spite of the often-revised fee tables, very high fees could be earned by the more skilled lawyers. Bepin Chandra Pal reported that his father, a pleader in the district court, earned Rs200–300 a month 'quite a high income in those days when a man generally counted rich Rs100 a month'. Mahajan reported that his first fee was Rs300. In those days (1913) when courts were held at different places as the collector toured, a lawyer could make 'good money' as 'fee for going on tour were substantial'. Lawyers' fees were much higher than the salaries of most police officials; in 1901 a police sub-inspector received less than Rs75 a month.

The biggest earners were men like C.R. Das and Motilal Nehru. In 1886, in his thirties, Motilal was averaging Rs2,000 a month and after some more years he was earning in lakh. He lived like a prince, had the first car in Allahabad and a palatial house. In the famous *Damraon Case* which he lost to C.R. Das he cleared rupees two lakh in eight months. C.R. Das did even better. From 1917 to 1919 he earned three lakh a year. In 1920 his earning was Rs50,000 every month. In January of the following year he gave all of this up and joined Gandhi's non-cooperation movement.

Though few lawyers earned as did these nabobs of law, many of them earned a good living. In 1914 a good lawyer could be retained for Rs20 in an appeal case and for Rs50 in a civil suit. Mahajan averaged Rs30 to 500 a month and hoped for the day when he could earn Rs1,000 a month as did the leading lawyer of the Gurdaspur Bar. After five years of practice, by 1914, Katju was making Rs400–500 per month, yet could not afford a carriage and went to court on a bicycle.

One reason that fee income was so high was that an average case moved very slowly. Cases were (and are) not heard on consecutive days but at wide intervals and only a fraction of the day was given to each hearing. Cases often lasted a generation. In 1955 the average duration of first appeal in the Allahabad High Court was 2,145 days. For this reason clients sometimes asked for a lump sum agreement. Mavalankar reported that his first case was the defence of a bigamist. His client asked for a lump sum agreement. Thinking it would last no more than three sittings he agreed to Rs15 (Rs3 a sitting being the low rate for cases in the lower court in those days). It lasted twenty. Another reason for high fees is the insistence of many litigants on having the most eminent counsel and the frequent unwillingness to compromise, even when urged to do so by counsel and judge.

There was little specialization at the Indian bar. Many advocates handled criminal and civil work, trial and appellate cases, commercial law and Hindu law at the same time, 'switching off from one subject to another'. Dr Kailash Nath Katju delighted in the variety of practice that challenged the Indian advocate and himself won famous cases concerning Hindu law, inheritance, business, and criminal matters.

Besides the prospects of making a good living, the prestige and honour shown to the successful members of the legal profession encouraged many to study law. Leading counsels of the high courts received many honours and promotions. The possibilities of rising in the profession were almost limitless. Mahajan, who as a college student had practised as a *mukhtar*, became an LLB in 1912 and practised as a vakil in the district court, then as a vakil in the Lahore High Court, judge of the High Court in 1943, Federal Court judge in 1948 and Chief Justice of the Supreme Court in 1954. The highest position of honour and responsibility open to an Indian during British rule was a cabinet post in the viceroy's council. In 1910 Mr Satyendra Prasanna Sinha, a leading barrister of Calcutta, was appointed as law member of viceroy's cabinet. This 'opened all positions of honour and dignity in the state to Indians of ability and integrity.'

GROWTH OF THE PROFESSION

Before 1920 more students studied law than all the other professions put together, as shown by the following table:

	Law Students	Students of Other Professions
1911–1912	3,036	3,135
1916–1917	5,426	4,595
1921–1922	5,234	6,755
1931–1932	7,151	7,954
1939–1940	6,749	10,378
1949–1950	9,464	31,170

As more territory was annexed by the British, the judicial system was extended and more and more lawyers were needed to practise in the newly opened courts and to advise the people in these new territories who had little knowledge of Anglo-Indian law and court procedure. In the Punjab in 1866 there were only eleven practising lawyers but in that same year there were 166,000 suits in the Punjab courts. By 1910 there were 1,277 lawyers to share in this volume of legal work and by 1918 the Punjab had 1,837 lawyers. There were different evaluations of this phenomenal growth. Spain refers to the lawyers of the Punjab as a horde of half-trained men who promoted litigation and kept the feuds of the Pathans alive. The editor of the *Lahore Law Journal* on the other hand attributed the growth of the profession to the lawyers' hard work, honesty, sympathy with the public, and usefulness to the people of the Punjab. Both views give only a partial picture. As great numbers came to be lawyers the most outstanding and capable of the ethical practitioners won great prestige for the profession at the same time that the unscrupulous promoters of litigation caused the 'lawyer to be regarded as a parasite feeding on society'.

Numerically India has the second largest legal profession in the world (after the United States). It has proportionately more lawyers than other non-Western countries. The great appeal of the profession which created this phenomenal growth in numbers very early led to overcrowding and unemployment at the bar. After 1890 the phrase 'briefless barrister' described the grim reality experienced by young lawyers. As brilliant a lawyer as C.R. Das, who joined the bar at Calcutta in 1893, spent the first fifteen years of his career experiencing the 'daily round of almost hopeless waiting at the Bar library in company of more than a hundred equally hopeless members of the learned brotherhood'. He took to writing to keep busy, fell into debt of Rs40,000 and was declared bankrupt by the court. He did not make a success of legal practice until he won sudden fame for his defence of Aurobindo in the *Alipore Bomb Case* in 1908. The more important the court, the more crowded was the bar. Although Madras Presidency had twenty-six district courts, nearly half of the advocates were practising in Madras City. The chances of starting practice in the villages at the taluk courts were very poor. An ambitious young lawyer could learn and progress in his profession only by working in close association with an experienced senior lawyer, and these men were found only at the district and high courts.

Without the help of a practising family member or relative many a well-trained talented new lawyer had little chance to show what he could do to succeed at the bar. A well-known vakil of Madras, Sivaswami Aiyar, referring to the very crowded conditions at the Madras bar writes, 'Unless a beginner has influential relations or connections or can get the chance of devilling to appreciative and generous leaders in the Bar, he has no means of making himself known to the client world or to the judges in the Courts'. . . . The failure of C.R. Das to get a good start as a barrister in the High Court of Calcutta is attributed to the retirement of his solicitor father which made it impossible for his father to see that legal business came his way. A practising father, interested in his son's legal career could spell the difference between failure and success at the bar.

Mahajan was more fortunate than Das. Although his father was only a *mukhtar* he had wide experience and knowledge of law and a busy practice. He trained a clerk in his office to be ready to serve his son when he finished his legal education. During law school vacations Mahajan worked in his father's office and learned how to accept and refuse briefs. He writes of his father, 'He taught me drafting of plaints, pleadings and petitions and made me draw out conveyancing documents.' For the first few months he worked as apprentice to his father and attended cases when his father was too busy to appear. In this way his ability came to be recognized by the bench, bar, and the public and his career was successfully begun.

Families with long and rich legal traditions supplied the Indian bar with an abundance of highly trained talented leaders who maintained high professional standards and won great honour for the bar.

CONCLUSION

In view of the impressive history of the legal profession, the place it holds in post-independence India is disappointing. It is an active and essential profession, but it no longer has the limelight. By the time of independence, widespread unemployment among the legally trained caused university graduates to seek training in other professions such as teaching, medicine, and engineering. No longer did the most talented men of the country study law. The prestige of the profession has greatly diminished. Katju, regretting this decline in the quality of the profession, has observed that previously only members of the higher classes, coming from families with a tradition of learning, studied for this profession. Now, however, students of law are drawn from all of society and often study law only because they cannot get seats in the other, more preferable professions.

The legal profession no longer offers the most honoured and profitable work that can be attained in India. It no longer draws the best students, and it no longer dominates the social and political life of the country. The monopoly it had on the leadership of the country for over a century is now gone. In a way the rest of society has caught up with the profession.

Still it can play a vital role in upholding individual rights, promoting more efficient and widespread justice, and acting as an integrating force in national life. It has great traditions on which to build. It now has a unified bar and controls the quality of its education, requirements, and ethical standards. It has an extensive literature and a great deal of experience. It is part of a 'modern legal system' which 'provides both the personnel and the techniques for effecting national unity'. The responsibility of this profession to the society of such a developing nation is indeed great, as has been its history.

7

Legal Profession and Society:
A Study of Lawyers and
their Clients*

K.L. SHARMA

This essay is based on the findings of my research project—'Relations Between Lawyers and Their Clients' which was sponsored by the Indian Council of Social Science Research, New Delhi. The project was completed in 1981. The study was carried out at Jaipur, the capital of Rajasthan (India). The study was confined to the lawyers of this city and their clients. Information regarding socialization, professionalization, stratification, and networks of lawyers as well as clients was gathered initially through an enumeration schedule in case of lawyers and later on through two separate interview guides for lawyers and clients. Sources such as census reports, bar council library, legislative enactments, university law school library literature, some reports, were also tapped as supportive base. In all, 140 out of 420 lawyers of Jaipur city, and 125 clients were interviewed. The norm of one client for one lawyer could not be met as only 125 clients were finally contacted. Depth interviews of some key informants were also conducted.

The questions explored in the study related to stratification within the bar, criteria of ranking, effect of clientele milieu on hierarchy among lawyers, and strains affecting solidarity and performance. Recruitment to the bar and training have been examined in relation to lawyers' socialization and professional achievement. In fact, our emphasis in this study is basically on the structure and processes among lawyers and clients in terms

*Excerpted from K.L. Sharma, 'Legal Profession and Society: A Study of Lawyers and heir Cleints', in S.K. Lal et al. (eds), *Readings in the Sociology of the Professions*, Delhi: Gian Publishing House, 1984, pp. 380–400.

of their position in society. Lawyers had contributed a lot to the emancipation of Indian masses from the British yoke, yet they have a colonial
legacy. They are called 'swindlers' and 'sharks'. Even today lawyers as a
'community' are represented more than any other group in Parliament
and state legislatures; lawyers have a great deal of professional autonomy
and they have also been guided by primordial and political constraints.
Why have law firms not emerged (except in metropolitan centres) in India
like it has done in the United States of America? Is the lawyer in India
'litigational', 'individualistic', and not so professional?' Why is the lawyer
in India not like a 'social engineer' as he is in England? With a view to investigate these and several other questions, the role of caste, rural–urban
background, parental heritage, family ties, law education, etc., have been
studied in detail.[1]

It goes without saying that sociology of legal profession is an inseparable
part of the sociology of law. Emphasis in sociology of law is on investigation
of the operation of interests, passions, and prejudices of lawyers, clients,
judges, citizens, etc. Sociology of law deals with the relationship between
law and society in terms of social background of the members and groups
in society, positive functions of law and also law as a tool serving vested
interests. Law can be viewed as a field of investigation which comprises
decision making (judicial behaviour) and latent grounds, hidden motives,
group interests, and extra-legal sources of hidden judicial decisions in
regard to judges, social background of lawyers, paralegal functionaries,
clients, etc.[2]

Legal practitioners in India are the second largest body of professionals
in the world, and are represented in the Parliament and state legislatures.
Galanter observes that the Indian lawyer's orientation is towards litigation
rather than in advising, negotiating, or planning. They have ability to
conceptualize in handling of rules. Further, they have individualism but
lack rigorous specialization. The lawyer plays the role of courtroom advocate rather than business advisor or negotiator, much less a social planner.
The ties with clients are not enduring but episodic. However, lawyers in
India have contributed to the national movement for independence,
framing of the Constitution, organization of mass movements, and
restoration of civil liberties.

Some more questions posed by Galanter are: (1) who uses lawyers?
(2) for what? (3) how do they contact them? (4) how widespread is the use
of touts and other intermediaries?, and (5) what does their presence
connote about the social organization of legal services? In fact, these questions refer to lawyer-practitioner, lawyer-scholar or lawyer-politician.
Galanter reflects upon several ethical questions related to legal profession.

He observes that Indian lawyers are court-centred and individualistic in orientation. They lack academic quality are not planners and agents of modernization. Legal education in India is of theoretical nature. It has no serious concern with people's problems. Anti-lawyer sentiment in India is found mainly due to negative image about the practitioners of law. However, Gajendragadkar pleads that lawyers should not confine themselves to their professional obligations and litigants, they should provide intellectual leadership to the country.[3] I have discussed evolution of legal profession in India from the ancient period upto the post-Independence era in my recent study of lawyers and their clients.[4]

Singh observes that the legal system, legitimation, and social change are interlinked processes and the historicity of the given society helps in shaping these interlinkages.[5] The legal system itself is a form of legitimation and may extend legitimation to other institutions. Singh here refers to three functions of law: as *indicator* of change, as *initiator* of change, and as *integrator* of change. Thus, according to Singh, law also performs an integrative function. He makes strong advocacy of the structural approach to the study of legal system, legitimation, and social change. He considers that the legal system in India is a historical product. But as I have stated that the history of legal system in India goes much farther back, continuity exists of ancient and oral indigenous law along with the modern legal system. Also dualism is part of the Constitution of India. The Constitution speaks of equality, social justice, freedom, and secularism. But at the same time the Constitution by its many provisions creates inequality, injustice, particularism, etc. This inner contradiction of India's Constitution has not been debated by law scholars and practitioners. Bi-legalism has become the norm today whether it refers to the Constitution or to the people of India.[6] Modern legal system historically as well as contemporaneously is a product of the political system.

There were about 75,000 lawyers in India in 1958 as per the Fourteenth Report of the Law Commission. However, the number increased to 99,988 in 1961. In 1971, the total of all categories of people in law profession went upto 1,47,662. The maximum lawyers per million inhabitants in India are found in West Bengal, and the minimum in Orissa, 263 and seventy-five respectively. In Rajasthan the number is 121 per million people. According to the 1971 census, there were 3,776 lawyers, 230 judges and magistrates, 170 law assistants, and 1,520 jurists in Rajasthan. Jaipur district had 426 legal practitioners and advisors in 1961 out of the total of 2,853. This was the maximum number found in any district in the state. The minimum was eight in Jaisalmer district. Even Jodhpur district had 324 lawyers though the Rajasthan High Court is located there.[7] Jaipur is not only the capital of Rajasthan, it is also the biggest town and largest district in terms of population. Jaipur was also the largest princely state in the erstwhile Rajputana. Thus, Jaipur town fulfilled the requirements of a fairly representative town for studying relations between lawyers and their clients. The fieldwork for the study was carried out in 1975–6. Through an enumeration schedule basic background information was gathered for all the 420 lawyers practising in various courts in Jaipur.

Of the 420 lawyers, 112 had rural background, fifty-three came from small towns, and the remaining 253 belonged to Jaipur city and some other urban centres. Out of seven categories of lawyers, the lawyers having specialization in taxation, civil, and criminal cases were found numerically preponderant. However, several lawyers practised in more than one area of specialization. There were also lawyers having specialization in revenue, transport, and labour problems. A sample of 140 lawyers was drawn ensuring equal, proportionate, and comparable representation. Of these 420 lawyers, 243 did not hold any office in professional, or political, social organizations. Two hundred sixty-one lawyers had their law education at the School of Law of Rajasthan University, Jaipur and ninety-three had their education from the universities of other states. Three hundred fifty-four lawyers were Hindus, fifty-two Jains, thirteen Muslims, and one Sikh. Only six belonged to lower castes, and 321 belonged to the upper castes. Eighty-five lawyers had mainly rural clientele, 166 had mainly urban, and the remaining 169 had clients from both rural and urban areas. As many as 265 lawyers had individual litigants as their clients whereas ninety-eight had institutions; thirty-two served governmental agencies, and the remaining twenty-one had mixed types of clienteles. Of these lawyers, 140 were selected based on the criteria of experience, rural–urban background and specialization.[8]

Since the universe of the clients of 420 lawyers could not be mapped out, it was decided to pick up one client per lawyer for the 140 selected lawyers. However, we succeeded in getting 125 clients, generally one for each lawyer, in some cases more than one client, and in some others none. Of the 125 clients, ninety-eight were Hindus, twelve Jains, three Sikhs, and twelve Muslims. Thirty-seven of them were illiterate, twenty-three were below matriculation, thirty-seven were educated upto matriculation and higher secondary, twenty-six were graduates and post-graduates, and no correct information could be ascertained in case of two clients. The clients belonged to various caste groups and were engaged in several occupations. Property and agricultural land were the main sources of discords and disputes.[9]

It was found that most of the lawyers took up legal profession not as the best alternative available to them but rather by accident, often against their own choice. In most of the cases, they had no possibility of employment at the time of graduation or post-graduation.[10] It is easier to get admission in India to an LLB course than to other professional courses and social science disciplines. Only a few who had an established practice of their family members opted deliberately for law education. After having obtained an LLB degree a large number of them worked hard to get into legal practice. Certainly some lawyers were impressed and inspired by some well-known luminaries in legal and administrative arenas.

About 50 per cent of our sample comprised lawyers-turned-politicians. They were members of Parliament, Rajasthan Assembly, leaders of political parties, and social and cultural orgainizations.[11] Generally, the politician-lawyers did not do so well in legal profession. The first five top lawyers out of a list of fifteen were not politically active. Also we have not found significant association between law academics and legal practitioners due to a lack of positive relationship between law education and legal practice. The law teachers lived in a world of their own and had no input of grass-roots experience in their theoretical and philosophical discourses on law. More than law teachers, the lawyers of our sample were influenced by their friends, caste, family members, relatives, and neighbours. However, most of the lawyers reported that hard work, sincerity, income, amenability, legal expertise, and political networks were the main criteria of their success. The number of clients was generally considered to be an accurate indication of the level of success achieved. Lawyers were found more successful as politicians because of their contact with the masses and professional autonomy.

Our data show that more than one-third of the clients had background of litigation as their fathers had fought one or more court cases, and majority of them were of upper castes, particularly Brahmins. Economic matters were the main cause for litigation. Criminal offences such as assault, rape, murder, burglary, etc., were the second most important reason. The third set of cases included defamation, negligence, and refusal to vacate houses by tenants, etc. The opponents included close kins, family and caste members, neighbours, relatives, tenants, state government, and business firms.

The clients have a full realization of the fact that litigation would take a long time. They know that they would have to spend a lot of money and waste time and energy. The people generally go to law courts for humiliating their opponents and for having a sense of satisfaction by dragging the opponents to the court of law for their misdeeds against them.

'Professional litigants' are also found in villages and towns. They, in a way, promote the 'culture of litigation' inadvertently.

The clients have a negative image of lawyers, magistrates, court clerks, and munshis. However, they do not have a negative image of their own lawyers in particular. One of the complaints against the magistrates is that they are not competent enough and also they come from upper and upper-middle class families and, therefore, do not do justice to the lower and 'untouchable' castes. Both court clerks and munshis are viewed as corrupt functionaries.

Of the 125 clients, seventy-five approached their lawyers directly, and only thirty-three through some contacts, and sixteen approached lawyers after having gathered requisite information about them. There is no uniform pattern or practice for paying fee to the lawyers. The fee is determined by the nature of the case and the professional calibre of the lawyer. Only three lawyers used touts or brokers to get clients. The opponents generally belonged to a lower caste than that of the litigants. Mainly cultivators, businessmen, and government servants were involved in litigation.[12] Both educated and illiterate fought court cases, hence there is no one-to-one tie between education and litigation. Seventy-one clients out of 125 had lawyers who either hailed from their neighbourhood, village area, or belonged to their caste/community. Clients are generally familiar with court culture, lawyer's tactics, and the role of munshi.

Law education, bar council, and legal practice are the pillars of lawyers' professionalization. The Law Commission of India in its fourteenth report observes that the legal profession is no more a distinguished public service. It is no more attractive as it was in the pre-independence period. Lawyers have lost their leadership in public life. The profession is crowded by young men who are hardly able to make a living.[13] These observations of the Law Commission are only partly true. Law education is somewhat open, but entry into law profession and, more so, the success in legal practice are not so open and easy as one would normally visualize. Who becomes a successful lawyer? This is a very difficult question to answer. The legal profession as it exists today is the outcome of the prevalent legal system, and the latter is an outgrowth of the British judiciary in India.

Lawyers come to know about legal practice from their family members and other independent sources. Mass media and teachers do not contribute much to their knowledge about the nature of legal profession. However, no direct relationship was found between source of knowledge and choice of legal practice as a career, in this particular study.

Out of 140 lawyers, 107 chose a legal career without the advice of parents or other relatives. Even those who already had some family members in law profession were not necessarily guided by them. Not all the lawyers started with legal practice as their first occupation. Fifty per cent were without any job, but the other 50 per cent switched to legal practice from a variety of jobs. A good number of them obtained their law degree as employed students.

Professional competence, honesty, integrity, and amiable personality are the main qualities/attributes necessary for a legal practitioner as viewed by the 140 lawyers themselves. Out of 140 lawyers we prepared a rank order of fifteen top lawyers, and found that lawyers having specialization in criminal and civil cases were included with the exception of one taxation lawyer.[14] The rank order of these fifteen lawyers does not refer to the income they earn from legal practice and political power they possess in society. This refers to the assessment of the lawyers of their own colleagues.

The lawyers admitted their weaknesses including that of toutism, malpractices, bribery, lack of punctuality, short temper, lack of proper attention to the clients, etc. For a young lawyer to be on his own needs some patronage of an established lawyer to come out of the phase of struggling in the profession. Lack of proper law education and professional control have also contributed to 'unprofessionalism' in legal profession. The Bar Council does not exercise very effective control over its members. Very often professionally competent members do not occupy the chairmanship of the Bar Council. Bar Council professionally controls its members. The control is not adequate since the Council's working is not satisfactory— it is not a very active body, nor does it take bold decision.[15]

In our study we found that most of lawyers considered themselves as custodians of their clients' legal interest. They thought this to be their legal as well as moral responsibility. Clients too do not have expectations of high idealism from their lawyers. Lawyers preferred relationship among colleagues more on professional plane rather than at interpersonal level. Lawyers also considered themselves as custodians and protectors of the legal apparatus of Indian society. Some of them thought that legal assistance to the poor should be their philosophy of life. It is upto the lawyers to expose loopholes in legislation. However, the lawyers were in favour of more autonomy for legal profession and reduction of interference in their professional activities by the high court. Besides the autonomy granted by the state, the other important factors conducive to autonomy are the lawyers' art, craftsmanship and ideas. In fact, the legal profession has a unity of its own. Legal standards of models also help to make it a unified system. Lack of autonomy is mainly due to continuity of colonial legal culture.

Law education, apprenticeship, and academic work by lawyers constitute the core of legal professionalism. It was reported that law courses were theoretically of a very high standard, but were not substantiated well by practical training. Some lawyers thought that input of morality and ethics should be added to law course besides theory and practice to make the courses wholesome and relevant. It was also stated that some courses on Indian society in general and on society in Rajasthan in particular be added to the course programme.

A large number of lawyers felt that legal apprenticeship was necessary for new entrants. They learn the 'tricks of the trade' and actual court procedures and practices by undergoing the apprenticeship. They also learn how to deal with clients and how to solve their legal problems. Apprenticeship is considered a period of learning and not earning. However, senior lawyers generally do not give much attention to the new entrants. It was suggested that as in the Supreme Court senior lawyers should appear with the juniors at the district courts. Apprenticeship period should be fixed uniformly. Apprentices should be paid at least some money to survive the period of training. They should be allowed to argue in the courts. However, some lawyers felt that confidence and competence can only be gained through independent practice. Apprenticeship also leads to dependency and exploitation.

Out of the 420 lawyers only thirty-five were reported to have written books, commentaries, and articles, etc. They wrote mainly on land tenancy, property, moneylending, and taxation. However, none of the lawyer-cum-writers have discussed the basic philosophical and academic issues related to the evolution of legal profession in India. In a large number of cases, the commentaries were written with a view to earn money. These writings do not reflect the social science skill as in the case of writings by some judges of high courts and the Supreme Court, hence academic professionalism is weak among the lawyers of Jaipur.

Indian lawyers were discriminated against the British barristers and citizens. Therefore, they fought not only for their own interests, but also for those of the unprivileged and helpless people. In the pre-independence period several lawyers attained a high level of professionalism and also proved equally proficient defenders of the human rights of Indian people. Professionalism and nationalist elan coincided. Our study shows that any lawyer who violated a canon of ethics was censured and suspended from carrying out legal practice in spite of the ineffectiveness attributed to the Bar Association.

There are certain contradictions in regard to theory and practice of legal profession. A lawyer, for example, advises his client not to be involved in unjust litigation, and the client may not heed to his lawyer's counsel and may insist on initiating litigation. The lawyer is supposed to accept the request of his client for defending him by using legal acumen. Such a situation ensues a conflict between the canons of professional ethics and the actual demands of individual practice. As regards getting business and dealing with courts and other official agencies, and in relations with clients, such a dilemma is often faced. However, professional ethics does not remain a strength if legal advice becomes a market commodity in India and also perhaps in a rich country like America.

We have stated earlier that Indian barristers were considered inferior to their British counterparts. Indian barristers were considered superior to Indian advocates who had their law education in India. Besides, there were pleaders of two grades and attorneys, solicitors, and *mukhtar*s etc. Even after independence there were as many as nine types of legal practitioners. Such a legacy of hierarchy within the bar has created obstacles in making the legal profession homogenous to a desirable level. Out of the 140 lawyers, seventy-five faced problems such as of getting clients, adequate income, books, stationary, and proper guidance. Lack of knowledge about court procedures, and cut-throat competition from other lawyers were other serious problems. The first five years were a period of real struggle for them. Sixty-four lawyers did not face such problems because they had someone in the profession to back them up.

The professional aspects of a lawyer's career centre chiefly around his commitment to professionalization which includes reading, writing articles for journals, purchase of books, apprenticeship, joint practice, understanding his profession, job performance, and the role of the Bar Council. All lawyers, with the exception of four, regularly read legal publications. Only ten lawyers had published articles in newspapers and magazines. Lawyers subscribed to a large number of legal journals and magazines because of professional necessity. Ten lawyers got most of the law magazines required for their practice. About 50 per cent of the lawyers visited the Bar Council library. Besides academic professionalization, lawyers considered themselves as specialists in specific and sub-fields. And this is how a lawyer is perceived different from a businessman. Legal practice is a profession as it is based on formal law education, apprenticeship, professional ethics, and service ideal whereas business lacks such attributes of a profession. More than 50 per cent of the lawyers felt that legal practice was better than medical, engineering, university teaching, and state-level services. Income and reputation are generally considered as the most important criteria for a successful lawyer.

Both lawyers and clients are stratified. Lawyers are stratified in two ways: (1) they are stratified in terms of their legal competence; and (2) they belong to various castes and communities. The two bases of social stratification are not unrelated. The clients are stratified in terms of their social background. Ideally, lawyers should serve all segments of society and should also belong to all sections of society. But lawyers serve mostly the upper and middle classes, and do not belong to the lower sections of Indian society. Only economically well-off people can avail lawyer's services, particularly of the one who is professionally reputed. Thus, the clientele of lawyers is distributed differentially along with social distinctions and divisions in Indian society.

Contrary to the situation in the pre-independence period now the legal profession is not confined to the upper caste and upper class alone. Pre-law schooling, and the type and quality of law education are not that important for a legal career while the nature of non-legal jobs and the type and status of legal practice are important. Internal stratification among lawyers is mainly due to the 'inheritance' of practice, non-legal support, and legal competence.

Today income and prestige of a lawyer are two important bases of stratification within the bar. The term 'leading lawyers' is used for those who have a combination of these attributes. Charles Morrison's categorization seems to be somewhat convincing. He refers: top lawyers, below top, average, below average, and briefless lawyers (beginners). They are sometimes also referred as: 'equals', 'juniors' and 'seniors'.[16]

Our analysis shows that there has been a distinct change in the class background of the legal practitioners. Pre-independence lawyers had more commitment to legal professionalism, national cause, and other altruistic objectives. They belonged to aristocracy by birth, but worked for the uplift of the people. Today, lawyers belong to wider sections of society representing all classes. Changes in law education and national situation, diversification of law and increased litigation have changed the nature of demands on lawyers.[17]

Some lawyers had the privilege of having patronage of influential friends, political leaders, senior lawyers, businessmen, and trade union leaders. Besides these networks, co-villagers, fellow caste men, and touts were also used by lawyers at the initial stage of their legal practice. These structural networks were required more at the initial stage of law practice. Father and village background have been found as very effective resources for getting clientele. Intermediaries and touts have generally been not encouraged by lawyers of Jaipur. However, about one-third of the lawyers worked for other senior lawyers.[18]

We have found that lawyers generally preferred clients who are not connected with political parties, and who do not belong to their own caste, community, village, and neighbourhood. Very few lawyers expressed a preference for businessmen and poor persons as clients in particular. A large number of lawyers were connected with well-known political leaders on the basis of affinal ties, friendship, and caste membership. A good number of these leaders were lawyers by training and politicians by profession and practice. Also lawyers sought help from senior lawyers and others for establishing their law practice, but generally did not seek help for winning a case for a client. More than 50 per cent of lawyers wanted their sons to pursue legal practice. However, about one-third of the lawyers did not want their sons to get into legal profession. The lawyers of the latter disposition were not as much satisfied with legal profession as the former category. Active participation in the affairs of Bar Council and other professional bodies was a source of strength for sixty-three lawyers out of the 140. Some lawyers were leaders of various political parties and activists and derived strength from them. Clubs, trade unions, caste associations, and welfare societies were other organizational networks for thirty-four lawyers. Twenty-nine lawyers extended free legal advice to various organizations, institutions, political parties, and persons.

Lawyers have linkages with their clients through many-sided structural channels. Lawyers have referred cases to other lawyers as they thought they did not have requisite competence in particular types of cases. Senior lawyers referred some cases to the junior ones. District lawyers have referred some lawyers at the high court level. However, in most cases lawyers have been referred by the old clients to the new litigants. Thus, both lawyers and clients become effective networks for each other. The clientele of the lawyers of Jaipur was found to be largely rural. Rural clients selected their lawyers based on legal specialization and caste affinity. Urban clients considered specialization and neighbourhood affinity as the criteria for choosing a lawyer. Urban clients comprise businessmen, professionals, government servants, landlords, and organizations and agencies. Rural clients have litigation related to land, property, crime, rivalry, etc.

Conclusion

We have discussed in the present paper the structure and process of legal profession in India based on our study of relations between lawyers and their clients. How lawyers are identified as 'superior' and 'inferior' or 'equal' within the bar, what criteria are used for making such a distinction, how a differential clientele milieu affects hierarchy among lawyers, and what are the strains affecting performance of lawyers—these are some of the questions attempted in this paper. Socialization of lawyers prior to their recruitment to law practice and its effect on recruitment, training, law practice, etc., have also been discussed. The main source of profession in India is not law education as such, but patronage and legal practice itself are the main source of successful professionalization. Finally, income and prestige become the main criteria of lawyers' position in the bar. Legal advice seems to be a market phenomenon, generally beyond the reach of the poor. There are contradictions in regard to legal ethics and law practice, lawyer–client relationship, and Bar Council and legal practice. A lawyer is different today from what he was before independence. However, lawyers in Jaipur are not for toutism and intermediaries. They take a lot of interest in social, cultural, and political activities. Choice of law profession was not clearly made out in many cases.

NOTES AND REFERENCES

1. Sharma, K.L., *Sociology of Law and Legal Profession*, Jaipur: Rawat Publications, 1984.
2. Vilhelm, Aubert, (ed.), *Sociology of Law*, Harmondsworth: Penguin Books, 1969; Gurviteh, Georges, *Sociology of Law*, London: Routledge and Kegan Paul, 1973.
3. Gajendragadkar, P.B., *Lawyers and Social Change*, New Delhi: National Forum of Lawyers and Legal Aid, 1976, p. 23.
4. Sharma, 1984, pp. 43–54.
5. Singh, Yogendra, 'Legal System, Legitimation and Social Change', in *Essays on Modernization in India*, Delhi: Manohar Book Service, 1978, pp. 136–7.
6. Jones, W.H. Morris, *The Government and Politics of India*, London: Hatchinson University Library, 1967, pp. 38–43; Galanter Marc, 'The Aborted Restoration of Indigenous Law in India', *Comparative Studies in Society and History*, vol. 14, no. 1, 1972, pp. 53–70; Rudolph, L.I., and S.H. Rudolph, *The Modernity of Tradition*, Bombay: Orient Longmans Ltd, 1967, pp. 251–930; Misra, B.B., *The Indian Middle Classes*, Bombay: Asia Publishing House, 1961.
7. Sharma, 1984, Chapters 2 and 3, for all the statistical information.
8. Ibid., Chapter 3.
9. Ibid.
10. Ibid., p. 84.

11. Ibid., pp. 85–7.
12. Ibid., p. 118.
13. *The Law Commission of India*, 14th Report, pp. 584–5.
14. Sharma, 1984, p. 118.
15. Ibid., pp. 120–1.
16. Morrison, Charles, 'Lawyers and Litigants in a North Indian District: Notes on the Informal Aspects of the Legal System', *Law and Society Review*, vol. III, no. 2, 1968–9, pp. 301–2; 'Kinship in Professional Relations: A Study of North Indian District Lawyers', *Comparative Studies in Society and History*, vol. 14, no. 1, 1972, pp. 100–25; Gandhi, J.S., *Lawyers are Touts*, Delhi: Hindustan Publishing Corporation, 1982.
17. Sharma, 1984, p. 158.
18. Ibid., pp. 185–7.

8

Social Organization at the District Courts

Colleague Relationships among Indian Lawyers*

CHARLES MORRISON

In addition to containing religious centres of pilgrimage, regional and local markets, and educational establishments, a district headquarters town in India is, virtually by definition, the seat of a whole complex of law courts. The personnel whose activities contribute to the pattering of social life in such towns include as an essential feature a small brotherhood of local legal practitioners. The present paper describes one such brotherhood: the advocates who practise in a district headquarters town in Haryana. The main problem with which I shall be concerned is that of isolating and describing the system of social relations, the interconnected set of behavioural patterns, that occurs in the daily interactions among a hundred or more professionals in the district courts. It follows that the paper looks to lawyers rather than law.

For the litigants of an Indian district, the courts are an important occasional social arena. For even the busiest of chronic litigants, however, they are only an *occasional* arena. The professional and administrative personnel of the legal system are necessarily somewhat marginal figures in the ligitant's world, of not as much concern to him as the allies and opposite parties of his numerous lawsuits. For a vast majority of district legal practitioners in India, on the other hand, the courts are the arena, the physical and social setting, for a lifetime's work.

*Excerpted from Charles Morrison 'Social Organization at the District Courts: Colleague Relationships among Indian Lawyers', in N. Jayaram and Satish Sabherwal (eds), *Social Conflict*, New Delhi: Oxford University Press, 1996, pp. 445–60.

In looking at the courts as the work context of the Indian district lawyer one can ask about some of the problems that occur in the description of any social system: How are relations distributed in space; what roles can be distinguished; what is the range of variation in role enactment, how does the purpose for which the system exists affect the formation of groups; how is authority distributed; and so forth. Not all these problems are dealt with in this essay; and many important facets of lawyers' lives, activities that take place away from the courts, are left largely out of account.

First, I comment on caste and the composition of the bar. Then I examine the setting in which the lawyers' interactions with their colleagues occur. Next I discuss three kinds of informal grouping that differentiate the bar and give shape to its internal political structure.

THE CASTE COMPOSITION OF THE BAR

All-India figures are not available, but knowledgeable metropolitan lawyers that Brahmins dominate the profession as a whole. There is a marked lack of importance that Brahmins as a community have in the public life of Punjab and Haryana. The castes that dominate the bar here (Aggarwal and Khatri) are those that also dominate the trading and business life of the town. The numerically dominant agricultural caste of the region is Jat, whose members comprise 40–50 per cent of the regional population.

In the day-to-day relations among members of the bar, caste is relatively unimportant as a determinant of social behaviour. It is, of course, a factor in recruitment to the profession. An urban Aggarwal boy stands a better chance than does a rural Chamar boy coming from a family in which literacy is high and other members are in government service or professions and where opportunities for law study are possible. But once both Chamar and Aggarwal become lawyers, their common professional identity tends to cancel the differences of caste identity. Of course, in the lives of lawyers outside the courts, caste is significant. For example, it is often a factor in regional political activity and in the management of various urban associations such as sectarian schools. In general, however, caste does not have the role-summation significance for city professionals that it has in village life.

THE COURTS AS AN OCCUPATIONAL SETTING

The lawyers' localization in the courts gives them a position there akin to that of merchants in a marketplace, and in fact both lawyers and clients sometimes refer to the court compound as a bazaar. I now turn to a description of physical environment and the ordering of social relations in the courts.

The district courts on which this paper is based are likely to give the casual visitor the impression of an improbable cross between a bustling, alfresco stock exchange at the peak of trading, a mainline platform before the express arrives, and a rural trade fair. Ramshackle kiosks, chairs, benches, tables, and lean-tos are scattered seemingly at random in the dusty and apparently undifferentiated compound that stretches forlornly between verandaed office buildings of various PWD vintages. Through the compound wanders a curious mixture of urban and rural types. It is difficult to distinguish the permanent population from the outsiders. An occasional figure arrives on horseback; others come in jeeps, cars, tongas, and the ubiquitous gaudy rickshaw. Listless crowds fill the verandas—are they litigants, witnesses, or just onlookers? Some doze among the chairs and benches of the compound or take part in innumerable discussions, consultations, and arguments. Many just sit and stare. Others work furiously at antique typewriters or with the tattered files, battered dispatch boxes, and the cloth bundles of Indian office life. From the rows of dilapidated tea stalls that fringe the compound, boys bring the inevitable refreshments. In season, a dust storm further enlivens the scene.

On entering one of the courtrooms, the visitor is likely to find the confusion only slightly abated. On a typical day, he will probably have difficulty even seeing the magistrate or judge, for the latter is usually obscured by a crush of advocates, witnesses, and others crowded round the bench. A succession of unhushed conferences are likely to be in progress between various secondary officials and lawyers and it is not unusual for parts of two cases to appear to be in progress simultaneously. The occasional efforts of police and chowkidars to impose order only add to the hubbub.

In such a setting, the Indian district lawyer spends between a half and two-thirds of his working time. In the course of a day at the district courts described here, an advocate passes back and forth between several segments of this setting. For each of these segments there are appropriate modes of behaviour and characteristic relationships. We will examine some of these distinctions in more detail.

First, however, a comment on the matter of confusion in juridical situations is relevant here. Anthropologists writing about law in the non-Western world have often noted the apparent disorder and informality of

court proceedings. For instance, Epstein observes that the seeming casual-
ness of African tribal courts is in marked contrast to the august atmosphere
of their English counterparts but adds that such informality does not
mean that the actual situation under inquiry is chaotic; rather it reflects
how closely the work of the courts is bound up in the daily lives of the
people. One of the admittedly minor differences between a 'traditional'
or tribal legal system and a 'modern' (i.e., westernized) law court such as
described here is that the latter is intended to cope, if not simultaneously,
at least in relatively rapid and continuous succession with very many
totally unconnected cases. Some of the seeming confusion in the district
courts arises from the nature of the system. The rules of procedure in such
a legal system necessitate the fragmentation of even the simplest case into
perhaps as many as five or six different hearings. This in turn multiplies
the frequency of interactions, if not the actual number of relationships,
in which lawyers and litigants are involved with court officials and the
judiciary. All this is relevant here not only because the fixing of dates for
future hearings consumes much of a lawyer's time, but also because one
of the skills of a successful lawyer is an ability to manipulate the court
calendar to his own advantage. We might usefully make a distinction between 'complexity' (the multi-stranded nature of the system) and 'confusion' (the possibility of ambiguous situations and the sheer difficulty of
stage management that results from the translation of this multiplicity
into actual social relations).

In the town described here, the district lawyer's professional use of
urban space has two clear divisions: home-office and courts. The latter has
three subdivisions which will be discussed later. The home-office is easily
accommodated by the domestic architectural conventions of north India.
All homes in the economic class to which lawyers belong possess a multipurpose public room usually provided with direct access to the street and
known here as a *baithak*. Depending on the size and stage of his career,
a lawyer's *baithak-office* may be more or less exclusively reserved for law
work. The ordering of behaviour associated with the baithak in the minds
of visitors and occupants provides, at least in this relatively prosperous
area, an interesting continuity between the urban and the rural. The
lawyer's office, the doctor's dispensary, and the politician's reception room
are all recognizable urban variants of the rural 'men's house' or guest quarters of this region. The baithaks of many substantial villagers here are
structurally and functionally identical with their urban variants. The
storage of simple agricultural equipment, lawyer's files, compounder's

medicines, and the accommodation of guests, clients, patients, or political supporters are all well within the range of uses for such places.

In this town, a routine weekday sight is the piecemeal morning procession of advocates on the road to the district courts. They can be readily distinguished by the uniform black coat and white trousers of their profession. Most lawyers walk to court. Sometimes an important client accompanies his lawyer from baithak-office to the courts. More often, a lawyer is joined by one or two colleagues, hence the impression of an informal procession.

In the court precincts, three distinct segments of social space can be recognized; the courts proper, the compound, and the Bar Association library. Each has a characteristic patterning of relationships. We are chiefly concerned with the last two. Activity in the courts proper is, as noted above, intense and bustling; but the behaviour is also highly repetitive and focused. For almost everything that goes on in the courtroom, there exists somewhere a set of written rules—government manuals on court upkeep and organization, textbooks on advocacy, codes, and case law. Colleague interactions here are highly legalistic in content and for the purposes of this essay of rather marginal relevance. Here my concern is with that area of the lawyer's identity that lies between this central, role-defining activity of court appearance and the broader field where professional identity merges with social class. In any case, it is *at* the courts rather than *in* court that the majority of district practitioners are to be found most of the time.

The second of the three segments is the compound; the third is the library. In both compound and library, lawyers interact with one another informally. The compound is, in addition, the chief area of lawyer–client interaction outside the courtroom. The compound also provides a place where potential clients can shop for lawyers, by observing their actions without entering into direct relations with them.

The special unit of identity in the compound is the *takht*, the platform table-bench that serves as an office and has some of the functions of a merchant's stall in a bazaar. Takhts themselves are not usually identified by name plates, although there is no actual rule against this. Many are ramshackle and there is no correspondence between the size or construction of a takht and the affluence or professional skill of its occupant. There is a seasonal rearrangement of takhts into more sunny or shadier parts of the compound, but this usually involves moves of only a few feet. Takhts are not equipped with partitions and consequently almost everything that occurs at one can be seen and often overheard from several others.

Not every lawyer practising at the district courts has a takht. Some lawyers use the library veranda and others share takhts with colleagues. Stamp vendors, stenographers, petition writers, and oath commissioners also occupy similar takhts in the court compound.

The Bar Association library at the courts described here is a collection of five or six rooms forming one of the buildings of the compound. The library also functions as a social club, general office, communications centre, mess hall, and consulting room. The place has the usual *baithak*-office atmosphere, achieved in part by portrait photographs of the late distinguished members. Sometimes clients come here but they are not encouraged to do so. In Goffman's terms, the library is a backstage area so far as lawyer–client relations are concerned. Clients are likely to become suspicious if they see their own counsel joking with the opposite party's advocate in the library building. Typically, client visitors stay only long enough to locate their lawyer, usually to let him know their case has been called. When a new magistrate or judge is appointed, he is expected to pay a semi-formal visit to the Bar Association premises. On his departure he may be invited by the bar to a tea party there. At all other times it is assumed that the judiciary will stay out of the compound and library areas and they appear to adhere quite strictly to this norm.

FRIENDSHIP SETS AND ETHNIC SECTIONS IN THE BAR

As already emphasized, members of the legal brotherhood spend much of their time in one another's company. Hours are consumed in informal conversation with colleagues while lawyers overtly wait for cases to be called or covertly wait for clients to materialize. In these sessions, as in the shorter courtroom confrontations, quick wit and verbal facility are valued. The peculiar ethos of this gossipy, single-purpose association is a somewhat paradoxical blend of egalitarianism, status consciousness, camaraderie, and mistrust.

In structural terms, three kinds of grouping can be discerned in the social relations of the lawyers described here. First, there are small, very informal, rather fluid, interconnected clusters or cliques of colleagues. Secondly, there is a more general grouping into two large sections on the basis of the ethnic distinction between 'refugees' and 'locals'. The refugees are men who moved (or whose families moved) to this district at Partition in 1947. Thirdly, there is a rather transient form of grouping which cross-cuts the broader, dual division of refugees and locals. I will refer to these three kinds of grouping as sets or cliques, sections, and alliances. Sets are the small day-to-day colleague groups; sections are the broad, permanent, ethnic divisions; and alliances are the occasional transient ties of political expediency and interpersonal rivalry. Informal social control and social-ization are achieved through sets for the most part; formal, internal poli-tical structure is chiefly expressed with reference to sections or alliances.

Although the section division of the bar here is explicitly recognized, it is felt to be 'wrong' and factionalistic. Not surprisingly in such a legal-istic atmosphere, some informants contend that there is no jural basis for such a division. Others simply argue that the distinctions of twenty years ago should now be forgotten. It is often said that the division into sections has no real significance. But despite such pious disapproval, the division continues and is clearly marked in space. Local advocates have their *takht*s clustered at one end of the court compound, just outside the Bar Asso-ciation library, near home as it were; refugees are clustered at the other side of the compound near the main entrance. A few isolated *takht*s dot the intervening space.

The basis on which sets or cliques are formed reflects the variety of associational ties available to educated urbanites. A common explanation for the origin of a bar friendship is the school tie. Involved here is a class or year identity rather than a differentiation based on competing insti-tutions. Most lawyers received their legal training at the main state law college. Beginners who join the bar at about the same time often become friends, even if they were not college mates.

Caste is on the whole unimportant in the organization of the bar but it does sometimes provide the basis for a set. There is a Rajput set, for ins-tance. Here the caste tie has been strengthened by a cooperative speculation in urban real estate. Common political interests (e.g., support of a local party candidate in a constituency election) provide another kind of the tie in the organization of some sets. Frequently, members of sets say they came together originally because they shared a common approach to life. It is difficult to specify what this means and there are sets whose members seem to have contrasting personalities.

Kinship links are sometimes a factor in set formation; a number of lawyers are distantly related to one another. Links of this sort should be distinguished from the ties that unite fathers and sons, between whom the norms of deference and respect preclude the possibility of informal clique formation. In the district courts, every lawyer belongs to some set but the degree of importance that such clique activity assumes in day-to-day life differs among individuals.

Some cliques of young advocates span the division between refugees and locals. Some sets of older lawyers, on the other hand, are explicitly based on shared refugee status. In the socially heterogeneous milieu of the courts, the refugee–local distinction does not have the same significance that it possesses in the larger society of this region where it is possible to distinguish broad, general, and contrasting stereotypic refugee–local patterns of outlook and lifestyle. In an anthropological account of commercial life in a small town of this area, the refugee businessman is depicted as an aggressive, extrovert, modernistic entrepreneur with a flair for manipulating the administration. The local bania, in contrast, is depicted as conservative, miserly, tradition-ridden, and fearful or indifferent of the administration. The common activities and training of the legal profession, however, prevent or blur the development of distinctions of this order. The characteristics are recognizable among the lawyers, but they cross-cut the section division. Thus, some who come close to the refugee stereotype sketched above are in fact locals; and there are some notoriously cautious and conservative refugee advocates.

There is little specialization in Indian district practice but this by itself does not seem a sufficient explanation for the poor development of partnerships. Sets or small cliques sometimes solidify into formal law partnerships but such firms are very rare at the district level where the joint family provides the basis for what little cooperative enterprise there is, inside and outside the courts. District lawyers often express the opinion that non-relatives are not likely to trust one another sufficiently to permit the widespread development of a partnership system. It is significant that where non-kin-based partnerships *do* exist at the district courts, income is usually divided between partners on a daily basis; where kinsmen are in partnership, professional fees usually go into a joint family purse.

The constant struggles of lawyers to prevent conflicting hearings from getting on their appointment books suggest that there is scope for some division of labour even if not amounting to formal specialization in fields of laws. But for partnership as a business style to develop, client acceptance of the pattern would be necessary and interviews with litigants suggest that many of them would be unwilling to trust multiple counsel. Paradoxically, mistrust of the lawyer's ability to 'be there on the day' leads a number of litigants to retain a second-string counsel, thus indirectly achieving one of the benefits that a partnership system might provide.

LEADING LAWYERS

Despite its egalitarian ethic, the bar is, of course, stratified. A tiny handful of advocates are recognized as 'leading lawyers'. This title is conferred on only five or six of the lawyers described in this paper. Below the level of the leading lawyer, three other ranks are sometimes explicitly recognized. One advocate labelled these as below top, average, and below average. At the bottom are briefless lawyers, e.g., struggling beginners or old, semi-retired practitioners. In the third rank are established lawyers who have had more than ten years of practice. The second rank is a category of men with many years of practice and often with some more or less important position in the community at large outside the bar but who lack the district-wide professional reputation of the top practitioners.

Leading lawyers are relatively isolated or setless, in my limited use of that term. They are rarely seen chatting about non-legal matters in small groups of advocates on the compound or in the library. In fact, one of the markers of the leading advocate status is infrequency of appearance in these locations. Unlike the majority of his colleagues, the leading advocate is found *in* court rather than *at* the courts. When he is not appearing before judges or magistrates he is usually to be found in his *baithak*-office dealing with a throng of clients. The difference between the size of a leading district lawyer's practice and that of the remainder of the bar is extreme and a day or two spent at the home of a leading lawyer leaves the visitor with the impression that half the litigants of the district must be in his hands.

Leading lawyers neither need nor can afford the time for minor informal interaction with colleagues. In the course of his career, a leading lawyer attracts a large number of juniors but these relationships tend to be perfunctory and not the basis of what I have called sets. Two of the leading lawyers of the bar were members of partnerships in the past but in both cases the other partner has died and not been replaced. Three of them have sons who are in practice with them. Although leading lawyers are relatively uninvolved in the formation of cliques, they are involved in the third kind of group I mentioned, the alliance.

It is useful to compare what I have called 'alliances' with what A.C. Mayer calls 'action sets' in his analysis of a municipal election in Dewas. Like the action set, the alliance is a purposive creation of an ego for the sole purpose of securing political support. In this respect, the alliance differs from the bar clique or set which need not be political and is often formed with no special end other than companionship in view. The section, of course, is not ego-centred and is an ascribed status group.

Unlike the linkages of an action set, the alliance does not have a variety of possible bases. All the ties that are used in alliances are those created by mutual involvement in the day-to-day working of the courts. This difference between action set and alliance is, I think, mainly one of complexity and context. Alliances are single relationships in a highly limited context. Action sets are complexes of linkage welded in the course of interaction in a large variety of contexts.

Lawyers, legal systems, and the legal profession can be usefully examined at a variety of levels and in several contexts. At the high level of grand theory there are such problems as why societies need lawyers (not all legal systems have them). In this paper I have looked at the other end of the continuum. I have attempted to see what can be said about the social relations that develop among lawyers in a particular legal system, given both the system and the lawyers.

III

Law and Religious Identity

The variety of cultures, customs, and faiths in India is indeed breathtaking. Perhaps the spirit of nation state demands that the law should be the same for every citizen of the entire country. But it is a debatable proposition whether this idea is practicable in a country like India. Since the time of India's independence it has been a burning issue whether there should be a uniform civil code for everyone or latitude is to be given for religious and ethnic sensibilities of various groups. This controversy is far from over and it is still emitting a lot of heat.

This is a complex problem and any simplistic solution is not likely to be satisfactory. It is not that the state does not recognize any ethnic identity. While it approves certain kinds of group identities it disapproves others. It is untenable, therefore, to insist that in accordance with the principles of nation state only one law should prevail all over the country for all ethnic and religious groups. At the same time some provisions in various sectarian laws which constitute a violation of human rights and run blatantly counter to the basic tenets of justice must not be left alone on the pretext of ethnic or religious identity. As John Mansfield rightly says: 'to put the choice as one between the personal law system and a uniform civil code is to put the issue too sharply'.

There already exist certain laws which affect religious prescriptions and age-old usages, but are considered necessary for general welfare and apply to all citizens of India irrespective of their religion or any other denomination. For instance, there is the Child Marriage Restraint (Amendment) Act 1978 which puts the minimum age of marriage for females at eighteen and that of males at twenty-one years. It may go against the personal laws based on religious texts but there were not many protests against the promulgation of this law. It is another matter that there are any number of marriages in violation of this law, because it runs counter to the age-old practices which have not yet been given up by large sections of the people. However, there has been stiff resistance to several bills moved to bring about similar social legislation such as the Hindu Code

Bill. That bill was later divided into a number of parts and after they became laws some of their provisions too are often violated. It needs serious sociological research to unearth as to why the factors which are responsible for resistance to certain measures of reform in personal laws do not lead to such resistance for other similar steps.

Soon after the dawn of India's independence, the idea of a uniform civil code was articulately mooted in the Constituent Assembly and it was widely accepted. Though there were some voices of dissent, these were largely quelled by an assurance that such laws will not be forced down the throat of any community. This idea of having a uniform civil code was embodied even in India's Constitution. Article 44 of the Directive Principles of State Policy proclaims that 'the state shall endeavour to secure for the citizens a uniform civil code throughout the territory of India'. Of course, like other Directive Principles it is not enforceable by any court of law but affirms a principle to be adopted by the state, and the state is expected to enact laws in its furtherance.

The underlying goal was to build a united India with a national identity. This objective was asserted all the more because during the national movement for independence, those who espoused India's struggle for freedom from colonial rule argued that it in the vested interest of British rulers to propagate the erroneous view that India was not a nation but a conglomeration of numerous castes, religious communities, tribes, and so on. However, the social fact of religious and ethnic diversity has to be reckoned with, and room has to be made in some way for the established usages of various groups. Otherwise, the edifice of national unity will remain threatened by the pressure of internal tensions.

Obviously, there are two sides to the issue. On the one hand it seems that personal laws of a community give a meaning to the life of the people who constitute that community, which citizenship of a nation state alone is unable to bestow. On the other, it can be argued that narrow loyalties to separate ethnic or religious practices put persons in bondage instead of liberating them from blind beliefs and usages.

A uniform civil code need not entirely obliterate all personal laws. Ways have to be explored in which their innocuous provisions may still be retained for those who wish to adhere to them. It has been suggested that there may be a common civil code but one should be free to opt out of it. This would also provide individual legitimation for their enforcement. Certain other ways too could be thought of.

The issue of personal laws versus a uniform civil code was brought to the centre of political debate and led to a lot of controversy and wranglings after the decision of India's Supreme Court in the Shah Bano case, and a subsequent enactment which amounted to its annulment. The judgment allowed Muslim widow the right of maintenance by her former husband. It also affirmed that this was in accordance with the dicta of the Muslim sacred law and with the principle that the state should strive to bring into being a common civil code which is enshrined in the Constitution. The judgment took to task the government for not doing enough to implement this Directive Principle.

There was a strident uproar against this judgment led by those who claimed to be the leaders of the Muslim community. They argued that the Supreme Court did not have the right to interpret the Shariat (the Muslim sacred law). They also voiced vehemently their opposition to a uniform civil code and set up organizations to ensure that it was not put in place.

It would seem that the Supreme Court could have avoided this controversy, which emitted more heat than light and led to an unnecessary hardening of attitudes on both sides, by merely affirming in their judgment that all widows, irrespective of their religious denomination, had a right to maintenance by their former husband in accordance with Section 125 of the Criminal Procedure Code. In hindsight, they need not have raised the question of the correct interpretation of Muslim sacred law in this context. The law conferring the right of maintenance to all widows irrespective of their religion had been in force for more than a century, and it had been generally accepted by everyone.

A new and unhappy twist was given to this problem by a subsequent enactment, the Muslim Women (Protection of Rights on Divorce) Act, 1986. According to this law, Section 125 of the Criminal Procedure Code which requires husbands to support their divorced wives was not applicable to Muslims. This was obviously in response to what was considered to be the angry reaction of the Muslim community to the Supreme Court Judgment.

This whole episode underscores the need for explorations in the field of sociology of law. In the first place, what was the response of the Muslim population to the judgment of the Supreme Court in the Shah Bano case? This is a question which requires empirical investigation. However, without any such investigation it seems to be taken for granted by most commentators, including John Mansfield, that there was very strong protest by the Muslim community as a whole to that judgment. Even Kavita Khory, who tends to argue that opinion was to some extent divided on this issue among the Muslims, cites only the opinion of some liberal or enlightened Muslims as the opinion of those who did not oppose the judgment. Khory concludes that 'one can assert with some certainty that a relatively large number of Muslims were against the judgment'. However, the picture is not so simple, Who has taken the opinion of ordinary Muslim women on this issue? A doctoral dissertation in sociology, the field work for which was conducted in Agra, brings out the fact that more than 70 per cent Muslim women respondents, the bulk of whom was neither educated not employed, said that Shah Bano should have got maintenance from her former husband. The point is that such matters need sociological investigation for reaching any reliable conclusion.

Secondly, this whole sequence of events brings out the necessity of systematic study of the sensibilities of various ethnic and religious groups. Such evidence would be useful to the courts and the statesmen. If the Supreme Court had some idea about the likely outcome of the observations made in their learned judgment, perhaps they would have considered some modifications in its content and phrasing.

Enactments too have to take into account their possible long-term consequences for different sections of the population. Ad hoc measures, taken for political expediency are prone to be counterproductive in the long run. Appropriate decisions for resolving such complex problems can only be taken in the light of the inputs from sound sociological study.

9

Religion, Law, and Secularism*

DONALD EUGENE SMITH

Traditional Hinduism and Islam were far more than 'religions' in the usual meaning of the word. Historically, both came very close to being total ways of life in the most literal sense; they prescribed detailed regulations for virtually every act of human existence, the great events which mark the life cycle and the day-to-day routine. All-pervasive religion regulated not only general social relationships but the whole area of what we now call criminal and civil law. In the Hindu or Muslim state the king had no legislative powers. The function of the state was to enforce the law but not to make it, since the law was already complete, enshrined in the sacred texts and in immemorial custom. Despite static conceptions of divinely ordained law, it did change by imperceptible degrees in response to new situations. Changes in practice generally came first, and these were later rationalized by the interpretations of the doctors of the law or the writers of commentaries. But the state had no direct role in this process.

Since the early nineteenth century, the impact of the West has produced drastic changes in countries where Hinduism and Islam are professed. The rise of Asian nationalism in some ways intensified the process of modernization begun by the European imperialist powers. The new independent states now seek to forge themselves into modern sovereign states after the Western pattern. While religion in many cases served as a useful ally of Asian nationalism, its role must now be circumscribed if these modern states are to emerge. And nowhere is the tension more evident than in the area of law, where the authority of traditional religion and the modern sovereign state lay claim to the same territory. The outcome

*Excerpted from Donald Eugene Smith, *India as a Secular State*, Princeton, New Jersey: Princeton University Press, 1967, pp. 265–91.

is not in doubt; one side represents the static past and the other the dynamic present and future. The secularization of law is thus an important facet of the modernization of the state. The consequent restriction of religion to the area of private faith and worship constitutes a religious reformation of the first magnitude, although imposed by the state.

India is the historic meeting place of these two great civilizations, Hinduism and Islam. Hindu and Muslim laws continue to regulate important civil matters such as marriage, divorce, adoption, guardianship, and inheritance. The existence of *two* major religious communities and systems of religious law within the state, and the consequent minority problem, inevitably produces complications in the process of modernization. A further complication is that India is committed to becoming not only a modern sovereign state but a secular state in the liberal democratic tradition. Some of the drastic, even ruthless, methods which have been elsewhere adopted to achieve the former objective (as in the case of Turkey) are thus denied to it. India must strive to attain the same ends within the procedural framework of parliamentary democracy. While the idea of the secular state certainly implies secular law, it also contains a conception of freedom of religion which for many present-day Hindus and Muslims has a direct bearing on the continuance of their respective religious laws. In order to understand this problem, it must be examined in historical perspective, both in relation to the West and in India itself.

EARLY LEGAL SYSTEM OF BRITISH INDIA

The seventeenth-century officials of the British East India Company had come to a country in which two ancient and very different systems of law prevailed, each rooted in a religion which claimed the totality of life for its proper jurisdiction. Law was an integral part of both Hinduism and Islam.

Hindu law is of great antiquity and is derived from several sources: (1) *Shruti*, that is, the divinely inspired Vedas, some of which date back to the middle of the second millennium BC; (2) the *Dharmashastra*s, or law codes, the oldest and most influential of which is the Code of Manu written sometime between 200 BC and AD 100; and (3) custom. The central conception of Hindu law is dharma, and it is important to grasp the essentials of this conception. S.V. Gupte wrote: 'The law of the Dharmashastras is a mixture of morality, religion and law. The distinction drawn by modern jurists between positive law and moral law is not observed in Hindu jurisprudence. According to Hindu conception, law in the

modern sense was only a branch of *dharma*, a term of the widest significance. The term *dharma* includes religious, moral, social and legal
duties and can only be defined as the whole duty of man; positive law was
therefore regarded as only a branch of *dharma*.' Indicative of the broad
meaning of dharma is the fact that it is impossible adequately to translate
it by a single English word, although duty, virtue, religious creed, religion,
justice, and law have all been used.

Muslim law shari'ah is derived from four sources: (1) the Koran;
(2) hadith, the teachings of the prophet Mohammed preserved by tradition and handed down by authorized persons; (3) *ijma*, the consensus of
those learned in Islamic law; and (4) *qiyas*, deduction by analogy from the
first three sources when they do not apply to a particular case. The comprehensive scope of this law was such that virtually every aspect of life was
brought under the regulation of the faith. Writing of the integrating
power of Islam among the Arab of an earlier period, W.C. Smith comments: 'The center of the unifying force was religious law, which regulated within its powerful and precise sweep everything from prayer rites to
property rights.' Islamic law, more than any other agency, effectively integrated the ethnically diverse peoples which later embraced the faith.

At first the East India Company permitted Muslim law officers, *kazis*
or muftis, to sit as judges in the criminal courts, and the British collectors
exercised only a general supervisory control over them. From 1790, however, the company directly assumed criminal jurisdiction, and the Muslim criminal law was continued as part of the public law of the land as it
had been under Muslim rulers. This law applied to Hindus as well as to
Muslims in Bengal, in Madras, and later on in other parts of India. British
officials became the judges, but the Muslim *kazis* continued to serve the
courts as authorized exponents of law, although the judges were able to
circumvent their opinions. Gradually, a substantial body of secular criminal law was developed through numerous regulations passed by the
government in order to supplement and amend the Muslim criminal law.
Regulation 6 of 1832 finally marked the end of the Muslim criminal law
as a system of general law applicable to all persons.

The revolutionary legal principle introduced by the British during this
period was that of equality before the law. This Western conception was
diametrically opposed to the basic assumptions of both Hindu and Muslim law. Hindu law assumed the hierarchical caste system, and the ancient
codes prescribed different penalties for the same crime, varying with the
respective castes of the offender and the person against whom the offence
had been committed. Muslim law assumed a basic distinction between

the Muslim and the Kafir (infidel). The radically new principle of the equality of all before the law was to lay a solid foundation for the establishment of a common citizenship in a secular state.

The *Diwani Adalats* established by Warren Hastings in 1772, were to apply civil law. In contrast with the decision by which Muslim criminal law became the law of the land, applicable to Hindus as well as to Muslims, Hastings' plan provided that 'in all suits regarding marriage, inheritance, the laws of the Koran with respect to Mohammedans, and those of the shastras with respect to Gentus (Hindus) shall be invariably adhered to.' Thus, Hindu law and Muslim law were treated equally, although the granting of this status to the former was bitterly resented by high-ranking Muslims as completely improper in a territory under the (nominal) dominion of the Mughal emperor. Nevertheless, Hastings's plan prevailed, and soon Brahmin pandits were appointed to expound the Hindu law in courts presided over by English officers of the company, just as the kazis interpreted and applied the Muslim law.

Hastings therefore obtained the services of ten learned pandits who prepared a Code of Hindu Law in Sanskrit, based on the most authoritative texts (1775). This was later translated into Persian and then English. As to Muslim law, Hastings also had an English translation made of the Arabic *Hidaya*. Later, under Governor-General Cornwallis, English translations of the Muslim laws of intestate succession and inheritance (1792) and the Hindu Ordinances of Manu (1794) were made by Sir William Jones. Jones began the preparation of a Digest of Hindu Law but died before its completion; the work was finally finished by his pandit Jaganath. Later scholars continued this work of codification and translation. However, it was not until 1864 that the government discontinued the services of the pandits and *kazis* in the courts of civil justice.

This, then, was the essence of Hastings' plan—the application of Hindu law to Hindus, Muslim law to Muslims, in all matters regarding 'inheritance, marriage and caste and other religious usages and institutions.' An act of 1781 added to this list cases of succession, contract and dealing between party and party. This system of personal law (as opposed to territorial law) was not without defects. It entirely ignored the fact that the Hindus were and are divided into numerous sects and subsects with differing laws and customs, and that different schools of Hindu law prevail in various parts of India. Similarly, there are two major divisions in Islam, the Shi'as and the Sunnis, as well as local variations in Muslim law and custom. Nevertheless, Hastings' basic plan, although modified in details, has continued in operation to the present time. As M.P. Jain states:

'To a very great extent this scheme holds the field today after a period of one hundred and eighty years. Today the Hindu law governs the Hindus in topics of marriage, adoption, joint family, debts, partition, inheritance and succession.'

It seems clear that the system evolved during the British period tended to rigidify Hindu personal law and to prevent its normal development in accordance with changing social custom. The pandits who served as law officers until 1864 were basically religious teachers, not lawyers, and were given no training for their official work. They tended to rely heavily on the most ancient texts and often neglected the role of usage and custom in Hindu law.

But the same was frequently true of the British judges; Mayne stated that, far from reading modern European legal principles into Hindu law, 'My belief is that their influence was exerted in the opposite direction, and that it rather showed itself in the pedantic maintenance of doctrines whose letter was still existing but whose spirit was dying away.' Referring to the great influence of the eleventh-century *Mitakshara* in the courts of south India, the same author commented: 'The consequence was a state of arrested progress in which no voices were heard unless they came from the tomb.' Furthermore, the British were most reluctant to modify Hindus or Muslim law by legislation, fearful of alienating their Indian subjects over religious questions. Thus the Second Law Commission reported in 1855 that it was not advisable to attempt to codify the personal laws: 'The Hindu law and the Mohammedan law derive their authority respectively from the Hindu and Mohammedan religion. It follows that as a British legislature cannot make Mohammedan or Hindu religion so neither can it make Mohammedan or Hindu law.'

THE PROBLEM IN PRESENT-DAY INDIA

Important areas of civil law, including marriage, divorce, inheritance, succession, remain under the religious personal laws. On a given point relating to inheritance, for example, three entirely different laws are applied by the courts to a Hindu, a Muslim, and a Christian. India is committed by its Constitution to the elimination of this system of personal laws. Thus, in the Directive Principles of State Policy, article 44, we find: 'The state shall endeavour to secure for the citizens a uniform civil code throughout the territory of India.' In this part of the chapter we shall discuss the steps which have been taken toward this objective and the issues which these steps have created for the secular state.

THE SPECIAL MARRIAGE ACT AND THE HINDU CODE BILL

The most important developments since independence concern the codification of Hindu law as a necessary step before Hindu, Muslim, and other personal laws can yield to a uniform code. At the same time a different, more direct approach is being made to a uniform civil code, based on legislation passed in the nineteenth century. We shall first consider this direct approach.

The Special Marriage Act of 1872 provided for a civil marriage before a registrar between persons neither of whom professed the Hindu, Buddhist, Sikh, Jain, Muslim, Jewish, Parsi, or Christian religion. The marriage could be solemnized in any form, provided that each party said to the other in the presence of the registrar and witness: 'I (A) take thee (B) to be my lawful wife (or husband). Before the marriage could be solemnized, both the bridegroom and the bride had to make declarations in the prescribed form that they did not profess any of the religions mentioned above. The basic object of the Act was to make legal provision for marriages celebrated in repudiation of personal laws. Inter-caste marriages among Hindus or marriages across religious lines (for example, a Hindu with a Muslim) were not permitted by personal laws. All who wished to marry under the Special Marriage Act were therefore compelled to renounce their religion in order to escape the restrictive provisions of their personal laws.

The Special Marriage Act of 1954 seeks the same objects as the old Act but does not require any denial of faith by the individual in order to come under its provisions. Furthermore, in the case of a valid marriage already contracted according to personal law, it is possible for the parties to apply for the registration of their marriage under the Act so that its provisions become applicable to them. Among these provisions are: liberalized grounds for divorce, the automatic severance from a joint family of a Hindu who marries under the Act, and a new legal basis for succession to property—the Indian Succession Act (based on English law) rather than the Hindu law of succession or other personal law. In the debate in the Lok Sabha, the law minister, C.C. Biswas, pointed out that when two people of different religions married, it would not be possible to apply the personal law of either party. It was therefore necessary to make some other provision in matters such as succession.

The Special Marriage Act of 1954 is thus, in a sense, a uniform civil code in embryo. Prime Minister Nehru described it as a first step toward bringing about uniformity in social observances. Those who voluntarily decided to come under the provisions of the Act became a kind of community to which all Indians could belong without giving up their religion in any way. In regard to certain important functions such as marriage and succession, they gave up their personal law but not their religion.

Although the Special Marriage Act is a direct step towards a uniform civil code, it is of course a voluntary and permissive piece of legislation which people may or may not accept. The number of Indian citizens who come under its provisions represents an extremely small percentage of the total population. In seeking to achieve the secularization of civil law, the major effort must therefore be directed at the modification of the personal laws themselves in the direction of uniformity. This brings us to the subject of the Hindu Code Bill and the bills which succeeded it.

During most of the British period the government rejected proposals that Hindu personal law be codified. Hindu law was thus far from uniform throughout India. Baroda had a Hindu Code different from that of the rest of India. In Kerala and Mysore the Hindu law with regard to women's property rights differed from that found in other areas. Two principal schools of Hindu law existed: (1) the *Dayabhaga* school, which prevailed in Bengal and Assam, and (2) the *Mitakshara* school, with four main subdivisions, throughout the rest of India. The two schools differed in the matter of joint family property and succession and inheritance laws, and the differences were by no means trivial. As one authority put it: 'Anyone who compare the Dayabhaga with the Mitakshara will observe that the two works differ in very vital points, and that they do so from the conscious application of completely different principles.' Clearly, the most pressing need was to introduce greater uniformity in the sphere of Hindu law itself before reaching out towards a uniform civil law for all communities.

The story of the Hindu Code Bill is worth recounting next. The draft Hindu Code Bill was introduced in the old Central Assembly in 1947 just before the partition of India, but the tremendous upheavals which accompanied the latter event made it necessary to shelve the measure for the time being.

The bill was finally taken up by the Select Committee of the Constituent Assembly (Legislative) in 1948, after which it was debated at length on the floor, with no little use of the filibuster and other delaying tactics by some orthodox Hindu members. Despite the able leadership of the law minister, Dr B.R. Ambedkar, the bill failed to reach the final stages of enactment, and in September 1951 it was dropped by the government. In announcing this decision, Prime Minister Nehru pleaded paucity of time as the reason, although a news article suggested that 'there was no doubt that government have responded, though only partially, to the pressure of public opinion against the bill'. Others believed that the real reason was simply the approaching general elections. The dropping of the bill was the occasion for Dr Ambedkar's resignation from the cabinet, and also for Swami Satyananda Saraswati's giving up his ten-day-old fast. The Swami had undertaken his fast outside the Parliament chamber to protest against the Hindu Code Bill.

In the general elections campaign of 1951–2, however, Nehru took a strong stand on the issue and repeatedly declared that he would never disown the Hindu Code Bill. In his statements he frequently emphasized the progressive social attitudes behind the provisions of the bill: "Thus, the Hindu Code Bill, which has given rise to so much argument, became a symbol of the conflict between progress and reaction in the social domain. I do not refer to any particular clause of the bill . . . but rather to the spirit underlying that bill. This was a spirit of liberation and freeing our people and, more especially, our womenfolk, from outworn customs and shackles that bound them.' Shortly after the election of the new Parliament, the main parts of the code were introduced as separate bills and were finally passed in rapid succession by huge majorities. In 1955 and 1956 the following bills received legislative approval: the Hindu Marriage Bill, the Hindu Succession Bill, the Hindu Minority and Guardianship Bill, and the Hindu Adoptions and Maintenance Bill. Having noted the background and the tortuous course of these measures through the legislative process, we may now turn our attention to their implications for the secular state.

Hindu Marriage, Divorce, Adoption and Succession

The debate on this legislation which took place both in Parliament and from public platforms was not centred in the issue of the secular state. Although the question of the effect on Hindu religion was generally present to a certain extent, the problems which engaged the attention of most participants in the debate were of a social nature. They were more concerned with the probable effect on the Hindu social structure of such provisions as divorce, inter-caste marriages, women's inheritance rights, and provisions affecting the joint family system. Codification of Hindu law was not the central issue; it was the progressive social provisions which sought to modify (some said 'destroy') the traditional Hindu social pattern. Thus the *Hindu* complained editorially: 'The object with which the Hindu Code Committee was first set to work was to codify and simplify the personal law of the Hindus, not to amend it in conformity with the promptings of social reform.' Although we are here concerned only with the aspects which touched upon the secular state, the discussion should not be interpreted as implying that these were the most prominent aspects of the debate.

One of the anomalous situations created by the debate in Parliament was the role assumed by the law minister who piloted the bills. An official of the secular state, he became an interpreter of Hindu religion, quoting and expounding the ancient Sanskrit scriptures in defence of his bills. In a speech on the Hindu Marriage Bill, H.V. Pataskar explained the Hindu concept of dharma and contrasted it with the elements of dogma in Christianity and Islam. He urged that the objections raised by opponents of the bill were based on a rigid interpretation of the Sanskrit texts, and this was attributable to the influence of these other religions which stressed their sacred scriptures as the final authority. The law minister quoted from the Bhagavad Gita, the *Arthashastra*, the *Manu Smriti*, and the *Narada Smriti* in order to support the provision for divorce in the bill.

Other members of Parliament were quick to take the minister to task for this approach. Acharya Kripalani pointed out that the search for religious authority for legislation was not in keeping with the secular state. 'We call our state a secular state. A secular states goes neither by scripture nor custom. It must work on sociological and political grounds.' V. Muniswamy decried the fact that both proponents and opponents of the bill based their arguments on the Vedas. He chided: 'I am submitting with all respect to the honorable minister of law that the trouble started only with him. I should submit that there was no necessity to bring in quotations from the Vedas to introduce the bill.' Once the law minister had chosen this approach, all the opponents of the bill very readily followed suit. Mr Muniswamy quoted a Tamil proverb: 'A man gave half an anna for a beggar to dance and then had to give one anna to stop the dance because it was so awkward.'

Furthermore, if the arguments in support of legislation are based on ancient scriptures, one must logically accept the authority in its entirety. Muniswamy pointed out that isolated verses in the Bhagavad Gita might be used, but the basic framework was totally opposed to progressive legislation. 'In the very first chapter of the Gita you will find Arjuna telling Krishna, 'If I start fighting against my friends, then there will be inter-caste marriages, therefore I will not fight.' . . . If you want to quote the Gita, therefore, you must be prepared to accept the caste system.'

Delivering the presidential address at the All India Convention on the Hindu Code in April 1955, Radhabinod Pal emphasized the same point:

'If the legislature is thinking of reverting to the Vedic age in respect of the Hindu law then I believe many other changes will have to be introduced and I do not think the particular change proposed in the code will be at all justifiable.' Muniswamy's attitude towards those who dreaded any alteration of ancient principles was humorously expressed: 'Some of the people say, do not touch the Vedas, do not touch the principles of the Vedas, and so on. I should like to tell them that I quite approve of what they say, and I would tell them, keep the Vedas untouched not only now but forever. Then only we shall be able to make any progress.'

The Hindu Marriage Bill contained three provisions which represented revolutionary departures from the principles of traditional Hindu law: inter-caste marriage, monogamy, and divorce. Inter-caste marriages had already been legalized by the Hindu Marriages Validating Act of 1949, and this position was reaffirmed in the new legislation. Hindu bigamous marriages had already been prohibited by state legislation in Bombay (1946) and Madras (1949), and the new bill sought to extend the principle to the whole country.

The provisions in the Hindu Marriage Bill for divorce elicited a lively debate in Parliament over whether Hindu marriage is a sacrament. N.C. Chatterjee, then leader of the Hindu Mahasabha, quoted many modern authorities on Hindu law to show that in the Hindu conception, marriage is regarded as one of the ten *sanskara*s or sacraments, necessary for the regeneration of men of the three highest castes, and the only sacrament for women and Shudras. According to this conception 'marriage is not a mere contract; it is a part of the life of the soul'. Chatterjee made a fervent appeal to the Parliament; 'Manu himself says that Vedic marriage is a *sanskara*. That is a solemn injunction. It is an inviolable union, an indissoluble union; it is an interminable union; it is an eternal fellowship. . . . In all humility . . . I appeal to all sections of the House, don't tamper with the Hindu sacramental marriage and introduce divorce into it.' Divorce was an institution completely foreign to the thinking of the ancient Hindu lawgivers, Manu and Yajnavalkya, who were 'God-given, God-intoxicated men, inspired by . . . intense devotion to eternal values.'

To these assertions the law minister replied, rather ineffectually, that the Sanskrit *sanskara* was not the exact equivalent of the of the English word 'sacrament' as generally understood by Christians. Prime Minister Nehru, on the other hand, readily admitted that Hindu marriage was sacramental, a sacrament being something which had religious significance, a religious ceremony. Nehru then went on to neutralize Mr Chatterjee's argument by insisting that not only marriage but all forms of human relationship should have an element of sacrament; more so in the case of the intimate relationship of husband and wife. but is it a sacrament 'to tie up people to bite each other and to hate each other?' The bill was passed.

During the debate on the Hindu Adoptions and Maintenance Bill, a much-disputed point involved the provision for the adoption of daughters as well as sons. The law minister, Pataskar, declared: 'It is as a result of wrong readings of some of the original Sanskrit texts that we have regarded the adoption of a daughter as something which is irreligious.' He then quoted from the texts *Dattaka Mimansa* and *Sanskar Kaustubha* in order to establish his point, and asserted that although not commonly practised among Hindus, the adoption of daughters was not inconsistent with any religious beliefs.

N.C. Chatterjee and other conservative Hindus, however, maintained that adoption among Hindus was based on a spiritual concept, namely, the necessity of having a son to offer *pinda*s (oblations) after the father's death, a function which could not possibly be performed by a daughter. Another member of Parliament, Mr Barman, stated: 'My objection is that after all this law of adopting a son as it obtains now under the Hindu shastras has been introduced into Hindu customs because of some religious beliefs, and in *Dayabhaga* it is said: "*Putrarthey kriatey Bharyya, Putra Pinda Prayojaka.*" That is, a man requires a son, a man marries because he requires a son, a son is required because of the religious performances, the oblations that the son can offer for the salvation of the father after his death. That is the religious foundation for adoption according to Hindu law and Hindu shastras, and it is for that reason that if a man has got a son, he cannot adopt another, and even if he had got no son, he cannot accept a girl.' Although Pataskar was again accused of trying to destroy the Hindu religion by this bill, he insisted that the *Dattaka Mimansa* was an authoritative Hindu text, and that the adoption of daughters was valid. What would have happened had no text been available to the law minister of a secular state can only be left to conjecture. The bill was passed.

The Hindu Succession Bill introduced another significant innovation, namely, the granting to the daughter of rights as a simultaneous heir along with the son, widow, etc. Under the old Hindu family system a daughter never received a part of the father's estate, the assumption being that she was either already a member of another family (if married) or soon would be. The Muslim law of succession, on the other hand, did grant such rights to daughters. In the debate in Parliament on the Hindu Succession Bill, several members claimed to see in the measure a wholesale engrafting of a principle 'more Mohammedan than the Mohammedan Law'. It was an attempt to impose certain aspects of the shari'ah (Muslim law) on Hindus. Despite such protests, the bill was passed.

The points raised over divorce and the Hindu sacramental marriage, the adoption of daughters, and the granting of succession rights to daughters, have been cited in order to illustrate the numerous religious implications of personal law. The critics who stressed the view that the Hindu law derives not only its authority but its content from the religious tenets of Hinduism are in fact supported by the unbroken tradition of Hindu legal scholarship. The constant effort of orthodox scholars has been to emphasize the spiritual and cosmic basis of the regulations of the law. The following definitions of *Dharmashastra*, found in a book published in 1952, illustrates the point: 'Dharmashastra is a comprehensive code to regulate human conduct in accordance with the unalterable scheme of Creation, and to enable everyone to fulfill the purpose of his birth. The whole life of man, considered both as an individual and as a member of groups (small and large) as well as man's relations to his fellow men, to the rest of animated creation, to superhuman beings, to the cosmos generally and ultimately to God come within the purview of Dharmashastra.'

J.D.M. Derrett, however, suggested that in the context of civil law, Hindu jurisprudence in some cases deliberately utilized religious doctrines in order to justify rules which on purely secular grounds were found to be sound and desirable. Furthermore, historically, Hindu law achieved an authority quite independent of its formal religious basis. The Buddhists ridiculed the alleged authority of the Vedas but apparently followed the regulations of the Hindu law regarding civil disputes and other matters. 'Thus, while the authority which justified the application of the law was admittedly religious, the rules themselves could and in fact did persist by virtue of their own merit and not merely by reason of a superstitious sanction attaching to their alleged source.' If this interpretation of Hindu law were to gain broader acceptance in present-day India, it would surely make the task of reform less painful to the religious-minded.

Most of the critics of the various bills which codified Hindu law could see only the negative aspects that the legislations would in one way or another prove detrimental to the interests of Hindu religion. They tended to see in the legislation the violation of freedom of religion. Acharya Kripalani, however, perceived an entirely different interpretation of the same facts—the secular state was giving special advantages to the majority religion and community. 'If they (members of the legislature) single out the Hindu community for their reforming zeal, they cannot escape the charge of being communalists in the sense that they favor the Hindu community and are indifferent to the good of the Muslim community or the

Catholic community in the matter of divorce. Do we want some one community to be in advance of other communities in India, simply because it happens to be in the majority? The charge levelled against Hindu communalists is that they want their community to be in a more advantageous position than other communities.' Kripalani's conclusion was inescapable: 'Whether the marriage bill favors the Hindu community or places it at a disadvantage, both ways, it becomes a communal measure.' If monogamy and divorce are good and desirable features of a marriage law, why favour the Hindus and withhold monogamy from the Muslims and divorce from the Catholics? If, on the other hand, these reforms are not so good and desirable, why punish the Hindus alone?

Legislations prohibiting the practice of polygamy among Hindus has been upheld as constitutional by the courts. In *State of Bombay* v. *Narasu Appa*, 1952, the Bombay High Court declared that polygamy could not be regarded as an integral part of Hindu religion. While Hinduism recognizes the necessity of a son to perform certain religious ceremonies after the father's death, Hinduism also provides the possibility of adoption if no son is born to him. The religious necessity of polygamy is therefore eliminated. The court held, furthermore, that such legislation (in this case enacted in Bombay state) did not discriminate against the Hindus and that it was not contrary to the principle of equality before the law. The constitutional position of the Hindu Marriage Act of 1955 is therefore not in question.

If we are thinking only of the *principles* involved, there can be little doubt but that the critics of this legislation are right. The enactment of civil laws for one community only is discriminatory, it does represent a communal approach, it does undermine the basic principle of equality before the law, it does place the state in a position where it is either persecuting Hinduism or promoting it, depending on one's point of view. Looking at the total picture quite objectively, it is true that the principles of secularism are not being adhered to. But several other comments are in order.

First, it must be remembered that the critics who represent the Hindu Mahasabha, the Jana Sangh, the Ram Rajya Parishad, and other communalist Hindu parties cannot be credited with any real concern for the maintenance of the secular state in India. Leaders of these parties who argued very cogently that the bills discussed above are opposed to the secular state, on other occasions argued that secularism is a curse and that India must become a Hindu state. Motivated largely by a deep-seated distrust of any efforts to change ancient Hindu social usages, these critics are quite willing to buttress their position with any arguments that are handy, including the secular state. Although they are calling for a uniform civil code rather than a codified Hindu law, it is certain that their opposition will be no less vociferous if and when a uniform civil code bill is introduced. The sacramental Hindu marriage and other Hindu socio-religious institutions are not likely to fare better under a uniform civil code than under the measures which have been enacted. Regardless of motives, however, we cannot dismiss arguments which are perfectly valid.

Second, many of the criticisms of the Hindu Code Bill and the bills which succeeded it are in reality criticisms of the whole structure of religious personal law inherited from the British. The communal nature of such personal law, the denial of equality before the law, the different provisions found in the various systems of personal law—these are not innovations introduced by the Hindu Code Bill, but an inherent part of the legal system which goes back to Warren Hastings' plan of 1772. Nehru's government cannot be blamed for a situation which it did not create but only inherited.

Third, it is clear that a uniform code is the answer to the whole problem. Why has it not been enacted? When asked this question the law minister, Mr Pataskar, replied that even these bills would apply to 85 per cent of the people, and would thus constitute a big step toward uniformity. The codification of Hindu law was regarded as a preparatory step towards the fulfilment of Article 44 of the Constitution. The following exchange with a member of Parliament brought out Nehru's approach. Commenting on the proposal of some that a uniform civil code be enacted, the prime minister declared:

'Well, I should like a civil code which applies to everybody, but . . .'

Mr More: What hinders?

Mr Nehru: Wisdom hinders.

Mr More: Not wisdom but reaction hinders.

Mr Nehru: The honourable member is perfectly entitled to his view on the subject. If he or anybody else brings forward a Civil Code Bill, it will have my extreme sympathy. But I confess I do not think that at the present moment the time is ripe in India for me to try to push it through. I want to prepare the ground for it and this kind of thing is one method of preparing the ground.

Nehru commented that arguments in favour of a uniform of a uniform civil code immediately might appear very progressive and advanced, but might prevent the nation from taking even one step in that direction.

Undoubtedly, much of Nehru's hesitation over a uniform civil code derives from his concern that nothing be done which would have an unsettling effect upon the minorities, especially the Muslims. The shari'ah (Muslim law) occupies an even more central place within Islamic religion that Hindu law does within Hinduism. As we have noted, Indian Muslims would be likely to regard any alteration at all of their personal law as a grave violation of freedom of religion. With clear memories of the tragic fratricidal Hindu–Muslim conflicts of the recent past, Nehru is understandably cautious. The situation is indeed paradoxical: in order to build up the confidence of religious minorities in the non-communal secular nature of the Indian state, Nehru is constrained to sacrifice for the time being other significant principles of the secular state such as a uniform civil code. But the day of such a uniform code is coming, and Indian Muslims, like their Hindu and Christian fellow-citizens, and as their coreligionists in other countries have done, should prepare themselves for these inevitable changes.

In conclusion, what can be said of India as a secular state with respect to its civil laws? The right objective of a uniform civil code is being aimed at, and considerable progress has been made through the codification of Hindu law; but serious difficulties remain. India's problem is by no means unique. Thus the state of Israel, despite the European origin of most of its leaders, has a system of rabbinical courts which control all cases of marriage, divorce, and guardianship. According to Pfeffer, the perpetuation of this system of religious courts which existed under Turkish and British rule 'has resulted in the continuation of laws that are grotesquely anachronistic and out of place in a modern, democratic republic with a distinctly Western orientation.'

India's progress must be measured in terms of its starting point, in terms of what has been done with the situation which was inherited in 1947. In this connection it is not inappropriate to compare the courses of action taken in India and Pakistan. In March 1957 an Indian Christian weekly, *The Guardian* of Madras, made some interesting comments in this regard. The editor referred to two news items which had appeared in the general press during that week. In Pakistan the government had just announced the appointment of a commission under the provisions of the 1956 Constitution to make recommendations 'as to the measures for bringing existing law into conformity with the Injunctions of Islam' (Article 198). In India the Allahabad High Court had just upheld the Hindu Marriage Act, although one of the petitioners contended that bigamy was an integral part of the Hindu religion. *The Guardian's* comment was: 'While Pakistan is reforming secular law to conform to traditional religion, India is legislating to change traditional practices to be brought into keeping with a modern, progressive outlook.'

10

Personal Laws or a Uniform Civil Code?*

JOHN H. MANSFIELD

PRESENT SITUATION

The idea that there should be a uniform law for India on subjects traditionally governed by personal laws of the different religious and ethnic communities—marriage, divorce, maintenance, adoption, guardianship, succession, and so forth—is of relatively recent origin. If early British administrators toyed with the idea, it was later discarded as utopian and unwise. The notion of separately codifying the different personal laws lingered longer, to be replaced by the more modest goal of changing aspects of these laws that conflicted with values the British held fundamental or when change was requested by important elements in the affected community.

The idea of a uniform civil code covering the traditional subjects of the personal laws does not seem to have been put forward until after independence. The Congress Party's pronouncements before that time did not advocate such a step, but some, on the contrary, took the position that there ought to be constitutional protection of the personal laws. So far as is known, the idea of a uniform civil code was first proposed during debate in the Constituent Assembly and its committees. But once the notion of a uniform civil code was put forward, it rapidly came to be accepted as an important part of the effort to construct an Indian national identity, over and against the separate identities of caste, religion and ethnicity.

Article 44 of the Directive Principles of State Policy in the Indian Constitution gives expression to the goal of a uniform civil code. It

---

*Excerpted from John H. Mansfield, 'Personal Laws or a Uniform Civil Code?' in Robert D. Baird (ed.), *Religion and Law in Independent India*, New Delhi: Manohar, 1993, pp. 139–77.

proclaims: '[T]he state shall endeavour to secure for the citizens a uniform civil code throughout the territory of India.' Like the other Directive Principles, this one 'shall not be enforceable by any court, but . . . [is] nevertheless fundamental in the governance of the country and it shall be the duty of the State to apply . . . [it] in making laws'. As will be discussed later, the Constitution did not abolish the system of personal laws and require that there be a uniform civil code; it only held forth a uniform civil code as an ideal towards which the state should strive.

During the years since the Constitution was adopted, voices have been raised repeatedly demanding to know why action has not been taken to bring about the fulfilment of the constitutional ideal. A famous example of such an utterance is the one made by the Supreme Court in its *Shah Bano* judgment. The intensity of the Muslim reaction to the Supreme Court's judgment in that case was partly explained by the inclusion of this utterance and the suggestion that what the government had failed to do, the Court itself might undertake. Criticism of the sort expressed by the Supreme Court may not be entirely justified. If one examines the debates in the Constituent Assembly on the subject of a uniform civil code, they include assurance that there was no intention to force a uniform civil code upon any community that was strongly opposed to it. The hope was, rather, that change would take place within communities, particularly within the Muslim community, that would bring the members to feel that their own interests would best be served by a uniform civil code. Perhaps it can be said that Article 44 imposed upon the state a duty to encourage such a change of attitude, and that successive governments, for reasons to which the Constitution gives no recognition, have shirked this duty. On the other hand, it equally can be argued that what has occurred—the absence of any significant movement towards a uniform civil code—is a situation that it was contemplated by the framers of the Constitution possibly to occur. If Hindu, Parsi, and Christian attitudes towards a uniform civil code may have changed to a degree, Muslim resistance has only stiffened as the years have passed. Consequently, it can be argued, in view of the legislative history of Article 44, it should not be the subject of severe criticism that the project for a uniform civil code has not gone forward.

Debate over the question of a uniform civil code has varied in intensity during the years since the Constitution was adopted. In the early 1970s there was a surge of activity: conferences, publications, reports. The last several years have seen a similar rise in activity, due in part to the *Shah Bano* judgment and the debate over the legislation to reverse it. Discussions about a uniform civil code have been indirectly affected by other matters:

the Ram Janmabhoomi–Babri Masjid controversy, the 1986 sati incident in Deorala, Rajasthan, and the anti-sati legislation that resulted from it; the conflicts in the Punjab and Kashmir; and the increase in communal violence in many parts of India.

Beginning in the mid-1980s an 'anti-secularist' critique of nationalist orthodoxy has emerged. The reasons for this phenomenon are complex, but some suggestions can be made. During the early years of independence, it was seen as important by leaders of the new nation that India should become a political entity as strong and unified as any. In the British period there had been those who had said that there was no such thing as 'India', and that what passed under that name was simply a congeries of castes, sects, and other religious and ethnic groups. The leaders of the new India felt it important to refute this proposition. The idea that India should be a nation state in the same sense and to the same extent as the strongest nations of the West, sprang certainly from a genuine concern for the welfare of the people of India, but it also had roots in a need for status and prestige. One characteristic of a true nation state, it was thought, was that it had a unified substantive law, not different religious and ethnic communities. The existence of different laws, whose applicability depended upon religion or ethnicity, was seen as a badge of inferiority; it suggested a political entity prone to distintegration, one that would have little influence in the world.

It is not necessary to take sides on the question of whether it was desirable for India to embrace the Western idea of a nation state. Gandhi certainly had stood against it. It is enough to note that in recent years there has been increasing controversy on the subject. A factor contributing to this change may have been the growing support around the world for the rights of religious and ethnic minorities within territorial states. This movement stresses the interest of these groups in preserving their distinctive cultures and in being protected against pressure to conform to the majority culture. The spectacle of large political entities in different parts of the world collapsing and giving place to smaller entities based on ethnicity, religion, language, or combinations of these factors, rather than strengthening the idea that a powerfully centralized, culturally homogeneous nation is essential for order and prosperity, may have confirmed for some the view that the pressing task for India is not to increase central power and cultural homogeneity, but to find an alternative to the 'nation state' model, an alternative that will sustain unity through some form of 'pluralism'.

The 'anti-secularist' critique of nationalist orthodoxy has been led by a group of eminent political scientists, sociologists, and historians.

Among these may be mentioned Ashis Nandy, T.N. Madan, and T.K. Oommen. It is possible that in some cases at least, the anti-secularists are converts from nationalist orthodoxy. Although the anti-secularists have not to any significant extent addressed the issue of a uniform civil code, their general criticism of orthodox nationalist ideology may have implications for this issue.

In his book published in 1990, Oommen summed up the major points made by the anti-secularists. The goal of a single secular national culture, Oommen thinks, was a mistake. Such a culture is not required for the unity that is needed to maintain order and achieve prosperity. Indeed, the aim of achieving it may have worked against these objectives. Oommen accepts the idea that there can be many 'nations' within India. These nations may be based on culture and language. Nations based on religion, on the other hand, involve an unacceptable risk of secession. In this latter opinion, Oommen is influenced, no doubt, by partition and the present troubles in the Punjab and Kashmir. He is supportive of religious 'pluralism' so long as it does not have a territorial basis. It may be that Oommen's belief that India does not need a single national culture neglects to some extent the necessity of some shared values if India is to exist at all. He seems to place his own faith in some rather vague humanistic values.

Oommen appears to approve the existing system of personal laws and to be opposed to a uniform civil code: '[C]ultural pluralism in India necessitates the recognition and operation of legal pluralism.' The 'timidity in evolving a uniform civil code' points to the fact that Indian 'secularism' meant not only non-interference in the affairs of other communities but also developing a positive appreciation of their distinct style of life'. Opposition to a uniform civil code on the part of the anti-secularists, if that is their position, could derive in part from an anti Western strain in their thinking, a tendency to reject what they see as an undesirable aping of the West and to embrace that which is indigenous and authentically Indian. Although there are those who suggest that a uniform civil code could embody the best of Indian ideas, the fact of the matter is that the content of a uniform civil code would almost certainly be inspired by modern Western values, just as were most of the legislative enactments during the British period—for instance, the Contract Act and the Transfer of Property Act—that touched upon subjects dealt with by the personal laws. Furthermore, the very idea of a single law applicable to all, regardless of community, on such topics as marriage and succession, is inescapably an import from the West.

Oommen considers it the function of the state to 'reform' the different religions in India and to remove from them 'obscurantist practices'

practices that are 'in violation of the principles of freedom, equality and justice'. He does not seem to appreciate the possibility of a conflict between the goal of 'reform' and the objective of maintaining 'cultural pluralism'. What is his position, for example, on Muslim polygamy, on the absence of a duty of a Muslim man to maintain his former wife, on unequal rights of inheritance for sons and daughters? Are these 'obscurantist practices' that stand in need of 'reform' or are they expressions of a healthy 'pluralism'?

With the attitude of the anti-secularists towards a uniform civil code, it would be interesting to compare the positions of various groups that are presently active in furthering the cause of Hinduism as they understand it. I have in mind such groups as the Arya Samaj, the Rashtriya Swayam-sevak Sangh (RSS), the Vishwa Hindu Parishad (VHP), and the Bharatiya Janata Party (BJP). The VHP, to speak of only one of these groups, seeks to create a Hinduism that will have strong links with tradition, but at the same time be able to compete successfully in the modern world with other religions and with secular ideologies. It seeks to unite a wide variety of castes and sects and to appeal to that increasingly numerous class of persons who wish to be both modern and Hindu. The Hinduism the VHP promotes is intended to have a certain dominance in India and to be recognized as more truly Indian than other religions. What would be the stance of the VHP on the subject of a uniform civil code? In view of its objectives, it might have a more ambivalent attitude on this issue than on certain others, such as special constitutional protection for minority educational institutions, the constitutional status of Kashmir and the removal of mosques allegedly built on sites sacred to Hindus.

If we assume that a uniform civil code would be entirely secular in its values, it might represent for the VHP too a complete break from tradition. Furthermore, a uniform civil code, applicable to all residents of India, would undermine the notion of the Hindus as a distinct community. It seems improbable that the VHP would favour a return to the *dharma-śāstra*s or to the Anglo-Hindu case law interpreting them. Such a return would involve giving up practices that provide bridges between orthodox Hinduism and modernity and which have become acceptable to many Hindus. In fact it may be the case that the present Hindu Code, adopted by Parliament in 1955–6, is a fairly good approximation of what the VHP would like for Hindus. Although the Code's values are predominantly secular, it retains a few traditional elements that may be of symbolic importance. Religious ceremonies, for instance, are still effective to bring about valid marriages and conversion to a religion other than Hinduism is ground for divorce. More important, the present code preserves the notion of the Hindus as a community. It seems improbable the VHP would wish to see this code made applicable to all residents of India. More likely, in line with ancient attitudes, it would prefer to hierarchize the different groups in India in accordance with their ways of life.

ADVANTAGES AND DISADVANTAGES OF THE SYSTEM OF PERSONAL LAWS

General Considerations

Assuming that Constitution neither requires that the system of personal laws be abolished nor that it be retained, the question of its desirability from a non-constitutional point of view must be confronted. In addressing this question, the teachings of the personal laws themselves of course can not be dispositive. It may well be that one or more of the religions in India require the state to enforce a particular body of rules upon the members of a community, or for that matter upon all the inhabitants of India, but this cannot be determinative for the Indian state. For the state, decision must be based upon its own ideology.

Strengthening national unity frequently has been cited as a reason for having a uniform civil code. Increased unity will mean less communal conflict and indirectly affect economic prosperity and national security. There is not likely to be any quarrel with the values stated. The difficulty lies in the proof. The comparative effect on national unity of different personal laws and a uniform civil code probably needs to be considered topic by topic, rather than generally. For example, what is the effect on national unity and communal conflict of the existence of different laws on polygamy? Do Hindus resent the fact that Muslims have a special privilege, or do they feel, rather, that the state's 'reform' of Hinduism has been a benefit conferred upon it? Do different laws of succession create hostility among religious communities? If there had been since independence a uniform code on the traditional topics of the personal laws, would there have been less communal violence than there has been? Some have noted that there have been uniform laws on a large number of subjects—for example, the criminal law and the law of contracts—for many years, and yet communal conflict has continued and indeed increased. If a uniform civil code were adopted today, what would be its effect on communal conflict in the next few decades? Its effect in the future might be different than what it would have been during the period since independence. Some believe that a uniform civil code would only increase communal tension. Certainly predominant Muslim reaction to the statement about a uniform code in the Supreme Court's *Shah Bano* jugment lends support to this view. A more effective way to assure national unity, it can be argued, is to reassure religious and ethnic groups that their personal laws will be respected. The empirical question of the effect on national unity and communal harmony of adopting or not adopting a uniform code should not be confused with the notion some national leaders had, and perhaps still have, that there is a sort of logical contradiction between the idea of a nation state and a system of different personal laws.

Probably the most interesting and important point to be considered in regard to the desirability or undesirability of a system of personal laws is the argument that such a system helps to affirm the distinct identities of ethnic and religious groups, and that this is a positive advantage. It is an advantage, it is suggested, because in affirming the identities of these groups, the state contributes to the well-being of the individuals who compose them. In particular, it contributes to their sense of existing and of having meaning in their lives. This sense of existing and having meaning, it is argued, is something that citizenship in a nation state along cannot confer. Although the anti-secularists, who have come to the defence of cultural 'pluralism', have not given a significant amount of attention to the question of the system of personal laws, the idea that such a system performs a useful function in confirming people's sense of existing and having meaning may be consistent with their general ideas.

Against the suggested argument in favour of the personal laws stands, of course, the opposite view that the individual is not enhanced but diminished by membership in most of the ethnic and religious groups that exist in India, and that the help he needs from the state is not reinforcement of these identities, but liberation from them. In supporting the system of personal laws, the state helps to keep these imprisoning identities alive. Quite apart from the question of the effect on national unity, the liberation of the human spirit, it is suggested, requires the elimination of the system of personal laws and the adoption of a uniform civil code.

Defenders of the system of personal laws cite in support of their position the example of different territorial laws. If territorial legal pluralism is desirable—and no one doubts that it is to some extent—why not nonterritorial ethnic and religious legal pluralism? All recognize that it would be an injustice for the conqueror of a territory to sweep away all the laws of the inhabitants and replace them with his own. To do so would be to deprive the inhabitants of an important constituent of their identity, to commit a kind of cultural genocide. So also in the case of the laws of non-territorial groups, it is argued. There is some force in the analogy. In the territorial case, although territory is an important aspect of identity, it is not the only one. Other factors, such as language, race, culture, religion, shared history, and law play a part. Why by removing the territorial factor should the whole force of the argument in favour of preserving identity through law be destroyed?

It is important to distinguish between affirming the law of an ethnic or religious group in the sense just referred to and upholding contracts and the laws of voluntary associations. What is affirmed in the latter situation is private ordering through individual choice. The enforcement of the law of a voluntary association finds justification in the choice made by each individual member to accept the law of the association. In the case of ethnic and religious groups in India, however, the application of their laws can seldom be justified on any such voluntaristic basis. Although some consideration of individual choice may occasionally appear—here we touch upon the complex subject of conversion—for the most part ascriptive elements are predominant. The fundamental question for the state, therefore, is whether, given its own ideology, there is value in maintaining the identities of ethnic and religious groups through the enforcement of their laws, even though these groups are predominantly ascriptive. Of course all identities that are received, or even imposed, rather than individually chosen, are not for that reason automatically to be condemned. The identity that comes from being a member of a family, or for that matter a citizen of a territorial state, are examples. Furthermore, the borderline between ascription and choice is often indistinct: if a young person elects to be initiated into a religious sect to which his family has long belonged, does he freely choose as an individual to be initiated into the sect, or is the reality more complicated than that?

State policy may exclude a particular subject, for example, the minimum age for marriage from all private ordering. In this situation both individual choice and the laws of ascriptive groups are ousted. On other topics, state policy may exclude, not private ordering as such, but only private ordering through the law of ascriptive groups. The state's readiness to enforce the consequences of individual choice may stand unimpaired. For example, an individual's decision to be governed by a particular law of intestate succession might be respected even though that same law would not be applied by reason of his membership in an ascriptive group.

A reason sometimes put forward for protecting the identities of religious and ethnic groups, which could include such groups recognized through their personal laws, is that when there are different cultures within a nation, improving dialogue is possible. If one group learns of the ways of another, it may become aware of its own deficiencies and decide to eliminate them, perhaps, by borrowing from the second group. Sometimes the suggestion is that the dominant culture, which is prone to the self-satisfaction that comes with power, will be humbled by what it learns from minority cultures. But the argument also can be directed against minority cultures: they must take into account the values of the dominant culture and consider whether their own ways stand in need of improvement. The emphasis on 'dialogue' can lead to an outcome quite contrary to respect for distinct cultural identities. It may be that the identity of a particular group consists precisely in keeping uncontaminated by the world the revelation it believes it has received, which may include specific rules regarding such subjects as marriage, divorce, and succession. Is this identity not to be respected because the group will not engage in give-and-take with the dominant culture, or in other words, will not submit to the view, probably the product of the dominant culture itself, that there can be progress in ideas about how to live?

The suggestion that the personal laws of ethnic and religious groups should be upheld because of the value of maintaining cultural identities could be argued to be especially applicable in the case of minorities. Minorities, defined either numerically or from the point of view of power, stand in special need, it may be thought, of having their cultures affirmed by the state. Their sense of worth may be fragile and, understandably, they may be sceptical of the ordinary political process. Furthermore, the argument that 'pluralism' is the best antidote to alienation and secessionist tendencies may be especially persuasive in the case of minorities. Article 30 of the Constitution, which gives special protection to minority educational institutionals, reflects this view. On the other hand, it is a notable feature of the present Indian scene that it is not the minorities alone that feel insecure and anxious about the future. Many Hindus share this anxiety and either attempt to reaffirm tradition or, like the VHP, to develop new forms that bind together past and future. Special protection of minorities is strongly opposed by such groups.

If the personal laws of the minorities were recognized, it is perhaps not quite correct to say that the personal law of the majority necessarily also would be recognized. It is true that if the minorities were exempted from the general law, what would be left would be the law applicable to the majority. But this law would not be the majority's personal law in the sense in which we have been using that term. The law applicable to the majority would as likely be imposed upon it as credited by it. Even though there is a 'democratic' political process, an important distinction still would be likely to remain between the state and the majority, especially in India, so that the law applicable to the majority would reflect the values of governing groups rather than those of the majority community or the congeries of communities that make up Hinduism. Everyone would agree that this is an accurate description of the circumstances attending the adoption of the Hindu Code of 1955–6. Even if Hinduism is seen to have a large capacity for development, it is not likely to be contended that in adopting laws for the Hindus in 1955–6, Parliament was simply striving to reflect a change that had already taken place among the mass of Hindus. Rather, it was seeking to draw Hindus on to a new path, one alien to their traditions. Still, because Hindus are in the great majority in India, and obviously have more influence with the state than the minorities, the adoption of the Hindu Code in 1955–6 may not have significantly undermined their sense of worth or alienated them from the state. But the matter is not free from doubt. The attitude of Hindu organizations such as the VHP towards the existing Hindu Code is unclear.

Is the Identity Value in Fact Upheld by Present Indian Law?

General Considerations

If the value of affirming the identities of ethnic and religious groups is the principal reason for the system of personal laws, it is worthwhile to consider the extent to which that value is in fact being supported. As has recently been observed, assertions concerning ethnic and national identity must be viewed with caution, for the processes of identity formation are not well understood. To the extent that the state is not simply recognizing an independently existing identity, but creating and shaping one, it cannot invoke in justification of its activity the identity value that we have been considering. If the identity value is not well supported by the law, changes perhaps can be made so that it will be better supported. On the other hand, if the identity value is not well supported and the reason for this is that importance is not really attached to it, the considerations claimed to outweigh this value should be brought into the open and submitted to careful examination.

Threshold Questions

In protecting the identity of cultural and religious groups through recognition of their personal laws, certain threshold ideas generated by the state's own ideology seem inescapably involved. For example, it is necessary for the state to decide what qualifies as a group for the purpose of receiving recognition through the enforcement of personal law: certain types of relationships may be judged not to qualify. Also it would seem unavoidable that the state has its own criteria regarding what constitutes membership in a group for the purpose of imposition of group law on an individual, although these criteria may make some reference to the attitudes held by the individual and the group. In addition, the state must have its own notion of what is meant by 'law' for the purpose of determining what the law of a group is. Although reference to sacred texts and seers long dead may be required, it seems doubtful that acceptance by the living will be left wholly out of account. At the same time, the state's notion of the 'law' of a group may point not simply to what a majority of the living members believe at a particular time, but to more enduring commitments. To the extent that the answers to these threshold questions flow from the state's own ideology rather than from ideologies that exist independently of the state, the state's system of personal laws will uphold the identity value in a way that is less than perfect.

Who Decides

What strikes many observers of the Indian legal system is not only that there are different laws for different religious and ethnic communities on certain topics, but that all these different laws are determined and administered by a single judicial system. That it is the courts of the state that perform this function undoubtedly affects the content of the laws that are administered.

It is common knowledge that however conscientiously the judges of the early British period tried to enter into the spirit of the classical Hindu law and the Islamic law, a consequence of their activity was, to some extent at least, to bring into existence something significantly different from those laws. The fact that the judges were British and carried in their heads ideas very different from those of the Hindu pundits and Muslims *kazis* who advised them, more or less foreordained this outcome. Also, as later became well understood, the very institutions and procedures that the British created to administer the laws were so different from those of the Hindu and Islamic legal traditions that the substance was bound to be affected. *Stare decisis* alone was a powerful engine for transformation, because it gave to the decisions of the state's courts a status that they had never enjoyed under either Hindu or Muslim rulers. The tendencies of the

British effort to find and apply the Hindu and Islamic laws, which had the effect of changing them, probably were only accentuated by the decision in 1864 to eliminate the court pundits and kazis and have the judges decide the legal questions unaided.

If the circumstances just mentioned are taken into account, the question naturally is presented to what extent the Anglo-Hindu case law, insofar as it is still applied by the Indian courts and not replaced by the Hindu Code of 1955–6, and the Anglo-Muslim case law, which is still fully administered, can be defended on the ground that they uphold identities that exist independently of the state. In order fully to uphold the identity of an ethnic or religious group through the enforcement of its laws, it would seem necessary to give effect to the institutions and processes created by the group to determine and apply its law, for these are as much part of the law as the substantive rules.

In India, not only are the laws of religious and ethnic groups determined by the courts of the state, but the judges of these courts frequently do not belong to the religion, the law of which they are to find. The suggestion that the judges assigned to hear a case should be selected on the basis of religion would be strongly resisted: selection on the basis of religion would be seen as seriously comprising the secular character of the state. The five-judge bench in the *Shah Bano* case, which determined among other issues the Muslim law of maintenance, was composed entirely of Hindu judges. If judges were assigned on the basis of religion, difficult questions of classification would arise. In a particular case it might not be enough that a judge was a Muslim: he might have to be of a particular school of Islamic law. And if customary law were involved, it might be necessary to find judges who belonged to the group whose custom was to be determined. Although it may be possible for a judge who is not of a particular religion to go a long way in entering into its spirit and presuppositions, to the extent that he is not able fully to achieve this, the identity value will not be perfectly upheld.

The Kazis Act of 1880 was the result of an effort by some Muslims to have the determination of questions of Islamic law placed in the hands of Muslims. But the effort failed and the British refused to confer judicial powers on the kazis. Instead, what was enacted was a strange exercise of state power. Among some Muslims it was thought that kazis could not function—and they were believed necessary for certain purposes—unless they were appointed by the state. This idea may have been based upon religious beliefs and influenced by experiences under the Mughal and early British regimes. The Kazis Act accommodated this sentiment by providing for state appointment of kazis when there were any considerable number of Muslims in an area who desired it. There was also to be consultation with the principal Muslim residents. But the Act carefully refrained from specifying what the duties of kazis might be, denied that they had any judicial powers, and specified that the Act should not be construed to prohibit anyone from acting as a kazi even if not appointed by the state. Thus the Act kept the authoritative decision of questions of Islamic law firmly in the hands of the state's judges, who might be of any religion or none at all, while at the same time authorizing the state to make appointments of kazis, implying some sort of link between the state and the kazis, a suggestion that could, perhaps, have a modest effect on the religion.

Conferring judicial powers on kazis needs to be distinguished from upholding their decisions as arbitrators selected by the parties to settle a dispute. In the latter situation there is state support for private ordering through individual choice, as distinguished from private ordering through the law of ascriptive ethnic or religious groups.

The debate over the Dissolution of Muslim Marriages Act, 1939, reproduced the controversy over the kazis. Quite apart from the issue of whether Islamic law permitted women to obtain divorce, and if so on what grounds, many of the ulema opposed the act because it allowed judges who were not Muslims to decide issues of Islamic law. But the effort to secure Muslim control of the administration of the law of divorce was unsuccessful.

The Parsi Marriage and Divorce Act, 1936, adopted, it is said, at the behest of the Parsi community, provides for special tribunals called Parsi Matrimonial Courts. The judges of these courts are judges of high courts or district courts, but the courts also include 'delegates', who must be Parsis. The delegates are chosen by the state government 'after giving the local Parsis an opportunity of expressing their opinions in such manner as the respective Governments may think fit.' The judges is to determine questions of law, the delegates questions of fact. Possibly the fact that the delegates are Parsis will give to their fact-finding a distinctive character: they may have background factual information that non-Parsis do not have. It is hard to avoid the belief, however, that such trouble would not have been taken to require that the delegates be Parsis unless it was thought that by this means Parsi views on matters of value would have some chance of having an influence on the case. Thus the Parsi Marriage and Divorce Act may present an instance in Indian law in which the state has made it possible for the adherents of a particular religion to play a role in the determination and application of their own law. But will the Parsis who serve as delegates be authoritative spokesmen for Parsi law or, because of the method of their selection, will they be primarily spokesmen for state values? As noted above, provision is made in the Parsi Act for consultation with local Parsis on delegate selection, but what assurance is there that those consulted will themselves be authentic spokesmen for Parsi values?

The recently authorized family courts, so far actually instituted in only a few large cities, may also throw into relief the question of who decides what the law is. Under the Act authorizing the creation of these courts, it is provided: '[I]f the Family Court considers it necessary in the interest of justice, it may seek the assistance of a legal expert as *amicus curiae.*' Under this provision may experts on the various personal laws be introduced into the functioning of the courts? It seems correct to assume that the personal laws will continue to be applied by the Family Courts, and that Parliament did not intend by the creation of these new institutions to effect a change in the substantive laws. Might the old court pundits and kazis make a reappearance in the family courts of modern India? There are those who believe that if this is not possible under the Family Courts Act as it stands, efforts should be made to amend the Act to assure that cases under the personal laws are decided by persons who are 'experts in those laws and can appreciate their letter and spirit.'

Particular Situations

The Shariat Act of 1937 provides an example of how difficult it can be in regard to the personal laws to determine whether the state is affirming the independently existing identity of an ethnic or religious group or asserting its own values. In that Act, which was a response to lobbying by certain Muslim groups, the state imposed the Shariat on all Muslims for most of the topics on the list to which the personal laws traditionally have been applied. The Muslims affected by the Act included a number of groups that had therefore followed the Hindu law on certain topics, such as succession. Those who had successfully campaigned for the Act believed it wrong to mix Islam with elements of Hindu or customary law. It is not certain what their view would have been if the groups in question had not only observed the Hindu law of succession, but had repudiated Islam entirely. Perhaps they would have thought that the members of these groups were no longer Muslims, and so there was no reason to bring them under the Shariat.

Did the application of the Shariat to the groups that had theretofore observed the Hindu law of succession uphold the identity value that we have been discussing? As noted earlier, in the application of the personal laws certain threshold questions unavoidably are presented that require resort to the ideology of the state. The issue of whether the groups that observed the Hindu law of succession should have been considered part of a larger group, 'Muslims', for the purpose of applying a particular law, would seem to be such a question. The answer to the question might involve difficult issues of history and interpretation, and not be provided simply by the fact that the groups considered themselves Muslims. Furthermore, were those who demanded that the Shariat be imposed upon these non-observant groups authentic spokesmen for Islam? To the extent that the answers to these questions are uncertain, it is not clear that the Shariat Act upheld the identity value. Possibly the British decided for purely pragmatic and political reasons to appease powerful Muslim interests by subordinating one group to another. It is interesting to note that although the Shariat Act suppressed the Hindu law to the extent that it had been observed by certain groups, it did not attempt to unify the various schools of Islamic law, all of which continued to be recognized as acceptable versions of the Shariat.

The Dissolution of Muslim Marriages Act, 1939, which allowed Muslim women to obtain divorce under certain circumstances, also presents the question whether the value of maintaining group identity is being supported by the state or some other value. There is a principle of Islamic law, recognized by one school at least, that under certain circumstances it is permissible to look to all of the schools of Islamic law to see if divorce is permitted under any of them. However, Professor Tahir Mahmood states that the Dissolution of Muslim Marriages Act contained some changes in the original proposals that had no support in any of the traditional schools of Islamic law. Thus, even though the legislature purported to rely on the views of the ulema and 'the Muslim community', possibly the Act represents now simply, as sometimes stated, a consolidation and clarification of Muslim law, but a 'reform' of that law in accordance with modern ideas about divorce and the equality of men and women.

The recent Muslim Women (Protection of Rights on Divorce) Act, 1986, which deals with the rights of divorced Muslim women to obtain maintenance, may represent an effort on the part of the legislature made on good faith to support the identity of a religious community by upholding its personal law. The purpose of the Parliament in adopting the Act was to reserve the Supreme Court's decision in the *Shah Bano* case, which some believed involved a departure from Islamic law. Professor Mahmood thinks that in the MW (PRD) Act, Parliament made some mistakes about Islamic law. To the extent that this is true, it cannot be said that the Act fully supports the identity value, even though the mistakes may have been inadvertent.

As already mentioned, the Hindu Code of 1955–6 is a difficult case in which to contend that the state has affirmed a group identity that exists independently of the state. The Code introduced a large number of rules—for example regarding divorce and adoption—that find no warrant either in the *dharmaśāstras* or in the Anglo-Hindu case law. No doubt Parliament thought it had a responsibility in respect to the Hindus, but the responsibility was, as already suggested, to separate them from their past and to provide them with a new identity. Thus many of the rules in the Hindu Code can only be justified from some point of view other than the identity value.

Options

Introducing an optional feature into the personal law system has the effect of undermining the identity value without appearing to do so. At least this is true if the personal law in question, fairly interpreted, does not permit the option. In 1972, an adoption bill without any religious limitations was introduced in Parliament. Some Muslims demanded that Muslims be excluded from the operation of the bill, since Islamic law does not permit adoption. There was Parsi opposition as well. Ultimately, the combined opposition led to the defeat of the bill. Professor Mahmood, commenting on this incident could not understand how reasonable persons, including Muslims, could be opposed to the bill or demand that any particular group be exempted. After all, he said, if adoption is a sin for Muslims, the bill did not require them to sin; it only permitted them to do so. How can it be justified, he asked, to seek the help of the state to prevent Muslims from sinning if they choose to do so? But the Adoption Bill without the exemption of Muslims could have undermined the identity value. If some of those who might wish to adopt would be properly classified as Muslims, and if under Islamic law adoption by Muslims is not permitted, if the state permits these people to adopt, it undermines the group and its identity. If the state supports individual choice in the matter, it elevates individual choice above the group's decisions. In fact, it supports an alternative Muslim identity that conflicts with the identity embodied in the law of the group, an alternative identity that combines aspects of Islamic law with the practice of adoption.

There is an optional feature in the Shariat Act. Although, as already stated, in regard to most topics the Act imposed the Shariat on all Muslims, including groups that had theretofore followed the Hindu law in certain matters, in regard to a few topics—adoptions, wills, and legacies—individuals were to be governed by the Shariat only if they made an election in its favour. The existence of this option did not please many of the ulema, who wanted full enforcement of the Shariat on all Muslims. At the same time the option tended to undermine the identity of the groups that had not observed the Shariat on these topics. This was so because the Act empowered individual members of these groups to opt out of the group's laws and accept the Shariat. Within these groups in fact there had been controversy about whether observance of the Shariat was consistent with their true identity. Ironically, the Shariat Act provides that if an individual elected to be governed by the Shariat on the optional topics, this decision bound his descendants as well. In other words, the very provision that exalted individual choice for one generation rejected it for the generations to come.

The MW (PRD) Act also has an optional feature. It permits a Muslim couple, when marrying, to submit themselves to the maintenance provisions of the Criminal Procedure Code, rather than to the Islamic law as expressed in the Act. The couple is thus provided with an opportunity to adopt secular ideas regarding maintenance following divorce while continuing, in the eyes of the state at least, to be Muslims.

The Special Marriage Act, 1872, was a pioneer legislation in the matter of options to escape from the law of the group. If two persons married under that Act, they were no longer governed by their personal law. In regard to succession, they became subject to the Indian Succession Act. In order to marry under the Special Marriage Act, the couple had to renounce their religion. For some communities, providing for this complete break from the group might not be inconsistent with the maintenance of the group's identity: the individuals do not threaten group identity because they are simply out of the group. Under the present Special Marriage Act, adopted in 1954, however, renunciation of religion is no longer required. Furthermore, in the case of two Hindus marrying under the Act, under a 1976 amendment they continue to be governed by the Hindu law of Succession. In other words, the state gives recognition to an alternative Hindu identity.

Professor Derrett suggested some years ago that all the personal laws might be made optional. That is, there would be a uniform civil code, which generally would be applicable, but individuals could opt out of it and into one or another of the personal laws. In 1987 Rajiv Gandhi's government, some thought in response to criticism of the MW (PRD) Act, announced it was considering introducing a bill for a 'voluntary civil code', but it then decided not to go ahead with the project. Of course these options would give supremacy to individual choice and turn the system of personal laws into a system of voluntary associations.

Professor Mahmood once suggested that there might be a referendum of each community and the majority could choose whether to continue with the personal law or accept a uniform civil code. This suggestion supports neither the group identity value, nor individual choice, but a regime of majority rule within each group. But majority rule may have nothing to do with the identity of a group from a religious and historical point of view. Under the law of the group, there may be no authority in the majority to determine the true way of life.

QUESTIONS IN THE MARGINS

The Personal Laws after the Adoption of a Uniform Civil Code

If the adoption of the Hindu Code in 1955–6 did not entirely eliminate the pre-existing Hindu personal law-for instance, it did not touch endowments, and although it affected the Hindu Undivided Family, did not abolish it—likewise the adoption of a uniform civil code might not entirely eliminate the personal laws. Indeed the question of the ways in which the personal laws might survive presents subtle and interesting points.

CONCLUSION

The foregoing discussion has sought to identify the various considerations relevant to a choice between the present system of personal laws and a uniform civil code. Among those that have been mentioned, particular attention has been given to what I have called the identity value, the value, that is, of an ethnic or religious group within a territorial state being able to maintain its distinctive identity and through this its members' sense of existing and having meaning. But giving weight to this value, it can be argued, is improper, because Article 44 on the Directive Principles embodies an adverse judgment against it. If there is legislative discretion under Article 44, it must be confined to prudential considerations, such as how much resistance there would be to a uniform code and what injurious consequences might flow from this resistance. However, what seems a permissible reading of Article 44 leaves open for consideration the weight and persuasiveness of the identity value, as it is presented in the Indian context. The framers of the Indian Constitution understood the complexity of the Indian social and religious situation and realized that an unforeseeable future might provide new insights into the problem of the personal laws, including the advantages and disadvantages of giving weight to the identity value.

But of course if the identity value is not well served by the existing system, unless there is some practical proposal on how the system might be changed to serve that value better, it cannot be invoked in justification of present arrangements. Features of the system that do indeed cast doubt on whether the identity value is well served have been pointed out. It has been noted, for example, that in the application of the personal laws, certain threshold questions necessarily are presented and answered, not from the point of view of the personal laws, but from the point of view of the state's own ideology, The state approves certain processes of group identity formation and not others. It has also been noted that the tribunals of the state, applying the personal laws from the outside so to speak, inevitably have difficulty entering into the spirit and presuppositions of the personal laws, so that their decisions are bound to reflect to some degree their own values. Instances have been pointed out where the identity value has certainly been undermined, although in a covert manner. For a final judgment on this question of the undermining of the identity value, a more thorough study of the personal law system than has been attempted here would be necessary. But enough has been done, perhaps, to suggest a possible conclusion that although compromises and limitations are to be found, the state administration of the system of personal laws does give substantial support to the identity value, so that the system should not be abandoned simply on the ground that it fails to achieve what it sets out to do.

More important, the foregoing discussion would seem to make clear that to put the choice as one between the personal law system and a uniform civil code is to pose the issue too sharply. In this connection the Supreme Court indeed may have done a disservice in its *Shah Bano* judgment in suggesting that a case concerning a Muslim woman's right to maintenance from her former husband involved the question of a uniform civil code. Even those who are clear that there should be such a code readily agree that certain groups, tribal groups for instance, should be exempt. This is a concession to the identity value. Furthermore, when pressed, they are likely also to concede that a reasonable case can be made out for excluding certain topics from a uniform civil code. The question is whether all aspects of the personal laws of ascriptive groups should be abolished if a uniform code is adopted. But even within the familiar list of personal law topics, it may be sensible to make distinctions. For instance, from the point of view of the identity value, the rules relating to marriage may be more important than the rules relating to succession. Likewise, from the point of view of state interests that compete with the identity value, a different importance may attach to different subjects on the familiar list. Such a particularizing approach, of course, has something in common with what has been going on since 1772. But the weight to be ascribed to the identity value, as well as that to be ascribed to other state interests, may be significantly different than in the past. With the benefit of intervening experience of a complex and ever-changing Indian society, an open-minded approach seems called for, one unconstrained either by the hesitancy of a foreign ruler to interfere in the laws and customs of subject peoples, or by a purely theoretical notion that a nation state cannot exist without a uniform substantive law on all subjects. The nation state that India needs is one that is adapted to its special circumstances.

11

The Personal Law Question and Hindu Nationalism*

DIETER CONRAD

Birth of a Problem

Warren Hastings' famous 'Judicial Plan' of 1772 in providing for the administration of their different traditional laws to Hindus and Muslims respectively has eventually had a major share in the development of the so-called *Two Nation Theory* in India. To recall the original wording of the provision, the East India Company's new civil courts or *diwani adalat*s to be set up in the province of Bengal were thereby directed

> . . . XXXIII That in all suits regarding Inheritance, Marriage, Caste and all other religious Usages or Institutions, the Laws of the Koran with respect to *Mahomatans*, and those of the Shaster with respect to *Gentoos*, shall be invariably adhered to; . . .

From that decision one has to date the establishment of personal laws on the plane of state legality in India: laws administered by the ordinary courts, jet applying not as common law of the land on a territorial basis (*yex loci*) but on account of personal status by membership in a social group defined by its religion. In view of later developments it ought to be clarified that this legal entrenchment of religious diversity did not at the time proceed from an intention to create rifts within the population. No insidious stratagem of 'divide and rule' was involved. The measure was largely a ratification of existing practices. It was motivated partly by administrative convenience, partly by a tolerant inclination to respect 'the

*Excerpted from Dieter Conrad, 'The Personal Law Question and Hindu Nationalism', in Vasudha Dalmia and H. von Stietencron (eds), *Representing Hinduism: The Construction of Religious Traditions and National Identity*, New Delhi: Oxford University Press, forthcoming.

rights of a great nation in the most essential point of civil liberty, the preservation of its own laws' fitting in a strategy to 'found the authority of the British government in Bengal on its ancient laws'. Nevertheless, the policy thus introduced, and since confirmed by a catena of statutory enactments, has proved to be double-edged. While it did fend off the wholesale imposition of foreign laws, its simplistic dichotomy inevitably has helped in course of time to create a perception of India as a country not so much '*a* great nation'—composed perhaps of a multiplicity of communities, languages, religions, peoples—but rather of *two* principal and compact socio-religious bodies, two *qaums* or nations. Conversely, when the demand for a uniform civil code was raised in the Indian Constituent Assembly, its supporters maintained: 'One of the factors that has kept India back from advancing to nationhood has been the existence of personal laws based on religion which keep the nation divided into watertight compartments in many aspects of life.'

PERSONAL LAW IN MUSLIM POLITICS

The political aspect of the diversity of personal laws has come out most prominently in the separatist propaganda of the Pakistan movement. From its founding manifesto by Rahmat Ali we find the claim to a separate Muslim nationhood supported by a reference to diversity of culture and laws:

> Our religion, culture, history, economic system, laws of inheritance, succession and marriage are basically and fundamentally different from those of the people living in the rest of India. . . . These differences are not confined to the broad basic principles—far from it. They extend to the minutest details of our lives. We do not inter-dine; we do not intermarry. . . .

This statement with its clear allusion to Hastings' formula has subsequently been repeated and rephrased a number of times, usually with a more generalized reference to the heterogeneity of laws. Thus the Joint Committee of the British Parliament considering the proposals for Indian constitutional reform in 1933–4 have this to say in their report: British India

> is inhabited by many races and tribes . . . often as distinct from one another in origin, tradition and manner of life as are the nations of Europe. Two-thirds of its inhabitants profess Hinduism in one form or another as their religion; over 77,000 000 are followers of Islam; and the difference between the two is not only one of religion in the stricter sense, but also of law and of culture. They may be said indeed to represent two distinct and separate civilisations.

This passage was later quoted by M.A. Jinnah in his article on the 'Indian Constitutional Question' published in *Time and Tide* of 19 January 1940, preluding the Muslim League's Lahore Resolution of March 1940. In a condensed paraphrase duplicating the quotation Jinnah finally draws the conclusion that Hinduism and Islam, as they represent 'two distinct and separate civilisations' . . . 'are in fact two different nations'.

Another rendering of the idea may be found in the petition by Aligarh scholars on 15 November 1939 which served as the source of Jinnah's presidential address at the Lahore session 1940: 'That the Hindus and Muslims belong to two different cultures, they have totally different religious philosophies, social customs, laws and literature. They neither inter-marry or interdine together and, indeed, belong to two different civilizations . . .' As late as 1972 it is echoed by Z.A. Bhutto in his interview with Oriana Fallaci:

> We are not brothers. We never have been. Our religions go too deep into our souls, into our way of life. Our cultures are different, our attitudes are different. From the day they are born to the day they die, a Hindu and a Muslim are subject to laws and customs that have no points of contact.

But even apart from such standard phraseology of the Two Nations Theory, Muslim concern with preservation of their personal law has always been politically prominent. It was asserted in the demands for constitutional protection of personal law in an All-India federation or in the Muslim Personal Law (Shariat) Application Act, 1937. In a recent study the basic attitude is described as 'Muslim perceptions of society as fundamentally heterogenous and immune to a system of common legislation for Muslims and non-Muslim'.

All this is, in principle, well known and has quite naturally been in the foreground of political attention. Less often it is realized that the adoption of 'personal law' as state law has had effects of a political nature on Hinduism as well. This latter aspect shall be the subject of the following discussion. It may be viewed, incidentally, as the primary aspect already in the reform of 1772, if we consider the operative change brought about by the new disposition: the elevation of Hindu laws to a status of parity with Muslim laws in the legal order of the emerging new state. The Mughal empire had tolerated the settlement of civil disputes among Hindus according to their own laws and customs through their unofficial panchayats or elders. But this did not imply recognition as law so much as rather a policy of non-interference. In the ruler's official courts Muslim law only was applied as being the law of the land. Against the new status given to

Hindu laws the Naib Diwan of Bengal province, Reza Khan, formally protested to the governor and his council.

Caste Integration in Hindu Law

The aspect of Hindu nationalism in Hindu law reform was unobtrusive at first. Legal reforms in matters of personal law broadly fell into the category of social reform. With its background of religious reform, social reform was perceived, as public debate developed, more and more as distinct from and in some respects almost antithetical to political reform. This very distinction, however, grew out of the peculiar condition of India, and was in itself a political phenomenon of primary significance. Indian society was prestructured in separate blocks by virtue of religious traditions, laws and customs. Social reform movements, therefore, almost inevitably tended to proceed within these socio-religious segments prompted by, and reacting on, the peculiarities of their respective institutions. The divisions of personal laws once established thus came to perpetuate and further entrench themselves.

When the newly founded Indian National Congress in its first sessions decided not 'to meddle' with questions of social reform it did so out of apprehensions that such social reform issues might prove to be too divisive. In effect, however, this meant avoiding the main issues of national integration, concentrating instead on superficial unity of 'political' purpose and leaving the great tasks of social regeneration to the religious compartments of society. The resulting tendency of tackling reform issues as internal matters of the communities—a term more and more understood, significantly, as denoting religious communities in the first instance— became fateful even for social reform movements which were originally motivated by broader 'national' concerns, such as Ranade's National Social Conference. Irrespective of the equivocal nation concept in reality the formation of national communities rooted in deeper layers of social structure took shape along religious lines, bound one day to tear asunder the veil of a purely political nation.

For the Hindu part of Indian society the very community basis of nationalism was problematical in view of the fragmentation into caste groups. Caste reform, therefore, became one of the foremost concerns of social reform not merely for humanitarian but also for political reasons. The political dimension was noted from the beginning. Rammohan Roy wrote in 1828 that 'the present system of religion adhered to by the Hindus is not well calculated to promote their political interest. The distinction of castes, introducing innumerable divisions and subdivisions among them has entirely deprived them of patriotic feeling. . .'. More radically, a Christian convert like K.M. Banerjea squarely put the blame for India's subjugation on the caste system: 'A people divided and sub-divided like the Hindus, can never make head against any power that deserves the name. This assessment was shared on the Muslim side, and Muslim leaders did not fail, in the developing rift between the communities, to point to the weak spot. Sir Syed Ahmed Khan, for instance, in his polemics against the Indian National Congress rubs it in: 'Is it supposed that the different castes and creeds living in India belong to one nation . . .'? And conversely, in a menacing tone: 'The Muslims are in a minority, but they are a highly united minority. At least traditionally they are prone to take the sword in hand when the majority oppresses them. The theme is fully developed as late as 1930 by Iqbal in his famous Allahabad address, when he dwells on the comparative homogeneity of the Muslim people in India: 'Indeed the Muslims of India are the only Indian people who can fitly be described as a nation in the modem sense of the word.' The Hindus, in comparison, are far less homogeneous; 'the process of becoming a nation . . . in the case of Hindu India involves a complete overhauling of her social structure.'

Quite naturally therefore, in the efforts at such 'complete overhauling' with a view to making Hinduism a nation-like, corporate entity, the caste issue figured prominently. There were theoretical endeavours to reduce the problem by reducing the number of castes to the classical four varna, re-interpreting, at the same time, the system as a mere division of functions without hierarchical meaning; Dayananda Saraswati, Vivekananda, and later also Gandhi, with somewhat misplaced sophistication, engaged in such apologetic exercises. Active reformers criticized such positions as being too compromising. There had been earlier practical, and more radical attempts at breaking down caste barriers by inter-caste marriages. The Brahmo Samaj took the lead, followed in a later context by the Arya Samaj. Both left their marks on the statute book. For in order to remove the restrictions of Hindu law against inter-caste unions legislation was required. A first initiative by the Brahmo reform movement led to the passing of the Special Marriage Act, 1872, often referred to as the Brahmo Samaj Marriage Act. As finally adopted, this was neither a truly secular, civil marriage law nor a measure of Hindu law reform, since its application presupposed a formal disclaimer of adherence to the Hindu or, for that matter, any other religion traditionally known in India. For the Hindus specifically, the then law member in the Governor General's council,

Sir Fitzjames Stephen, had lectured in typical Tory fashion about this requirement of disowning one's religion when contracting a civil marriage, about the necessity to choose between being a Hindu or not—one thing or the other: 'Leave your *law and religion*, if you please, but do not play fast and loose with your *law and religion*.' In other words: loosening the bonds between religious groupings and family laws was not in the British interest. Hindu reformers thought otherwise and after two unsuccessful attempts in 1911 and 1918 finally secured an amendment in 1923 which permitted Hindus (and adherents of related religions generally subject to Hindu law) to marry under the Special Marriage Act without renouncing their religion. This clearly was a step, if a modest one, towards Hindu communal unity, creating an opening for social integration among the segments of the Hindu community, and only among them. It was odious to Hindu traditionalists who considered it as 'varnashankarism', but the Bill in the words of its mover Sir Hari Singh Gour, 'would be of great political advantage for the Hindus'.

RECLAIMING THE 'UNTOUCHABLES'

In view of the foregoing an interesting exchange before the Simon Commission in 1928 may be noted in which Sir Hari Singh Gour tried to elicit a statement from the untouchable leader Dr Ambedkar to the effect that the untouchables were not 'outside the pale of Hinduism'; in support he pointed to the advantages which the untouchables could derive from the Special Marriage Act, 1923, for inter-caste marriage, provided they were classed as Hindus. Indeed the position of the untouchable castes, or so-called depressed classes, turned out to be the crucial and most sensitive issue of Hindu national integration. Earlier efforts by Hindu reformers to work for the betterment of their condition owed a great deal to a sense of religious rivalry and shame stirred by Christian missionary activities among these sections. Later with the growth of political Hindu revivalism and with the prospect of political reforms introducing elective principles the problem took on political significance in the context of communal representation. There was a natural apprehension that these numerous and hitherto suppressed classes might look for political support from outside Hinduism and might not be counted, under the new numerical rules of political grammar, as part of the Hindu community. The Arya Samaj first turned its attention to the task of 'winning back' these neglected and estranged classes to Hinduism, just as it undertook to reconvert Christian

and Muslim converts to Hinduism in the 'purification' or *shuddhi* movement. From the turn of the twentieth century Arya samajists began to
'purify' low-caste and untouchable groups in the Punjab and to admit
them into the Arya Samaj on the level of twice-born caste status, according to Hindu social ranking. Significantly, this led to immediate dissension
with the Sikh reformist Singh Sabhas with whom the Arya Samaj had
initially cooperated. The Sikhs feared that 'their' untouchables were lured
away from Sikhism and converted into the Hindu fold. The seeds of Sikh
separatism were sown in these years.

The Arya Samaj persevered in its efforts which gathered momentum
under the leadership of such national figures as Lala Lajpat Rai and Munshi Ram, the later Swami Shraddhanand. In 1909 the All India Shuddhi
Sabha was established. The connotations of aggressive Hindu nation
building were unmistakable. It is interesting to observe how the 're-
clamation' of low-caste Hindus prompted attention to inter-caste community, and again, inter-caste marriage in general. From 1922 this was made
a major plank by the Arya Samaj. Bhai Parmanand. In 1937, a Central Act
was secured validating inter-caste marriages by Aryas; in contrast to the
earlier Brahmo Marriage Act, or Special Marriage Act of 1872, this law
shows no collateral interest in social reform issues as monogamy or raising
the marriage age, but is simply concerned with legalizing inter-caste or
even inter-religious unions within the context of the new Arya-Hindu
community.

The shuddhi approach to the problem of the depressed classes was, in
substance, not a peculiarity of the Arya Samaj. Most important, Gandhi's
attitude was fundamentally similar though with characteristic inversion:
in his view it was Hinduism and particularly its upper castes, rather than
the untouchables, which had to be purified by removing the 'blot' or 'sin'
of untouchability. This perception of the problem as 'an essentially Hindu
question' proved to be of great consequence. Gandhi's attitude, whether
in times of his formal position as a Congress leader or in his later independent Harijan campaign, was influential with the Congress and had its
more or less official backing. When in 1931 at the Round Table Conference in London he announced his resolve 'to resist with (his) life' the
introduction of separate electorates for the untouchables he did this as the
sole and authorized representative of the Indian National Congress—
though he took care to specify that in this matter he was speaking 'not
merely on behalf of the Congress' but also on his own behalf'. This and
the following actions—his Poona fast against the Communal Award in
1932 and his subsequent Harijan campaign proceeded upon the basic
assumption that the task essentially was re-integration of the untouchables

into Hindu society. The evil apprehended from separate electorates, in particular, was 'vivisection' of Hinduism rather than of the Indian nation. The untouchables' emancipation as citizens, irrespective of religion, was implicitly relegated to a secondary position, possibly envisaged as a by-product but clearly subordinated to the primary religious concern. The very name 'Harijan'—*lit.* man, devotee of God (i.e., the Hindu god Vishnu or Hari)—a term borrowed by Gandhi from a Gujarati bhakti poet and introduced as a generic designation for all untouchables bears testimony to this religious approach. Equally significant is the prominence given to the campaign for opening Hindu temples for the untouchables. If Gandhi described the whole anti-untouchability movement as 'essentially religious', he was not merely acting under the constraints of his prison or release terms prohibiting him from direct political activity; the very political implications of his campaign which he reluctantly owned were in themselves also of religious significance, since the objective was the saving of Hinduism or, more practically, the creation of an integrated Hindu' society.

Undoubtedly untouchability originally has been a phenomenon of Hindu society. But it is one thing to recognize Hindu notions of ritual impurity as the root cause of the peculiar social degradation suffered by the untouchables, but quite a different matter to insist that redress is only to be had *within* Hinduism and to prescribe, as sole remedy for a social disease produced by Hinduism, a closer integration with a Hindu society which can only be hoped to be reformed in the process. While Gandhi's religious attack on the taboos defining untouchability may have been a promising and even indispensable strategy to alleviate the social pressures on the untouchable castes, as it were, from within, the message of a truly national Indian Congress had to be a different one: that irrespective of their religious affiliation and irrespective of the hoped-for egalitarian sea change of Hinduism these classes were to be assured equal status in the political context of the Indian nation and its civil society. Such a secular, political alternative is not an ex-post construct, advanced with the benefit of hindsight and in disregard of actual historical options. It was, on the contrary, postulated in express terms by the untouchables' organizations and especially argued by the untouchable leader B.R. Ambedkar. Ambedkar insisted that the untouchables were interested not so much in religious reforms such as temple entry, but in political power and political safe-guards for their civic rights, and above all, in the recognition as a separate element in the national life of India (separate, that is, from Hindus), en-titled to independent representation. The gist of Gandhi's endeavours, on the contrary, was to prevent such an independent position from emerging, in order to forestall alliances of an autonomous untouchable group with non-Hindu groups and to work for their national integration via their primary integration into the Hindu socio-religious body. This, in all clarity, was the issue in the Poona confrontation of 1932 and its aftermath.

Later, through his prominent role in framing the Indian Constitution, Ambedkar was able to vindicate some of his claims for special constitutional rights of the untouchables or, with the technical legal term, scheduled castes. But the influence of Hindu nationalism has left questionable traits in the legal regime. The dogma that untouchables are, and have to remain, Hindus was incorporated into the presidential order defining and enumerating the scheduled castes: '. . . no person who professes a religion different from the Hindu religion shall be deemed to be a member of a Scheduled Caste'.

The Hindu Code

The main direction of the codification is towards the twin goals of unification of the Hindu community and uniformity of its personal law. It seeks to do away with all legal divisions of castes and corresponding distinctions of legal rules. But it also abolishes the derogatory effect of customs which in Anglo–Hindu Law had been recognized in principle albeit hedged in by procedural requirements of proof. The Acts of 1955–6 take overriding effect over customs and usages unless express reservations are made by specific provisions for customary variation, such as, for instance, customary rites and ceremonies for a Hindu marriage. In the result the reform, as far as it goes, completes the transformation of Hindu Law begun under the British administration from a complex and flexible framework providing some coherence and interconnection between a multitude of communities governed by their own customary laws to uniform law uniting one great legal community. The boundaries of this community are marked by the definition of 'Hindu' contained in the statutes.

The change appears most clearly in the Hindu Marriage Act. For the first time it introduces a uniform matrimonial system for all castes and classes of Hindus, namely monogamy coupled with the possibility of judicial divorce. There are no caste barriers anymore for the selection of spouses. But the removal of caste restrictions also implies that objections against inter-religious marriages are now removed within the sphere demarcated by the broad statutory definition of 'Hindu'. A Hindu thus may marry a Buddhist, Jaina, or Sikh, but cannot marry a Christian or

Muslim under the Act. A later conversion by one of the 'Hindu' spouses to another religion within the range of 'Hindu'-ness (e.g., of a Hindu to Buddhism or vice-versa would have no effect on the matrimonial tie, whereas conversion to an alien religion would be a ground for divorce.

Other provisions even more clearly show the character of being a sanction against leaving the statutory 'Hindu' community. All claims of maintenance under the Hindu Adoptions and Maintenance Act, 1956—by spouses, children, parents, etc.—are lost upon conversion to a non-Hindu' religion. A wife who may on various grounds have a right to sepa rate residence and maintenance from her husband looses both 'if she is unchaste or ceases to be a Hindu by conversion to another religion'— a truly remarkable juxtaposition of ground. A parent loses the natural guardianship of a Hindu minor, if he or she has ceased to be a Hindu.

It may be logical that under the Hindu Adoptions and Maintenance Act only Hindus may adopt; the restriction of the capacity to be adopted to Hindus is less plausible in view of the extended definition of 'Hindu'. It is, however strange that a married Hindu should not need the consent of his spouse to either adopt or give in adoption a common child, if the spouse 'has ceased to be a Hindu'. The children of a former Hindu born after his conversion 'to another religion' are disqualified from inheriting property from their Hindu relatives; for the case of their reconversion the law offers the premium of lifting the disqualification.

The constitutional validity of all these provisions is very doubtful in view of Articles 15 and 25. The point to be made here is, however, that all legal disabilities attached to the fact of conversion do not arise in the case of conversion between Hindu religion proper, Jainism, Sikhism, or Buddhism. The concern of the law is exclusively directed to conversion from one of these native religions to 'alien' religions like Christianity, Islam, Judaism, or Zoroastrianism. This is obvious religion-based discrimination, very questionable in a secular state. What the law does is to create a privileged position for indigenous religions forming a community the members of which are known by the artificially expanded designation 'Hindu'—a kind of religious 'son of the soil'. This seemingly technical terminology is in striking correspondence to the famous definition of 'Hindutva' by V.D. Savarkar. Nor is the affinity accidental. In its conse-quence modern Hindu law is creating something which traditional Hinduism has never been: one single territorially based community welded together to a coherent socio-religious body by unity of status and *connubium* (as one *jati*, to use Savarkar's term), by uniformity of laws overriding particular customs and by legal sanctions against withdrawal.

The unitarian legal concept seems even to engender attempts at defining a religious unity. Contours of the latter appear in certain *dicta* by Indian courts, for instance in Chief Justice Gajendragadkar's definition of Hinduism in the so-called Satsangi case where he outlines certain common fundamentals of 'the Hindu religion' expressly referring to the broad inclusive definition of 'Hindu' in the Constitution (Art. 25) and the Hindu Code Acts.

CONSTITUTIONAL ASPECTS

The enactment of the 'Hindu Code' is generally reckoned as a major achievement of the first Parliament elected under the Indian Constitution. But this should not obscure the fact that its roots, as we have seen, go far back in the days of British rule. The first actual moves for a comprehensive codification were made after difficulties experienced with the Hindu Women's Rights to Property Act 1937, leading to the appointment of a Hindu Law Committee (Rau Committee) by the Government of (British) India in 1941 and, eventually, to the introduction of the Hindu Code Bill in the Central Legislative Assembly in April 1947. With its origin clearly antedating the Constitution and even independence the great legislative venture can hardly be conceived, as is often done, as a step towards implementing the constitutional directive for a uniform civil code. This is more or less an afterthought, apologetical or optimistically misconstruing the historical forces at work. The codification of Hindu personal law rather belongs to the line of separate social reform within the communities. A parallel development on the Muslim side had earlier taken shape with the passing of the Muslim Personal Law (Shariat) Application Act, 1937. Its stated motivation showed the same characteristic mixture of communal consolidation and social reform: establishing the primacy of canonical Islamic law and thus its uniformity over variations of local (frequently Hindu) custom, and at the same time reintroducing the more liberal Islamic rules of female inheritance in derogation of such customs. A similar admixture of the political has to be noted in the accompanying piece of social reform legislation, the Dissolution of Muslim Marriages Act, 1939, giving rights of unilateral divorce to Muslim women. Whatever the relative weight of orthodox unification and social reform, it is ironic to see reforming efforts aimed at improving women's rights in parallel on both sides of the communal divide in the same year 1937 which also witnessed the definitive turn towards political separation. One is tempted to recall the statement by the supposed pioneer of Muslim separatism. Sir Syed

Ahmad Khan, that it was social questions on which Hindus and 'Mahomedans' could unite and ought to unite. But by 1937 separate social reform had become inextricably interwoven with divisive tendencies emphasizing intra-communal consolidation. One may ponder over the fact that the first Parliament of independent secular India used its newly acquired authority to take a further step in that fateful tradition, and to enact a comprehensive measure of such separate reform, with the result of one-sided consolidation of the majority community.

The result of these developments, in any case, is politically unfortunate. The two major communities have unified their laws of personal and family status, have removed internal differentiation as well as areas of overlapping and mediating customs. They now stand side by side as solidified blocs as far as legal regimes are concerned. A somehow concerted development towards common goals has not taken place, the differences having become more accentuated rather than diminished. One might raise a general objection that statutory reforms of the kind described do not practically reach the majority of the population and their real significance accordingly is not as great as it might appear on paper. But this view would dangerously underestimate the long-term consequences of the structural changes initiated. The overall direction of these changes is transfer of the reference for collective self-identification from the intermediate customary group to the largest encompassing religious community, or religious 'nation'. Such changes resulting from statutory innovations will not surface overnight, but are bound in the long run to influence the pattern of social relations profoundly and lastingly. If the realization of personal law reform is seen as a slow but steady movement, present signs seem to point the direction of further cleavage between the religious communities. This tendency is potentially explosive.

Nor does the present dispensation stand on firm ground in terms of constitutional principles. There is a fundamental contradiction in a secular state's forcing upon its citizens a mandatory disjunction of personal laws based on differences of religion. Put in more legal terms: it is doubtful whether the binding adscription of personal law regimes according to religion can permanently survive attacks based on the constitutional guarantee against religious discrimination (Art. 15, Cl. 1).

This basic question—whether the system of different personal laws for the religious community can as such be accepted as constitutional— seems never to have directly been brought before the courts. Constitutional complaints have in a number of cases been raised against recent legislative changes in Hindu law. The principal target has been the introduction of monogamy as the only legal form of marriage for Hindus, and the corresponding punishment of Hindus for bigamy. This was challenged as religious discrimination in view of the continuing freedom for Muslims legally to marry more than one wife.

In all cases the complaints have been rejected by the high courts involved. The arguments used to achieve the result were mainly three:

(a) The word 'discriminate' in Art. 15 (1) was interpreted to mean an adverse, individuous distinction only. Introduction of strict monogamy in Hindu law was then qualified as a progressive measure of social reform beneficial to the community concerned. Punishment for bigamy, being but incidental to this generally beneficial reform, could not be attacked as discrimatory.

(b) In order to fall under Art. 15(1) discrimination must be based on grounds *only* of religion, etc. The legislative changes in Hindu law were not based on a religious classification alone but also on the pre-existence of complex bodies of personal law corresponding to the differing social traditions and perceptions of the communitites. These pre-existing socio-legal systems are implicitly recognized by the constitutional directive to introduce a uniform civil code *in the future*; they may therefore be taken into account as an additional basis of classification. In particular, the legislature could enact social reforms in stages considering the differences of development and acceptance of reform in different communities.

(c) In addition, the Bombay High Court ventured a third and very far-reaching line of reasoning. According to this view, uncodified personal law are not subject to the fundamental rights chapter of the Constitution at all. This is concluded from the omission of the expression 'personal law' in a clarificatory clause defining the extent of 'law' to be affected by fundamental right's part by expressly including certain kinds of sub-statutory laws. This interpretation would lead to the unlikely result that personal law, so far as it is in statutory or customary form, is to be subject to fundamental rights, while the generalized personal law taken from the old scriptures is exempt—unless, of course, modified by statute or custom. With great respect, the Court seems to have overlooked the fact that legal validity is imparted to the old personal laws by the statutes providing for their applicability in certain matters—from Bengal Regulation II/11772 and the later Civil Court Acts to the Muslim Personal Law (Shariat) Application Act, 1937. It is this statutory law and its blanket references to the old sources which have become subject to the fundamental rights and, to the extent of inconsistency , void.

The last-mentioned doctrine advanced, somewhat hesitatingly, by the Bombay High Court has been discussed here mainly because it seems to have encouraged, though in an unacknowledged manner, a tendency of the courts to consider the personal laws as per se exempt from the impact of fundamental rights. Statements to this effect have been made by the Supreme Court in a case concerning uncodified Hindu law and, with respect even to statutory Hindu law, by the Delhi High Court. Both statements are, strictly speaking, obiter dicta, not required for the decision of the cases in question and rather unsupported by legal reasoning. It is submitted that they have no basis in the Constitution and ought to be retracted at the earliest opportunity. They create a dangerous lacuna in constitutional legitimacy by telling the citizen—that is, in most cases the female citizen—that in some of the most important and vital aspects of life he or she is not protected by the constitutional guarantees of fundamental rights but is left to be governed by the unbridled orthodoxy of past times.

We may then come back to grounds (a) and (b) which have come to be taken as generally accepted, or rather, have not been subjected to closer scrutiny. I would, however, maintain that these grounds also suffer from serious infirmities.

(a) To interpret 'discrimination' as adverse or invidious distinction only, is certainly a possible, but not the only possible reading. Courts have not been consistent in this and also sometimes applied the wider meaning ('any differentiation'). It is indeed somewhat disconcerting to find the very same bench of the Bombay High Court who decided Narasu Appa's case only half a year later striking down a land acquisition scheme in *favour* of Harijans as a forbidden caste discrimination under Art. 15. The inherent difficulty is that discrimination in favour of someone in most cases involves discrimination *against* another: the difference then dissolves into a question of *standing*: who is entitled to complain? Furthermore, the difference between adverse and beneficial discrimination will often be a matter of subjective judgment. The cases under discussion are telling examples for this. To a man sentenced to jail under a discriminatory law it is cold comfort bordering on the cynical to be told that this discrimination is really to his benefit because it qualifies as a measure of social reform. The concept of social reform taken, as a legal term, from Art. 25 has no independent validating force in the context of Art. 15: if the effect of a law is discriminatory, the object of the law, however laudable, will not obviate the constitutional prohibition. In sum, if put to test in concrete cases of differential treatment the adverse/beneficial dichotomy will not prove much of a shield for religious discrimination in the administration of personal laws.

(b) The argument that discrimination in personal laws is not based on grounds of religion *only*, therefore, assumes crucial importance. But is the pre-existence of different systems of personal law in the great communities a social fact independent of religion? It is elementary that religion has always been at the core of the distinction of personal laws. As noted in the beginning of this essay, the British reluctance to interfere with native religious usages was the determining factor in introducing the system. Its ambit was again determined by its supposed affinity to religious convictions. Legal reform in these areas was always resisted by orthodox opinion in the respective community as an attack on religion. If there had remained any doubt as to these basic sentiments the religious agitation against the *Shah Bano* judgment of the Supreme Court ought to have dispelled it. Moreover, the classification by which application of personal law is determined is entirely based on religion, and perhaps even more so today than before. It is no answer to say that Hindu law applies to many persons not professing the Hindu religion; because the additional classes included are again defined in religious terms (Jain, Sikhs, etc., or even 'any other person . . . who is *not* a Muslim, Christian, Parsi or Jew by religion). The whole argument then amounts to this: discrimination by a rule of personal law in a given case is not based on religion only, because it is part of a wider, systematic discrimination based on religion. The inherent weakness of such an argument hardly needs elaboration.

The most relevant constitutional ground, for a continuation of the regime of separate personal laws may be, paradoxically, the constitutionally expressed intention to abolish it. The Directive Principle enjoining the state 'to endeavour to secure for the citizens a uniform civil code' appears to militate against the notion of a wholesale, automatic abolition of the regime by force of Art. 15 (1). This has been noted in all the judgments discussed and been interpreted as indicating the Constitution makers' intention to reserve this matter to the legislature. There are, of course, overwhelming practical grounds recommending such a solution as against the chaotical consequences of a *tabula rasa* created by a sudden judicial verdict. The interpretation is reinforced by the history of Art. 44: the original motion had been for a fundamental right to a uniform civil code; this was deliberately changed to a directive principle by the Constituent Assembly, thus excluding automatic enforcement by the courts. The legal construction, nevertheless, presents difficulties. A directive principle cannot abrogate the enforceable right under Art. 15 (1), but can only be used as a means of interpretation. The interpretation of Art. 15 with the help of Art. 44 can hardly lead to the result assumed by the Bombay High Court, namely that uncodified personal law is totally exempted from the impact of Art. 15, e.g., also with respect to specific instances of sex, or caste-based discrimination. Art. 44 is solely concerned with the wholesale replacement of personal laws by a unified code. It could only be invoked to support an interpretation that pending preparation of such code the courts are not supposed to effect virtual advance enforcement of the code by application of Art. 15(1): discrimination by temporary continued enforcement of personal laws could be said to be based *not only* on religion, but on the additional ground of a constitutional mandate to await enactment of the civil code. Such an interpretation is not without strains, but has the advantage of reflecting the real pragmatical constraints involved. It must be evident, however, that it looses some of its force with every year the constitutional mandate remains unfulfilled. The constitutional time, in other words, as granted by Art. 44, is running out.

This brings us face to face with the earnest of the constitutional directive for a code, if at all it is to be taken seriously rather than a mere *alibi* for doing nothing. It also brings to mind the tremendous political difficulties. It is well known that the Muslim community would regard the imposition of a civil code as an attack on their religion, and it may be that a total obliteration of the Muslim personal law would amount to a violation of their religious liberty in suppressing religious practices considered essential by their religion. The acceptance of the Hindu community is by no means to be taken for granted, in view of the difficulties experienced in enacting the reform legislation of 1955–6, and of the effective resistance against abolition of the *Mitakshara* joint family. A further argument has lately been advanced: according to this view personal laws are part of the 'culture' guaranteed to any section of citizens by Art. 29 (1) and are not, therefore, at the free disposal of the legislature. While this argument would not seem to be valid against limited statutory reforms in view of the express powers reserved for such reforms in Art. 25 it is not without force if it comes to a total abrogation of personal law systems intrinsically interwoven with the communities' way of life.

The arguments from religious freedom and freedom to preserve one's culture, therefore, have to be taken seriously from the legal point of view apart from political considerations. But it must not be overlooked that all such arguments are arguments based on fundamental rights: they presuppose an act of personal choice to avail oneself of such rights. They cannot come in the way of optional systems. Enforcement of personal laws as such has not been guaranteed by the Constitution. This is one, and perhaps the primary, proposition to be deduced from Art. 44, and it represents, as any student of constitutional history knows, a deliberate decision taken by the Constitution makers in the face of repeated Muslim demands for such a guarantee. It follows that there is no constitutional obstacle to making the application of personal laws voluntary. On the contrary the present system of forcing personal law on the members of the respective communities is open to grave constitutional doubts, under aspects of equality as well as religious freedom itself. In particular the religious communities as such have no constitutional mandate to exercise authority over their individual members in this matter. There is no reason why the concurrence of traditional and self-appointed community leaders should be required even for reforms of an enabling character. The reference to 'section of citizens' in Art. 2 cannot be interpreted in this way unless the whole system of individual fundamental rights is to be subverted by collective guarantees. On the contrary the aim should be to reverse the trend towards communal consolidation which today is threatening to disrupt the Indian nation, and to give more leeway to individual choice.

The way out of the constitutional tangle would then seem to be the introduction of some kind of optional system. Suggestions for an optional civil code have often been made. A detailed review of this discussion is impossible here. Obviously there are two main alternatives. First, the more traditional model, would require a positive option to come under the regime of the general code. In support of this solution it could be said that an important part of such a code is already in existence, namely the Special Marriage Act, 1954. At the same time, experience gathered with the application of this Act seems to indicate that the practical impact of such optional code would be marginal since such an option would require a distinct active sophistication ready to venture what to most common people might appear as a leap into the dark. The second alternative would appear to be more in tune with the Constitution: a uniform civil code generally to apply as a matter of course, unless there is an express option of a person (or for that matter, of a couple contracting a marriage) to come under one's personal law either generally or in certain matters. For this also there is a precedent in the optional clause of the Muslim Personal Law (Shariat) Application Act, 1937. Here the choice would be a conscientious exercise of religious freedom or a conscientious judgment how far one considers the personal law to be an essential part of one's religion and way of life. It would moreover be a decision for the well-known and traditional and, therefore, more easy to take. Again, details cannot be discussed or worked out here. It may also be a sound policy to begin with introduction of the first alternative and switch over to the second at a later state.

CONCLUSION

In the present context I may confine myself to three concluding observations:

(a) The element of individual choice would remove the constitutional objections against the personal laws as presently applied. Differential treatment would then no longer be based on grounds only of religion, but on the additional fact of a deliberate option by the person concerned.

(b) This might also go a long way answering constitutional objections against particular rules of personal laws in their present condition—and may, paradoxically, save some of these laws from being 'reformed out of existence or identity. In the context of compulsory application many details of the personal laws are not likely to survive constitutional review on length. The position of women in particular under some of these laws is untenable if measured by human rights' standards; and constitutional scrutiny will one day have to begin in earnest. The only constitutional way to save some of the peculiarities of the traditional laws for people cherishing them as essential for their personal philosophy of life may well be to require an act of personal submission and, thereby, individual legitimation for the enforcement of these laws.

(c) The main political decision which will have to be made, however, is whether the present trend towards ever more rigid compartmentalization of Indian society in terms of its religious groups, is to be stopped or even reversed. The dangerous potential of this in-depth drift towards a religious line-up is becoming visible today. It is no accident that Sikh separatists have lately raised the demand for a personal law of their own. What some minority leaders do not seem to see is the increasing marginalization of their communities including their personal law by the legal consolidation of the majority community—legal Hindutva, as it were. It would seem to be in the interest, not last, of minorities, if some more open legal space for choices of common personal and civic status was created. Finally, Hinduism, as a religion or as an ensemble of religions, would stand to benefit by being relieved of the function to serve 'as a uniting principle' in law as well as in 'generating true national feeling'.

12

The Shah Bano Case: Some Political Implications*

KAVITA R. KHORY

INTRODUCTION

In April 1985, the Supreme Court of India ruled that under Section 125
of the Criminal Code, Ahmed Khan, a Muslim from Indore in Madhya
Pradesh, was required to pay maintenance to his former wife, Shah Bano.
This seemingly innocuous event generated tremendous controversy and
hostility amongst the Muslims in India and raised fundamental questions
about the nature of Indian politics. Almost immediately, the Congress
party government as well as other political parties and a wide range of
social and political organizations in India were embroiled in the ensuing
debate on key issues encompassing religion, law, and politics.

This essay examines the linkage between religion and politics in India
as exemplified by the Shah Bano case. It should be noted at the outset that
the Shah Bano case is by no means a unique example of the nexus between
religion and politics in South Asia. Historically religion has played a central role in the politics of the region. While the partition of India and the
creation of Pakistan on the basis of Islam in 1947 is the most critical example of this phenomenon, the significance of religion in the political arena
did not end with the division of the subcontinent. In fact, it raised a new
set of questions regarding the role of religion in Pakistan and India's
political systems. While Pakistan continues to debate the role of Islam in
defining its social, economic, legal, and political structures, it appears that
the Indian state is also far from resolving the apparent conflict between

*Excerpted from Kavita R. Khory, 'The Shah Bano Case: Some Political Impli-
cations', in Robert D. Baird (ed.), *Religion and Law in Independent India*, New
Delhi: Manohar, 1993, pp. 121–37.

aspirations of religious communities and the secular notion of the Indian polity. Although there are obvious and significant differences between India and Pakistan's religious concerns and their management, it is clear that religion remains a contentious issue in the politics of both countries.

Issues of caste and religion are at the forefront of contemporary Indian politics. While one cannot deny the continued salience of religious issues and symbolism after 1947, India in the 1990s seems to be confronting a renewed and more powerful politicization of religion. The more conspicuous examples of religious and caste conflict in recent times include the Babari Masjid–Ram Janmabhoomi dispute in Ayodhya, the controversy over the Mandal Commission report that played a large part in bringing down V.P Singh's government in November 1990, and the so-called Hindu militancy or revivalism in some parts of India.

While important in its own right the Shah Bano case provides us with an excellent vehicle for examining the broader trends in Indian politics that are signified by these events; First, it forces us to re-evaluate the continued salience of religious identity in the political arena. Second, it raises a series of questions regarding the rights of minority groups, whether ethnic, linguistic, or religious, within a democratic system. Third, and perhaps most importantly, the Shah Bano case has revived the debate over defining secularism in the Indian context, particularly in the way it guides state policy towards the demands of religious communities. Lastly, the case has brought to the forefront lingering antagonisms, common misperceptions and a pervasive sense of insecurity shared by both Muslims and Hindus in India. The Shah Bano case is particularly useful for examining relations between the two communities, as well as the related and much discussed, but vaguely defined phenomenon, described variously as Hindu 'fundamentalism', 'militancy', and even Hindu 'nationalism'.

Our discussion of the Shah Bano case is divided into two parts. First, a brief summary of the case is followed by an examination of the diverse responses to the judgment from within and outside the Muslim community. As we shall see, the judgment generated varied and often conflicting reactions amongst the Muslims, members of the government, the Congress party, and other political parties and organizations. I intend to explain why many Muslims vehemently opposed the Supreme Court's decision, as well as the government's initial decision to support it. Because the Shah Bano case led to renewed debate over replacing Muslim personal law with a common civil code, we shall examine the controversy regarding the continued use of Muslim personal law based on the Shariat. We are concerned mainly with the political dimensions of the issue rather than its legal ramifications

The second part of the essay focuses on the Congress government's attempts to contain the negative electoral implications rising from the Muslim community's opposition to the judgment. By implementing the Muslim Women's Bill, which, in effect, overturned the Supreme Court's earlier decision, the government hoped to stem some of the Muslim hostility. In doing so, however, the Congress generated considerable opposition amongst its own party members, moderate Muslims and women's groups, and the Hindu community at large, which had welcomed the judgment. What motivated Rajiv Gandhi's government to undertake such an action despite its initial support of the Supreme Court's decision? To answer this question, we focus in particular on the Muslim community's relationship with the Congress and the extent of its electoral influence. We need to consider whether the government was simply reacting to the immediate circumstances of the Shah Bano case, or was it guided by more complex and perhaps less obvious reasons.

Finally, we shall briefly explore the varied notions of secularism in India with reference to government policy on religious issues in general, and the Shah Bano case in particular. To what extent has the Indian state succeeded in managing, if not resolving, the conflict between the prerogatives of religious identity and the demands of an ostensibly secular polity?

Ahmed Khan, Shah Bano, and the Supreme Court

Although the Shah Bano case first assumed prominence in the Indian media in 1985, it originated in 1978 when Ahmed Khan of Indore in Madhya Pradesh divorced Shah Bano, to whom he had been married for forty-four years. Ahmed Khan returned Rs3,000 (about $300) which had been her *mehr* or marriage settlement from her family, as required by Islamic law. Rather than accept the settlement based on Islamic tenets, Shah Bano sued her former husband for maintenance under the Criminal Procedure Code of India. As a result of this appeal she was awarded Rs180 per month for maintenance purpose. The Shah Bano case gained national attention when Ahmed Khan appealed against this judgment to the Supreme Court of India on the basis that as a Muslim he had to obey the Shariat, which required only that he pay her maintenance or iddat, for three months. The Supreme Court upheld the Madhya Pradesh High Court's decision granting Shah Bano continued maintenance from Ahmed Khan. The Supreme Court ruled that under Section 125 of the Criminal Code a husband was required to pay maintenance to a wife without means of support.

While the Supreme Court decision in itself challenged the more conventional interpretations of Islamic law, Chief Justice Chandrachud's disparaging comments regarding the practice of Islamic law and the status of Muslim women further intensified Muslim opposition to the judgment. The Supreme Court gave not only its own interpretation of the Shariat but it also exhorted the government to implement a uniform civil code which would replace Muslim personal law. In his conclusion Justice Chandrachud stated

> It is also a matter of regret that Article 44 of our Constitution has remained a dead letter. It provides that 'The State shall endeavour to secure for the citizens a uniform civil code throughout the territory of India.'. . . A common civil code will help the cause of national integration by removing disparate loyalties to laws which have conflicting ideologies. . . . It is the state which is charged with the duty of securing a uniform civil code for the citizens of the country and, unquestionably, it has the legislative competence to do so.

The Supreme Court's decision was significant for the Muslim community in two respects. First, in formulating its judgment, the court made several disparate references to Islamic law and indicated that its decision to grant maintenance to Shah Bano was in accordance with the Shariat. In doing so, the court was essentially interpreting Islamic law, which drew considerable ire from the Muslim community, particularly members of the clergy, who argued that it was not only inappropriate for a secular court to interpret religious law but that it set a disturbing precedent whereby the Ulema's interpretations could be overruled by secular jurists. Second, Justice Chandrachud's appeal to introduce a uniform civil law in the country was viewed by the Muslims as a challenge to their continued practice of Islamic law in India as it pertains to issues of succession, inheritance, marriage, and divorce.

It was difficult for the Congress government to remain aloof from this controversial and much publicized decision, particularly in view of Justice Chandrachud's reference to Article 44 of the Constitution and the call for implementing a uniform civil code in India. What seemed to be a relatively trivial issue concerning the maintenance of a divorced Muslim woman became a national issue that polarized individuals, groups, political parties, and the government.

Muslim Reactions to the Judgment

We need to stress at the outset that the Muslim community was by no means completely united in its opposition to the Supreme Court judgment. While it appears that most Muslims responded in varying degrees against the Shah Bano decision, it would be incorrect to assume that all Muslims reacted similarly. Given that Muslims in India are deeply divided by linguistic, cultural, social, and regional differences, it is not improbable that they would react differently to the Shah Bano case as well. Therefore, we will also look at the responses of those Muslims, who were perhaps not as vocal, but nonetheless significant, in their support of the Supreme Court's decision.

Muslim reactions against the Supreme Court verdict ranged from numerous meetings and conferences organized by several Muslim groups, such as the Jamiate Ulema-e-Hind, the Jamia Millia Islamia, and the All-India Muslim Personal Law Board to mass protests in various regions of India, including Uttar Pradesh and Bihar, which have a significant Muslim population. The large-scale demonstrations against the judgment led to the common perception that most Muslims opposed the decision as well as any discussion of formulating a common civil code. The strongest attacks against the decision were voiced by the Muslim clergy, who believed that the Supreme Court's attempt at interpreting Muslim law directly challenged their authority. The clergy's prominence in leading the attack against the judgment was not entirely welcome by the more moderate segments of the community. For example, Shahid Siddiqui, editor of the leading Urdu weekly *Nai Duniya*, claimed: 'Every small-town maulana has become a leader now with narrow objectives and narrow interest. If the controversy is not resolved quickly, these people will take the community behind by two or three decades.' Regardless of how the more moderate elements amongst the Muslims viewed the clergy, it is clear that the Ulema's stance against the judgment was shared by a large number of Muslims. The Shah Bano case brought together disparate segments of the community, who could agree on little other than the claim that the Supreme Court's decision was a direct intervention in the fundamental religious rights of the Muslims in India.

Those Muslims who opposed the judgment argued that the Supreme Court's decision and its statement on the need to create a uniform civil code threatened their religious autonomy and their Islamic identity. Syed Shahbuddin, an aspirant for national leadership of the Muslim community and a Janata member of the Lok Sabha expressed this widely shared sentiment. 'Ours is not a communal fight. It only amounts to resisting the inexorable process of assimilation. We want to keep our religious identity at all costs.'

While the judgment itself was sufficient to rouse the Muslims, several other events heightened the community's sense of insecurity. Some of the more notable examples in this regard include the national Hindu reaction in 1981 to the local conversion of a few untouchables to Islam; the killing in Assarn of more than a thousand Muslims during the 1983 state elections; the terms of Rajiv Gandhi's settlement in 1985 of the Assam regional agitation, which deprived some Muslim immigrants of their citizenship and others of the right to vote for ten years; and lastly the reopening, by an order of the local court, of the Ram Janmabhoomi temple at Ayodhya in Uttar Pradesh, regarded by Hindus as the birthplace of Rama but claimed by local Muslims to be the Babari Masjid, a mosque reputedly built by the Mughal Emperor Babar. Taken in conjunction with the Sikh–Hindu confrontations in north India, many Muslims viewed these events as part of a larger pattern of Hindu revivalism and nationalism. Under these circumstances, the Muslim community's strong reaction against the judgment was not surprising.

Whereas religious and/or political challenges may evoke the strongest response amongst Indian Muslims, we cannot ignore the impact of economic concerns on the community's sense of well-being and security. It is argued that a large number of India's eighty million Muslims remain at a disadvantage in terms of literacy, education, and job and business opportunities. Although these problems are not restricted to the Muslims, they have heightened the perception that the community is isolated from the mainstream of national life. While economics does not entirely explain the politicization of religious identity, it is one of the more commonly used rallying points for mobilizing groups on the basis of religion, ethnicity, language, or regional affiliation in India and elsewhere. For the Muslims in India, the Shah Bano case reinforced the perception that their lack of economic development as a community inevitably weakened them in the national political arena. The implicit threat to the practice of Muslim law as manifested in the Supreme Court's decision was seen as an attempt to assimilate Muslims within the larger 'Hindu' culture and to deprive them of the autonomy to manage the personal affairs of the community members.

Although the more conservative elements amongst the Muslims seemed to dominate the community's response to the judgment, there were several individuals and groups, mainly members of women's organizations within the community, who supported the decision. For them the ruling was a significant step in their struggle against those who abused and misused Koranic laws to justify the exploitation of women. For example, Zoya Hasan, an active campaigner for reform and codification of Muslim personal law, argues that the varied and often conflicting interpretations of the Shariat provided by the Muslim clergy creates more confusion and leads to discrimination against women. While disagreeing with the common belief that the majority of Muslims, particularly women, are with the Ulema on the issue of maintenance, she claims that most of the Muslim women, particularly in the villages, are reluctant to speak out in favour of the decision. What is apparent, however, is that there is considerable ambivalence regarding the decision even amongst the educated, urban Muslim women. Although many women as well as liberal men in the community feel the need for formalizing Islamic personal law, they are not all in favour of establishing a common civil code.

THE GOVERNMENT'S RESPONSE

The government initially supported the Supreme Court's verdict in the Shah Bano case. Arif Khan, a Muslim and a minister of state expressed the government's position when he claimed that the Supreme Court had made a 'progressive and correct interpretation of our religious law'. Rajiv Gandhi's support of the decision seemed to fit his image of a moderate and progressive politician, who was particularly concerned with the rights of women in India. Although the government formally agreed with the decision, there was considerable dissension even within the Congress party. For example, Maulana Ziaur Rehman Ansari, the Union minister of state for environment conducted a three-hour long tirade in parliament against the judgment. Similarly, Maulana Asad Madani, president of Jamiate-ul-Ulema-e-Hind and the Congress (I)'s key Muslim campaigner wrote a strong letter to the prime minister indicating how upset the Muslims were with the party. As Muslim protests against the judgment gained momentum, Rajiv Gandhi found it increasingly difficult to maintain his support of the decision and his minister Arif Khan, who had acted as the government's spokesman on the issue.

OTHER VIEWS OF THE JUDGMENT

For the most part, the Hindus responded favourably to the Supreme Court's judgment in the Shah Bano case. Again, while one should be cautious about assuming that all Hindus in India responded uniformly to the decision, it appears that most of them were particularly satisfied with the Supreme Court's emphasis on the need to create a uniform civil code. Many Hindus had not forgotten the bitter battle waged in the 1950s when the Hindu Code Bill was enacted, which reformed the Hindu law on marriage and inheritance and simplified divorce. The Hindus have repeatedly argued that if their laws could be reformed by state policy, why should not Muslim laws undergo similar codification and reform.

The Hindu reaction may be explained in part by what Shekhar Gupta terms 'the paradox of a majority's minority complex'. He argues that the Hindu community which constitutes more than 80 per cent of the population regards itself as a minority in India. For instance, Hindu organizations claim that

> The Hindus are being discriminated against—being denied their share of power by minorities voting as blocs, witnessing a dilution of their religious values by a liberalization that has spared other religious faiths, and being ill-treated in those parts of the country where they are themselves a minority or close to becoming one.

While it is beyond the scope of this essay to delve into the perceived grievances of some Hindu groups and organizations, it is, however, a significant factor in understanding the way in which the Hindus reacted to the Supreme Court ruling. Moreover, Muslims regard the more militant manifestation of Hindu grievances as a threat to their religious identity and autonomy. For many Muslims, the Shah Bano judgment was in some respects an indication of Hindu efforts to assimilate other religions within the fold of Hinduism. The Hindus, on the other hand, viewed the decision as a way of bringing about a more uniform approach to the diverse religious groups and practices in India, particularly in the realm of personal law.

Apart from the Bharatiya Janata Party and the Marxists, who openly supported the judgment, the other political parties, such as the Janata Dal refrained from opting for one side or the other. The Janata Dal was particularly optimistic about receiving some of the Muslim vote, alienated from the Congress. To some extent, the Janata Dal's calculations paid off when its candidate Syed Shahbuddin won a by-election in north Bihar in December 1985. A year earlier, Rajiv Gandhi's Congress (1) had won the Kishanganj constituency, which spreads along the India-Bangladesh border and has a large number of Bengali-speaking Muslim peasants. The constituents rejected the Congress candidate by a large margin although he was the general secretary of Jamiat-ul-U1ema-e-Hind; a religious organization. While it is difficult to establish whether there were other reasons for the Congress candidate's defeat, it seems that the government's support of the Supreme Court decision contributed to its loss of Muslim votes in this by-election. The Congress' election defeat in north Bihar was important for two reasons: one, it indicated that the party's Muslim constituency was dissatisfied with its stand on the Shah Bano case; and two, it contributed to Congress's decision to re-evaluate its earlier support of the judgment.

THE GOVERNMENT RECONSIDERS ITS STAND

Within a year of the Supreme Court's judgment the government was reconsidering its earlier support of it. The Congress government modified its stance in response to several important factors. First, it was clear that Muslim protests against the decision were growing rapidly and showed few signs of abating unless the government altered its position on the issue. Second, and perhaps more importantly, the Congress party suffered electoral setbacks in a number of constituencies throughout the country. In region with significant numbers of Muslims, opposition parties successfully exploited the Shah Bano case and the perceived threat to Muslim identity in India. For example, in Assam, the newly constituted United Minorities Front (UMF) won eighteen assembly seats. Almost all of these constituencies has a Muslim majority. The UMF campaigners focused on two key issues: one, the threat to immigrant Muslims from the Assam accord; and two, the threat to Muslim identity all over the country from the Shah Bano judgment. Similar instances of Muslim votes going to other parties were reported from Bijnore, parts of Orissa, and West Bengal. Although it is not easy to gauge exactly how the Muslims voted, it seems that sufficient numbers of Muslims voted against the Congress as a result of its support of the Shah Bano judgment.

It was clear to the Congress party that the Muslims' electoral support had diminished considerably following the judgment. Although in the Lok Sabha the Muslim vote can by itself win no more than fifty seats, it can affect electoral outcomes decisively in about a hundred other constituencies. Moreover, in Bihar, Utttar Pradesh, West Bengal, and Assam, no national party can assume office without a reasonable share of the Muslim vote.

Since before independence the Congress party has had the political support of the orthodox and conservative elements amongst the Muslims, particularly from the Jamiate-Ulama-e-Hind, an organization of Muslim clerics associated with the famous Islamic university at Deoband. The Jamiyat's cooperation with the Congress is based on a tacit agreement under which the Ulema would give their support provided that the Muslim personal law is maintained, as would endowments, mosques, and other institutions and aspects of Muslim culture. The Congress's liberal and secular approach under Nehru and later Mrs Gandhi also drew the secular, liberal and even Marxist Muslim politicians to the Congress party. In most general elections since 1947, Muslims have predominantly voted for the Congress party. It is evident that in siding with the Supreme Court's ruling the Congress alienated a large segment of its traditional Muslim electoral support. Given the strong electoral compulsions, it was inevitable, that Rajiv Gandhi would eventually modify his party's stand on the Shah Bano case.

In order to ensure the continued support of Muslim voters and to prevent further outbreaks of violence, Rajiv Gandhi's government introduced a bill in Parliament that effectively abrogated the precedent set by the Supreme Court's award of maintenance to Shah Bano. According to the bill, Section 125 of the Criminal Procedure Code which requires husbands to support their divorced wives, was not applicable to Muslim marriages. In the proposed legislation, known as the Muslim Women (Protection of Rights on Divorce) Bill, maintenance to a Muslim divorced woman is to be provided by her former husband only during the *iddat* period, and the *mehr* (marriage portion) or other properties given at the time of marriage to be paid at the time of divorce. After the *iddat* period, it is the responsibility of the woman's family to provide for her. If relatives do not have the means to pay such maintenance, the woman could appeal to the *waqf*, the charitable trusts maintained for pious purposes. The bill was in accordance with the ulema's interpretation of the Shariat, which held that when the marriage contract is terminated by divorce, the husband's financial responsibilities cease. The bill was passed by both Houses of Parliament in May, 1986. Arif Khan, who had eloquently defended the judgment, resigned from the government in protest.

The prime minister defended the bill, claiming that it would further secularism in India by ensuring religious communities of fundamental rights. There was no indication in his speech that at the time of independence the Congress had strongly favoured the creation of common laws to enhance the secular nature of Indian society. While the bill may have appeased Muslim religious leaders, it was criticized by many liberals, both Muslims and Hindus. Whereas Muslim and Hindu critics of the bill agreed that it severely undermined the rights of Muslim women, they differed on key implications of the bill. First, and most important, they seemed at odds over what the bill meant for the rights of religious communities in India. For example, most Hindus believed that the bill weakened Indian unity by catering to Muslim separatism and allowing them to place membership in their religious community over their national allegiance. Needless to say, this kind of response alienated even moderate Muslims from the Hindus. Regardless of their support for or opposition to the bill, most Muslims were concerned about their status and rights as a religious minority in India.

Second, when Hindus, such as the journalist Arun Shourie, faulted the bill for its injustice to Muslim women, many Muslims, both liberal and conservative, believed that it was a thinly disguised attempt on the part of Hindus to express contempt for the Muslims and their religious practices. Muslims who opposed the bill were often hesitant to voice their views for fear of seeming to agree with Hindu intolerance.

Those Muslims who were against the bill argued that it perpetuated social injustice and undermined the rights of Muslim women. Zoya Hasan's comments are representative of this view:

> The bill was not at all necessary at the moment. It is against women. It undermines the right of Muslim women. It exonerates the main culprits – the husbands who divorce their wives. It seeks to pass on the responsibility to maintain the divorced Muslim woman to her natural family. . . . It is not the question of the personal law of a community, but that of the abandoned getting social justice.

Madhu Kishwar, editor of *Manushi*, a feminist journal in India, highlights the complex and controversial nature of the bill. While recognizing the broader implications of the bill, she maintains that it has intensified hostility and violence against the Muslims. In questioning the Hindu community's belief that the Muslims were in fact more powerful and influential than their numbers or economic and political status in society suggests, she forces her readers to confront widely held but unsubstantiated perceptions:

> Most Hindus are being led to believe that this bill demonstrates the sinister designs of those Muslims who want to 'break up the country.' For instance, a prominent Hindu politician is supposed to have remarked that this bill is proof that the mullahs and the Muslim League are running the country. This is indeed a bizarre distortion of reality. The Muslim community may occasionally be given some token concession because they represent an important vote bank. However, in reality, they are in no position even to protect themselves from continued pogroms and riots. They are continually losing even the precarious foothold they once had in the country's political economy.

It has been suggested that Rajiv Gandhi responded to electoral pressures by attempting to appease both Hindus and Muslims. The introduction of the Muslim Women's Bill in Parliament almost coincided with the opening of the Babari Masjid–Ram Janmabhoomi site in Ayodhya in February 1986. As noted before, the site was disputed by both Hindus and Muslims. In the past, the local court had restricted both Muslims and Hindus from entering the area in order to prevent any outbreak of violence. In January 1986, Rajiv Gandhi directed the chief minister of Uttar Pradesh to ensure that this time the restrictions would not be implemented. On 1 February 1986, the district judge ordered the gates opened. Further, the magistrate's statements appeared to endorse the claims of the Hindus to the site. It appeared that Rajiv Gandhi was trying to keep both communities satisfied. On one hand, Muslim protests against the Shah Bano judgment resulted in the introduction of the Muslim Women's Bill, on the other hand, sensing Hindu opposition to the bill, the prime minister attempted to appease them by reopening the disputed site.

Rajiv Gandhi's actions in this regard exemplified the way in which religion and politics are linked in India, whether in specific communities or at the national level. His policies were not unique; his mother and predecessor, Indira Gandhi, had certainly pandered to religious sentiment during the latter part of her tenure in office. Her approach to the Sikh conflict in Punjab, and her attempts to mollify the Hindus in Haryana for electoral purposes, brought religious issues to the forefront of national politics. To an extent, her actions contributed towards further politicizing religion and almost guaranteed the continued significance of religious issues in the national arena. Rajiv Gandhi's election campaign in 1984 also emphasized religious themes and symbols drawn primarily from Hinduism. This is by no means a new trend in Indian society. Much has been written, for example, about Mahatma Gandhi's liberal use of religious symbols for political purposes.

CONCLUSION

The Shah Bano case is indicative of three key trends in contemporary Indian politics. First, it is an important example of the inextricable link between religious and political issues in India. For the Muslims, Islam provides comprehensive guidelines for conducting oneself in the so-called secular or political realm. Therefore, any efforts to extract forcibly the religious element from the political sphere is resisted. Muslims in India are not the only ones to oppose state intervention in what they believe are their fundamental rights as citizens of secular India. Christians and Parsis have expressed similar reservations regarding the implementation of a uniform civil code. While this is not a new or significantly different trend in Indian politics, it is certainly reinforced by the controversy surrounding the Shah Bano case and the Muslim Women's Bill.

Second, the Shah Bano case amongst other demonstrates the weakening 'secularism of India's centrist consensus'. Whereas secularism may not have been defined more precisely under Nehru and his peers, there was a certain degree of consensus amongst them regarding secularism as an ideology and a constitutional arrangement. The most important goals were the creation of a common national identity and economic development. As recent events indicate, these goals may be more elusive than anticipated originally. In many ways, the consensus of the first twenty-five years after independence has been replaced by strong, often violent, disagreements over the fundamental principles of the Indian polity. Although the banner of secularism is raised frequently to justify pluralist practices, it is also used to condemn minority demands as a threat to national integrity. Such criticisms are levelled against those Muslims who wish to abide by the Shariat's tenets in matters of personal law. Sikh demands for recognition of Sikhism as a religion distinct from Hinduism evoked similar responses.

Third, and perhaps most important, the Shah Bano case is representative of the way in which group divisions within Indian society are increasingly manipulated for political reasons. As noted before, Rajiv Gandhi and his mother before him did not hesitate to use religious sentiments for garnering electoral support. For example, Mrs Gandhi frequently stressed that Muslim safety against Hindu fundamentalists could be preserved only by the Congress party. Moreover, with the recent prominence of the BJP and its 'Hindu oriented' message in Indian politics, it is unlikely that we shall see a significant change in this particular mode of politicking.

Despite the prominence accorded to religious identity in this paper, it is only one amongst several variables in South Asia's political culture. Regional, linguistic and ethnic identities and also class affiliations are equally important. While these identities are dynamic and their significance may vary according to the context, they are vital for our understanding of South Asian politics. Identities are formed, modified, and exercised in the political realm in response to several key factors that include urbanization, mass communication, the spread of education, and growing social mobility. Moreover, they may be reinforced by the way in which policy makers respond to group demands. For instance, government policies in the form of preferential treatment or quota systems encourage groups to organize on the basis of particular identity in order to derive maximum benefits from such programmes. Lastly, group identities are strengthened when challenged by others. These challenges may come from other groups in society in the form of migration and/or economic and political competition, or they may result from government efforts to impose a common national identity on diverse groups. The recent rise in ethnic nationalism in South Asia and in other parts of the world may be attributed in part to such processes.

Meanwhile, India continues in its struggle to define secularism and, more importantly, to resolve what role the state should play in issues and disputes concerning religious groups in India. Although the debate over formulating a common civil code continues, it seems that the efforts of individual religious groups to reform their own laws may be more acceptable and effective in the long run rather than relying on state initiatives. The important point, however, is not whether we can separate religion and politics but how to structure their relationship in the Indian context.

IV

Law and the Disadvantaged Groups

The Indian Constitution and the policies based on it seek to make some provision for extending special help to the educationally and socially weaker sections of society so as to promote their upliftment. Marc Galanter employs the remarkably appropriate term 'compensatory discrimination' for this policy.

Such sections include the depressed castes which have been subjected to exploitation and degradation for thousands of years; the scheduled tribes which live mostly in inhospitable areas; and the 'Other Backward Classes' (OBCs) which include a diversity of castes, from the ones that are considered to be rather low to the middle castes whose sections often possess substantial landholdings. Women, who constitute about one half of the total population, too have suffered from various disadvantages. Their status has been traditionally low as compared to that of men in all the religious denominations at almost all rungs of social hierarchy, and in most parts of the country.

It merits systematic investigation by the sociologists of law to assess how far such constitutional provisions and pieces of legislation have been effective in achieving their objectives, and what latent functions have resulted from them. It would be naïve to assume that all such provisions always serve the purpose of helping only those who are even now suffering from economic and social handicap. While some of these provisions may have helped the deserving sections, some are prone to be employed by certain people for their own gain at the cost of those for whom such benefits were intended.

For instance, among the scheduled castes and tribes certain sections which were advantageously placed have been enjoying the benefits of the reservations over a long time, for one or more generations, and have become comparable to other sections in the middle classes in their educational and economic level. But they continue to take the advantage of the reservations meant for those who are educationally and socially backward in the real sense. They subject to unfair competition those poor people who happen to come from the higher castes. What is worse, they deprive the vast majority of the exploited and impoverished people of the scheduled castes and tribes of the advantage of reservations by influencing policies in this regard.

They constitute important pressure groups in political and administrative circles and claim to represent the interests of the scheduled castes and tribes as a whole. They use their influence to mould policies in such a way that they deprive those who really need special protection and support. For example, they insist on reservations for persons belonging to the scheduled castes and tribes in the higher echelons of administrative services and in postgraduate education in fields like medicine. Reservations in such areas hardly have any relevance for the overwhelming majority of the scheduled caste or tribal people who are largely landless labourers or have to live in remote and inhospitable regions under miserable conditions. They cannot even dream of attaining such heights. The influential and prosperous sections that are included in the reservation categories have little concern for such things as literacy, basic health, and nutrition, which really matter for the vast majority of these disadvantaged segments of society.

Similarly, reservations for the other backward classes (OBCs), apart from arousing a good deal of jealousy and resentment among the middle-class people in general, may lead to certain consequences which tend to accentuate the oppression and exploitation of the most impoverished section of our society. In large parts of the country the middle castes own big landholdings and employ a large number of farm labourers. Most of these labourers are from the scheduled castes. Quite a few of the land-owning middle castes are included in OBC category, for whom there is provision of reservations in educational institutions and government services.

There is an understandable clash of interest between the landowners and the farm labourers, and this frequently assumes the form of caste conflict. The landowning castes usually have the upper hand and they mercilessly crush any signs of revolt or claims for justice. Since the overwhelming majority of landless labourers belong to the so-called 'untouchable' castes, such excesses take the form of atrocities against the Harijans. In many such cases the people perpetrating these atrocities belong to the middle castes which are included among the OBCs. It is worth sociological investigation whether their further acquisition of administrative and political clout through reservations for the OBCs goes against the interests of the most oppressed section of our society, the depressed classes.

This is an example of the necessity of inputs from research work in the field of sociology of law, so that the laws and policies are shaped in such a way that justice is done to all sections of society. Without inputs from scientific field investigations, all aspects of this and similar matters cannot be revealed. These are therefore essential for informed and equitable decision making. In one of the readings that follow, the eminent lawyer, Ram Jethmalani, has brilliantly argued the case in favour of reservations for the OBCs. However, on such comprehensive social policy matters more is required by way of systematic empirical research in the field.

Perhaps the most numerous amongst the disadvantaged people in society are the women. In almost all strata of society women suffer from some disadvantages as compared to the menfolk of their class. It is not only 'a result of women's economic dependence. Economic factors are undoubtedly important. But there are other factors as well, which have their own importance. There are factors related with social structure and social values. All these factors are, of course, inextricably interwoven in the sociocultural fabric.

The family plays an overwhelmingly important part in the life and status of women. All laws which impinge upon the family system, such as the Hindu Marriage Act, 1955, the Special Marriage Act, 1954, the Hindu Succession Act, 1956, and the Muslim Women (Protection of Rights on Divorce) Act, 1986 are immensely important for women. But the degree and nature of the impact of such legislation can only be found out through scientific empirical research in the field. Unless such research work is carried out, we do not know how much use is really being made of the laws which seek to raise the status of women, and how far they are being ignored, flouted, or circumvented in devious ways. Similarly, the reaction of Muslim women to the law passed in 1986 can be reliably known only through empiric investigation.

When a piece of social legislation does not seem to be effective, we have to look for the structural and valuational factors that may be responsible for this. For identifying these factors sociological analysis and research are needed. It seems, for example, that the patriarchal joint family system which has been the pivot of Indian society and other peasant civilizations, may be at the root of the low status of woman. This family system is not peculiar to India. As Sorokin, Zimmerman, and Galpin (1930) have shown in their monumental, but rather neglected work, *A Systematic Sourcebook in Rural Sociology,* all societies based on subsistence plough agriculture have in common certain features, like large size of family based on peasant household, authority of the father (or the eldest male in the family), low status of women, low age of marriage of girls, and so on. The

Indian joint family shares fully all these common features. Similarly, this work brings out the fact that such societies are marked by the gestalt of familism and that the family constitutes the hub of social life. This again is true of India as well.

Just as the ancient Chinese law prescribes *Three Successive Obediences* for women, so also the *Manusmṛti* lays down that a woman has to obey her father in childhood, husband in her youth, and son in her old age, and that she is incapable of being independent.[1] It seems that such mores serve the function of maintaining solidarity of the joint family, which consists of a number of married couples. Unless the women obey their husbands and other elders in the family they can become a cause of break-up of the joint family. Since they come from different households and have a relationship of rivalry with each other, they are prone to quarrel. Such quarrels, if not kept in check by a strong hand, may damage the solidarity of the joint family. Low age of marriage for girls which is a common feature of peasant families has also been practised since ancient times in India. *Smṛti*s, the books of sacred law of the Hindus, prescribe that a girl must be given away in marriage before she attains puberty. This too seems to be functional for the solidarity of this type of family. Unless the daughters-in-law become a part of the family at a tender age, they are likely to have developed attitudes which may not be congenial to the family that they join.

In Indian society and culture the values of the patriarchal family have been in the commanding position. So much so, that this has been reflected not only in mythology but also in metaphysics. Shrirama (1966) has shown how even a system of philosophy, the Sāṅkhya provides an example of the influence of the patriarchal values. The story of Lord Ram has been the most revered myth of Hindu culture. It has been told in many languages and in many ages. It appears that the distinguishing point in Ram's character is that he obeyed the command of his father; even though it was unjust, he had to leave the throne and go to the jungle for fourteen years, and it was not even conveyed fully in so many words. Ram is deified chiefly because of his unquestioning obedience to his father. This is the cardinal virtue of the patriarchal family, and it is ingrained in the minds of everyone through this myth.

When attempts are made to uproot such values and mores through legislation, it would be naive to expect that the laws which are intended to do this will be accepted readily by sizeable numbers. Many other social, economic, and cultural forces will have to combine to make such laws really operative.

However, some measures do seem to have promoted to a certain extent the empowerment of women. The policy of reserving one-third of the elective posts for women in the panchayats appears to have paid dividends. In the initial stages of its implementation it was widely commented that this provision had not made any real difference: Even though a woman may have been elected as a *panch* or sarpanch, the effective power was still exercised by her husband or some other male. But as time passed, some of the women *Panche*s and sarpanches became aware of the procedures, gained self-confidence, and began to take decisions on their own. But only systematic field investigation can bring out how far this has happened in different parts of India. Such research work would also reveal the other consequences of this measure.

NOTE

1. Such prescriptions are the same both in ancient Chinese and Indian laws. Both countries basically had the same type of patriarchal family and stable peasant civilizations for thousands of years. To my mind the only error in Sorokin, Zimmerman, and Galphin's outstanding work is that they have termed this type of family as 'rural family'. The fact is that essentially the same type of family is found also in urban centres in the peasant civilizations. It would therefore be more appropriate to call this type of family 'the family of peasant civilizations'.

13

Pursuing Equality in the Land of Hierarchy*

MARC GALANTER

Independent India embraced equality as a cardinal value against a background of elaborate, valued, and clearly perceived inequalities. Her constitutional policies to offset these proceeded from an awareness of the entrenched and cumulative nature of group inequalities. The result has been an array of programmes that I call, collectively, a policy of compensatory discrimination. If one reflects on the propensity of nations to neglect the claims of those at the bottom, I think it is fair to say that this policy of compensatory discrimination has been pursued with remarkable persistence and generosity (if not always with vigour and effectiveness) for the past more than fifty years.

These policies of compensatory discrimination entail systematic departure from norms of equality (such as merit, even-handedness, and indifference to ascriptive characteristics). These departures are justified in several ways. First, preferential treatment may be viewed as needed assurance of personal fairness, a guarantee against the persistence of discrimination in subtle and indirect forms. Second, such policies are justified in terms of beneficial results that they will presumably promote: integration, use of neglected talent, more equitable distribution, etc. With these two—the anti-discrimination theme and the general welfare theme—is entwined a notion of historical restitution or reparation to offset the systematic and cumulative deprivations suffered by lower castes in the past. These multiple justifications point to the complexities of pursuing such a policy and of assessing its performance.

India's policy of compensatory discrimination is composed of an array of preferential schemes. These programmes are authorized by constitutional

* Excerpted from Marc Galanter, *Law and Society in Modern India*, New Delhi: Oxford University Press, 1989, pp. 185–207.

provisions that permit departure from formal equality for the purpose of favouring specified groups.

The benefits of compensatory discrimination are extended to a wide array of groups. There are three major classes. First, there are those castes designated as Scheduled Castes (SCs) on the basis of their 'untouchability'. They number nearly eighty million (14.6 per cent of population) according to the 1971 census. Second, there are the Scheduled Tribes (STs) who are distinguished by their tribal culture and physical isolation and many of whom are residents of specially protected scheduled areas. They number more than thirty-eight million (6.9 per cent of the population in 1971). Third, there are the 'backward classes' (or, as they are sometimes called 'Other Backward Classes') a heterogeneous category, varying greatly from state to state, consisting for the most part of castes (and some non-Hindu communities) low in the traditional social hierarchy, but not as low as the SCs. Also included among the other backward classes are a few tribal and nomadic groups, as well as converts to non-Hindu religions from the SCs and in some areas the denotified tribes. It has been estimated that there were approximately sixty million persons under the OBC heading in 1961—roughly the magnitude of the scheduled caste population at that time (sixty-four million). (Today the portion of the population designated under this heading is probably larger).

For the most part, preferences have been extended on a communal basis. Members of specified communities are the beneficiaries of a given scheme and all members of the community, however prosperous, are entitled to the benefits. However, some schemes use a means test to supplement the communal one—only members of the listed communities with incomes below the specified ceiling are eligible. In a few instances, the communal test has been replaced by an economic one—income or occupation or a combination of the two—and a few schemes use tests neither communal nor economic.

Preferences are of three basic types: first, there are reservations, which allot or facilitate access to valued positions or resources. The most important instances of this type are reserved seats in legislatures, reservation of posts in government services, and reservation of places in academic institutions (especially the coveted higher technical and professional colleges). To a lesser extent, the reservation device is also used in the distribution of land allotments, housing and other scarce resources. Second, there are programmes involving expenditure or provision of services— e.g. scholarships, grants, loans, land allotments, health care, legal aid— to a beneficiary group beyond comparable expenditure for others. Third, there are special protections. These distributive schemes are accompanied by efforts to protect the backward classes from being exploited and vic-timized. Forced labour is prohibited by the Constitution (Act 23 [2]) and in recent years there have been strenuous efforts to release the victims of debt bondage, who are mostly from scheduled castes and tribes. Legislation regulating moneylending, providing debt relief, and restricting land transfers attempt to protect scheduled castes and tribes from economic oppression by their more sophisticated neighbours. Anti-untouchability propaganda and the Protection of Civil Rights Act attempt to relieve untouchables from the social disabilities under which they have suffered. This legislation is not compensatory discrimination in the formal sense of departing from equal treatment to favour these groups; it enjoins equal treatment rather than confering preferential treatment. But in substance it is a special undertaking to remedy the disadvantaged position of the Untouchables.

Alleged Costs and Benefits

Few in independent India have voiced disagreement with the proposition that the disadvantaged sections of the population deserve and need 'spe-cial help'. But there has been considerable disagreement about exactly who is deserving of such help, about the form this help ought to take, and about the efficacy and propriety of what the government has done under this head.

There is no open public defence of the ancien regime. Everyone is against untouchability and against caste. Public debate takes the form of argument among competing views of what is really good for the lowest castes and for the country. These views involve a host of assertions about the efforts—beneficial and deleterious—of compensatory discrimination policies.

Here, I would like to sketch in the most general terms the full range of claims that are made as to benefits and costs—the various ways in which the policy of compensatory discrimination allegedly helps or hurts the protected groups, others, and India as a whole.

Rough and redundant as it is, this anthology of claims will provide us with a checklist that will help in devising appropriate standards for eva-luating specific schemes. For convenience, each claimed benefit is paired wit the opposite claim of cost. It would simplify matters if each of these pairs represented points on a single dimension that could be unambiguously measured. Unfortunately, the most that can be claimed for them is that each is a composite of sometimes reinforcing but occasionally conflicting qualities that may conveniently be grouped together. Since the lines between the claimed effects are not always distinct, some overlap and redundancy is unavoidable.

A Costly Success

Have these policies 'worked'? What results have they produced, and at what costs? Our assessment of alleged costs and benefits suggests the complexity hidden in these apparently simple questions. Performance is difficult to measure: effects ramify in complex interaction with other factors. Compensatory policies are designed to pursue a multiplicity of incommensurable goals in unspecified mixtures that very from programme to programme, from time to time, and from proponent to proponent. Evaluation of a specific scheme for a specific groups during a specific period is itself a daunting undertaking. In other places, I have attempted to use this checklist of claims in evaluating specific schemes.

What I want to do here is draw a crude sketch of the effects of the compensatory discrimination policy in their largest outline. What has the commitment to compensatory discrimination done to the shape of Indian society and of lives lived within it?

The limited clarity of such a sketch is dimmed by the necessity of distinguishing between compensatory discrimination for the SCs and STs on the one hand and for the OBCs on the other. The following summary focuses on programmes for SCs and STs and adds some qualifications in the light of the experience with schemes for the OBCs.

Undeniably, policies of compensatory discrimination have produced substantial redistributive effects. Reserved seats provide a substantial legislative presence and swell the flow of patronage, attention, and favourable policy to SCs and STs. The reservation of jobs has given to a sizeable portion of the beneficiary groups earnings and the security, information, patronage, and prestige that go with government employment. At the cost of enormous wastage, there has been a major redistribution of educational opportunities to these groups. (Of course not all of this redistribution can be credited to preferential policies, for some fraction would presumably have occurred even without these.)

Such redistribution is not spread evenly throughout the beneficiary group. There is evidence for substantial clustering in the utilization of these opportunities. The clustering appears to reflect structural factors (e.g., the greater urbanization of some groups) more than deliberate group aggrandizement, as often charged. The better situated among the beneficiaries enjoy a disproportionate share of programme benefits. This tendency, inherent in all government programmes—quite independently of compensatory discrimination—is aggravated here by passive administration and by the concentration on higher echelon benefits. Where the list of beneficiaries spans groups of very disparate condition—as with the most expansive lists of other backward classes—the 'creaming' effect is probably even more pronounced.

The vast majority are not directly benefited, but reserved jobs bring a many fold increase in the number of families liberated from circumscribing subservient roles, able to utilize expanding opportunities, and support high educational attainments. Although such families comprise only a tiny fraction—an optimistic guess might be 6 per cent—of all scheduled caste families, they provide the crucial leaven from which effective leadership might emerge.

Reserved seats afford a measure of representation in legislative settings, though the use of joint electorates deliberately muffles the assertiveness and single-mindedness of that representation. The presence of SCs and STs in legislative settings locks in place the other programmes for their benefit and assures that their concerns are not dismissed or ignored. Job reservations promote their presence in other influential roles and educational preferences provide the basis for such participation. Of course, these positions are used to promote narrower interests—although we should not assume automatically that those they displace would bestow the benefits of their influence more broadly. If, for example, legislators from reserved seats are disproportionately attentive to the concerns of those of their fellows who already have something, it is not clear that this is more the case with them than with legislators from general seats.

Legislative seats are occupied by members of national political parties. They must aggregate broad multi-group support in order to get elected and, once elected, must participate in multi-group coalitions in order to be effective. In the office setting, too, there are relations of reciprocity and interdependence. The broad participation afforded by reserved seats and reserved jobs is for many others a source of pride and warrant of security.

If the separate and special treatment entailed by preferential programmes wounds and alienates the members of beneficiary groups, this is amplified by the hostility experienced on being identified as a recipient. As sources of alienation, these experiences must be placed against the background of more devastating manifestations of hostility, such as the much publicized assaults and atrocities perpetrated on scheduled castes.

At the policy-making level, reserved seats have secured the acceptance of scheduled castes and tribes as groups whose interests and views must be taken into account. In every legislative setting they are present in sufficient numbers so that issues affecting these groups remain on the agenda. Anything less than respectful attention to their problems, even if only lip service, is virtually unknown. Overt hostility to these groups is taboo in legislative and many other public forums. But there is evidence that scheduled castes and tribes are not accepted politically. Very few members of these groups are nominated for non-reserved seats and only a tiny number are elected. There is massive withdrawal by votes from participation in election for reserved seats in the legislative assemblies. Apparently large numbers of people do not feel represented by these legislators and do not care to participate in choosing them.

In the long term, education and jobs help weaken the stigmatizing association of scheduled castes and tribes with ignorance and incompetence, but in the short run they experience rejection in the offices, hostels, and other settings into which they are introduced by preferential treatment. Resentment of preferences may magnify hostility to these groups, but rejection of them obviously exists independently of compensatory programmes.

Compensatory programmes provide the basis for personal achievement and enlarge the beneficiaries' capacity to shape their own lives. But in other ways the programmes curtail their autonomy. The design of the legislative reservations, the dependence on outside parties for funds and organizations, and the need to appeal to constituencies made up overwhelmingly of others, tend to produce compliant and accommodating leaders rather than forceful articulators of the interests of these groups. The promise of good positions offers a powerful incentive for individual effort. But reservations in government service—and educational programmes designed to provide the requisite qualifications—deflect the most able to paths of individual mobility that remove them from leadership roles in the community. Constraints are intruded into central issues of personal identity by eligibility requirements that penalize those who would solve the problem of degraded identity by conversion to a non-Hindu religion.

Although preferential treatment has kept the beneficiary groups and their problems visible to the educated public, it has not stimulated widespread concern to provide for their inclusion apart from what is mandated by government policy. (This lack of concern is manifest in the record of private sector employment—as it was in public undertaking employment before the introduction of reservations.) Against a long history of such lack of concern, it is difficult to attribute its current absence to the policy of compensatory discrimination. But this policy has encouraged a tendency to absolve others of any responsibility for the betterment of SC and ST on the ground that it is a responsibility of the government. The pervasive overestimation of the amount and effectiveness of preferential treatment reinforces the notion that enough (or too much) is already being done and nothing more is called for.

Compensatory preference involves a delicate combination of self-liquidating and self-perpetuating features. Reservations of upper-echelon positions should become redundant as preferential treatment at earlier stages enables more beneficiaries to compete successfully, thus decreasing the net effect of the reservations. A similar reduction of net effect is produced by the extension to others of benefits previously enjoyed on a preferential basis (e.g. free schooling). Judicial requirements of more refined and relevant selection of beneficiaries (and of periodic reassessment) and growing use of income cut-offs provide opportunities to restrict the number of beneficiaries.

Reserved seats in legislatures are self-perpetuating in the literal sense that their holders can help to produce their extension, but extension requires support from others. The periodic necessity of renewal provides an occasion for assessment and curtailment. Programmes for SC and ST are for a delimited minority and pose no danger that the compensatory principle will expand into a comprehensive and self-perpetuating system of communal quotas. Although restrained by the courts, the provisions for the OBC are open-ended: a majority may be the beneficiaries and the dangers of self-perpetuation cannot be dismissed.

The diversion of resources by compensatory discrimination programmes entails costs in the failure to develop and utilize other talents. The exact extent of this is unclear. It seems mistaken, for example, to consider compensatory discrimination a major factor in the lowering of standards that has accompanied the vast expansion of educational facilities since independence. The pattern in education has been less one of excluding others than of diluting educational services while extending them nominally to all. Similarly, the effect of SCs and STs on the effectiveness of a much enlarged government bureaucracy is overshadowed by a general lowering of standards combined with the assumption of a wide array of new and more complex tasks.

The most disturbing costs of preferential programmes may flow not from their exclusion of others but from their impact on the beneficiaries.

What do the programmes do to the morale and initiative of those they purport to help? The numbers who fall by the educational wayside are legion. How rewarding is the educational experience of those who survive? Compensatory discrimination policies are not the source of the deficiencies of Indian education which impinge with special force on the beneficiaries.

As a forced draft programme of inclusion of SCs and STs within national life, compensatory discrimination has been a partial and costly success. Although few direct benefits have reached the vast mass of landless labourers in the villages, it has undeniably succeeded in accelerating the growth of a middle class within these groups—urban, educated, largely in government service. Members of these groups have been brought into central roles in the society to an extent unimaginable a few decade ago. There has been a significant redistribution of educational and employment opportunities to them; there is a sizeable section of these groups who can utilize these opportunities and confer advantages on their children; their concerns are firmly placed on the political agenda and cannot readily be dislodged. But if compensatory discrimination can be credited with producing this self-sustaining dynamic of inclusion, there is at the same time a lesser counter-dynamic of resentment, rejection, manipulation, and low self-esteem. And these gains are an island of hope in a vast sea of neglect and oppression. This mixed pattern of inclusion and rejection, characteristic of urban India and of the 'organized' sector, is echoed in the villages by a pattern of increasing assertion and increasing repression

Since independence India has undergone what might crudely be summarized as development at the upper end and stagnation at the bottom. With the boost given by compensatory discrimination a section of the SCs and STs has secured entry into the 'modern' class manning the organized sector. What does this portend for the bulk of untouchables and tribals who remain excluded and oppressed? Are they better or worse off by virtue of the fact that some members of their descent groups have a share in the benefits of modern India? The meaning of these achievements ultimately depends on how one visualizes the emergent Indian society and the role of descent groups in it

Even this kind of crude characterization of the overall impact of policies is not possible in dealing with measures for OBCs. Policies diverge from state to state, and very different groups of people are involved. In some states the OBC category is used to address the problems of a stratum of lowly groups who are roughly comparable in circumstance to the SCs and STs. In other places this category has been used to tilt the distribution of government benefits in favour of a major section of the politically dominant middle castes. The latter doubtless produce substantial redistributive effects, if less in the way of including the most deprived. But these expensive preferences for OBCs are of immense consequence for the SCs and STs. They borrow legitimacy from the national commitment to ameliorate the condition of the lowest. At the same time they undermine that commitment by broadcasting a picture of unrestrained preference for those who are not distinctly worse off than non-beneficiaries, which attaches indiscriminately to all preferential treatment. And because the OBC categories are less bounded and are determined at the state rather than at the Centre, they carry the threat of expanding into a general regime of communal allotments.

FAIRNESS AND HISTORY

Arguments about the utility of compensatory preference entwine with arguments about its fairness. Apart from the other costs, is compensatory preference so tainted by unfairness that it is illegitimate to promote the general welfare by this means? We have encountered several arguments about the fairness and unfairness of these programmes. We shall examine four here: (1) Is it unfair to depart from judgments on 'individual merit' to favour the beneficiaries over contenders for valued resources? (2) Is it unfair to compensate members of some groups for injustice perpetrated on their ancestors? (3) Is it unfair to compensate some victims and not others? (4) Is it unfair that some should bear more of the burden of compensation than others? Before taking up these fairness arguments it may be helpful to recall the justifications that may be advanced for the compensatory discrimination policy. Although they are often entwined in practice, we can separate out three sorts of justifications for these measures, which I label the non-discrimination, the general welfare, and the reparations themes.

The Non-discriminatory Theme

Compensatory discrimination may be viewed as an extension of the norms of equal treatment, an extension invited by our awareness that even when invidious discriminatory standards are abandoned there remain subtle and tenacious forms of discrimination and structural factors which limit the application of new norms of equality. Aspiring members of previously victimized groups encounter biased expectations, misperceptions of their performance, and cultural bias in selection devices; they suffer from the absence of informal networks to guide them to opportunities; entrenched systems of seniority crystallize and perpetuate the results of earlier discriminatory selections. Thus norms of non-discrimination in present distributions are insufficient to erase or dislodge the cumulative effects of past discrimination. Compensatory preference operates to counter the residues of discrimination and to overcome structural arrangements which perpetuate the effects of past selections in which invidious discrimination was a major determinant. In this view compensatory preference serves to assure personal fairness to each individual applicant. Group membership is taken into account to identify those individuals who require special protection in order to vindicate their claim for selection on 'merit' grounds. (The justification for much American affirmative action is often cast in these terms—as an extension of classical individualistic non-discrimination principles.)

The General Welfare Theme

On the other hand, compensatory discrimination may be advocated not as a device to assure fairness to individuals, but as a means to produce desired social outcomes—e.g. to reduce group disparities, afford representation, encourage the development of talent, and so forth. Arrangements for reservations in British India were justified on such 'functional' grounds as are the various preferences for 'Oriental' Jews in Israel today. Americans are familiar with the 'balanced ticket' and other arrangement by which shares are apportioned among various constituencies with the exception that abrasive disparities are kept in bounds, participation is spread out, representation is secured, and responsiveness assured. The units in such functional 'welfare' calculations are groups rather than individuals. The chances of individuals are affected by the rearrangement of the chances of groups. But the purpose is not to rectify discriminatory selection among individuals, but to introduce a standard quite apart from personal deservingness.

The Reparations Theme

In some cases, compensatory policies have another root—that a history of invidious treatment has resulted in accumulated disabilities which are carried by certain groups. No matter how fair and unbiased the measures presently employed for distributing benefits, the victims of past injustice will not fare well in terms of current performance. To distribute benefits by neutral standards will perpetuate and amplify unjust exactions and exclusions in the past. Fairness then demands that present distributions be arranged to undo and offset old biases, not to perpetuate them.

Like the non-discrimination theme, this is a fairness argument rather than a welfare argument. But it emphasizes groups as the carries of historic rights rather than as indicators of individual victimization. And it looks to a very different time frame. Welfare arguments are prospective; non-discrimination looks at the present situation and seeks to refine out lingering inequalities. The reparations theme sees the present as an occasion to reckon accounts for past injustice.

Do preferential programmes unfairly confer benefits on grounds that depart from even-handedness, merit, etc., that should govern the distribution of opportunities and resources? Along the lines referred to above as the 'non-discrimination theme', proponents might respond that some of the preference accorded is not departure from even-handedness but its extension in substance rather than form to individual members from the beneficiary groups. In this view, compensatory discrimination arrangements counter subtle discriminations and overcome the structural arrangements which entrench the results of past selections from which the beneficiaries were excluded.

In the Indian setting, few would argue that compensatory discrimination seeks only to protect merit against subtle or structural bias. Preferential treatment is accepted as a departure from merit selection in order to promote such goals as redistribution, integration, and representation. Is it unfair to combine these with merit as a basis for distributing benefits?

Let us take merit to mean performance on tests (examinations, interviews, character references, or whatever) thought to be related to performance relevant to the position (or other opportunity) in question and commonly used as a measure of qualification for that position. (In every case it is an empirical question whether the test performance is actually a very good predictor of performance in the position, much less of subsequent positions for which it is a preparation.) Performance on these tests is presumably a composite of native ability, situational advantages (stimulation in the family setting, good schools, sufficient wealth to avoid malnutrition or exhausting work, etc.) and individual effort. The latter may be regarded as evidence of moral deservingness, but neither native ability nor situational advantages would seem to be. The common forms of selection by merit do not purport to measure the moral deservingness dimension of performance. Unless one is willing to assure that such virtue is directly proportionate to the total performance, the argument for merit selection cannot rest on the moral deservingness of individual candidates.

Instead it rests upon the supposed consequences: those with more merit will be more efficient or productive; awarding them society's scarce resources will produce more indirect benefits for their fellows. A regime of rewarding merit will maximize incentive to cultivate talents; the demoralizing effects of departing from merit outweigh supposed advantages, based on calculations of imponderables. The argument for merit is an argument for production of more social well-being.

Many sorts of effects flow from any allocation of resources: benefits are multiple, they include not only tangible production, but symbolic affirmations and the creation of competences. The allocation of education, government jobs, or medical careers arguably has consequences for the distribution of incentives, levels of participation, and disparities in the delivery of services. Which dimensions of benefit are to be taken into account in designing a given selection? In setting where there has been a broad concensus that a single-minded test of performance is appropriate, what is the argument for a shifting to a broader, promotional basis of selection? Compensatory discrimination schemes involve enlargement of the basis of selection to include other criteria along with the productivity presumably measured by 'merit'—representation, integration, stimulation, and so forth. This enlargement is justified on the ground that without it society would be deprived of the various benefits thought to flow from the enhanced participation of specified groups in key sectors of social life. The argument is that the combination maximizes the production of good results. Of course there is always the empirical question of whether the promised results are indeed produced, but the supplementation of merit with other instrumental bases of selection hardly seems unfair in principle. Pursuit of other worthy results can be balanced against merit, as one result-oriented justification for unequal allocations against another.

Compensatory discrimination is both more and less than a reformulation of selection criteria. It is less because typically merit (in narrow performance terms) is left intact for the main part of the selection. The criteria are modified to require the inclusion of certain groups, an inclusion thought to produce a wide spectrum of beneficial results. But the new mixed standards are not applied across the board to the whole selection. So compensatory discrimination involves something more: the demarcation of those groups on whose behalf the broader promotional standards should be employed.

To prefer one individual over another on grounds of caste, religion (or other ascriptive criteria) is specifically branded as unfair by the anti-discrimination provisions of the Indian Constitution. The ban on the use of these criteria is, as we have seen, qualified to allow preferential treatment of a certain range of groups, whose history and condition seemed distinctive. There was agreement that some groups were burdened by a heritage of invidious discrimination and exclusion (and/or isolation) that made their condition distinct from that of their fellow citizens; the deprivations of their past and present members were thought to justify a special effort for their improvement and inclusion.

Spokesman for backward classes sometimes call for measures specifically to remedy the wrongs of the past. If one thinks of the blighted lives, the thwarted hopes, the dwarfing of the human spirit inflicted on generations of untouchables, or of the oppression and exploitation of tribal peoples, the argument for measured vindication of these historic wrongs has an initial appeal. But there are many kinds and grades of victimization; deprivations are incommensurable Perpetrators and victims sometimes stand out in stark clarity, but infirm and incomplete data often leave unclear precisely who were brutally exploitative, who willing or reluctant collaborators, who inadvertent beneficiaries of what we now see as systems of oppression. These arrangements interact with many other factors—climate, invasions, technology—in their influence on the present distribution of advantages and disadvantages. The web of responsibility is tangled and as we try to trace it across generations, only the boldest outlines are visible. Without minimizing its horrors, the past provides a shaky and indistinct guide for policy. It is beyond the capacity of present policy to remedy these wrongs: in the literal sense these injustices remain irremediable.

But if our perception of past injustice does not provide a usable map for distributing reparative entitlements, it can inform our vision of the present, sensitizing us to the traces and ramifications of historic wrongs. The current scene includes groups which are closely linked to past victims and which seem to suffer today from the accumulated results of that victimization. In a world in which only some needs can be met, the inevitable assignment of priorities may take some guidance from our sense of past injustice—thus providing the basis for a metaphoric restitution.

All remedies involve new distinctions and thus bring in their train new (and it is hoped lesser) forms of unfairness. Singling out these historically deprived groups for remedial attention introduces a distinction among all of the undeserved inflictions and unfairnesses of the world. One batch of troubles, but not others, are picked out for comprehensive remedy using extraordinary means. Those afflicted by other handicaps and misfortunes are left to the succour and aid that future policy makers find feasible and appropriate within the framework of competing commitments (including commitments to equal treatment). But drastic and otherwise outlawed remedies were authorized for victims of what was seen as a fundamental flaw in the social structure. The special quality of the commitment to correct this flaw is dramatized by the Constitution's simultaneous rejection of group criteria for any other purpose.

The line of distinct history and condition that justifies compensatory discrimination is of course less sharp in practice than in theory. There are borderlines, grey areas, gradual transitions. There is disagreement about just where the line should be drawn. And once it is drawn, the categories established are rough and imperfect—summations of need and deservingness; there are inevitable 'errors' of under-inclusion and over-inclusion.

We arrive then at an ironic tension that lies at the heart of the compensatory discrimination policy. Since the conditions that invite compensatory treatment are matters of degree, special treatment generates plausible claims to extend coverage to more groups. The range of variation among beneficiaries invites gradation to make benefits proportionate to need. Those preferential policies create new discontinuities and it is inviting to smooth them out by a continuous modulated system of preferences articulated to the entire range of need and/or deservingness. But to do so is to establish a general system of group allotments.

Compensatory discrimination replaces the arbitrariness of formal equality with the arbitrariness of a line between formal equality and compensatory treatment. The principles that justify the preference policy counsel flexibility and modulation. We may shave away the arbitrary features of the policy in many ways. But we may dissolve the arbitrary line separating formal equality and preferential treatment only at the risk of abandoning the preference policy for something very different.

If there is to be preferential treatment for a distinct set of historically victimized groups, who is to bear the cost? Whose resources and life chances should be diminished to increase those of the beneficiaries of this policy? In some cases, the costs are spread widely among the taxpayers, for example, or among consumers of a 'diluted' public service. But in some cases major costs impinge on specific individuals like the applicant who is bumped to fill a reservation. Differences in public acceptance may reflect this distinction. Indians have been broadly supportive of preferential programmes—e.g., the granting of educational facilities and sharing of political power—where the 'cost' of inclusion is diffused broadly. Resentment has been focused on settings where the life chances of specific others are diminished in a palpable way, as in reservations of jobs and medical college places.

There is no reason to suppose that those who are bumped from valued opportunities are more responsible for past invidious deprivations than are those whose well-being is undisturbed. Nor that they were disproportionately benefitted by invidious discrimination in the past. Reserved seats or posts may thus be seen as the conscription of an arbitrarily selected group of citizens to discharge an obligation from which equally culpable debtors are excused. The incidence of reservations and the effectiveness with which they are implemented tends to vary from one setting to another. Reservations impinge heavily on some careers and leave others virtually untouched. The administration of compensatory discrimination measures seems to involve considerable unfairness of this kind. If some concentration of benefits is required by the aims of the perference policy, it seems clear that more could be done to distribute the burden among non-beneficiaries more widely and more evenly.

SECULARISM AND CONTINUITY

Fairness apart, to many Indian intellectuals compensatory discrimination policies seem to undermine progress towards the crucial national goal of a secular society. Secularism in this setting implies more than the separation of religion and state (religious freedom, the autonomy of religious groups, withdrawal of state sanction for religious norms, and so forth). It refers to the elimination (or minimization) of caste and religious groups as categories of public policy and as actors in public life. In the 1950s and 1960s this was frequently expressed as pursuit of a 'casteless' society. Proponents of such a transformation were not always clear whether they meant the disestablishment of social hierarchy or the actual dissolution of caste units. But at the minimum what was referred to was a severe reduction in the salience of caste in all spheres of life.

The Constitution envisages a new order as to the place of caste in Indian life. There is a clear commitment to eliminate inequality of status and invidious treatment and to have a society in which government takes minimal account of ascriptive ties. But beyond this the posture of the legal system towards caste is not as single-minded as the notion of a casteless society might imply. If the law discourages some assertions of caste precedence and caste solidarity, in other respects the prerogatives previously enjoyed by the caste group remain unimpaired. The law befriends castes by giving recognition and protection to the new social forms through which caste concerns can be expressed (caste associations, educational societies, political parties, religious sects).

If the legal order's posture towards caste is ambivalent, public denunciation of caste has universal appeal. For lower castes it provides an opportunity to attack claims of superiority by those above them; for the highest castes it is away to deplore the increasing influence of previously subordinate groups, either the populous middle castes that have risen to power with adult suffrage or the lowest castes whose inclusion is mandated by compensatory discrimination programmes. Looking up, the call for castelessness is an attack on the advantages retained by those who rank high in traditional terms; looking down, it denies legitimacy to the distributive claims of inferiors and insists on even-handed application of individual merit standards.

The use of caste groups to identify the beneficiaries of compensatory discrimination has been blamed for perpetuation the caste system, accentuating caste consciousness, injecting caste into politics and generally impeding the development of a secular society in which communal affiliation is ignored in public life. This indictment should be regarded with some scepticism. Caste ties and caste-based political mobilization are not exclusive to the backward classes. The political life within these groups is not necessarily more intensely communal in orientation; nor are the caste politics of greatest political impact found among these groups. Communal considerations are not confined to settings which are subject to compensatory discrimination policies but flourish even where they are eschewed. Although it has to some extent legitimated and encouraged caste politics, it is not clear that the use of caste to designate beneficiaries has played a preponderant role in the marriage of caste and politics. Surely, it is greatly overshadowed by the franchise itself, with its invitation to mobilize support by appeal to existing loyalties. But the avowed and official recognition of caste in compensatory discrimination policy combines with the overestimation of its effects to provide a convenient target for those offended and dismayed by the continuing salience of caste in Indian life.

The amount of preference afforded to the scheduled castes and tribes is widely overestimated. The widespread perception of ubiquitous and unrestrained preferment for these groups derives from several sources. First, there is the chronic overstatement of the effects of reservation: large portions of reservations (especially for cherished higher positions) are not filled; of those that are filled, some would have been gained on merit; diversion of benefits to a few may be perceived as a deprivation by a much larger number. The net effect is often considerably less than popularly perceived. Second, ambiguous nomenclature and public inattention combine to blur the distinction between measures for SCs and STs and those for OBCs. The resentment and dismay engendered by use of the OBC category to stake out massive claims on behalf of peasant middle groups (particularly in some southern states) are readily transferred to discredit the more modest measures for scheduled castes and tribes.

If caste has displayed unforeseen durability it has not remained unchanged. Relations between castes are increasingly independent and competitive, less interdependent and cooperative. 'Horizontal' solidarity and organization within caste groups have grown at the expense of 'vertical' integration among the castes of a region. The concerns of the local endogamous units are transformed as they are linked in wider networks and expressed through other forms of organization—caste associations, educational societies, unions, political parties, religious societies.

If secularism is defined in terms of the elimination of India's compartmental group structure in favour of a compact and unitary society, the compensatory discrimination policy may indeed have impeded secularism. But one may instead visualize not the disappearance of communal groups but their transformation into components of a pluralistic society in which invidious hierarchy is discarded while diversity is accommodated. In this view compensatory discrimination policy contributes to secularism by reducing group disparities and blunting hierarchic distinctions.

The development of a secular society in which the hierarchic ordering of groups is not recognized and confirmed in the public realm is a departure from older Indian patterns. The compensatory discrimination policy is a major component in the disestablishment of a central part of the traditional way of ordering the society. But this break with the past itself is conducted in a familiar cultural and institutional style. The administration of preference programmes reflects older patterns in the fecund proliferation of overlapping schemes, the fragmentation of responsibility, and the broad decentralization of authority under the aegis of unifying symbols. When these policies encounter the judiciary, what purports to be a pyramidal hierarchy establishing fixed doctrine turns out to be a loose collegium presiding over an open-textured body of learning within which conflicting tendencies can be accommodated and elaborated.

The compensatory principle of substantive equality is added to the constitutional scheme of formal equality but it does not displace it. This juxtaposition of conflicting principles is an instance of what Glanville Austin admiringly describes as one of

India's original contributions to constitution-making [that is] accommodation . . . the ability to reconcile, to harmonize, and to make work without changing their content, apparently incompatible concepts—at least concepts that appear conflicting to the non-Indian, and especially to the European or American observer. Indians can accommodate such apparently conflicting principles by seeing them at different levels of value, or, if you will, in compartments not watertight, but sufficiently separate so that a concept can operate freely within its own sphere and not conflict with another operating in a separate sphere. . . .

With accommodation, concept and viewpoints, although seemingly incompatible, stand intact. They are not whittled away by compromise but are worked simultaneously.

The expectation that these principles could coexist has been ful-filled. The compensatory principle has been implemented but it has not been allowed to overshadow or swallow up opposing commitments to merit and to formal equality.

The compensatory discrimination policy is not to be judged only for its instrumental qualities. It is also expressive: through it Indians tell themselves what kind of people they are and what kind of nation. These policies express a sense of connection and shared destiny. The groups that occupy the stage today are the repositories and transmitters of older patterns. The advantaged and the disadvantaged are indissolubly bound to one another. There is a continuity between past and future that allows past injustice to be rectified. Independence and nationhood are an epochal event in Indian civilization which make possible a controlled transformation of central social and cultural arrangements. Compensatory discrimination embodies the brave hopes of India reborn that animated the freedom movement and was crystallized in the Constitution. If the reality has disappointed many fond hopes, the turn away from the older hierarchic model to a pluralistic participatory society has proved vigorous and enduring.

14

Jurisprudential Foundation
of Reservations*

M.P. SINGH

THE NEW CHALLENGES

In view of the fact that the Constitution sanctions reservations for the advancement of backward sections of the society, it could reasonably be expected that no further justifications were needed to defend any legislative or executive effort in that direction. Experience has, however, belied our expectations. Soon after the commencement of the Constitution a lacuna was found in the reservation provisions and that had to be remedied by an amendment of the Constitution. Even after the amendment the provisions are not wide enough to comprehend all situations requiring affirmative action. Inadequacy of these provisions, even in the limited area which should have most genuinely fallen within them, has been amply demonstrated in *State of Kerala v. N.M. Thomas*. Express provisions for affirmative action may be subjected to narrow interpretation applying the maxim *expressio units exclusio alterius*. Moreover, advanced or privileged sections of the society, precluded from the benefits of reservations recommended by Mandal Commission have, under the garb of challenging the implementational aspect of the constitutional provisions sanctioning affirmative action, started in reality questioning the constitutional policy itself as a result of which the country had to face violent and widespread demonstrations. Momentum against the constitutional policy appears to be gathering strength day by day under different pretexts.

For these reasons we shall have to travel beyond the letter of the Constitution to defend and justify affirmative actions that are urgently needed

*Excerpted from M.P. Singh, 'Jurisprudential Foundation of Reservations', *Indian Bar Review*, vol. 17, nos 3 and 4 and vol. 18, no. 1, 1990–1, pp. 245–74.

either to remove the existing grossly unjust inequalities in our society or at least to raise all sections of society to the level of human existence and to assure them their due 'dignity' expressly envisaged in the preamble to the Constitution.

THE QUESTION OF MERIT

According to the meritarian principle of distribution, which can be traced back to Aristotle and was as its peak during the nineteenth century under the influence of individualist thinkers, social goods should be allotted on the basis of one's merit on ability, whether natural or acquired. Leaving aside the general intricacies in the application of the principle, in such matters as admission to institutions of higher education or appointment to state services it will require that the candidates are selected on the basis of their individual merit, i.e., their ability in terms of achievement of certain grades or marks in an objective test—generally a test of intelligence plus knowledge—held for that purpose. Supporters of this principle claim that it assures best justice in so far as it allocates the rewards or goods on the basis of an objection criterion having nothing to do with such personal characteristics of an individual as his birth, race, colour, sex, caste, etc. They say that it also satisfies the justice precept of 'treat like cases alike and different cases differently' in so far as it provides a criterion of immediate relevance to the goods to be distributed. This principle assures the selection of the ablest persons from amongst a large number for the limited goods or opportunities available for distribution. It also assures a strong society and its overall progress in so far as it provides incentive for hard work and the development of superior mental and physical capacities.

Though on their face these arguments appear to be attractive, a close examination will expose that they suffer from a number of serious weaknesses. To begin with, the notion of merit itself is not as objective as it might appear. It is rather subjective. What is merit? Merit has no fixed or definite meaning free from variations. It is nothing but a criterion to achieve some predetermined social objective or value or to satisfy certain perceived social need. It does not control the objective, value, or need, but is controlled by them. Thus the merit must vary according to the variations in the social objective, value, or need set for achievement or satisfaction. For example, in a society suffering from under population due to long-term war or any other reason, production of more children may be a merit and parents may be rewarded for producing more children because the society needs an increased growth of population. Production of more than one or two children may, however, become a demerit in an overpopulated and underdeveloped society. Similarly, high grades or percentage of marks in educational examinations may be a merit for teaching assignment because the object is to have intellectually sound persons, but for a police or defence job where predominantly physically strong men are needed, physical strength and not the grades in examinations may be the merit.

To take one more example, suppose there are three boy claimants for one ticket of a cricket match show. To whom out of these should the ticket go on the basis of merit? To one who has the highest score in the last examination, or the one who has demonstrated exceptional potentiality to obtain better scores in future, or the one who does not fall in either of these two categories but has demonstrated immense interest in cricket? An answer to these questions would depend on what our ultimate objectives are. If we want to encourage talent and effort by rewarding it, the boy with highest marks should get the ticket, If we want to encourage the effort and potential, the second boy must get the ticket. And if we want to encourage sports, particularly cricket, the ticket must go to the third boy.

No more examples are necessary to bring home the point that the so-called merit is subjectively determined in terms of the perceived social objectives, values, or needs and is bound to change with the changes in the latter.

This analysis of merit leads us to two conclusions. First, since merit is dependent upon the value, goal, or the objective to be achieved, a society or the dominant group in a society may set such objectives or goals for which the members of that group are most suitable and thus use the apparently objective-looking criterion of merit to exclude other groups from the social good. For example, a warrior class or race in power may say that they need physically strong and well-built men in all walks of public life and administration and accordingly all positions will be filled on the basis of physical strength or prowess. On the face of it physical strength appears to be an objective criterion, but in fact it may result in constant and uniform exclusion of the undernourished and the poor from these positions because there is a close proximity between being well-fed and well-built and between undernourished and weak.

Second, since merit is determined for serving the perceived social needs (or values) of the day, satisfaction of such needs is the end and merit is simply a means to achieve that end. For example, efficiency in public administration may be an end and to achieve that end standards that may ensure such efficiency may be set as merit A society may find that having met the ordinary common needs of the community, it needs highly intelligent and sophisticated doctors, engineers, or lawyers to meet the special needs. To achieve that end it may decide that to these courses persons must be admitted solely on the basis of their intelligence measured through a pre-admission test or on the basis of marks or grades achieved in the previous school examination or both. Conversely, a society may find that it does not need as much intelligent and sophisticated doctors, engineers, or lawyers, as it needs the ones who can serve the day-to-day ordinary needs of the rural and tribal people and may accordingly decide that persons to these courses should not be admitted on the basis of intelligence alone, but also on the basis of their suitability to serve the rural and tribal people. And if the society finds that persons with urban or affluent background are not suitable for the job because of their unwillingness to serve the rural and tribal people as well as their attitude towards them, it may decide that persons with rural or tribal poor background only will be admitted to these courses or that preference will be given to them. Thus while in the first case intelligence is the merit for becoming a doctor, engineer, or lawyer, in the second, rural or tribal poor background acquires priority over intelligence and becomes merit.

To take one more example: suppose a country is not interested in high-class quality cloth but it wants that everyone must be clad even if the cloth is coarse. In such a situation those entrepreneurs who can produce cheap cloth even if it is coarse should have priority, if a question of granting a textile industry licence arises, over those who have highly sophisticated machinery and technical knowhow to produce fine quality cloth beyond the common men's reach. Thus the capacity to produce coarse but cheap cloth becomes a merit as against the capacity to produce high quality cloth.

These examples should leave no doubt that merit varies with the variance in the social needs. A society has to first determine and find out its needs and then determine the best means to ensure their satisfaction. It cannot talk of merit in the abstract. A society like ours which is under a constant and serious threat of disintegration because only certain classes or groups are dominating in every walk of life leaving no place or even hope for the rest of the classes or groups may find that keeping the society together is much more important than high standards of efficiency and accordingly it may look for the means that ensure its integration and prevent disintegration. One such means may be larger induction of excluded groups in all walks of public life so that they also develop a sense of involvement and stake in the present societal arrangements. Operationalization of this means may temporarily require reservation for the excluded groups: whether the reservation should be one hundred per cent or less is then a matter for determination. But whatever method is adopted, membership of an excluded group, and not intelligence, becomes the merit for selection to the seats in educational institutions and positions in public services. A society must make this kind of decision on the basis of clearly and objectively ascertainable facts lest the decisions lead to injustice, bad blood and even quicker disintegration. But that is a different matter altogether. What is necessary to be remembered at this juncture is the fact that merit changes with the context and that it is simply a means to achieve certain ends and not an end in itself.

Whether we look at the existing social structure or at the structure towards which our society is fast moving the meritarian principle of social justice is incongruous. Pressing for the application of that principle to the exclusion of others is out of place, more so when its application has been diluted in view of its weaknesses and new social arrangements are being worked out even in those societies which were dominated by it for quite sometime. In a society based on vast and well-rooted inequalities of birth, sole application of the meritaraian principle will mean nothing but legitimizing such inequalities and ensuring the lion's share to the privileged few and a very small or no share to the disadvantaged masses. To minimize the existing inequalities and bring about a just social order we shall have to give due recognition to the claims and needs of those unfortunate sections of share which have been denied equal share and equal opportunities for centuries. Demand for the application of meritarian principle of social justice coming from those sections of the society who have been enjoying for long all the benefits and privileges based on birth regardless of any individual ability or merit is certainly unfair and unjust.

SOCIAL JUSTICE AND THE CONSTITUTION

By the time our Constitution makers began their deliberations the weaknesses of the meritarian concept of market and individualistic society leading to widespread social injustice had already been exposed by thinkers like Saint-Simon, Durkheim, the Webbs, Tawney, Laski, and Green. These thinkers had also drawn an alternative plan for a new society which will assure greater equality to all and take into account the existing disabilities of the people. Laying down the foundations of a social welfare state they emphasized that 'social good results from the national coordination of the activities of altruistic men, rather than from the free play of individual self-interest'. These ideas had immensely impressed the leading figures in our freedom struggle as well as the Constitution makers. They thought that the solution to Indian problems lay in the implementation of these ideas.

The same concept has been expressed with greater vigour and clarity in the Directive Principles of State Policy contained in Part IV of our Constitution. The directives in no uncertain terms require the state, inter alia, to promote the welfare of the people by securing and protecting a social order in which justice, social, economic and political, should in form all the institutions of national life;[1] to reduce economic disparities; to make available adequate means of livelihood; to distribute the ownership and control of material resources so as to subserve the common good; to operate the economic system in such a way that it does not result in the concentration of wealth and mean of production to the common detriment; to protect health and strength of workers and children of tender age against abuse;[2] to provide for legal assistance and aid, to provide right to work, to education and to public assistance in cases of unemployment, old age, sickness, and disablement and in other cases of undeserved want;[3] to secure just and humane conditions of work and provision for maternity relief;[4] to provide for living wages and conditions of work ensuring decent standard of life and full enjoyment of leisure and social and cultural opportunities;[5] to promote with special care the educational and economic interests of the weaker sections of the people and their protection from social injustice and all forms of exploitation;[6] and to raise the level of nutrition and the standards of living and public health.[7] These principles can be enforced notwithstanding the general right to equality in Article 14 and right to the six freedoms in Article 19.[8]

The Constitution also ensures due representation of the weaker sections (scheduled castes and scheduled tribes) in Parliament and state legislatures through reservation of seats.[9] It also directs for their induction into state services and provides special administrative safeguards for them.[10] A backward class commission to make recommendations for improving the conditions of the backward classes and a commission to report on the administration of scheduled areas has also been conceived.[11] Special provisions have also been made for such minorities as Anglo-Indians.[12]

All these provisions make it amply clear that our Constitution does not leave the individual at the mercy of *matsya nyaya*, representative of a competitive model of society. It assigns a prominent role to and imposes heavy responsibility upon the state to assure a dignified life to each individual irrespective of what he deserves on meritarian considerations. It envisages equal respect and concern for each individual in the society and if the attainment of that goal requires special attention to be paid to some that ought to be done. The provisions requiring special attention are not an exception to the general scheme of the Constitution but are an integral part of it and may be called a basic structure in *Kesavananda Bharati* terms. They in fact represent the central ideology that worked in the mind of the Constitution makers for eradicating our age-old social injustices through an enlightened constitutional order.

RESERVATION

Some people argue that affirmative action is not bad but quota or reservation is. They would like the state to provide all kinds of facilities such as financial help, more educational avenues, better health care, improved living conditions, free coaching for equipping them to get into higher education, jobs, etc. to the backward groups so that they may have equality of opportunity in open competition with others. The argument is good in so far as it supports affirmative action minus quota or reservation, but it has its own limitations and cannot be accepted as such for more than one reason. First, under the existing social arrangements it is impossible to think of absolute or near-absolute parity in opportunity. Family background, environment, heredity, and many other things, which are beyond social regulation, have an important bearing upon one's personality and abilities. Facilities of the kind envisaged above cannot completely remove the impact of these factors. Second, there is no qualitative difference between the policy of quotas or reservations and providing other facilities. Special facilities can also be attacked on the same grounds as quotas or reservations.

Third, due to resource constraints, the state is unfortunately not in a position to provide all the inputs to enable the disadvantaged segments of society to uplift themselves and compete from a level of equality with the privileged and the advanced ones. Indeed the state is not able to meet even the barest necessities of food, shelter, and health care, what to say of other facilities. Fourth, at the present stage, while certain groups are almost completely unrepresented in all walks of public life (such as higher education and administration), their induction cannot be postponed indefinitely to an uncertain future. Last, the special facilities programme, so long as it is based on caste lines, does not in any way support those who oppose quota or reservation on the ground that they compartmentalize society and harm the cause of social integration in the long run. For these reasons it may be submitted that the special facilities argument is by and large an argument to divert the attention of the policy makers from the immediate and important task of realizing the goal of social justice in our society.

THE EFFICIENCY ARGUMENT

Although, the argument of efficiency advanced against affirmative action does not require separate treatment, it is necessary to counter the general impression created by its protagonists, especially because of the observation of Pathak J. in *A.B.S.K. Sang (Rly)* v. *Union of India*,[13] that efficiency of administration is the 'paramount need' to whose 'primacy all else is subordinate'. We submit with respect that the paramountcy of efficiency over everything else as a social value or need of our society is neither empirically tested nor clearly supported by the constitutional text. Though efficiency is an important value in so far as it assures greater production and better services, its importance has to be compared with and ultimately set against the significance of such other values as integration, prevention of discrimination, or eradication of stark social injustice. Through that exercise we might find that for us integration and rectification of socially harmful deprivation and injustices are as, if not more, pressing needs as efficiency. That was the demonstrable perception of the Constitution makers of the Indian reality and social needs which have not yet materially changed. Reference to 'maintenance of efficiency of administration' in Article 335 was not intended to project the paramountcy or primacy of efficiency over the need expressed in that article, namely, the induction of the scheduled castes and tribes into the state services so as to give them due representation therein.[14]

Even if we assume the paramountcy or primacy of efficiency, the connection between the existing tests for entry into the services and the efficiency of administration has not been empirically established. To quote Marc Galanter, who has been closely studying the affirmative programmes for over a quarter of a century:

> The translation of lower academic accomplishment into inefficiency in administration is difficult to trace. It is not clear how well academic performance correlates with administrative talent. Nor is it clear that differences in the level of such talents are directly reflected in efficiency or inefficiency of administration.

Moreover, he says: 'In part the higher scores of others may reflect cultural disadvantages which are irrelevant to the business at hand; in part, the lower scores of beneficiaries may reflect a remediable lack of polish and experience rather than lack of native ability.' Similarly the Supreme Court, in the scintillating and inimitable style of V.R. Krishna Iyer J. has rejected the argument that the existing tests for entry into state services are true indicators of merit or suitability. 'Unfortunately,' said Krishna Iyer J., 'the very orientation of our selection process is distorted and those like the candidates from the SC & ST who, from their birth, have had a traumatic understanding of agrestic India have, in one sense, more capability than those who have lived under affluent circumstances and are callous to the human lot of the sorrowing masses.' According to him '[e]litists whose sympathies with the masses have dried up are, from the standards of the Indian people, least *suitable* to run Government and least *meritorious* to handle state business, if we envision a Service State in which the millions are the consumers.' In his opinion, a 'sensitized heart and a vibrant head, tuned to the tears of the people, will speedily quicken the development needs of the country' and a '[s]incere dedication and intellectual integrity, . . . not degrees from Oxford or Cambridge, Harvard or Stanford' or similar Indian institutions are the major components of merit or suitability.

In making these remarks Krishna Iyer J. is not laying down any infallible alternative test of judging the suitability of the entrants who will assure the most efficient administration. But certainly he is passionately exhorting us to relate efficiency to our developmental needs and is exposing the irrelevance and inadequacy of the existing tests to the kind of efficiency of administration we need. Had the existing tests been directly linked to efficiency of administration, our central administration would have been most efficient and a negligible percentage of the scheduled castes and tribes only in recent years would have not eroded its efficiency to the extent alleged. 'In the light of the many forces which effect administrative inefficiency,' says Galanter, 'it seems appropriate to confront to guard against assertions about the effect of reservations with some skepticism, if only the widespread tendency to attribute any inefficiency in governmental operations to the presence of Scheduled Castes.'

An additional allegation attributing inefficiency in the administration to reservations is made on the plea that they adversely affect the morale of other public servants who are actually superseded or work under the constant fear of such supersession by their supposedly less qualified colleagues. But here again, as Galanter rightly suggests, without a careful empirical study it is difficult to say how much of the effect on morale is because of reservations and how much due to our prejudice towards the scheduled castes and tribes. It may reasonably be assumed that our centuries-old heritage of treating the scheduled castes and tribes as a subhuman, inferior lot must be working, at least subconsciously, in forming our attitude towards them when they participate with us as equals whether on the basis of reservation or otherwise. This attitude has nothing to do with the quality of the scheduled caste or tribe incumbents.

Finally, recalling the constitutional scheme outlined above, we respectfully agree with O. Chinnappa Reddy J. that in the name of efficiency we cannot introduce 'the vestiges of the doctrine of laissez faire and create . . . a new oligarchy. Efficiency has many facets and one is yet to discover an infallible test of efficiency to suit the widely differing needs of a developing society such as ours.' And further, in the words of Varadarajan J. 'public employment . . . should not be monopolised by any particular section of the people of this country in the name of efficiency, though efficiency cannot altogether be ignored.'

CONCLUSION

The limited objective of this essay is to identify the moral and philosophical justifications for affirmative action—justifications which sustain and transcend the constitutional text and policy. We have carefully avoided the implementational aspects of such action, not because they are less important but because we did not want to mix up the two. Once we accept the soundness of the policy of affirmative action the implementational aspect can be sorted out. Failure at the implementational front should not be the reason to discard the policy itself. The policy is intended to help the historically disadvantaged or discriminated groups. Even among the historically disadvantaged groups only, it must be ensured that a fortunate few do not monopolize its benefit for ever. A constant endeavour has to be made that the theoretical justifications are matched by effective implementation.

NOTES

1. Art. 38.
2. Art. 39.
3. Art. 41.
4. Art. 42.
5. Art. 43.
6. Art. 46.
7. Art. 47.

8. Art. 31C.
9. Arts 330 and 332.
10. Art. 335.
11. Arts 164 and 338.
12. Arts 339 and 340.
13. A.I.R. 1981 S.C. 298 at 332.
14. See Iyer J. in *A.B.S.K. Sangh* at 310. He reads a positive and a negative aspect in that article. While the former requires the claims of the scheduled castes and tribes to equalization of representation in services to be taken into consideration the latter tells 'that measures taken by the State, pursuant to the mandate of Articles 16(4), 46 and 335 shall be consistent with and not subversive of "the maintenance of efficiency of Administration".'

15

Mandal Revisited*

RAM JETHMALANI

While those allergic to the Mandal report or its implementation are entitled to a forceful expression of their views, it is certainly not evidence of their much vaunted merit or intelligence that valuable public property should be burnt or normal working of the social and economic mechanism be brought to a grinding halt by violence and hooliganism. The major arguments of the agitationists however require to be rationally exposed and repelled.

It is said that the Mandal Commission report was going to be implemented as a vote-catching gimmick and it smelled of a political sleight of hand. Ignorance of India's historical sickness and our constitutional prescriptions implicit in this calumny is amazing. The bewildering and unjust caste system of India was conjured up neither by Mr Mandal nor by Mr V.P. Singh. The framers of the Indian Constitution were not looking for vote banks. Those great and wise men had realized that India has to be welded into one nation and the bonds of nationhood would require to be reinforced. The invisible glue which binds masses of people into a single composite identity distinct from others is principally composed of an intense longing to live and die together in preference to any others based on mutual affection and cooperation in the pursuit of common political and social objectives. That feeling cannot arise or for long remain in the hearts of those condemned to appalling poverty while they observe a few amongst them wallowing in obscene wealth. Those who beat the drums of twenty-first century may well ponder that at the close of the twentieth there will be five hundred million of us living like swine, searching in hunger for putrified edibles in the dumps of trash discarded

*Excerpted from Ram Jethmalani, 'Mandal Revisited', *Indian Bar Review*, vols 17–18, 1991, pp. 193–7.

by the rich. Why should these swine have a longing to live, die, or fight alongside those whom they must see as robbers or at best as heartless self-seekers? Some of these swine are sentenced for ever to degrading occupations like collecting carcasses of dead animals and carrying basket of human shit on their head. It is absurd to expect a feeling of national solidarity from humans whose self-esteem, self-confidence, motivation, and ambition are all destroyed by social injustice.

True, enough poverty is endemic for a vast majority of our countrymen. They all need to be rescued from its quagmire. But the poverty relevant to this discourse is not the general poverty resulting from general causes like colonial exploitation, paucity of natural resources or inefficient management of the economy. What is relevant is a special kind of poverty which is the direct result of unspeakable atrocities perpetrated by small number of privileged individulals on the vast majority of their own countrymen. This unfortunate majority has been wounded and permanently crippled. It has suffered this fate by accidental birth in one or the other of the denigraded and degraded castes. The Constitution makers took cognizance of the tragic historical realities and promised to the people, justice—social, economic, and political. They promised dignity of the individual as a step towards integrity and unity of the nation. The Preamble of the Constitution does talk of merit or effeciency. It preferred justice as a superior goal and made it a fundamental principle of governance of the country that:

> The State shall promote with *special* care the educational and economic interests of weaker sections of the people, and, in particular, of the Scheduled Castes and the Scheduled Tribes, shall protect them from social injustice and all forms of exploitation (Article 46 of the Constitution).

The article notices the existence of an abnormal kind of 'weaker sections' of society. They are weaker not because of general causes effecting the entire nation but because of their specifically being victims of social injustice and manifold forms of exploitation through the long course of history, The obligation of all governments is to promote their educational and economic interests with special care.

Our great classics provide the best example of our historical callousness. Manu enjoined obedience to caste rules as the very essence of dharma. The Ramayana tells us that Shambuk, a Shudra, was beheaded because he committed the sacrilegious act of meditation. The Mahabharata familiarizes us with the tribal boy Ekalavya who made himself an archery expert but being a tribal was compelled to lose his thumb as *Gurudakshina* to Dronacharya. The Mandal Report draws poignant attention to harsh current reality. A Madrasi Tiyan must keep himself at a distance of thirty steps from a Brahmin and the Mahar in Maharashtra might not spit on the road lest a high-caste Hindu should be polluted by touching it with his feet. The Constitution makers found an antidote in what an American scholar called 'compensatory discrimination'. I wish Article 14 of our Constitution should have more realistically read: 'All men are born un-equal and each as to be right to be unequally treated to make them as equal to others as possible.' India can never become a nation unless the high castes are prepared to make penance by willingly acquiescing in the state pursuing the policy of compensatory discrimination with persistence and generosity. It may sound odd to some ears but the truth is that in some way we are accountable as well as punishable for the sins of our ancestors. Our young men in particular need to be educated that merit they are talking of is only inherited ability or ability acquired in unfair circums-tances. Such fortuitous merit is not relevant from the point of view of social justice. Under a political and social system in which the voice of the downtrodden has been unconsionably suppressed, a few privileged ones have succeeded in setting the criteria of merit for their own benefit, and then they have proceeded to put unfair price tags on their own brand of supposed merit. Actually, there is no intrinsic or compelling reason why a sweeper should not get more than a soldier or a soldier get more than a minister.

The argument or meritocracy is thus a myth. Minimum professional standards are not being diluted. Professional schools operating under quota system do not profess to certify incompetents. Indeed it is possible that handicapped students having demonstrated their ability to overcome handicapes imposed by their caste or the resulting backwardness will develop their abilities more rapidly than the other class. Social Darwinism is both immoral and unconstitutional. Indian society will have to firmly reject it.

The Supreme Court in a 1985 decision speaking through Mr Justice O. Chinnappa Reddy has firmly and irrefutably put the merit argument to rest:

> . . . One of the results of the superior, elitist approach is that the question of reservation is invariably viewed as the conflict between meritarian principle and compensatory principle. No, it is not so. The real conflict is between the class of people, who have never been in or who have already moved out of the desert of poverty, illiteracy and backwardness and are entrenched in the oasis of convenient living and those who are still in the desert and want to

reach the oasis. There is not enough fruit in the garden and so those who are in, want to keep out those who are out. The disastrous consequences of the so-called meritarian principle to the vast majority of the undernourished poverty-stricken, barely literate and vulnerable people of our country are too obvious to be stated. And, what is merit? There is no merit in a system which brings about such consequences. Is not a child of the Scheduled Castes, Scheduled Tribes or other backward classes who has been brought up in an atmosphere of penury, illiteracy and anti-culture, who is looked down upon by tradition and society, who has no books and magazines to read at home, no radio listen, no T.V. to watch, no one to help him with his homework, who goes to the nearest board school and college, whose parents are either illiterate or so ignorant and ill-informed that he cannot even hope to seek their advice on any matter of importance, a child who must perforce trudge to the nearest public reading room to read a newspaper to know what is happening in the world, has not this child got merit if he with all his disadvantages is able to secure the qualifying 40% or 50% of the marks at a competitive examination where the children of the upper classes who have all the advantages, who go to St. Paul's High School and St. Stephen's College, and who have perhaps been specially coached for the examination may secure 70, 80, or even 90% of the marks? Surely, a child who has been able to jump so many hurdles may be expected to do better and better as he progresses in life . . .

(1985) Suppl. SCR 394 - KCV Kumar v. Karnataka.

Reservations do not perpetuate caste. They destroy its ugly manifestations. When a scheduled caste chap becomes a sub-inspector—maybe not a brilliant one—the high-caste constable would salute him. That becomes the first significant step towards creating a classless society. Democracy without social justice is hypocrisy without limitation. Implementation of the Mandal report is a valiant fight for substituting a real for a sham democracy.

The duty of political parties who swear by the Constitution is thus obvious. For sordid political reasons they must not foment social tensions. They are appealing to the basest in human nature. They are exalting self-interest of the few above the pressing needs of many that have suffered in silence for centuries and are only now beginning to experience some self-expression and be unified for dignity and fairness. Never for example has merit been the operative principle of our political life. Is it possible for any one to suggest seriously that any government, past or present, is composed of the most efficient and meritorious ministers? Is the bureacracy composed of men of the highest integrity and honesty? Are our superior courts composed of the best legal brains of the country? Are our armed force composed of the best soldiers available? Is it not that sychophancy and ability to manipulate have become qualifications for many appointments and promotions?

It behoves all political parties to impress upon the young that real talent of the high caste has vast, almost limitless, scope for growth and achievement. The whole of the private sector is available to them. The liberal professions are wholly open to them. The business, commerce, industry in the rest of world outside India are open to them. Even in the field of public employment vast chunks like defence and atomic research have been left out for them. In, the net result, the controversy dwindles into a fight for about forty thousand jobs the overwhelming majority of which fall in Classes IV and III. The choice before our young men of merit is clear. Do they want to tear apart the social fabric acting on blind selfish impulse or do they wish to cement Indian society and make of it a powerful nation in which the most backward of us will be able to proclaim one day that they no longer need special care? Yes, the Mandal report is not and does not even pretend to be a solution or the general poverty and backwardness that constitute our major national headaches. In fairness, it is not even the final solution of the ills that beset our historically weaker sections. The real solution is to increase the size of the national cake by expansion of educational facilities and the job market. The real solution is to produce more wealth by sound economic management. Above all the most effective solution is effective control of numbers that want a slice of the cake. But until that happens the weak and the meek shall not wait.

16

Empowerment of Women: Legal Strategies*

S.P. SATHE

Although the pursuit of gender justice spans over the last nearly 175 years, one finds that, barring a few pockets of modernized and liberated sections of women, by and large gender injustice and inequality have continued though in some respects, they have become much more visible due to increased access to mass media and greater consciousness among women. Religious revivalism has rejuvenated some old forms of gender exploitation as is seen by the resurgence of sati in Rajasthan. Rapes, dowry deaths, female infanticide, as well as female foeticide have proliferated which are symptomatic of greater marginalization and commoditization of women. What can the law do to achieve gender justice? Besides protecting a woman from discrimination and atrocities, it can empower her in various ways by equipping her with rights and power so as to enable her to fight against male hegemony. Women empowerment is to be seen as a concomitant of the total process of social change leading to a just society and therefore its success will depend upon the success of the supportive socio-economic policies and simultaneous changes in the political process. We propose to examine various legal strategies of women empowerment.

Before we undertake this exercise, it will be in the fitness of things to understand what we mean by gender justice and empowerment. The Constitution uses the expression 'justice' in a number of provisions. The Preamble says that justice—social, economic, and political—shall be the aim of the Indian Republic. Article 38 says that the state shall strive to promote the welfare of the people by securing and protecting, as effectively

*Excerpted from S.P. Sathe, 'Empowerment of Women: Legal Strategies', in *Towards Gender Justice*, SNDT University, Bombay, 1993, pp. 56–88.

as it may, a social order in which justice—social, economic, and political—shall inform all the institutions of national life. In Article 39 A, the State has been asked to secure that the operation of the legal system promotes justice. Although the word 'justice' has not been defined in the Constitution it has been articulated through various directive principles of state policy, particularly those contained in Article 39 and the guarantee of fundamental rights contained in Part III of the Constitution.

The Constitution does not use the word 'gender'. It uses the word 'sex' in Articles 15(1), 16(2), or 325 which prohibits discrimination on ascriptive grounds. It has a sexist provision in Article 15(3) which enables the state to provide specially for women. Although the word 'sex' has a narrower meaning than the word 'gender', and the above provisions merely guard against discrimination on the basis of 'sex', the 'gender' justice which aims at much more than mere absence of discrimination has to be part of the constitutional agenda. In the words of Cardozo, a written constitution states or is intended to state not rules for the passing hour but principles for an expanding future. The Constitution is therefore continuously required to be restated and reinterpreted. We therefore hold that the concept of gender justice is incorporated in the concept of social justice. It means that in the new social order based on justice—social, economic, and political—as visualized by Article 38 of the Constitution, men and women must equally participate in decision making and must have equal access to the resources of the community. It will also mean that the gender constructs which are the basis of the role allocations and role perceptions in a patriarchal social order will have to undergo change in favour of gender neutral constructs. It means elimination of women subordination and establishment of gender equality. Equality does not mean similarity. Women need different rights and entitlements with regard to their reproductive function. Gender justice must be preceded by the existence of a pluralistic and democratic social culture. Another pre-condition for gender justice is the existence of a democratic, liberal, and secular polity. Gender justice does not thrive in a fundamentalist regime.

The empowerment of women is an input which is intended to eliminate their subordination and establish gender equality. Empowerment is a positive concept. It requires affirmative state action in support of those who are to be empowered. The Constitution doubtless envisages state intervention on behalf of the disadvantaged sections of society.[1] By empowerment we mean creating and strengthening through various inputs the capacity of a person to impose duties arid liabilities on other persons. In the Hohfeldian sense such a person must have rights and power in order to create their respective correlatives, namely, duties and liabilities in another person.[2] Law can create such empowerment through three methods. These are as follows:

    I. It can cause empowerment directly by conferring rights on the person whom it intends to empower or by imposing liabilities on other persons towards the person to be empowered;

    II. It can cause empowerment by strengthening the institutional infrastructure for enforcing such rights and liabilities; and

    III. It can cause empowerment by supporting, stimulating and monitoring the attitudinal and value changes in society.

The success of the first method of legal intervention depends upon the success of the second method and the success of both these methods depends upon the success of the third method of legal intervention. We shall consider each of these methods in detail.

EMPOWERMENT THROUGH CONFERMENT OF SUBSTANTIVE RIGHTS/POWER

There are four methods of empowerment through conferment of rights or power on persons to be empowered: by creating penal sanctions against certain types of behaviour that violate the dignity or liberty of women; by creating new proprietary entitlements for women such as giving them a share in matrimonial property or assuring them a right to work and on equal wages, etc.; by providing preferential treatment to women or providing for compensatory discrimination in their favour by reserving jobs or seats in local self-governing institutions and by facilitating the exercise of liberty or freedom by such persons.

Penal Sanctions Against Acts Violative of Women's Rights

Violence is used for reinforcing women subordination and is usually an exercise of power by men against women. Sexual assaults or domestic violence have to be understood against the perspective of power relation in a patriarchal society. Penal sanctions are invoked to impose liabilities on persons who use violence.

Sexual Assaults

As a result of the women's agitation against the decision of the Supreme Court in the *Mathura* case,[3] the law of rape was significantly altered in 1983 by the Criminal Law (Amendment) Act of that year. The alterations made were as follows: (i) new offences were created by Sections 376-A to 376-D and a new concept called 'custodial rape' came to be defined in Cl. (2) of Section 376; (ii) minimum statutory punishments were prescribed and the maximum of those punishments were enhanced to add greater deterrence against sexual assaults; and (iii) changes were made in the laws of evidence and procedures with a view to imposing greater burden of proof on the accused and to confer some protective privileges on the victim of the assault. Let us consider each of these more elaborately.

New Offences

Offence Against Judicially Separated Wife

Section 376-A made sexual intercourse with a judicially separated wife without her consent an offence and provided two years' imprisonment and fine as punishment. The original IPC did not contain such a provision because there was no provision at that time for judicial separation. Now that there were provisions for such judicial separation, this new offence had to be created. Since sexual intercourse without consent with the wife did not amount to rape, it was necessary to provide for the judicially separated wife who would technically continue to be the wife and yet ought not be made subject to such sexual intercourse. Again, since sexual intercourse with the wife even without her consent is not rape, sexual intercourse with the judicially separated wife could not be rape within the meaning of that word as used in Section 375 of the Penal Code. Therefore, even though it is not rape, it is now punishable by the new section.

Custodial Sexual Intercourse

Sections 376-B, 376-C, and 376-D deal with sexual intercourse committed by custodial authorities against women in their custody. The offences mentioned in these sections are not called rape. They are acts involving sexual intercourse committed by inducing or seducing the woman to consent by using his official position by the accused. The requisites of these offences are: (i) the accused must have been a public servant or the superintendent or manager of a jail, remand home, or other place of custody or must have been on the management of a hospital or must have been on the staff of a hospital; (ii) he should have taken advantage of his official position; (iii) the woman with whom such sexual intercourse was had must have been in the custody of the accused; (iv) she must have been induced or seduced to give consent to such intercourse, and (v) he should have had sexual intercourse with her. In the offence of rape, the prosecution is required to prove that the woman did not consent or that the sexual intercourse had been against her will. In the offences of custodial sexual intercourse, the prosecution does not have to prove that the woman consented or that the sexual intercourse had been against her will. Instead, it is required to prove that the accused took advantage of his official position to induce or seduce the woman to consent to such intercourse.

Custodial Rape

Although custodial rape was included within the definition of rape, the 1983 amendment specifically defined what custodial rape was. Section 376, (2) defined custodial rape in the following ways. One type of custodial rape is that which is committed by policemen. It deals with rape committed by a police officer 'within the limits of the police station to which he is appointed': or 'in the premises of any station house whether or not situated in the police station to which he is appointed': or 'on a woman in his custody or in the custody of a police officer subordinate to him'. This definition is wide enough to cover all acts of rape committed by the police either in a police station or anywhere while the woman is in his custody. The second type of custodial rape is committed by a public servant or such other custodial authority as is described above in connection with custodial sexual intercourse by taking advantage of his official position. In all these cases, the accused can put forward the defence that the woman against whom rape is alleged, consented to the sexual intercourse.

Punishments

Sexual intercourse with a judicially separated wife is punishable with imprisonment which may extend to two years and also with fine.[4] Punishment for custodial rape can extend to five years imprisonment and fine.[5] In both of these offences, only the maximum of the period of imprisonment has been prescribed. There is no statutory minimum punishment which a court has to pass. In respect to the offences of rape and custodial rape however, the minimum mandatory period of imprisonment has been prescribed. It has been provided by Section 376 as amended in 1983 that the punishment for rape shall not be less than seven years imprisonment but which may extend to life or for a term exceeding ten years.[6] The court, however, has been given power to impose a sentence less than seven years 'for adequate and special reasons to be mentioned in the judgment.'[7] The section further provides that punishment for rape committed by a police officer on a woman in his custody or by a public servant taking advantage of his official position on a woman in his custody or by a person on the management of a remand home or other place of custody on an inmate of such place of custody or by a person on the management of a hospital on a woman in that hospital or by a person on a woman known to be pregnant or by a person committing rape on a woman who is under twelve years of age or in case of gang rape 'shall not be less than ten years' but which may be for life.[8] The court has been given the power to impose a sentence less than ten years for 'adequate and special reasons'.[9] Section 376 was amended mainly to provide higher sentence against rapes committed by policemen on women subject to their control and by other custodial authorities against women under their custody or against rape on a pregnant woman or a girl below 12 years of age or against gang rape. The cases such as that of *Maya Tyagi* or *Mathura* were instrumental in spearheading a movement for such reform. In the last two decades, rapes committed by policemen have increased in number. Usually, women belonging to poorer sections and particularly those from the weaker sections of society become victims of rape. Amendments to Section 376 were made with a view to providing deterrents against such rapes. The success of such amendments depends upon how they are operationalized by the courts. Judges must be sensitized to the problems faced by rape victims and persuaded against taking hyper-technical positions on the assessment of the evidence. In *Suman Rani*[10] the Supreme Court reduced the punishment of the accused held guilty of custodial rape from ten years to five years on the ground that the peculiar facts and circumstances of the case and the conduct of the rape victim justified such lesser sentence. The Court stuck to its decision even on a review petition.[11] The judges defended their judgment by saying that they were not guided by the past sexual history of the rape victim but because of the delay on her part to report the crime. It is submitted that the justification given by the judges is not convincing. The decision to reduce the sentence below the minimum of ten years prescribed by statute was clearly wrong.

Domestic Violence

Dowry had its genesis in *vardakshina*, which meant a gift voluntarily given by the girl's father to the bridegroom. It is a consideration for the marriage either in money or in kind. Dowry became a means of exploitation when social taboos developed against a girl remaining unmarried. The girl's father is under pressure to marry off his daughter as early as possible. Even though the sex ratio in India shows a decline in the number of women as compared to men, the rates as well as frequency of dowry has been going up. The lower social position of the woman is mainly responsible for the evil of dowry. Young married women have been subjected to physical and mental torture in order to extract dowry from their fathers. In some cases, such girls have either committed suicide or have been burnt to death by the husband or other in-laws. This phenomenon is popularly known as dowry death. The Dowry Prohibition Act, 1961, was passed to curb the dowry menace. The definition of dowry in the Act was rather too restrictive. Nothing could be dowry which was not demanded at the time of the marriage. The post-marriage demands for dowry were not covered by this definition.[12] The definition was therefore amended by the Amendment Act passed in 1984 which replaced the words 'as consideration for the marriage' in Section 2 of the Act by the words 'in connection with the marriage'. The original Act exempted presents freely given to either of the spouses at the time of the marriage from the definition of dowry.[13] The Amendment Act provided that the presents be entered in the list maintained in accordance with the rules made under the Act and provided further that the presents given by or on behalf of the bride or any person related to her should be of 'customary nature' and the value thereof should not be excessive, having regard to the financial status of the person by whom they are given.[14] Section 6 deals with the recovery of the dowry. It provides that if any person other than the woman in connection with whose marriage it is given receives the dowry, he shall return it to the woman within a specified period and until so returned he shall hold it in trust for her benefit. If he fails to do so, he is liable to punishment provided under the Act. The Supreme Court had held in *Pratibha Rani* v. *Suraj Kumar*[15] that a Hindu married woman was the absolute owner of her *stridhan* property and the husband who had ill-treated her and ultimately turned her out of the house without returning her dowry articles was guilty of the offence of criminal breach of trust as defined by Section 406 of the IPC. This principle seems to have been applied to the retention of dowry in Section 6 of the Dowry Prohibition Act. In spite of such deterrent provisions, the menace of dowry has increased in recent years. Usually, the girl's father or other relations are reluctant to complain about the demands for dowry from the boy's side. They fear that the lodging of such a complaint might prejudice the chances of finding a match for their daughter. Most cases prosecuted under the Act have been those where complaints against dowry extraction were made only after all other methods of peaceful resolution of the conflict were found to be unsuccessful. In most cases, the girl's father or other relation had complied with such demands and yet those demands went on increasing and a time came when they were forced to call a halt to those incessant demands. In some cases, the marriage had already broken down and the girl had come back to her parental home. In some other cases, the girl had committed suicide or was killed. The meagre number of cases reported under the Act show that not enough use of the law has been made for women in distress.[16]

The menace of dowry which was essentially a high-caste/upper-class Hindu societal phenomenon has spread to lower-caste groups among Hindus as well as the Muslims and Christians. The Dowry Prohibition Act is a secular legislation and applies to all communities. However, the dowry menace has increased phenomenally in recent years. The alarm caused by the increase in the number of dowry deaths prompted Parliament to make several changes and add several provisions to the IPC, the Cr.PC, and the Indian Evidence Act. Two provisions were made in the IPC against domestic violence.

(i) Section 498-A was added which makes cruelty to a married woman by her husband or by her in-laws punishable with three years of imprisonment. Cruelty for the purpose of this section means (a) any wilful conduct which is of such a nature as is likely to drive the woman to commit suicide or to cause grave injury or danger to life, limb, or health (whether mental or physical) of the woman; or (b) harassment of the woman where such harassment is with a view to coercing her or any person related to her to meet any unlawful demand for any property or valuable security, or is on account of failure by her or any person related to her to meet such demand. Section 198-A was added to the Cr.PC saying that the cognizance of an offence of cruel treatment under section 498-A of the IPC must be taken on police report or upon a complaint made by the aggrieved person or by her father or mother or brother or sister, or by her father's or mother's brother or sister, or with the permission of the court by any person related to her by blood, marriage, or adoption. Why should a complaint made by her friend or a women's organization not be entertained?

(ii) Section 304-B was added to the IPC by the Criminal Law Amendment Act passed in 1986. This section starts with the title 'Dowry Death'. It provides that where the death of a woman is caused by any burns or bodily injury or occurs otherwise than under normal circumstances within seven years of her marriage and it is shown that soon before her death she was subjected to cruelty or harassment by her husband or any relative of her husband for, or in connection with, any demand for dowry, such death shall be called 'dowry death' and such a husband or relative shall be deemed to have caused her death. The punishment for such offence as provided in Subsection (2) is imprisonment for a term which shall not be less than seven years but which may extend to imprisonment for life. In the Indian Evidence Act, it was provided by the Criminal Law (Amendment) Act, 1986, that once it is shown that soon before her death, the woman had been subjected by the accused to cruelty or harassment for, or in connection with, any demand for dowry, the court shall presume that such person had caused the dowry death.[17] Section 306 of the IPC defines the offence of abetment of suicide. Whoever abets the commission of suicide shall be punished with imprisonment for a term which may extend to ten years and shall also be liable to fine. The husband or any relation of his who forces a woman to commit suicide or facilitates such commission of suicide by her could be charged with the offence of abetment of suicide under this section. The Criminal Law (Amendment) Act, 1983, inserted a provision whereby it is provided that once it is shown that the woman committed suicide within a period of seven years from the date of her marriage and that her husband or relative of her husband had subjected her to cruelty, the court would presume, having regard to all other circumstances of the case, that such suicide had been abetted by her husband or by the relative of the husband, as the case may be.[18] These provisions impose burden of proof on the accused which earlier lay on the prosecution. Section 174 of the Cr. PC was amended to provide that in case a woman dies or commits suicide within seven years of marriage. a post-mortem report and other investigations must be made. Thus we have three provisions dealing with the problem of domestic violence. Section 498-A is invoked when there is mere harassment and cruelty against the woman, Section 304-B is invoked when such cruelty or harassment specifically made with a view to extracting dowry results in the abnormal death of the woman and Section 306 is invoked when a woman commits suicide.

The very nature of these offences requires a less technical and socially sensitive approach by various components of the criminal justice system. The Supreme Court dealt with such a question in *Stree Atyachar Virodhi Parishad* v. *Dilip Nathumal Chordia* in an appeal against the decision of acquittal given by the Bombay High Court. The Supreme Court observed.

> We are referring to these provisions . . . only to emphasize that it is not enough if the legal order with sanction alone moves forward for protection of women and preservation of societal values. The criminal justice system must equally respond to the needs and notions of the society. The investigating agency must

display a live concern The Court must also display greater sensitivity to criminality and avoid on all counts 'soft justice'.[19]

Such concern for making the criminal justice system respond to the ghast-liness of the dowry deaths, which usually take place in the privacy of mat-rimonial life, is reflected in some recent judgments of the courts. In *Public Prosecutor, A.P. High Court* v. *T. Basava Punnaiah*[20] the Andhra Pradesh High Court dilated on the subtle distinction between Section 304–B and 306 of the IPC. The fact that the deceased had been treated cruelly was proved beyond doubt. She died of asphyxia. It was alleged that the three accused, namely the husband, his father, and mother had strangulated her neck and subsequently made it appear as suicide by hanging. The addi-tional sessions judge held that the death had been by suicide. He held the accused guilty of abetment to suicide under section 306. On appeal it was argued by the counsel of the accused that Section 304-B did not apply where a person committed suicide. The Court observed:

> Section 304-B is a special provision which is inserted by the amendment in 1986 to deal with dowry deaths. It applies where the death of a woman is caused by any burns, or bodily injury or occurs otherwise than under normal circumstances, if the other conditions are satisfied. Since the deceased died on account of the hanging, the death occurred otherwise than under normal circumstances. We are, therefore, of the view that even if she had committed suicide by hanging, still the death comes within the scope of section 304-B IPC, if it is shown that she was subjected to cruelty or harassment by her husband or any relative of her husband in connection with any demand for dowry.[21]

Creating Proprietary Entitlements for Women

Another method of empowerment is of conferring property rights and other entitlements on the persons to be empowered. Powerlessness arises essentially out of lack of access to resources. Empowerment means facilitating access and ensuring rightful shares in the material resources of the community.

The National Perspective Plan for Women AD 1988–2000 for the first time recognized that women should not be viewed as a weaker segment of society or as passive beneficiaries of the development process, but as a source of unique strength for reaching the national goals.[22] The Plan re-commended the following changes in the laws with a view to conferring additional proprietary rights on women:

(a) All matrimonial property should be registered in the joint names of husband and wife. Where it is not in the joint names, the wife should have the right to ask for, injunction, until the matter is settled, if the marriage breaks down.

(b) The parents should be prevented from denying daughters their rightful share of property by making wills disinheriting them.

(c) The right of the wife to the matrimonial home must be guaranteed.

The recommendations contained in (a) and (c) pertain to matrimonial property. We have so far not even legislated to give equal inheritance rights to women. The Perspective Plan rightly recommended that there should be a uniform civil law by the year AD 2000. The right to matrimonial property is a further step towards empowerment of women. Meanwhile, the right to maintenance of the discarded and divorced wife has to be strengthened. The Law Commission has made some sound suggestions for legal reform in this respect.[23] The Supreme Court held that the second wife of a Hindu was not entitled to maintenance under Section 125 of the Cr.PC.[24] Under the Hindu Adoption and Maintenance Act. 1956, however, the Court has granted maintenance to the second wife.[25] Since Hindu marriages are not registered, a woman may enter into a wedlock without the knowledge that the man whom she marries has a living spouse. The denial of maintenance to such a woman might prove to be unfair. The Perspective Plan recommended that the minimum amount of maintenance should be calculated on the basis of basic needs of the woman and that the upper limit of the amount of maintenance as provided in Section 125 of the Cr.PC should be removed. The Law Commission has also made a similar recommendation regarding the upper limit of the amount of maintenance. In a recent study of the decisions of the trial courts on maintenance,[26] it was found that the amount of maintenance had rarely a nexus with the needs of the woman or the financial capacity of the husband.

The Equal Remuneration Act, 1976, was enacted to provide equal remuneration to male and female employees. The Act provides in Section 4 that 'no employer shall pay to any worker, remuneration at rates less favourable than those at which remuneration is paid by him to workers of the opposite sex.' The Act was amended in 1987 to provide for more deterrent punishment and to prohibit discrimination not only in initial recruitment but also in any condition of service subsequent to recruitment such as promotion, training, or transfer. However, in spite of this Act, women continue to be discriminated in jobs and conditions of service.

Employers are reluctant to employ women because of the additional financial liability that such employment entails. If there are thirty or more women employees, provision for creches is required to be made.[27] Further, they have to be given maternity leave.[28] In a leading Government of India public utility, a circular had been issued asking women employees applying for maternity leave to produce evidence of their marriage. Women employees often prefer to keep their marital status confidential in view of the policy of the employers not to recruit married women. When they apply for maternity leave obviously they contradict themselves. But why should being married be a disqualification for employment? Why should being married be a qualification for getting maternity leave?[29] Such irritants will continue to frequent women's job opportunities as long as the long-standing prejudice against women employment stays. The Supreme Court held that a settlement arrived at between the management and the employees through negotiations could not be a valid ground for discrimination in remuneration between male and female employees.[30] This shows that trade unions are also willing to sacrifice the interest of the female employees. There is a mistaken belief that a woman has lesser requirements and responsibilities than a man. Further, there is an assumption that a woman's efficiency is lower. The traditional division of work allocates household work for women which is not quantified and therefore a housewife is considered to be non-productive. Most of these assumptions have now been proved to be false. Women are vital and productive workers in India's national economy. They make up one-third of the labour force, though this is rarely quantified through statistical data that are available because two sectors, namely domestic work and the unorganized sector in which women mostly work, are not included in such statistical surveys.[31] In a recent study,[32] it has been pointed out that among poorer families there is greater dependence on the women's earning. It has been found that Indian women contribute a much larger share of their earnings to basic family maintenance than do men. Therefore, increases in women's income translate more directly into better health and nutrition for children. Women's empowerment regarding access to work would doubtless facilitate the anti-poverty efforts.

Empowerment Through Positive Discrimination

We have described how under Article 15(3) of the Constitution, the state can make special Provisions for women. Education is free for women. Women also are a preferred group for the dispensation of free legal aid by the state agencies. In some recent statutes, women's participation has been ensured by providing them with preferential appointments to decision-making bodies. For example, under the Consumer Protection Act, a lady social worker is to be one of three members of the District Forum,[33] and one woman of ability and integrity with special knowledge of industry, law, economics, etc., has to be on the State Commission as well as the National Commission.[34] The Family Courts Act, 1984, which provides family courts for the adjudication and settlement of family disputes also provides that while appointing judges for that court, preference shall be given to women.[35] We have already said that seats have been reserved for women in panchayats as well as local self-governments. However, while the effects of reservations in jobs are mixed and the positive feedbacks are slow and uncertain, those of the reservations for women in the local self-governing institutions or panchayats seem to be more reassuring. Gail Omvedt[36] had narrated how one Usha Nikam had to struggle to get an all-women's panel elected to a panchayat. The recent success story of an all-women panel in Brahmanghar village in Bhor taluka of Pune district is much more encouraging.[37] Reservations of seats for women in the panchayats or local self-governing institutions could doubtless go a long way towards womens empowerment. That might also ultimately reveal that induction of the powerless groups into the political process might be a surer and quicker method of empowerment of such groups than their mere induction into the services.

Legislation Facilitating Liberty

The law on abortion has been a subject of heated debate in several countries including the United States of America. A liberal law on abortion doubtless facilitates women's liberty. In India, the liberalization of the abortion law came through without much controversy. The Medical Termination of Pregnancy Act, 1985, was a step towards the liberation of the woman. It secured to her the right to decide about abortion.[38] While the technology of contraception has liberated her from the tyranny of nature, among the poorer section of women the problem lies as much as in their lack of awareness of the available technology as in ignorance of their rights. Therefore, a well-conceived programme on adult education could be the first step towards informing a woman of her rights—which includes rights over her body—the liberty to conceive or terminate a pregnancy. A well-informed woman would want to limit her procreation and that would doubtless help arrest the population growth. The population control programme must be an integral part of a comprehensive health care scheme. The right to health care must be recognized as a basic human right. The law of adoption for all communities must be passed to facilitate adoptions. Universalization of education, and particularly women's education, could go a long way towards liberating women.

EMPOWERMENT THROUGH INSTITUTIONAL INFRASTRUCTURE

All disadvantaged sections of society suffer from lack of access to institutions of grievance redressal. Therefore, one of the important strategies of empowerment is to facilitate access to grievance redressal and rights-enforcing institutions. The Committee on the Status of Women recommended the creation of family courts to settle disputes pertaining to family matters.[39] Family Courts Act, 1984, was passed to provide for the establishment of family courts with a view to promoting conciliation in and securing settlement of disputes relating to marriage and family affairs.[40]

Family courts are part of the tribunal system that is emerging as an alternative to the court system and is intended to be less formal, policy-oriented and less expensive than the courts. The formal courts follow the adversary procedures which tend to be technical and lead to prolonged proceedings. The family courts are supposed to have greater freedom of procedures and they have to promote conciliation wherever possible.[41] Unlike the adversary procedure where the role of the judge is limited, the judge in a family court is supposed to act positively. The appearance of lawyers is optional and only with the permission of the Court.[42] The Act therefore makes provisions for association of social welfare agencies and counsellors to assist the family court in settling disputes through conciliation.[43]

It is too early to say whether family courts have been successful or not. However, the opinion prevailing among many is not favourable.[44] Informality of procedures is a double-edged weapon. In the hands of a judge who shares the concerns of the law and is just and fair, it can become a tool of social justice. However, in the hands of a judge who does not share such concerns and is brought up in the tradition of black letter law, it can become an instrument of oppression. Formal procedures at least make the law predictable. Informalization of procedures must therefore be preceded by intensive gender sensitization training programmes for the judges who have to decide these matters.

Traditionally, marriage is an institution based more on a hierarchical relationship between man and woman than an egalitarian one. The Family Courts Act requires that the judges should be committed to the institution of marriage.[45] It is feared that the judges' commitment to the protection and preservation of marriage may prevail over their concern for women's right to equality within the marital world. Moreover, the state governments have not given a fair trial to the Act. The judges and courts under this Act have not been given basic infrastructural facilities. Besides, family courts have not been set up everywhere. The Act itself limits the establishment of family courts to cities or towns the population of which is more than one million,[46] and the state governments have been given the discretion to establish them in other places.[47]

Another forum for grievance redressal was set up recently by the National Commission for Women Act, 1990. This Act created a National Commission for Women which consists of (a) a chairperson, committed to the cause of women to be nominated by the Central government; (b) five members to be nominated by the Central government from amongst persons of ability, integrity, and standing who have had experience in law or legislation, trade unionism, management of an industry or organization committed to increasing the employment potential of women, women's voluntary organisations (including women activists), administration, economic development, health, education, or social welfare; and (c) one member-secretary to be nominated by the Central government who shall be (i) an expert in the field of management, organizational structure, or sociological movement, or (ii) an officer who is a member of a civil service of the Union or of an All-India service or holds a post under the Union and has the appropriate experience.[48] The Commission is free to regulate its own procedure.[49]

The Commission has three types of functions. It has purely recommendatory functions such as: (a) to make in its reports recommendations for the effective implementation of the safeguards provided for women under the Constitution and the laws; (b) to review the provisions of the Constitution and the laws affecting women and recommend amendments thereto; (c) to make periodical reports to the Government on any matter pertaining to women and in particular regarding various difficulties under which women toil. The Commission will have executive-cum-judicial functions such as (a) to take up cases of violation of the provisions of the Constitution and of other laws relating to women with the appropriate authorities; (b) to look into complaints and take *suo moto* notice of the matters relating to (i) deprivation of women's rights; (ii) non-implementation of the laws enacted to provide protection to women and also to achieve the objective of equality and development; (iii) non-compliance of policy decisions, guidelines, or instructions aimed at mitigating hardships and ensuring welfare and providing relief to women; and (c) to inspect or cause to be inspected a jail, remand home, women's institution:

or other place of custody where women are kept as prisoners or otherwise, and take up with the authorities concerned, any remedial action, if found necessary.[50]

The Commission has been given certain powers of a civil court such as of summoning and enforcing the attendance of persons, requiring the discovery and production of any document, receiving evidence on affidavits, issuing summons for the examination of witnesses and documents, etc.[51] The chairperson and members of the Commission are to be public servants for the purpose of Section 21 of the IPC.[52] Appointments of chairperson and other members of the Women's Commission have now been made and the Commission has started its work. The National Commission for Women is intended to act as an ombudsman in women's matters. Similar commissions at the state levels are also being contemplated.

Strengthening of the institutional infrastructure for facilitating access to decision making and remedial institutions is very important. In the absence of such an efficient infrastructure, the substantive rights conferred by law become ineffective.

Public interest litigation (PIL), has been another device through which access to justice on the part of the disadvantaged sections is facilitated. PIL which has been described by Justice Bhagwati as a strategic arm of the Legal Aid Movement in India[53] has doubtless played a significant role in making justice more accessible to the disadvantaged sections of society. However, unless the mainstream system of justice, i.e. the courts, is reformed, women and all disadvantaged sections of society will continue to suffer. What is the use or giving new rights and entitlements if the system continues to be corrupt, inefficient, expensive, and dilatory? Tribunals and informal grievance redressal inputs can merely provide relief if the mainstream system functions efficiently. They are not alternatives to courts but are supposed to complement the work of the courts.

Supporting, Stimulating and Monitoring the Attitudinal and Value Changes in Society

Although law can catalyze change in social behaviour, the real change can come only through the efforts of those who struggle for change. Education plays a very important role in bringing about social change. In a country where more than 50 per cent of the people are still illiterate, and tradition as well as religion reinforce women subordination, neither equality not justice is within sight for a majority of women. With the growth of religious fundamentalism, as seen in the *Shah Bano* case or in the revival of sati, women's subordination is further legitimized. A major cultural renaissance therefore must precede and be implicit in a women's movement in India. The fact that almost all political parties are now espousing women's issues in their manifestoes and that women are now being given a share in decision-making is a positive sign, not of the change in man's attitude but of the compulsions of democracy. The law plays an important role in supporting and monitoring the women's movement for their rights. The Constitution of India guarantees certain fundamental rights which the State cannot take away or abridge either by legislative or executive action.[54] All citizens, including women, have the right to freedom of speech and expression, freedom of assembly, freedom of association, freedom to move within the territory of India and freedom to reside and settle in any part of the territory of India[55] Women are entitled to vote.[56] All disadvantaged sections, including women, can use these rights to organize their movements.

The main task of those who are crusading for gender justice will be to educate both men and women about it. The movement to change public opinion and societal attitudes and values can at the most be catalyzed by law. But such change cannot come merely through legal prescriptions. India needs a new movement for change. It should aim at promoting humanism and respect for individual dignity and liberty. The law can help by protecting the freedom of those who crusade for such change and by firmly preventing those who try to subvert it. Gender justice will be an important item on this agenda. It is a long journey indeed.

APPENDIX

Provisions of the Criminal Law (Amendment) Act 1983 regarding Rape.

Section 375

A man is said to commit 'rape' who, except in the case hereinafter excepted, has sexual intercourse with a woman under circumstances falling under any of the six following descriptions:

Firstly—Against her will

Secondly—Without her consent

Thirdly—With her consent, when her consent has been obtained by putting her or any person in whom she is interested in fear of death or hurt.

Fourthly—With her consent, when, the man knows that he is not her husband, and her consent is given because she believes that he is another man to whom she is or believes herself to be lawfully married.

Fifthly—With her consent, when, at the time of giving such consent, by reason of unsoundness of mind or intoxication or the administration by him personally or through another of any stupefying or unwholesome substance, she is unable to understand the nature and consequences of that to which she gives consent.

Sixthly—With or without her consent, when she is under sixteen years of age.

Explanation

Penetration is sufficient to constitute the sexual intercourse necessary to the offence of rape.

Exception

Sexual intercourse by a man with his own wife not being under fifteen years of age, is not rape.

Section 376

(1) Whoever, except in the cases provided for by subsection (2), commits rape shall be punished with imprisonment of either description for a term which shall not be less than seven years but which may be for life or for a term which may be extended to ten years and shall also be liable to fine unless the woman raped is his own wife and is not under twelve years of age, in which case, he shall be punished with imprisonment of either description for a term which may extend to two years or with fine or with both:

Provided that the Court may, for adequate and special reasons to be mentioned in the judgment, impose a sentence of imprisonment for a term of less than seven years.

(2) Whoever,
   (a) being a police officer commits rape—
      (i) within the limits of the police station to which he is appointed: or
      (ii) in the premises of any station house whether or not situated in the police station to which he is appointed; or
   (iii) on a woman in his custody or in the custody of a police officer subordinate to him; or
   (b) being a public servant, takes advantage of his official position and commits rape on a woman in his custody as such public servant or in the custody of a public servant subordinate to him; or
   (c) being on the management or on the staff of a jail, remand home or other place of custody established by or under any law for the time being in force or of a women's or children's institution takes advantage of his official position and commits rape on any inmate of such jail, remand home, place or institution; or

(d) being on the management or on the staff of a hospital, takes advantage of his official position and commits rape on a woman in that hospital; or

(e) commits rape on a woman when she is under twelve years of age; or

(f) commits gang rape shall be punished with rigorous imprisonment for a term which shall not be less than ten years but which may be for life and shall also be liable to fine:

Provided that the Court may, for adequate and special reasons to be mentioned in the judgment, impose a sentence of imprisonment of either description for a term less than ten years.

Explanation 1

Where a woman is raped by one or more in a group of persons acting in furtherance of their common intention, each of the persons shall be deemed to have committed gang rape within the meaning of this sub-section.

Explanation 2

'Women's or children's institution' means an institution, whether called an orphanage or a home for neglected women or children or a widow's home or by any other name, which is established and maintained for the reception and care of women or children.

Explanation 3

'Hospital' means the precincts of the hospital and includes the precincts of any institution for the reception and treatment of persons during convalescence or of persons requiring medical attention or rehabilitation.

Section 376-A

Whoever has sexual intercourse with his own wife, who is living separately from him under a decree of separation or under any custom or usage without her consent shall be punished with imprisonment of either description for a term which may extend to two years and shall also be liable to fine.

Section 376-8

Whoever, being a public servant, takes advantage of his official position and induces or seduces, any woman, who is in his custody as such public servant or in the custody of a public servant subordinate to him, to have sexual intercourse with him, such intercourse not amounting to the offence of rape, shall be punished with imprisonment of either description for a term which may extend to five years and shall also be liable to fine.

Section 376-C

Whoever being the superintendent or manager of a jail, remand home or other place of custody established by or under any law for the time being in force or of a women's or children's institution takes advantage of his official position and induces or seduces any female inmate of such jail, remand home, place or institution to have sexual intercourse with him, such sexual intercourse not amounting to the offence of rape, shall be punished with imprisonment of either description for a term which may extend to five years and shall also be liable to fine.

Explanation 1

'Superintendent' in relation to a jail, remand home or other place of custody or a women's or children's institution includes a person holding any other office in such jail, remand home, place or institution by virtue of which he can exercise any authority or control over its limits.

Explanation 2

The expression 'women's or children's institution' shall have the same meaning as in Explanation 3 to sub-section (2) of section 376.

Provisions of the Indian Evidence Act Regarding Presumption

a. Suicide

Section 113-A

When the question is whether the commission of suicide by a woman had been abetted by her husband or any relative of her husband and it is shown that she committed suicide within a period of seven years from the date of her marriage and that her husband or such relative of her husband had subjected her to cruelty, the Court may presume, having regard to all the other circumstances of the case, that such suicide had been abetted by her husband or by such relative of her husband.

Explanation

For the purposes of this section, 'cruelty' shall have the same meaning as in sec. 498 A of the Indian Penal Code (45 of 1860)

b. Dowry Death

Section 113-8

When the question is whether a person has committed the dowry death of a woman and it is shown that soon before her death such woman had been subjected by such person to cruelty or harassment for, or in connection with, any demand for dowry, the Court shall presume that such person has caused the dowry death.

Explanation

For the purposes of this section 'dowry death' shall have the same meaning as in s. 304-8 of the Indian Penal Code.

c. Rape

Section 114 - A

In a prosecution for rape under Cl.(a) or Cl.(b) or Cl.(c) or Cl. (d) or Cl. (e) or Cl.(g) of sub-section (2) of sec. 376 of the Indian Penal Code (45 of 1860), where sexual intercourse by the accused is proved and the question is whether it was without the consent of the woman alleged to have been raped and she states in her evidence before the Court that she did not consent, the Court shall presume she did not consent.

NOTES

1. Art. 46, Constitution of India.
2. Hohfeld, *Fundamental Legal Conceptions*, Walter Wheeler Cook (ed.), New Haven: Yale University Press (4th Printing), 1966.
3. *Tukaram* v. *Maharashtra*, All India Reporter, 1979, SC 125. *See* Upendra Baxi, 'Taking Suffering Seriously: Social Action Litigation in the Supreme Court of India' in R. Dhavan, R. Sudarshan, and S. Khurshid (eds), *Judges and the Judicial Power*, London: Sweet and Maxwell, 1985, 289–315.
4. S. 376-A.
5. S. 376-B, S. 376-C, and S. 376-D.
6. S. 376(1).
7. Id. Proviso to Cl(1).
8. S. 376(2).
9. Proviso to ibid.
10. *Premchand* v. *Haryana*, (1989) 1 SCC 286.
11. (1990) 1 SCC 249. *See* S.V. Joga Rao 'Premchand v. State of Haryana, An Epitome of Soft-Justice Syndrome', *National School of Law Journal*, 186, 1986. *Also see* 'Sub-Minimum Sentence in a Rape Case' 33 *Journal of the Indian Law Institute* 439 (1991).
12. *L.V. Jadhav* v. *Shankarrao Abasaheb Pawar* (1983), 4 SCC 231: All India Reporter, 1983, SC 1219.
13. The Dowry Prohibition (Amendment) Act, 1984; see *Vinod Kumar* v. *State*, All India Reporter 1982, P&H 373.
14. S.3(b) ibid.
15. (1985) 2 SCC 370. Also see *Madhusudan Malhotra* v. *Kishore Chand Bhandari* (1988), Supp. SCC 424.
16. *See* 'Violence Against Women', *The Lawyers Collective*, March 1987, p. 4.
17. Section 113 B, The Indian Evidence Act, 1872.
18. S.113 A, ibid. *See* Appendix.
19. (1989) 1 SCC 715, 718. *See* B. Sivaramayya, 'Women and the Law' in XXV *Annual Survey of Indian Law (Indian Law Institute)* 1989 at p. 321, 326–7.
20. (1989) 2 *Criminal Law Journal* 2330 (AP).

21. Id, p. 2333.
22. Government of India National Perspective Plan for Women AD 1988–2000, New Delhi: Dept of Women and Child Development, Ministry of Human Resources Development, 1988, p. 1.
23. Law Commission of India, 132nd Report on Need For Amendment of the Provisions of Chapter IX of the Code of Criminal Procedure 1973 in Order to Ameliorate the Hardship and Mitigate the Distress of Neglected Women, Children and Parents (Govt. of India, 1991);*Also see* Flavia Agnes, 'Maintenance for Women: Rhetoric of Equality', *Economic and Political Weekly*, vol. XXVII, no. 41, 10 October 1992, p. 2231.
24. *Yamunabai Anantrao Jadhav* v. *Anantrao Shriram Jadhav* (1988) 1 SCC 530; All India Reporter 1988, SC 644. *See* Jaya Sagade 'Polygamy and Woman's Right of Maintenance, A Survey of Judicial Decisions' 31 *Journal of Indian Law Institute* 336, 1989, 345.
25. *Vaijayanti Bai* v. *Keru Ananta*, II (1991) DMC 548 (Bom); *Reddi* v. *Reddi*, All India Reporter 1976, AP 43.
26. Sagade, Jaya 'A Comparative Study of Woman's Position Under the Indian Family Law with Special Reference to Right to Maintenance', A thesis ap proved by the University of Poona for the Degree of Doctor of Philosophy in Law (Unpublished).
27. S. 48 of the Factories Act, 1948.
28. The Maternity Benefits Act, 1961.
29. Sarkar, Lotika 'Gender Justice in Legislation: Nehru Era One Step Forward, One Step Backward', in Upendra Baxi (ed.), *Dimensions of Law, Festschrift in Honour of Prof. S.P. Sathe*, Bombay: Tripathi, 1992, p. 186.
30. *Mackinnon Mackenzie & C.* v. *Audrey D'Costa* (1987), 2 SSC 469: All India Reporter 1987, SC 1281.
31. Government of India, Shramshakti: Report of the National Commission on Self-Employed Women In the Informal Sector, 1988.
32. Bennett, Lynn, 'Women, Poverty and Productivity in India, EDI Seminar Paper No. 43, 1991. The author concludes that 'the labour force participation of women and their proportional contribution to total family income are the highest in households with the lowest economic status'. She further observes that 'the poorest families are the most dependent upon women's economic productivity', p. 59.
33. The Consumer Protection Act, 1986, Section 10(1)(b).
34. Section 16(1)(b) and Section 20(1)(b), ibid. 20(1)(b).
35. The Family Courts Act, 1984, Section 4(4)(b).
36. Omvedt, Gail 'Women and Maharashtra Zilla Parishad Elections', *Economic and Political Weekly*, vol. XXII, no. 47, 1987, p. 1991–2.
37. *The Indian Express*, 22 November 1992, p. 1. This is a story of a panchayat in a place called Brahmaghar in Bhor taluka of Pune district in Maharashtra.

38. S. 3(4), The Medical Termination of Pregnancy Act, says that no pregnancy shall be terminated without the consent of the pregnant woman.

39. Government of India, Towards Equality: 'Report of the Committee on the Status of Women in India', Dept. of Social Welfare, 1974, Ministry of Education and Social Welfare, p. 141.

40. The Family Courts Act, 1984 (Act No. 66 of 1984).

41. Section 10 of the Family Courts Act allows the family court to lay down its own procedure with a view to arriving at a settlement. S. 14 allows the family court to receive evidence irrespective of whether it is admissible under the Indian Evidence Act.

42. S. 13 FCA.

43. S. 5 provides for association of social welfare agencies and S. 6 provides for conciliation officers and other employees of the family court.

44. *See* S.P. Sathe, 'Family Courts and Reality', *The Lawyers*, Sept. 1990, p. 7; *also see* cover story 'Family Courts: From the Frying Pan into Fire', *The Lawyer*, Sept. 1990, p. 4; D. Nagassaila 'Family Courts: A Critique', *The Economic and Political Weekly*, vol. XXVII, no. 33, 1992, p. 1735.

45. S. 4(4)(a) FCA.

46. S. 3(1)(a) ibid.

47. S. 3(1)(b).

48. S. 3(2), The National Commission for Women Act, 1990.

49. S. 9(2) ibid.

50. S. 10(1) ibid.

51. S. 10(4) ibid.

52. S. 15 ibid.

53. *P.U.D.R.* v. *India*, All India Reporter, 1982, SC 1473, 1476–7.

54. Art. 13 (2).

55. Art. 19 (1)66. Article 325.

56. Art. 325.

V

Societal Role of Judiciary

The existing legal system in India is not of much use to the vast majority of its citizens who are predominantly uneducated, poor, and helpless. It is generally used only by those well-to-do persons who have a lot of time and money to spare. In fact this system of law is often employed by the powerful, wealthy, and scheming persons to heap injustices on the ordinary people, in the assured belief that their victims have neither the guts nor the means to go to a court of law against them.

Numerous helpless people have been languishing in prison because they have been accused of a crime which they may not have committed at all, just because their cases have not yet been decided by a court of law. Many a time, such 'undertrials' spend a longer period in jail than the maximum term of sentence prescribed for the crime of which they had been accused.

Such a state of affairs can be remedied basically and in a lasting manner only through focused reform of the entire system of law, which has to be grounded in fresh thinking and systematic field investigations. This objective can be achieved only through close collaboration between those who understand deeply the legal system and the sociologists well versed in research methodology. It cannot be attained merely through good intentions or by patchwork measures and ad hoc remedies.

However, some perceptive judges of the Supreme Court who had a deep concern for the needy and the helpless, like Justice V.R. Krishna Iyer and Justice P.N. Bhagwati, thought out certain ways which go beyond judicial procedures.

The rise of judicial activism shows the realization among some sections of the judiciary that the present legal system is not adequate for giving justice to the people who need it most. Judicial activism is an effort on the part of the judiciary to establish a result-oriented credibility of the system. As Justice V.R. Krishna Iyer puts it: 'India was waiting for judicial activist,

social action litigation, people-oriented jurisprudence and a vaster jurisdiction with broader access to justice.'

Judicial activism, and public interest litigation (PIL) signal a departure
from the combatant culture inherent in our legal system. Any socially
conscious person can bring to the court of law such matters as the bondage
and exploitation of a certain groups of people, cases of high-level corruption in public affairs, and damage being caused to the environment or to
the monuments which embody our cultural heritage. It is not necessary
that the person who brings up the matter should have himself or herself
suffered injustice or injury. Thus the age-old requirement of a locus standi
for a person who becomes a party to litigation has been obviated.

Such a requirement, though time-honoured, is hardly tenable in the
face of the abundantly prevailing social realities in a country like India.
How can one expect a bonded labourer, *bandhua mazdoor*, working in a
brick kiln in a remote area to go to a court of law against the brutality and
merciless exploitation to which he or she is being subjected? Such cases of
oppression, cruelty, and virtual slavery are innumerable. The victims who
are condemned to such injustice have neither the know-how nor the
means to take their cases to a court of law. To make it a condition that the
person who is being subjected to injury or injustice alone has the right to
be a party to litigation is to shut for the vast mass of people the doors of
justice through law.

However, there seems to be a need to provide a stable structure and to
institutionalize the procedures of judicial activism. Otherwise too much
would depend upon the disposition of different judges. For quite a long
time there have been differences of opinion on such matters among the
Supreme Court judges themselves. For instance, Justice P.N. Bhagwati,
Justice R.S. Pathak, and Justice A.N. Sen delivered separate judgments in
the Bandhua Mukti Morcha case. Both Justice Pathak and Justice Sen
were of the view that although in exceptional circumstances a letter or
some other communication may be treated as a writ petition, it must not
be addressed to a particular judge; it has to be submitted to the court as
a whole, and not to any individual judge. Seervai expressed the opinion
that permitting to address such letters and communications to a particular judge would amount to allowing the petitioner to choose the judge
who will take up his case. It appears however that as far as possible an attempt should be made to ensure that judicial activism and public interest
litigation are not bogged down in too many formalities. Serious endeavour is called for to find suitable ways out. For example, in a case like the
one mentioned above, it can perhaps be provided that when such a letter

or any other communication is received by a particular judge, he or she will forward it to the Chief Justice to assign it to any judge or bench. That would obviate the possibility of such letters of communications being rejected without any consideration of their merit, and at the same time avoid allowing a petitioner to choose the judge. A step in this direction seems to have been taken with the establishment of a cell in the Supreme Court for dealing with public interest petitions.

It is also important to remember that in its enthusiasm for judicial activism, the judiciary should not take over unnecessarily the powers of the legislative and executive arms of the state. This is essential because the judiciary may not always have the benefit of the understanding of people's opinion which the legislators are expected to have; and it may not necessarily have the feel of ground realities which the executive wing of the state is likely to possess. We may mention one judgment as an instance. Some years ago the Supreme Court ordered that all the streets in Delhi should be swept and all the garbage should be removed in the night so that the city is clean by the morning. Eminent urban administrator and planner, M.N. Buch, who has a long experience in the field, wrote an article giving the reasons why this was not feasible because of a number of factors. In that article, he also asked, *inter alia*, as to why the Supreme Court does not order some day that all the cases pending in various courts shall be decided by a particular date.

We must not expect too much from the judicial system. There are certain deep-seated maladies in the economic and sociocultural system as a whole. All of these cannot be remedied by the legal system alone. Perhaps the entire social system will have to change to get rid of them.

17

Towards an Indian Jurisprudence of Social Action and Public Interest Litigation*

V.R. KRISHNA IYER

THE DIALECTICS OF PUBLIC INTEREST LITIGATION

The central concern of law and justice is humanity and its happy, orderly advance, their focus. But in actual fact, notwithstanding emphatic rhetoric in constitutional parchments, equal protection of the laws and a just social order remain paper projects for the have-nots of society. The rule of law is but pleasing illusion if the judicial process does not serve as a delivery system of social justice 'in widest commonalty spread'. Litigation, the curial modus operandi for securing rights of citizens, may well lose its curative potency vis a vis the indigents, agrestics, and illiterates. For them it may survive for some time as the tantalizing opium of remedial hope if the court, by its performance, blesses the rich but betrays the poor. How can the judicative system command the confidence of the humbler millions if law-in-action marginalizes the masses, even menaces the many who hunger for right and justice? In an exploitative system the anonymous lines below ring a bell:

> The law locks up both man and woman
> Who steals the goose from off the common,
> But lets the greater felon loose
> Who steals the common from the goose.

Anatole France acidly expressed the truth of the lie that law is the agent of justice: 'To disarm the strong and arm the weak would be to change the

*Excerpted from V.R. Krishna Iyer, 'Towards a Burgeoning Indian Jurisprudence of Social Action and Public Interest Litigation', *Indian Bar Review*, vol. 16, no. 2, 1989, pp. 132–50.

social order which it's my job to preserve. Justice is the means by which established injustices are sanctioned.' The portentous poignancy of this unhappy reality is writ large on the state of justice in India. This ominous scenario is mitigated by fresh signs of humanism, tho' with halting steps. Law is what law does and so, a performance audit of the legal system alone can tell whether it fills the bill of securing to the people what the Constitution solemnly pledges: 'Justice, Social, Economic and Political; . . . Equality of Status and of Opportunity; and . . . the dignity of the individual.' The present study is confined to the judicial system which, in any society, is but a superstructure, the hard socio-economic equations being the foundation. I have often quoted a profound thought of Seton Pollock relating to my theme here and so I borrow it again:

> The law itself, though of crucial social importance, is only one element in the total human task. That task is to meet and master those frustrations that diminish man in his humanity and obstruct the realisation of his freedom and fulfilment within the human society. Those frustrations stem from ignorance, poverty, pain, disease and conflicts of interest both within the person (the field of psychological medicine) and between persons (the territory of the law). These manifold and interacting frustrations cannot be met by any one discipline but only by a co-ordinated attack upon the problem through enlightened political and administrative initiatives and by educational, medical, psychological *and legal remedies.*

Only a judicial culture which, in its texture, has social justice, human dignity and egalite woven into it can make the judicature in a Third World country, based on a socialistic democratic order, functional. The raw realities of Indian society today are colossal literacy, intractable indigency, and countless chronic injustices, intended with a militancy generated by the preambular rhetoric of the Constitution. The feudal–colonial status quo ante received its legal death sentence with Indian independence. The tryst with destiny Indians made, when the country awoke to freedom, 'to wipe every tear from every eye' and to underwrite 'a social order in which justice, social, economic and political shall inform all the institutions of the national life', is still a pious wish.

This sublime sentiment, consecrated in the Constitution, is distancing itself from the still sad music of Indian humanity whose life, for considerable numbers, remains a tale of blood, toil, tears, and sweat. The political watershed was marked by Indian independence. The great divide between the colonial legal system and free India's value-laden jurisprudence must be grasped if one is to approach the story of judicial developments in the domain of public interest litigation. The political

compulsions and socialistic imperatives, which ignited processes of transformation in the administration of Indian justice, desiderated creative
adaptations and mass-based mutations in manifest fulfilment of the
constitutional mandate that 'the State shall secure that the operation of
the legal system promotes justice, on a basis of equal opportunity, and
shall . . . ensure that opportunities for securing justice are not denied to
any citizen by reason of economic or other disabilities' (Art. 39 A), The
judiciary, being one of the three principal instrumentalities of the state,
is also bound by this command to slough off the dated dogmas of colonial
vintage and so to shape the processes of law as to enrich the national resolve to secure equal justice to all, regardless of economic and other disabilities.

It needs no dialectical materialist to conclude that the social dimensions of jurisprudence when it makes a quantum jump from a dying, im-
perial order to a living democratic order must undergo a people-oriented
radicalization. The people of India are illiterate, around 70 per cent, indigent, around 50 per cent being below the poverty line, primitive, more
than 20 per cent being depressed classes and tribal miserables. A land
where gender injustice is religiously practised by all the religions, where
sati or pressure to leap into the husbands funeral pyre, child marriage,
bride-burning, deadly dowry ubiquity, gang rape, bonded labour, and
marketing of tribal women and dedicating them to godesses as a pious
device to push them into prostitution—these and other besetting vices
mar the human map, agonizing realities cannot but summon the robed
brethren to catalyse the constitutional processes and make social justice
a fact, not a fiction. The writ of court must raise the conscience of the
social forces, or else it is dope, not hope. The pariah sector is silent victim
of countless privations and human rights violations. The judicature cannot be a jejune and jaundiced limb inertly witnessing the Constitution
being stultified.

Environmental pollution, toxic effluents, and deforestation by industrial irresponsibles, public corruption by 'privatized' power processes and
a host of other mafia operations vitiate the social milieu, violate public
morals and deflate the faith of the mute millions in the legal system as a
corrective instrument. In sum, the lowliest, the lost and the last, who are
the Fourth World within the Third World, wait in vain for social justice,
in its comprehensive connotation. A chapter on fundamental duties casts,
inter alia, a constitutional obligation on every citizen 'to protect and improve the natural environment including forests, lakes, rivers, and wild
life, and to have compassion for living creatures and to safeguard public

property and to abjure violence'. If a poor person, unable to stop pollution although affected by it, seeks the help of the court to decree its eradication, the judicial process cannot slumber. Similarly, when public property is squandered, plundered or, by corrupt means, siphoned off for illegitimate ends, a helpless citizen must be able to arrest the process through judicial aid. If a tribal finds the State funds for his tribe's rehabilitation looted by political dacoits or his forest precincts dubiously snatched away by moneyocrats, the court should issue firefighting writs or rescue directives because his fundamental duty to safeguard public assets can be enforced only through court orders. Equal wages for equal work, regardless of sex, is a constitutional and statutory duty of the employer. If there is breach, judicial power must offer effective shelter. Even if a legislation hurting or hampering the backward sector is passed, the higher courts have to declare the statute void, if it be contra-constitutional. In sum, the judicial process, in its functional fulfilment, must be at once a shield and sword in defending the have-nots when injustice afflicts them. And this must be possible even if the humbler folk, directly aggrieved, are too weak to move the court. Access to justice, as will be explained later, is fundamental to fundamental rights. For a right without a remedy is writ in water, being but printed futility. And when the battle is between India (Private) Limited and Indian (Public) Unlimited, the court, with large constitutional authority, must act. 'To be or not to be' is the question before a dynamic judiciary.

Human rights are inalienable values which make for the dignity and worth of personhood. In a feudal universe and colonial cosmos India is, alas, a blend of both—fundamental freedoms are a casualty or a formality. Freedom of speech and of the press, freedom of association, of labour's right to strike and people's right to protest are jural marijuana in a court system of slow responses. For landless tillers and other deprived and underprivileged categories, for ill-treated prisoners and victims of police torture and lock-up liquidation, for child labour, homeless floatsams, sufferers of custodial cruelties and unspeakable forms of indignity and shame for the socio-economic 'deprived' abounding in India, social justice is constitutional cant and judicial justice a rope of sand unless enforceability is easy and the forensic process committed to compassionate realism in the grant of relief. The suprema lex of India promises most of what the Universal Declaration of Human Rights inscribes; the Supreme Court and the high courts, under solemn oath, swear to do Justice, using the legal process as a means towards that end. If the judges take the Constitution seriously, they are bound to accelerate the process of forensic *perestroika* geared to the goal of affirmative relief within the reach everyone, be he backward, primitive, tongueless, or suppressed. Justice, in the constitutional connotation, embraces many dimensions, not mere adjudication between two litigants visualized by the gladiatorial scenario of the adversary system. A radical rupture with that 'combatant' culture, transplanted into India and nurtured by the Indo-Anglian judicature, is thus inevitable. Moreover, the tasks which functionally belong now to the forensic system are far beyond the mimic battles carried on according to medieval rules and indifferent to the inequality of the weaker sector. According to the anglophilic institutional vision, the judge is but an umpire, and the better boxer, not the juster party, wins the game. Obviously, he who needs help to present his case finds himself at the losing end. This shall not be. Third World jurisprudence, in its processual, remedial, and substantive dimensions, must inspire a result-oriented credibility in the Lazarus sector and Abel bracket. Then only will the rule of life legitimize the rule of law.

The Constitution of India, like other national charters of our times, has a progressive hue. Here a few major provisions in Parts III and IV need emphasis. Equality and equal protection, when enforceable as law (Art. 14), gives the court a power to wipe out the terrible inequalities and iniquities rampant in a feudal–colonial society. Freedoms of speech and association, of movement inside and outside the country, of profession and business, guaranteed under Art. 19, vest in the judges vast powers to interdict state authoritarianism and ensure individual autonomy. Most importantly, human life and personal liberty are made impregnable, subject, of course, to legal procedure (Art. 21). Though seemingly vulnerable to legislative invasion, this protection has been rendered an inviolable rampart against executive and legislative breaches through rulings of the Supreme Court.

For emphasis, let me recapitulate the inhumanity of life, despite the humanism of the Constitution. India lives simultaneously in several centuries. Some practices still flourish, though not extensively, which are survivals from ages of human bondage. Women are suppressed, trafficking in human beings, including servitude, flourishes, child labour in factories and risky enterprises is piteously extant. The numerous backward brackets, living in shanties and pavement dwellings and shocking subhuman social and economic conditions, are in no mood to vanish, what with caste wars in Bihar, bonded labour in feudal estates, and dispossessed tribals, harassed in their forest habitats, roaming homeless in despair. A gathering storm is bound to blow unless a creative rule of law, socially sensitive, operationally dynamic, and remedially prompt and potent comes into being. The proprietariat versus the proletariat confrontation must generate a progressive jurisprudence out of the creative tension. The grim urgency of the summons for a radical, humanist version of the jurisprudence of justice, cadres of justices and techniques of justicing is evident from the frequent reports about terrible injustices on a macro scale. Otherwise, human rights of the hungry militants become non est. This is the social essence of the battle of the tenses. The Raj past still holds the Republic prisoner. A struggle for peaceful deliverance is possible only if law and court conspire to change this sorry scheme of things entirely and remould it nearer to our heart's desire. In British Indian days, poverty itself was a crime and a wandering indigent could be bound over as a security suspect by the criminal law. Independence brought ideological winds of change, and humans without rights were clothed with guarantees of fundamental rights. But where was the Promised Land? Progress had been made, mass awareness had been infused, of courts with extra ordinary powers had incarnated, but the actualization of rights remained distant. India was waiting for the judicial activist, social action litigation, people-oriented jurisprudence, and a vaster jurisdiction with broader access to justice.

The jurisdiction of the Indian Supreme Court is the widest in the world; the challenges of India's social changes are the sharpest: the dynamics of a functional jurisprudence is the creative expression or judicial response to the crisis of hunger for justice. Public interest litigation is the offspring of these social forces. This burgeoning process, seminal and innovative, makes the court a catalyst of social justice, a defender of the constitutional faith and the protagonist in the drama of human rights for the common man.

Judicial power, as the constitutional sentinel on the qui vive, has vigilant, versatile functions as the interface between a billion people and the moguls of power. Here is a rising revolution of justice expectations, ignited by independence, which may burst as an angry explosion of frustrations if the judiciary, by omission and commission and conservative tradition, fail in its mission as a radical fiduciary and redemptive instrumentality of the people.

DEMOCRACY OF JUDICIAL REMEDIES

This role transformation democratizes judicial institution—both process and personnel—and banishes the cult of the court as imperium in imperio. Judge Jerome Frank aptly sums up for his country what obviously applies to India:

The robe as a symbol is out of date, an anachronistic remnant of ceremonial government. . . . A judge who is part of a legal system serving present needs should not be clothed in the quaint garment of the distant past. Just as the robe conceals the physical contours of the man, so it needlessly conceals from the public his mental contours. When the human elements in the judging process are covered up, justice operates darklingly. Now that the Supreme Court has declared the judiciary a part of candid democratic government, I think that the cult of the robe should be discarded.

There has to be a paradigm shift if the march from despair to hope is to take place—a new way of thinking about old problems, a shift of the judicial centre of gravity from the affluent to the indigent which, in truth, is the fulfilment of the Constitution. Statesmen of the law must surely dynamize the forensic methodology with creative intelligence and consciousness of social dimensions, and democratize its institutional accountability so as to ensure the Third World mendicants for justice, in their millions, meaningful remedial alms!

True, economic transformation is the primary function of the executive and the legislature. But where justice is the end product and its content has socio-economic components, the Constitution, which is the nidus of all power, commands the judges to catalyse and control, monitor and mandate by writs, and directions—vide Articles 32 and 226—so that they may bear true faith and allegiance to the Constitution and say 'Thy shall be done'.

Public interest litigation (PIL) is the product of creative judicial engineering. The first obstacle to the people-oriented project 'PIL' is the blinkered adversary praxis. Friedman was right when he said: 'It would be tragic if the law were so petrified as to be unable to respond to the unending challenges of evolutionary or revolutionary changes in society.' Lord Scarman likewise hit the nail on the head in his Hamlyn lectures 'I shall endeavour to show that there are in the contemporary world challenges, social, political and economic, which, if the system cannot meet them, will destroy it. These challenges are not created by lawyers; they certainly cannot be suppressed by lawyers; they have to be met either by discarding or by adjusting the legal system. Which is to be?' Legal justice must not operate in a soundproof, lightproof court room with obsolete chants, mystiques, and techniques but discern the social changes and redesign its delivery system, so as to accelerate people's access to effective, litigative justice. The tension between heritage and heresy will, if neglected for long, tear down the tower of justice. In truth, the law lags behind contemporary advances. When we deny this gap, the law becomes 'the government of the living by the dead'. The 'ayatollahs' of the law are negative navigators of the old order. Commonwealth Secretary General, Ramphal once observed:

> The law has a greater, more positive, more exciting role in discerning change and legitimising progress. It is a role played consistently over the ages as the law fulfilled its noblest purposes with consummate discretion in such areas as human bondage, the right of dissent, desegregation and women's rights. There will assuredly be other roles ahead for which you will need wisdom, perception and courage but most of all a vision of change and sensitivity to its arrival. Only thus will you secure your validity and fulfil your deepest duty in our changing world.

PATHOLOGY OF ADVERSARIASIS

The social credential of the justice system and its functional potential desiderate a remedial jurisprudence which is the cutting edge of court justice, breaking the bigotries of the current 'adversarial' ideology and other forms of 'robesque' rituals lest a dinosaur fate should overtake the justice system.

The adversary regime, a legacy of Anglo-American legal culture, is splendid in principle in many respects and is a victory in practice for human rights, viewed historically with Star Chamber memory, but is hostile to current expectations from court justice unless necessitous innovations are wrought into the system. A court *where man matters* is the goal. 'Appropriate judicial technology' for human justice is the desideratum.

In recent years the cost-intensive features of the adversary system and the way in which it closes the door against lesser mortals has provoked daring departures by jurists of the eminence of Lord Devlin, Professor Zeidler has suggested conference-like procedures and elimination of gladiatorial features. Some judges have proposed reforms by making the judge not a referee but one who seeks to reach the truth. The disabilities of one of the disputants in producing evidence should not and would not, if the judge were activist, weaken his case if truth is on his side. Justice must be rounded on truth, not mere 'proof' which depends, in an adversary milieu, on the strength of the party. Consequently, a wave of change is blowing over the Indian judicial terrain.

EASY ACCESS TO JUSTICE

Any discussion of this nascent jurisprudence in social locomotion must begin with the lucid thought of Cappelletti;

The right of effective access to justice has emerged with the new social rights. Indeed it is of paramount importance among these new rights since the enjoyment of traditional as well as new social rights presupposes mechanisms for their effective protection. Such protection, moreover, is best assured by a workable remedy within the framework of the judicial system. Effective access to justice can thus be seen as the most basic requirement—the most basic 'human right'—of a system which purports to guarantee legal rights.

Access to, justice today is confined to a 'person aggrieved' and having 'standing' or cause of action by alleging a direct personal injury. In Third World conditions this restricted approach defeats the object of justice to the voiceless for whom the court is 'untouchable' and 'unapproachable'. Access to courts is not an abstract conception but a reified project with mutations and adaptations according to the exigencies of society. Class actions, test cases, representative suits, public interest litigation, social action groups going into courts initiators or intervenors, and so on are some of the forms. The subject matter in such cases may be environmental pollution, public nuisance of other sorts, oppression of socially weaker groups, violation of social welfare legislation, evasion of legal controls by the corporate sector, illegitimacy of appointments to high offices, executive excesses by public functionaries, administrative delinquencies, and so on. Civil rights litigation, consumer protection, fight against deprivation of liberty of the poor, over-incarceration, torture in custody, unjust death penalties, etc.—these classes of cases have more impact on the weaker section of society and take much less time and expense than property litigation, tax cases, and corporate battles put together. Public law must develop in this direction at the procedural level so that justice may come within the reach of the common classes directly or vicariously. 'Standing' is the legal entitlement or a person to invoke the jurisdiction of the court or tribunal regardless of his personal injury. The adjectival law must be broadened to bring within the orbit of 'standing' any person, who has a *real concern* in the cause. 'Concern' is a word without definite legal connotation such as is possessed by 'interest'. The use of 'real', emphasizes that busybodies are not to have standing and the word is itself a flexible one which may operate as a regulator in this context; it transforms the concept of 'concern' into one which is clearly objective. Indeed, the jurisprudence in this branch is of great promise despite the exaggerated apprehensions deliberately generated by some 'yesterday' jurists and judges who are allergic to the dawn of the new public law. The 'floodgates argument', often urged on the score that busybodies will flood our courts with frivolous cases, is a phoney bogey. 'The idle and whimsical plaintiff, a

dilettante who litigates for a lark, is a specter , which haunts the legal literature, not the courtroom.'

Properly used, the poor become strong through an independent,
dynamic national legal services authority, with a network of duties from
educating and arming the weak with legal missiles and helping them use
litigative artillery for vindicating rights. Otherwise, the poor will dismiss
the justice system as an expensive inconsequence.

How can a bonded labourer working in a stone quarry ever know of
moving the Supreme Court of India?; 'bonded labourers are non-persons,
exiles of the system, living a life or animals. The bonded labourer has no
home, no shelter, no food, no drinking water. He has no hope. A human
being without hope has no Supreme Court. Says Nandita Haksar, an
activist,

> It is only a socially committed individual or politically aware organisation that
> can speak on his behalf. Such an individual or organisation may be deeply
> moved by the misery he sees or by a report he reads. Such a person (or orga-
> nisation) does not suffer the disabilities himself but he feels for the poor and
> reacts to injustice. Can such a person (or organisation) move the court on
> behalf of the poor, . . . the jurisdiction of the Supreme court 'can be invoked
> by a third party in the case of a violation of the constitutional rights of another
> person or determinate class of persons, who, by reason of proverty, helpless-
> ness, disability or social or economic disadvantage is unable to move the court
> personally for relief.

In fact, public interest cases, ignited by social action campaigners, involve
the rights of humble people at one go, unlike traditional litigation which
deals with disputes between individuals. And a single case may reach relief
to thousands of people instead of driving them to separate cases which
would have to be heard separately.

SEMINAL JUDICIAL TRENDS

The Supreme Court of India in the *Fertilizer case* accepted this people-
oriented broad-based perspective. The actual case arose when a damaged
plant was sought to be sold by a public sector factory for an allegedly low
price causing loss to the exchequer. The workers of the factory challenged
the proposed sale. The Court observed:

> Two questions, incidentally arise: Have the workers locus standi under
> Art. 32, which is a special jurisdiction confined to enforcement of fundamen-
> tal rights? What, if any, are the fundamental rights of workmen affected by

the employer's sale of machinery whose immediate impact may be conversion of permanent employment into precarious service and eventual exit? Lastly, but most importantly, where does the citizens stand, in the context of the democracy of judicial remedies, in the absence of an ombudsman? In the face of (rare, yet real) misuse of administrative power to play ducks and drakes with the public exchequer, especially where developmental expansion necessarily involves astronomical expenditure and concomitant corruption, do public bodies enjoy immunity from challenge save through the post-mortem of Parliamentary organs. What is the role of the judicial process, read in the light of the dynamics of legal control and corporate autonomy? This juristic field is virgin . . . law must meet life on this critical yet sensitive issue. The active co-existence of public sector autonomy, so vital to effective business management, and judicial control of public power tending to go berserk, is one of the creative claims upon functional jurisprudence.

* * *

While it is unnecessary fur us to spell out in greater detail the emergence of a new branch of administrative law in relation to the national plan and the public sector of the economy, it is important to underscore the vital departure from the pattern of judicial review in the Anglo-American legal environment because the demands of development obligated by Part IV compel creative extensions to control jurisprudence in many fields, including administrative law, contract law, penal law, fiscal law and the like.

* * *

A pragmatic approach to social justice compels us to interpret constitutional provisions, including those like Arts. 32 and 226, with a view to see that effective policing of the corridors of power is carried out by the court until other ombudsman arrangements—a problem with which Parliament has been wrestling for too long—emerges.

* * *

The learned Attorney General challenged the petitioner's locus standi either qua worker or qua citizen to question in court the wrong doings of the public sector although he maintained that what had been done by the Corporation was both bona fide and correct. We certainly agree that judicial interference with the Administration cannot be meticulous in our Montesquien system of separation of powers. The court cannot usurp nor abdicate, and the parameters or judicial review must be clearly defined and never exceeded.

* * *

Assuming that the Government company has acted mala fide. or has dissi-
pated public funds, can a common man call into question in a court the
validity of the action by invocation of Art. 32 or 226 of the Constitution?

* * *

We have no doubt that in competition between courts and streets as dispenser
of justice, the rule of law must win the aggrieved person for the law court and
wean him from the lawless street. In simple terms, locus standi must be
liberalised to meet the challenges of the times. *Ubi jus ihi remedium* must be
enlarged to embrace all interests of public-minded citizens or organisations
with serious concern for conservation of public resources and the direction
and correction of public power so as to promote justice in its triune facets.

* * *

Law, as I conceive it, is a social auditor and this audit function can be put
into action only when some one with real public interest ignites the jurisdiction. We cannot be scared by the fear that all and sundry will be litigation-
happy and waste their time and money and the time of the court through false
and frivolous cases. In a society where freedoms suffer from atrophy and
activism is essential for participative public justice, some risks have to be taken
and more opportunities opened for the public-minded citizen to rely on the
legal process and not be repelled from it by narrow pendantry now surrounding locus standi.

The foundation for court action is no longer the personal injury of the
plantiff, and a liberalized rule for seeking relief, in categories of cases now
well established, through surrogates, good Samaritans and public-spirited organizations, is now integral to the processual jurisprudence of India.
A radical democracy of judicial remedies is now taking shape in the forensic universe of Third World countries. This litigative avatar as the deliverer
of social justice is the crimson phenomenon of public interest forensics.
Now considerable liberties are taken with vintage procedures. For instance, instead of formalized pleadings even letters setting out grievances
are treated as sufficient to trigger judicial action. Why? The illiterate indigents and rural primitives suffer injustices but are out of bounds for
expensive lawyers' offices and exotic legalese. Hence what has been called
epistolary jurisdiction is in vogue in PIL cases whereby an ignorant victim
or lay social activist is permitted to lay information before the court.
Thereupon the court moves on its own in a compassionate jurisdiction to
inhibit wrongs and to enforce rights.

However, certain safeguards are being institutionalized; letters are processed by legal aid societies who pass them on to advocates for conversion into proper writ petitions which are filed through the registry so that they often are represented in a more satisfactory shape. When a socially conscious individual or a voluntary organzation moves the court on behalf of the poor it does so mostly on the basis of newspaper reports or scanty personal knowledge. The court needs facts, statistics, affidavits, and evidence before it can come to a conclusion on violation of fundamental rights. The contest is always unequal, On the one side is the government, with the entire administration at its command and an army of lawyers of the might of a corporation or moneyocrat. On the other side is a social activist seeking justice without any idea of court procedures or requirements or an indigent priced out of the judicial theatre. Often for such an individual or organization, obtaining an affidavit from a bonded labourer, a woman in a rescue home, or a jailed trade union leader is in itself a hard task. Other procedural abracadabra, familiar to the bar, may baffle them. In such predicaments, juristic realism suggests new recipes, forges new tools, devises new methods, and adopts new strategies for the purpose of making human rights meaningful for the large masses of people. Social workers, journalists, engineers, law teachers, advocates, and welfare organizations have been involved in such undertakings and their reports have become mines of information on the condition of the people. People who have no forum for redressal of their grievances have now some access to justice, This is a new dimension to the forensic process. Public interest litigation is not, to borrow a court ruling, 'in the nature of adversary litigation but a challenge and an opportunity to the government and its officers to make basic human rights meaningful to the deprived and vulnerable sections of the community to assure them social and economic justice which is the signature tune of our Constitution.'

While a broader perspective regarding locus standi is a desideratum more radical procedural reforms are essential if the marginalized masses are to regard the justice system as theirs, Judicial justice must be liberated from the sclerosis of the adversary process, for the sound reason that between unequals that procedure fails to be just and handicaps the underdog. Procedural fair process based on principled pragmatism must govern our choice. Prof. Dr W. Zeidler has pinpointed the controversy thus:

> Amongst the procedural systems the common law (adversary) procedure is what a shining Rolls Royce car is amongst automobiles whereas the German procedure may be compared with a dusty small Volkswagen, I agree, But the question remains: What is it you can afford to pay for, and how often and in what situations are you in need of a Rolls Royce or a Volkswagen?

The greatness of the adversary system (including the accusatory process, as it is popularly known in the criminal jurisdiction) and its revolutionary part in the progressive story of human justice cannot cover up its current anti-poor aberrations, its chronic elitism, and soft response to exploitative interests as their rescue shelter. I view the court process as a value weighted ally of the people's process and suggest a reform project on the basic assumption that the democratic politics of justice (in the higher sense) desiderates humanist procedural mutants with activist egalitarian bias. The creed of social justice sanctions the swing towards the have-nots.

Whole truth become the major concern of the judge. Indian courts have now established the praxis, subject to rules or natural justice, of collecting evidence through its own agencies like commissions. In *Sunil Batra II* where the court acted on a letter from a prisoner complaining about the torture of a fellow prisoner, a senior advocate was deputed to enter the Delhi prison, question officers and prisoners, examine entries in books and make a report to the court. This measure unearthed a horrendous torture which the prisoner could never have established. In Mehta's cases a legal action was started by a public-spirited citizen on the ground that hazardous manufactures by a private company should be forbidden. A major leakage of oleum gas affecting a large number of persons led to the litigation. The court, to judge the issue of toxic emanations, appointed a team of experts and got their reports. The Supreme Court, in this case, expanded the concept of locus standi even in the area of environmental preservation. Further, the judges resorted to collection of independent information on a technical subject through the agency of a Commission. The relevant observations are excerpted here:

> There is also one other matter to which we should like to draw the attention of the Government of India. We have noticed that in the past few years there is an increasing trend to the number of cases based on environmental pollution and ecological destruction coming up before the Courts. Many such cases concerning the material basis of livelihood of millions of poor people are reaching this Court by way of public interest litigation. In most of these cases there is need for neutral scientific expertise as an essential input to inform judicial decision making. These cases require expertise at a high level of scientific and technical sophistication. We felt the need for such expertise in this very case and we had to appoint several expert committees to inform the Court as to what measures were required to be adopted by the management of Shriram to safeguard against the hazard or possibility of leaks, explosion, pollution of air and water, etc., and how many of the safety devices against this hazard or possibility existed in the plant and which of them, though necessary, were not installed. We had great difficulty in finding out independent experts who would be able to advise the Court on these issues. Since there

is at present no independent and competent machinery to generate, gather and make available the necessary scientific and technical information, we had to make an effort on our own to identify experts who would provide reliable scientific and technical input necessary for the decision of the case and this was obviously a difficult and by its very nature, unsatisfactory, exercise. It is therefore absolutely essential that there should be an independent Centre with professionally competent and public spirited experts to provide the needed scientific and technological input. We would in the circumstances urge upon the Government of India to set up an Ecological Sciences Research Group consisting of independent, professionally competent experts in different branches of science and technology who would act as an information bank for the Court and the Government departments and generate new information according to the particular requirements of the Court or the concerned Government department.

The voice of the Third World asking for social justice is heard in Gupta's case relied on in *Mehta*. The rationale of the new development is spelt out:

Where a legal wrong or a legal injury is caused to a person or to a determinate class of persons by reason of violation of any constitutional or legal right or any burden is imposed in contravention of any constitutional or legal provision or without authority of law or any such legal wrong or legal injury or illegal burden is threatened, and any such person or determinate class of person is by reasons of poverty or disability or socially or economically disadvantaged position unable to approach the Court for relief, any member of the public or social action group can maintain an application for an appropriate direction, order or writ in the High Court under Art. 226 and in case of breach of any fundamental right of such person or class of persons, in this Court under Art. 32 seeking judicial redress for the legal wrong or injury caused to such person or determinate class of persons. This Court also held in S.P. Gupta's case (supra) as also in the *People's Union for Democratic Rights* v. *Union of India*, and in Bandhua Mukti Morcha case (supra) that procedure being merely a handmaiden of justice it should not stand in the way of access to justice to the weaker sections of Indian humanity and therefore where the poor and the disadvantaged are concerned . . . this Court will not insist on a regular writ petition and even a letter addressed by a public spirited individual or a social action group acting pro bono publico would suffice to ignite the jurisdiction of this Court. We wholly endorse this statement of the law in regard to the broadening of locus standi and what has come to be known as epistolary jurisdiction.

Nor should the Court adopt a rigid stance that no letters will be entertained unless they are supported by an affidavit. If the Court were to insist on an affidavit as a condition of entertaining the letters the entire object and purpose of epistolary jurisdiction would be frustrated because most of the poor and disadvantaged persons will then not be able to have easy access to the Court and even the social action groups will find it difficult to approach the Court.

The concept of state itself has been broadened to encompass every enterprise which is under the control of the state. Even prisons, hospitals, rescue homes and other like sanctuaries have come within the court's newfound ombudsmanic jurisdiction. The old 'hands off' doctrine is dead. For instance, wages for prisoners who work in the prisons are now made obligatory by an order of the high court of Gujarat. A report was called for by the Court before the hearing of the case and relief granted linking up the remedy of wages with the constitutional prohibition of forced labour. Similarly, the same high court issued a commission to a task force headed by a jurist to investigate into and report on the working conditions of the Surat textile workers and based thereon, protective measures in favour of the workers were mandated by the court. The Supreme Court itself has, after investigation and hearing through unorthodox methods, got juveniles lodged unlawfully in the prisons of India released. Mental hospitals which were torture homes were invigilated by the Supreme Court and affirmative action, through a scheme approved by the Court, gave relief to those miserables. Likewise, after getting expert reports, the Supreme Court gave positive directives to prevent quarrying of stones from the Doon Valley to protect the environment. Prisoners of Bihar, who were blinded by police torture, women who were sold like chattel and undertrials who were unjustly languishing in custody were liberated by the Court. A host of such humanist instances is issuing from the higher judiciary breaking away from ancient judicial obscurantism but firmly based on the Indian Constitution, expansively and imaginatively interpreted. In short, revolutionary changes are taking place in Judicial technology, and judicial law-making. Epoch-making social dimensions are being added to the judicial process. Law with a heart, court with a human face, is the serendipity.

Another facet of forensic innovation. The *Ratlam Municipality Case* is a path-breaker even like the *Rickshaw Pullers* case. Specific schemes were prepared in both these cases under the authority of the court. Dynamic developments in the field of relief, not by mere decree for money or declaration or right, but by regular schemes being framed and judicially monitored, are the new discovery. How fascinating and heart-warming to read these creative pages of judicial history in the making! In *Sunil Batra* a whole code to protect prisoners was made by the court not merely for the prison which figured in the case but for all prisons in the country, and sessions judges were directed to visit penal institutions periodically to investigate prisoners' grievances. In *Sheila Barse cases*, the court called for a report, through the head of a college of social work, about the fate of female inmates of police lock-ups in Bombay and issued directives for the police stations *in the whole states*. In environmental pollution and like situations, this dynamic dimension to remedial justice, of framing projects and operating them under judicial monitoring, is reflected in court judgments. Even so, the pace is slow; dissenting voices make the process zigzag; tradition is a *vis inertia; vigoroso tempo* is still a wish, not the finish. But judicial perestroika is no longer anathema. The court is now a sentinel of the nation, but operationally it has 'miles to go' and 'promises to keep' even though 'the woods are lovely, green and deep'. The robed brethren cannot afford to live in several centuries simultaneously, nor be colonial and free, black and white. *Fiat justicia* is a constitutional command for India of a billion humans, most of whom are alienated from the system.

Cappeletti's lovely cynicism has a message:

> Our judicial system has been aptly described as follows: Admirable though it may be, (it) is at once slow and costly. It is a finished product of great beauty, but entails an immense sacrifice of time, money and talent. This 'beautiful' system is frequently a luxury, it tends to give a high quality of justice only when, for one reason, or another, parties can surmount the substantial barriers which it erects to most people and to many types of claims.

The elusive beauty of exotic justice which is beyond reach for the Fourth World can no longer tantalize, and Operation Public Interest Litigation, pruned and disciplined, structured functionally and inspired jurisprudentially, is the Indian legal Lamarkism evolved by the Constitution interacting with the militant environment.

> Our judges are not monks or scientists, but participants in the living stream of our national life, steering the law between the dangers of rigidity on the one hand and of formlessness on the other. Our system faces no theoretical dilemma but a single continuous problem: how to apply to ever-changing conditions the never-changing principles of freedom.

The frontiers-persons of the Indian judiciary may patriotically remember Brougham's words:

> It was the boast of Augustus that he found Rome of brick and left it of marble. But how much nobler will be the sovereign's boast when he shall have it to say that he found law dear and left it cheap; found it a sealed book and left it a living letter; found it the patrimony of the rich and left it the inheritance of the poor; found it the two-edged sword of craft and oppression and left it the staff of honesty and the shield of innocence.

18

Public Interest Litigation*

MAHABALESHWAR N. MORJE

The public interest litigation (PIL) is one of the most important facets of the administrative law and administrative justice. The preamble, the directive principles, and the fundamental duties of our Constitution are essentially the summary of the views and ideas which are found in *Gitanjali* of Rabindranath Tagore and other important Indian commentaries. These commentaries refer to obligations and duties towards the neglected poor and weaker sections of the society. The judgment of the Supreme Court in *Bandhua Mukti Morcha* is one of the cases which refers to socio-economic problems and that appears to be the reason why the Supreme Court referred to Rabindranath Tagore's views in the above judgment.

PIL is considered as an instrument which extends legal aid to the poor masses and weaker sections of the society. In a country like India, where more than 40 per cent of the people live below poverty line the state or public authorities against whom PIL is brought by social workers or by public institutions are expected to welcome such litigations as it would result in ensuring basic human rights, constitutional as well as legal, to those who are in a socially and economically disadvantageous position.

What is meant by a PIL petition? Who can file such petitions? Who are expected to finance them? Is it required to be filed under Article 32 in the Supreme Court of India, or under Article 226 in the high courts? Against whom can such petitions be filed? Can all ordinary postcard or telegram be sufficient to file such petitions? What should be the approach of the government and other corporations? What is the view of the Supreme Court and various high courts when entertaining such petitions? Is

*Excerpted from Mahabaleshwar N. Morje, 'Public Interest Litigation', *Indian Bar Review*, vol. 15, no. 142, 1988, pp. 59–68.

it possible for PIL to be misused, say for publicity or for political purpose? What precautions should be taken to achieve the real objective of PIL? How far does PIL fulfil the objective of the directive principles of state policy and fundamental duties?

LEGAL AID TO POOR

Article 39A was added to the directive principles in order to ensure equal justice promised to all citizens by the preamble. Article 14 guarantees equality before law. Article 39A was added in 1976 when it was found that, though several welfare, laws were enacted under our Constitution to realize the goal of social justice, these have remained only on paper without being properly implemented. The total indifference and failure of the legislative wings in the implementation of such socio-economic legislations gave rise to certain issues. Non-implementation of these legislations affected the poorer sections of society. The judiciary therefore was expected to set right the situation of changing the century-old 'outlook'. It was said that while reaching the decision in implementation of socio-economic legislations, the operators of the state organizations, including the judiciary, failed to examine the social climate in interpreting the welfare laws. Some of the courts still continue to stick to old rules of construction without any regard to new constitutional jurisprudence and human rights. The old rules on locus standi and cause of action are required to be liberalized in the backdrop of socio-economic changes contemplated through various social welfare legislations. It created more and more new categories of rights in favour of masses and a corresponding new category of duties on the public authorities.

VIOLATION OF LABOUR LAWS

The scope and nature of public interest litigation has been decisively laid down by the Supreme Court in the *Asiad Workers'* case. The matter was brought to the notice of the Court by means of a letter which was treated as a writ petition on the judicial side. The Court started enquiry into the allegations of violations of various labour laws in relation to workmen employed in the construction works of various projects connected with the Asian Games. In the course of the judgment, P.N. Bhagwati J. (as he then was) made certain revealing statements such as 'mere initiation of social and economic rescue programmes by the Executive and Legislature would not be enough and it is only through multi-dimensional strategies, including public interest litigation, that these and economic rescue programmes can be effective.' About the role of judiciary, he said:

The time has now come when the courts must become the courts of the poor and the struggling masses of this country. They must shed their character as upholders of the established order and the status quo. They must be sensitivised to the need of doing justice to the large masses of people to whom justice has been denied by a cruel and heartless society for generations. It is through public interest litigation that the problems of the poor are now coming to the forefront and the entire theatre of law is changing. It holds out great possibilities for the future.

He spoke about the legal profession as well:

There is a misconception in the minds of some lawyers, journalists and men in public life that public interest litigation is unnecessarily cluttering up the files of the court and adding to the already staggering arrears of cases which are pending for long years and it should not therefore be encouraged by the court. This is, to our mind, a totally perverse view smacking of elitist and status quoist approach.

PRO BONO PUBLICO

PIL has developed its institutional roots by the judgment of the Supreme Court in *Judges* case which held:

Any member of the public can maintain an application or an appropriate direction, order or writ in the High Court under Article 226 and in case of breach of any fundamental right to such person or determined class of persons in this court under Article 32 seeking judicial redress for the legal wrong or injury caused to such person or determined class of persons, where the weaker sections of the community are concerned, such as undertrials languishing in jails, inmates of the protective home in Agra or Harijan workers engaged in road construction in the Ajmer District, who are living in poverty and destitution, who are barely eking out a miserable existence with their sweat and toil, who are helpless victims of an exploitative society and who do not have an easy access to justice, this court will not insist on a regular writ petition to be filed by the public spirited individual espousing their case and seeking relief for them. This court will readily respond even to a letter addressed by such individual acting pro bono publico.

DUTY OF GOVERNMENT

When the petitions are filed in the interest of the public the governments are not expected to raise technical objections saying that no fundamental rights of the petitioners or the workmen on whose behalf the petition has been filed, have been infringed. On the contrary, the government should welcome an inquiry by the court if it is found that the citizens are deprived of their legitimate rights under the Constitution. In this regard, it would be necessary to mention the petition filed on behalf of the bonded labourers in the country. The system of bonded labour has been prevalent in various parts of the country since long, prior to the attainment of political freedom and it constitutes an ugly and shameful feature of our national life. This system based on exploitation by a few socially and economically powerful persons trading on the misery and suffering of large numbers of men and holding them in bondage is a relic of a feudal hierarchical society which hypocritically proclaims the divinity of man but treats large masses of people belonging to the lower range of the social ladder or economically impoverished segments of society as dirt and chattel. This system under which one person can be bonded to provide labour to another for years and years, until an alleged debt is supposed to be wiped out which never seems to happen during the lifetime of the bonded labourer, is totally incompatible with the new egalitarian socio economic order which we have promised to build and it is not only an affront to basic human dignity but also constitutes gross and revolting violation of constitutional values.

CHALLENGE TO THE GOVERNMENT

While deciding this case, the Supreme Court has held

> Public interest litigation is not in the nature of adversary litigation but it is a challenge and an opportunity to the Government and its officers to make basic human rights meaningful to the deprived and vulnerable sections of the community and to assure them social and economic justice which is the signature tune of our Constitution. The Government and its officers must welcome public interest litigation, because it would provide them an occasion to examine whether the poor and the down-trodden are getting social and economic entitlements, or whether they are continuing to remain victims of deception and exploitation at the hands of strong and powerful sections of the community and whether social and economic justice has become a meaningful reality for them, or it has remained merely a teasing illusion and a promise of unreality, so that in case the complaint in the public interest litigation is found to be true, they can, in discharge of their constitutional obligation, root out exploitation and injustice and ensure to the weaker sections their rights and entitlements. When the Court entertains public interest litigation, it does not do so in a cavilling spirit or in a confrontational mood, or with a view to tilting its executive authority or seeking to usurp it,

but its attempt is only to ensure observance of social and economic rescue programmes, legislative as well as executive, framed for the benefit of have nots and the handicapped and to protect them against violation of their basic human rights, which is also the constitutional obligation of the executive. The Court is thus merely assisting in the realisation of the constitutional object-ives.

The Supreme Court further states:

Article 21 assures the right to live with human dignity, free from exploitation. The State is under a constitutional obligation to see that there is no violation of the fundamental right of any person, particularly when he belongs to the weaker sections of the community and is unable to wage a legal battle against a strong and powerful opponent who is exploiting him. Both the Central Government and the State Governments are therefore bound to ensure observances of various social welfare and labour laws enacted by Parliament for the purpose of securing to the workmen a life of basic human dignity in compliance with the Directive Principles of State Policy.

Writ Petition under Article 32

While interpreting the maintainability of writ petitions under Article 32 of the Constitution, the Supreme Court further held:

It must be borne in mind that the court's approach must be guided not by any verbal or formalistic canons of construction but by the paramount object and purpose for which this article has been enacted as a fundamental right in the Constitution and its interpretation must receive illumination from the trinity of provisions which permeate and energise the entire Constitution, namely, the Preamble, the Fundamental Rights and the Directive Principles of State Policy. It is clear on the plain language of Clause (1) of Article 32 that whenever there is a violation of a fundamental right, anyone can move the Supreme Court for enforcement of such fundamental right. Of course, the Court would not, in exercise of its discretion, intervene at the instance of a meddlesome inter-loper or busy body and would ordinarily insist that only a person whose fundamental right is violated should be allowed to activise the Court. Where, however, the fundamental right of a person or class or persons is violated, but who cannot have resort to the Court on account of their poverty or disability or socially or economically disadvantaged posi-tion, the Court can and must allow any member or the public acting bona fide to espouse the cause of such person or class of persons and move the Court for judicial enforcement of the fundamental right of such person or class of persons. This does not violate, in the slightest measure, the language of the constitutional provision enacted in Clause (I) of Article 32.

SERVING PUBLIC PURPOSE

While deciding the *Pavement Dwellers* case the Supreme Court has held:

> The Constitution is not only the paramount law of the land but, it is the source and sustenance of all laws. Its provisions are conceived in public interest and are intended to serve a public purpose. The doctrine of estoppel is based on the principle that consistency in word and action imparts certainty and honesty to human affairs. This principle can have no application to represent-ations made regarding the assertion or enforcement of fundamental rights. There can also be no waiver of fundamental rights. No individual can barter away the freedom conferred upon him by the Constitution. A confession made by him in a proceeding, whether he does not possess or will not enforce any particular fundamental right, cannot create an estoppel against him in that or any subsequent proceedings. Such a confusion, if enforced, would defeat the purpose of the Constitution. Were the argument of estoppel valid, an all-powerful State could easily tempt an individual to forgo his precious personal freedom on promise of transitory, immediate benefits.

RIGHT TO LIVELIHOOD

The Supreme Court further observed

> The right to life includes the right to livelihood. The sweep of the right to life conferred by Article 21 is wide and far reaching. It does not mean merely that life cannot be extinguished or taken away as for example, by the im-position and execution of death sentence, except according to procedure established by law. That is but one aspect of the right to life. An equally im-portant facet of that right is the right to livelihood because, no person can live without the means of living, that is, the means of livelihood. If the right to livelihood is not treated as a part of the constitutional right to life, the easiest way of depriving a person of his right to life would be to deprive him of his means of livelihood to the point of abrogation. Such deprivation would not only denude the life of its effective content and meaningfulness but it would make life impossible to live. And yet, such deprivation would not have to be in accordance with the procedure established by law, if the right to life is conceded. That which alone makes it possible to live, leave aside what makes

life livable, must be deemed to be an integral component of the right to life. Deprive a person of his right to livelihood and you shall have deprived him of his life.

These writ petitions were filed on behalf of persons who live on pavements and in slums in the city of Bombay. They constitute nearly half of the metropolitan population. The first group of petitions relate to pavement and *basti*s of slum dwellers. Those who have made pavements their homes exist in the midst of filth and squalor, which has to be seen to be believed.

Rabid dogs in search of stinking meat and cats in search of hungry rats, keep them company. They cook and sleep when they ease, for no conveniences are available to them. Their daughters come of age, bathe under the nosy gaze of passers-by, unmindful of the feminine sense of bashfulness. The cooking and washing over, women pick lice from each other's hair. The boys beg, men folk, without occupation snatch chains with the connivance of the defenders of law and order; when caught, if at all, they say: Who does not commit crimes in this city?

Prevention of Misuse of Provision

The Supreme Court however has always taken care to see that persons under the pretext of public interest are not misused. In one of the cases directives were issued to government in a petition filed by the parents of a student for taking steps against ragging in a medical college in the State of Himachal Pradesh. In this case, the Supreme Court has held that public interest litigation is a weapon which has to be used with great care and circumspection and the judiciary has to be extremely careful to see that under the guise of redressing a public grievance, it does not encroach upon the sphere reserved by the Constitution to the executive and the legislature.

On receiving a letter written by a guardian of a student of medical college in Shimla, the high court treated it as a petition and issued notices to the college authorities and the government. The court gave various directives, including a directive to constitute a committee for reporting in the matter. On the submission of the report which contained a recommendation for legislation, the high court directed the chief secretary to inform the court as to what action the government proposed to take on the recommendation to initiate legislation for curbing ragging. This directive was given in spite of the chief secretary's categorical assurance in that regard.

SMALL MAN AND BIG INDUSTRIALIST

While referring to PIL and the rights of the small men to have their rights adjudicated under Article 136 read with Article 32, the Supreme Court has observed that the special leave petitions of 'small men' are as much entitled to consideration as special leave petitions of 'big industrialist'. In fact, the Supreme Court has always regarded the poor and the disadvantaged as entitled to preferential consideration than the rich and the affluent, the businessmen and the industrialists. The reason is that the weaker sections of Indian humanity have been deprived of justice for long, they have had no access to justice on account of their poverty, ignorance, and illiteracy. The strategy of PIL has brought justice within the easy reach of the poor and the disadvantaged sections of the community. It is, therefore, not correct to say that the Supreme Court is not giving to the 'small men' the same treatment as it is giving to the 'big industrialists'. In fact, the concern shown to the poor and the disadvantaged is much greater than that shown to the rich and the well-to-do.

TRANSFERING OF MARKSHEET AT MBBS EXAMINATION

A petition was filed by Dr Mahesh Gosavi against Shivajirao Nilangekar Patil, the then chief minister of the state of Maharashtra alleging his involvement in tampering with the grade sheets of MBBS examination to further the career of his daughter. The petitioner alleged that this was done at the behest of the chief minister of the state. The Supreme Court held that though the affidavit filed in support of the petition was of unreliable credence, it was proper. The allegations made in the petition disclosed a lamentable state of affairs in the University of Bombay. The petitioner might have moved the court for furthering his private interest but enquiry into the conduct of the examiners of the university was a matter of public interest as well. When such state of affairs are brought to the notice of the court, it is the duty of the court to enquire into the allegations to find out the truth. In such a situation all enquiry into the state of affairs of a public institution becomes necessary and private litigation assumes the character of public interest litigation and such an enquiry is necessary and essential for the administration of justice.

MANUFACTURE OF HAZARDOUS PRODUCTS

A public interest litigation was filed raising some seminal questions concerning the true scope and ambit of Articles 21 and 32 of the Constitution. They related to the principles and norms for determining the liability of large enterprises engaged in manufacture and sale of hazardous products; the basis on which damages in case of such liability should be quantified; whether such large enterprises should he allowed to continue to function in thickly populated areas; and if they are permitted so to function, what measures must be taken for the purpose or reducing to a minimum the hazard to the workmen and the community living in the neighbourhood. These are questions of the greatest importance particularly since the leakage of methyl isocynate (MIC) gas from the Union Carbide plant in Bhopal. Lawyers, judges, and jurists are now considerably exercised as to what controls, whether by way of relocation or by way of installation of adequate safety devices, need to be imposed on corporations employing hazardous technology and producing toxic or dangerous substances. Further, if any liquid or gas escapes which is injurious to the workmen and the people living in the surrounding areas, on account of negligence or otherwise, what should be the extent of liability of such corporations and what remedies can be devised for enforcing such liability with a view to securing payment of damages to the persons affected by such leakage.

Contract to Bottle Arrack

A public interest litigation was brought for setting aside grant of contract to bottle arrack. It was established that the executive action was arbitrary. The High Court set aside the contract in spite of the fact that the allegation of bias against the chief minister was found to be false.

While deciding this case the Supreme Court held that it is true that in a public interest litigation, those professing to be public-spirited citizens cannot be encouraged to indulge in wild and reckless allegations besmirching the character of others but, at the same time, the court cannot close its eyes and persuade itself to uphold publicly mischievous executive actions which have been so exposed. When arbitrariness and perversion are writ large and brought out clearly, the court cannot shirk its duty and refuse its writ. Advancement of the public interest and avoidance of the public mischief are the paramount considerations. As always, the court is concerned with the balancing of interests.

Right to Road in Hilly Areas

While deciding the question or providing road to the people in hilly areas in public interest litigation, the Supreme Court has held that affirmative action in the form of some remedial measure in public interest in the background of the Constitutional aspirations as enshrined in Article 38, read with Article 19 and 21 of the Constitution by means of judicial directions in cases of executive inaction of slow action is punishable within the limits. By the process of judicial review, if the high court expedites or energizes executive action, it should do so cautiously. Remedial action in public interest must be with caution and within limits.

Views of the Chief Justice of the Supreme Court

While referring to the importance of PIL R.S. Pathak, CJ has observed that PIL has come to stay. While justifying the importance of PIL, the Chief Justice further said:

> Public interest litigation is suggestive in itself. It refers to matters in which the public, or a significant identifiable section of the public, are interested. Public Interest Litigation has served to highlight the problems suffered by the poor and the weaker sections of the people, and if employed appropriately it can, in certain cases, result in bringing relief to them with an expeditiousness and directness not ordinarily conceivable through the traditional procedures of litigation. I believe that, used wisely and subject to the limitations of the Court's jurisdiction, it can be of much benefit as a vehicle for focusing judicial attention on matters affecting the public welfare. Public Interest Litigation has come to stay, a conviction expressed by me some years ago in the Bandhua Mukti Morcha Case.

With the benefit of the experience the Court have had since, it may be time for the court to lay down some broad norms and principles, which without adversely affecting the flexibility necessary to the proper consideration and disposal of such matters, may provide some guidance in their task. The need arises because a mystique appears to have surrounded this jurisdiction. It is desirable to analyse the concept, to evaluate its degree of success and to put in on a firmer constitutional fooling. PIL cannot be put into a straight jacket, but it is certainly amendable, as all judicial proceedings should be, to the observance of certain principles—principle which will promote and guarantee its healthy development without regarding its effectiveness as a vehicle of justice. It is only proper to dispel the misgivings of those who feel that PIL is 'the unruly horse which will unsettle public faith in the administration of justice, as well as to remove the fear of those who apprehend that this chapter in the Court's jurisdiction is drawing to a close.'

VI
Law and Social Change

Sociologists consider law to be one of several social codes. The primary function of social codes is to sustain the social order by upholding the basic values and norms of society. Besides law, social codes include religious codes, institutions, customs, and rules of etiquette and manners. Each kind of social code is backed by its own type of sanctions. Any violation of religious codes is believed to result in supernatural sanctions. Social institutions, like the institution of marriage, are so established that they become a condition of behaviour in the society. Violation of customs is punished by social disapproval and censure. Flouting of rules of etiquette of the group invites ridicule. Similarly, violation of laws is expected to lead to penalization or punishment by the state. Since the state alone has the legitimate power of violent punishment, the breaking of law invites the ultimate sanctions which the society can inflict. In an extreme case, this can even be the sentence of death.

Like all social codes, values and norms underlie law also. Thus laws too exercise the function of social control, that is the upholding of the existing sociocultural system. However, in modern times law is also being used as an instrument for bringing about social change. This is all the more true of countries like India which aspire to change at a high pace. In this process, the laws that are brought into being for this purpose often come in conflict with the traditionally accepted norms and values of large and dominant sections of society. While such laws are necessary if social change is to be our goal, it has to be recognized that like potent medicines these may evoke certain unsavoury reactions and unforeseen side effects.

Just as controlled experiments have to be carried out to gauge the effectiveness of new medicines, and the reactions and side effects that they may causes, so also there is the need of systematic sociological research for assessing the effectiveness of laws that are promulgated, and the reactions and non-intended consequences that they may lead to.

Indian society and culture have a long and continuous, though significantly changing, tradition. Many of the mores have deep roots in historical circumstances that prevailed thousands of years ago. If these mores are sought to be changed we must have a good understanding of the sociocultural forces that have shaped them. Just as a surgeon cannot hope to perform an operation successfully unless he has thorough knowledge of human anatomy and physiology, so also it would be futile to expect to bring about beneficial social transformation without proper understanding of the structures and processes that have developed through the ages. Without understanding how the fabric has been woven and how the knots have been tied, we cannot hope to untie the beliefs and attitudes that we wish to untie. One of the major tasks of sociology of law is to unfold and bring out the social forces and cultural configurations which have shaped the judicial values and institutions in society.

The opening reading in this part, therefore, summarizes the findings of a long-drawn research endeavour to trace the growth of judicial values and institutions in India since the earliest times (Indra Deva and Shrirama, 1980). This piece of research is based on a sociological interpretation of Sanskrit texts right from the *Ṛg Veda* to the later *Smṛtis*. The values and attitudes, which lead to disdain and discrimination against women and the lower castes which we now seek to eliminate through social legislation, seem to have their roots in the clash of races and cultures between the Aryans and the non-Aryans. This is reflected vividly in the *Ṛg Veda*, and carried forward through *Dhama Sūtras* and the *Smṛtis* in multifarious changing forms. For example, the attitude of contempt and suspiciousness towards women seems to have something to do with the fact that the Aryan hordes, who were naturally short of women, had to take wives from the alien non-Aryans whom they considered low and despicable. In the *Ṛg Veda*, the word *Vadhū* is used for female slave, as well as for wife or daughter-in-law.

Similarly, the disdain for the Sudras seems to owe its origin to the contempt which the victorious Aryans had for the dark-skinned *Dāsa*s, whom they subjugated (Shrirama 1999). The Aryans were very proud of their fair complexion and sharp nose, and of their culture and religion. They called the *Dāsa*s, *Kṛṣṇa varṇa* (dark-complexioned), *anāsāh* (without noses, meaning snub-nosed), and *śiśnadevāh* (worshippers of phallus), and ordained that they must not come near *Ṛta* (the Aryan law that underlies and upholds all phenomena, physical as well as social). In this way the Sudras, who appear largely to be the descendants of the *Dāsa*s, were cast out of the sphere of law for the higher Varnas a long time ago. Thus a duel system of law emerged.

In the *Ṛg Veda* the *Dāsa*s are referred to as *amanuṣya* (non-human). This attitude seems to have assumed a legal shape in the *Dharma Sūtra*s which are aphorisms composed around the sixth century BC, and the *Smṛti*s which came into being between the second century BC and AD sixth century. The *Dharma Sūtra*s and the *Smṛti*s are the main texts of the elite Hindu juristic tradition. The thread of disdain and discrimination against the low-castes runs through all these works which were composed over such a long span of time.

In the hierarchical Hindu society everyone was not equal before the law. Inequality between persons belonging to different castes in the hierarchy is embodied into the law in various ways. Thus, the Brahman can marry women of all the four varnas, including a Sudra woman. When he marries a Sudra woman no mantras are to be recited. However, a Sudra is allowed to marry only a Sudra woman. Persons belonging to the Sudra varna were not to be permitted to own property. The *Dharma Sūtra*s of Gautama and Āpastamba prescribe that a Sudra who intentionally reviles a twice-born man by abuse shall be deprived of his tongue. But if a Brahman reviles a Sudra not even a fine is to be imposed upon him. Following the *Dharma Sūtra*s, the *Manusmṛti* prescribes that the very limb by which a Sudra offends a twice-born person should be cut off. Manu goes to the extent of prescribing that if a Sudra even raises his hand to beat a high-caste person, his hand should be cut off. Killing a Sudra is treated lightly. The *Parāśar Smṛti* prescribes the same rites of purification for killing a Sudra as those for killing mice and other minor creatures. The *Smṛti* attributed to Parāśara belongs to the same period as the *Smṛti*s of Bṛhaspati, Kātyāyana, and Nārada, which constitute 'the grand trio' of traditional Indian jurisprudence.

Traditional Hindu law went through many changes. Many Vedic norms were given up and new ones which were despised by early Aryans were adopted. There also was a vast change in the procedures and the complexity of the legal system. From the simple rules of the *Ṛg Veda*, jurisprudence reached great heights of sophistication and refinement in the later *Smṛti*s. But the discrimination among persons belonging to different strata of society, both in privilege and punishment, continued through the ages in various forms.

If we seek to establish equality for all before the law, a lot more than mere legislation will have to be undertaken. So long as social, cultural, and economic inequalities of immense magnitude continue to exist, law alone cannot bring equality and justice. For instance, so long as the most down-trodden people of the Indian society—the landless labourers working on the farms of others—who belong overwhelmingly to the scheduled castes continue to live in that condition, no real upliftment of the scheduled castes is possible. And this can happen only if there is a more equitable distribution of land through genuine land reforms. But that perhaps is a tall order.

19

Growth of Traditional Legal System: The Perspective of Change through the Ages*

INDRA DEVA AND SHRIRAMA

Any objective assessment of judicial values and institutions in Indian tradition must reckon with the fact that this tradition has not remained unchanged and static. It has been long and growing. It encompasses several thousands of years and it has gone through many basic changes. When essentials of social structure and culture are transformed, the legal system cannot remain unchanged. Adequate understanding of legal values and norms even at a particular point of time is not possible without the perspective of change. Traditional judicial norms as we find them are products of numerous processes of socio-economic and cultural change.

Sufficient attention has, however, not been given to the processes of change in the discussion of traditional legal norms. It is understandable that when a lawyer argued his case in a court of law, he amassed all evidence that could be cited in its favour from various traditional texts without much regard to the period of their composition. He has neither the time nor the inclination to delineate the social forces that shaped these legal codes and brought about changes in them.

But even monumental scholarly works on traditional judicial values and institutions have not paid much attention to the pattern of transformation of the traditional legal system through successive historical eras. The tendency has been to deal with one particular topic at a time and

*Excerpted from Indra Deva and Shrirama, 'Judicial Values and Institutions in Indian Tradition', *ICSSR Research Abstract Quarterly*, vol. VIII, no. 1, January–March 1979, pp. 39–50.

to put together all related evidence drawn from diverse texts. The picture that emerges thus represents no real social or legal system as it actually existed or functioned in any historical era. It is a picture made up of patches drawn from texts representing different types of social structure and cultural ethos, separated from each other by centuries and even millenia. These patches can hardly be expected to form any coherent whole; and attempts to impute consistency to them understandably lead to distortion of data. Here our attempt has been to draw the broad outlines of the social forces that lent distinctive characteristics to judicial values and institutions at various phases of the genesis and growth of Indian civilization. We see how rudimentary prejudices generated by clash of races and cultures were legitimized later on and established into intricate patterns of hierarchy through subtle provisions in sacred and secular law. It is also seen how the judicial system responded to the growing needs of commerce and industry and developed a high degree of complexity and sophistication in the era of later smritis.

The immigrant Aryans who started pouring into India some two thousand years before Christ were militant and proud of themselves. The Dāsas and Panis whom they attacked and overpowered were so different from them, both racially and culturally, that they hardly regarded the latter as human beings. Indeed, the Vedas refer to them as *Amanuṣya*.[1]

Under such circumstances it was only natural that a dual system of law came into being. There was one set of norms for the Aryans, and another for the subjugated non-Aryans. Such a situation tends to exist in all cases of large-scale invasions. But in India it seems to have crystallized into an institutionalized arrangement that has continued through millenia. In the Vedas, the division is basically twofold: Aryans and Dāsas. In early Vedic times there was no clear and hereditary differentiation between Brahmans and Kshatriyas. Both of these categories belonged, of course, to the Aryans. In the fourfold varna system that developed later the bulk of Sūdras came from the Dāsas.[2]

The system of law that developed subsequently shows a good deal of discrimination among persons of different varnas, both in punishment and privilege. This discrimination is evident in a variety of provisions right from the *Dharmasūtras* to the Smritis and their commentaries. Killing a Brahman is considered to be the most serious crime in all legal treatises. According to the *Apastamba* and *Baudhayāna Dharmasūtras*, if a person of a lower varna kills a Brahman not only is he to suffer capital punishment but his entire property is to be confiscated. But killing a Sūdra is treated lightly. The *Paraśarasmṛti* prescribes the same rites of purification for killing a Sūdra as those for killing a bird and other minor creatures.[3]

Discrimination on the basis of varna is obvious also in the provisions regarding abuse and assault. Gautama and Baudhayāna provide that a Sūdra who intentionally reviles twice-born men by abuse shall be deprived of his tongue.[4] If a Vaisya abuses a Brahman he has to pay a fine of 150 Karṣapaṇas; the Kshatriya has to pay 100 Karṣapaṇas for the same offence. But a Brahman has to pay only fifty Karṣapaṇas, if he abuses a Kshatriya; for abusing a Vaisya he has to give twenty-five; and if he abuses a Sūdra no fine is to be imposed upon him.[5] Manu and Yajñavalkya inherited the rules provided by Gautama and Baudhayāna.[6]

Following Gautama, Manu prescribes that the very limb by which a Sūdra offends a twice-born should be cut off. Manu prescribes the same punishment for a Sūdra who even raises his hand to beat a high-caste. Following Manu, Bṛhaspati and Nārada too have included this provision together with a milder one.[7]

Provisions regarding adultery also bring out varna discrimination. If a woman commits adultery with a man of a lower caste the king shall cause her to be devoured by dogs in a public place according to Gautama. The adulterer also should be put to death.[8] If a Sūdra defiles an Aryan woman, his organ shall be cut off, and all his property should be confiscated. If the woman is with a protector, the guilty person should be awarded death after having undergone the punishment prescribed.[9] Baudhayāna prescribes death sentence for all men guilty of adultery. But he takes care to exclude Brahmans from this punishment. For a Sūdra adulterer, he explicitly ordains that he should be burnt alive in straw fire.

Similar discrimination is also obvious in matters related to property. For example, the lawgivers prescribe smaller shares for a son born to a Brahman from wives of lower varnas. Thus Baudhayāna prescribes that sons born of wives of lower varnas inherit four, three, two, and one share according to caste hierarchy. Gautama and Vasiṣṭha do not at all include sons from a Sūdra wife among heirs.

Aryans believed in Ṛta or the order which regulates the world. Any deviance from the right path was believed to be punished mercilessly by its protector Varuṇa. Of course this law was applicable only within the Aryan fold. In the seventh Mandala of *Ṛg Veda*, Vasiṣṭha says: 'The worshippers of Phallus should not come near Ṛta.'[10]

In *Taittiriya Saṁhitā* the Sūdra is equated with the horse, and utilizing him is considered quite justified. It says that 'these two, the horse and the Sūdra are conveyance of being.'[11] The *Satapatha Brāhmaṇa* is even more harsh when it says that in woman, Sūdra and crow, falsehood, sin, and darkness reside.[12] *Aitareya Brāhmaṇa* prescribes the duties of the Sūdra thus: Sūdras are to be disciplined by others, they have to get up on order (of the master) and they are to be killed (by the order of the master).[13] The attitude of disdain towards Dāsas or Sūdra is obvious. By the time of the Brāhmaṇas the colonizers had turned them into a docile servile class which could be exploited to any extent. The social system of India was founded on force and behind it a kind of racialism was at work.

In the Vedic age woman did not enjoy a position of equality with man, despite the fact that we find some women composers of Vedic hymns. The Aryans had a strong patriarchal society. Indra, the hero-god refers to the Dāsa Sambara with contempt, because his army consisted of women soldiers. 'The Dāsa Sambara made women his instrument, what can his vigourless (*abalā*) army do to mine?'[14] The word *abalā* later became a synonym for woman and is still in use. The invading Aryans were under standably short of women and they had to take women from the people whom they subjugated. It is not surprising therefore that in the *Ṛg Veda* *vadhū* is used both for 'bride' and a 'female slave'.[15]

In *Gṛhyasūtras*, we do not find that Aryan militancy which is perceptible in the Vedas. This indicates a peaceful state of society. Though four varnas are mentioned, marriage among different varnas is allowed in the direct order, besides in one's own varna. Thus a Brahman can have wives from all the four varnas, a Kshatriya from three, a Vaisya from two and Sūdra only from his own varna.[16] While marrying a Sūdra wife mantras were not to be recited. Meat is the chief food. Beef was considered most delicious. A special guest was offered a cow to be killed or set free at the guest's descretion.[17] Feeds of fowls and fishes were considered capable of producing special qualities in a six-month-old child.[18] *Sura* or wine is also mentioned in *Śankhāyana Gṛhyasūtra* as a common drink.[19]

The householder of the *Gṛhyasūtras* is supposed to perform a lot of household rituals and odd jobs which indicate that in the Sūtra period Aryans were colonizing extensive areas. The requirements of colonization of vast lands did not permit the huddling together of a large number of kinsfolk in large households. In fact the rituals prescribed in these aphorisms do not presume the presence of any other adult in the family except the husband and wife.

In the *Gṛhyasūtras* the woman entering the household of a man as his wife was looked upon with suspicion. It seems that she often came from the subjugated race. She was suspected to be carrying with her some destructive elements for her husband's family. She was also considered unfaithful towards him. In view of these dangers, the husband performed rituals and prayers to divert the evil elements towards his wife's earlier lover or spouse.[20] This further suggests that the wives of the Aryan house-holders did not belong to the same stock.

Though the four varnas were introduced long before the Sutra period, it appears that getting a servant was difficult. A ritual has been prescribed in Sutras to retain a servant who is prone to run away. It is obvious that servants were kept by force and they ran away often.[21] It is interesting to note that judges while entering courts of justice used to perform prayers, so that their adversaries in the bench could not speak against them.[22]

The *Dharmasūtras* seem to contain material of widely different eras. While some portions because of their Vedic language appear to be in the direct line of the Vedas, others strike as post-Buddhist and products of the age of Brahmanical revival. The latter are quite close in their spirit and content to the Smritis. It is remarkable that the *Dharmasūtras* do not claim a divine origin. They are avowedly composed by human beings. This is in sharp contrast to the Smritis.

The *Dharmasūtras* are primarily the law books of the Aryans. The an-cient Aryan law is closely connected with the social structure and ethical norms. Any deviance from the path of traditional social norms was con-sidered as infringement of law.

The four classes had quite hardened by the time of the *Dharmasūtras*. Apart from the four varnas some mixed castes have also been mentioned. The people of Brahman varna are considered highest while Sūdras the lowest. It seems that by the time of *Dharmasūtras* the Brahman had esta-blished their complete supremacy over all sections of society. The Brah-man stood to gain by all sorts of rituals—whether they were meant for gaining royal positions and merit or for getting rid of some sin. Numerous rites and ceremonies were prescribed. Some of these had to be performed daily, some fortnightly, some monthly, and still others annually. Besides these, there were rituals for diverse specific occasions for the fulfilment of particular desires for regaining ritual purity, and for attainments of glory. In all these rituals the Brahman priest was the sole beneficiary. *Baudhayāna Dharmasūtra* declares that whatever learned Brahman propounded even in jest is the highest law.[23] Even the king should give due respect to the Brahmans. On the road the king should make way for the Brahmans.[24]

The *Dharmasūtras* prescribed a specified code of conduct for Sūdras. The *Gautama Dharmasūtra* says that are *kṛṣṇavarṇa*. They together with their families should serve the Aryans for the remnants of food, cast-off shoes, umbrellas, garments, and mats. When they become unable to work it is their master's duty to support them.[25] On this provision, we find a mutual understanding between the employee and the employer, which is absent in *Vasiṣṭha Dharmasūtra*. Vasiṣṭha is not so liberal towards Sūdras. He considers the Sūdras as a burial ground, therefore no food should be given to them. He quotes Yama in his support, who inter alia says that remnants of food must not be given to Sūdras.[26]

The Sūdra were declared the servile class for whom law books prescribe no justice. They could not own any property. Generation after generation, serving the twice-born was their job. Baudhayāna says that as the Vaisyas and Sūdras are not particular about their wives, so the *Gāndhava* and *Paisacha* forms of marriage respectively are prescribed for them. According to Baudhayāna these types of marriage rites are in tune with their occupation which are animal husbandry and service respectively.[27]

The Vaisya and the Sūdra varnas are often grouped together. Vaisyas though included in the Aryan society, are placed lowest among the twice-born. They had to pay taxes to the king on one hand and to satisfy the priests on the other. Probably due to this the Buddhist religion became most popular among these two varnas who were exploited the most.

Certain practices in the *Dharmasūtras* are forbidden by the Smṛitis. These include carrying a waterpot. *Niyoga*, widow remarriage, etc. Baudhayāna prescribes that every twice-born man should carry a waterpot for his personal purification (toilet) as well as for sipping water while performing *sandhyā* and drinking, though after pouring some water on the ground. It has also been affirmed that no wise man should doubt the sanctity of this practice, as the self-existent (Brahman) himself came into existence with a water vessel. Baudhayāna further asserts that just as the sacrificial cup, *Camasa*, remains pure (though many participants in sacrifice drink *Soma* from it) because of the contact with the Soma juice, in the same way the water vessel is constantly pure through its contact with water.[28] Because of such explanations it becomes quite clear that even at that time some opposition existed towards this old practice, which was later on totally rejected and declared as *Kalivarjya*.

Vasiṣṭha and *Baudhayāna Dharmasūtras* reject the old *śaulka* form of marriage, or marriage after giving bride price, which has been prescribed by *Mānava Gṛhyasūtra*. They quote a verse of Kashyapa that a purchased wife cannot assist at sacrifices as she is a slave. Vasiṣṭha names it *manuṣya* rite instead of *śaulka*, which is of course a more refined term.[29]

Dharmasūtras give a more liberal treatment to widows as compared to smritis. The sutras ordain that a widow shall avoid taking honey, meat, liquor (*madya*), and sat, and should sleep on the ground for one year after the death of her husband. Baudhayāna and Vasiṣṭha quote Maudgalya who prescribes a six-month period. A sonless widow can bear a son to her husband by a brother-in-law after the expiration of that period, with the permission of elders.[30] This practice was also prohibited by *Manusmṛti*. The *Vasiṣṭha Dharmasūtra* recommends widow remarriage in case the marriage has not been consummated.[31]

Another remarkable provision that we find in the *Dharmasūtras* is related to the taking back of the sons of persons who have been ex-communicated from society. An *abhiśasta* is a person who has been turned out from caste for offences like murdering a Brahman, or a person of the two higher varnas, or a Brahman woman, or causing an abortion. But killing a learned Brahman in self-defence does not pollute. The Sutras do not permit the taking back of the person guilty of murdering a male Brahman but their sons can be readmitted in the community. The reason given for the re-entry of sons of the *abhiśastas* is interesting. It is argued that the guilt of the father need not be passed on to the son, just as a person deficient in limbs does not necessarily beget similar sons. However, a reference is also made to the opinion of Hārita which is contrary on this point.[32]

Baudhayāna and Gautama declare that the four orders (ashramas) are not in the Aryan pale,[33] as the Vedas mention only one order. Moreover they argue that in other orders people do not beget offsprings Baudhayāna attributes an *asura* origin to this fourfold scheme. He says that an Asura, Kapila the son of Prahlāda, in his struggle with gods made these divisions; a wise man should not heed them. Baudhayāna further argues that in Vedic texts the word 'four paths' refers to four sacrificial rites: *Iṣitis*, animal sacrifices, *Soma* sacrifices, and *Darbhahomas*. Baudhayāna speaks of the greatness of these sacrifices. Āpastamba and Baudhayāna assert that a person should fulfil duties of studentship and of householder; he who praises other (than these) duties is turned to dust and perishes.[34] This clearly shows that the lawgivers were conscious and uneasy about the non-Aryann influence on the Aryan people and they rejected the theory of four ashramas because it had been introduced by non-Aryans.

The *Dharmasūtras* closely follow the ancient Vedic norms. The old practices were regularized and given the shape of formal treatises on law. Through these provisions, it can be concluded that these cater to a civilization with the supremacy of Brahmans. In these, not only the codes of conduct for each Varna have been laid down but also responsibilities of the king, taxation, sources of ownership, treasure trove, inheritance, guardianship of minor's wealth, punishment for libel, abuse, assault, adultry, etc., rules of moneylending and usury, and adverse possession are prescribed. The sutras mark the stage of transition from the Vedic period to the period of the Smritis. While the legal concepts and procedures seem to be quite simple in the Vedic period, the smritis show a good deal of juristic refinement. This is particularly evident in the later smritis. While these discuss the authenticity of documents in great detail, we do not find any mention of written documents in the *Dharmasūtras* (except in *Vasîṣṭha Dharmasūtra*, which is of later origin) even as an evidence of moneylending and other such transactions. This also suggests that writing was not practised in the period of the early *Dharmasūtras*.

The rise of Buddhism provided a major challenge to the Vedic tradition. Buddha preached a doctrine of equality. He did not accept the divinity attributed to the Brahmans. He puts forth examples of other people, like the 'Greeks' and the 'Kamboja' where the master could become a slave and vice versa.[35] Buddhism asserted the fundamental equality of all the four varnas. In a passage in *Digha Nikāya*, it has been concluded that classes evolved through different occupations. Originally the king was the chosen leader, the *Mahāsammata*, approved by the majority of people.[36] The Buddhist literature is in the common man's language, Pali, and has a simple style. This was in sharp contrast to Brahmanical orthodoxy which was the preserve of the elite.

Though Buddhism revolutionized the whole society, the caste which benefited the most from it was the prosperous commercial caste, the Vaisya. In a verse of *Digha Nikāya*, we find a practical suggestion for being wealthy:

Making money like a bee
Who does not hurt the flower,
Such a man makes his pile
As an anthill, gradually
The man grown wealthy thus
Can help his family
And firmly bind his friends

To himself, he should divide
His money in four parts;
On one part he should live,
With two expand his trade,
And the fourth he should save
Against a rainy day.[37]

The Buddhist Jatakas portray a society well developed in industry and commerce. We find a vivid description of different manufacturers such as blacksmiths making razors, axes, ploughshares, and needles.[38] The leatherworkers, potters, ivory-workers, workers of precious stones, all are described as living and working in special sectors. Each group was organized in a *seni* (*Śreṇi* in Sanskrit) or corporation. Jetthaka (*Jetthaka* in Sanskrit) or an elderly worker was called *pamukha* (*pramukha*) or the chief of the corporation. He held an important position in the king's court.[39]

The Jatakas provide striking evidence of the existence of market mechanism in that period. There is ample material to show that the value of goods was determined by bargaining between the buyer and the seller. Competition also played its part. This is in marked contrast to the common idea that in traditional Indian society the payments for goods and services were settled traditionally.

The *Manusmṛiti* seems to have spearheaded the response of Brahmanical tradition to the challenge of Buddhism; and it is perhaps because of this that it occupies a position of pre-eminence among the traditional texts which propound the fundamentals of law. The work was attributed to the primeval father, Manu, in order to give it the authority of the original doctrine. However, to wean away the masses from Buddhism, many non-Vedic practices prevalent among them had to be accepted by the Brahmanical lawgivers. At the same time many old Aryan customs such as *Niyoga*, widow remarriage, carrying a water pot by *Snataka*s, and taking beef had to be rejected. *Manusmṛiti* laid the foundations of a new era, and all the later Hindu law books follow it in one way or the other.

One important device of legitimizing deviation from Vedic percepts and practices was that of declaring them to be 'Kalivarjya'. This means that because of the degenerate *Kali* age people had become unfit for following the old Vedic norms. Thus on the one hand new values were substituted for the old, and on the other reverence to the authority of Vedas was not given up. The opening passages of almost every smriti indicate that it had become necessary to lay down the laws because of the prevalence of disorder. Each smriti is attributed to some ancient mythical sage, thereby bestowing traditional authority on its dicta.

The flowering of judicial literature in the era of Brahmanical reassertion against Buddhism seems deeply significant. There is ample evidence in the *Ṛg Veda* of the marked distaste of the Vedic Aryans for commercial values. They considered despicable the expectation by the indigenous Pani to receive something in return for everything that was taken from him. Even after the Aryans established themselves as the dominant elite stratum in the social order, they continued to look down upon the commercial and serving classes. As the *Satapatha Brāhmaṇa* puts it, they are live horses for riding on. *Dharmasūtra*s do not mention any commercial usages. It is only *Manusmṛiti* which mentions forgery of documents of contract and warns that documents should be examined properly. It seems that the commercial and industrial life which had already developed in the pre-Aryan city civilizations, had continued to thrive. But the elites accorded no recognition to it earlier. It is only the Atharva Veda which gives importance to commerce. This Veda belongs to the Viś. It is significant that most of the Sanskrit terms connected with commerce including those for value, money, and commodity, are derived from the word '*paṇi*'. However law concerning commercial transactions was largely ignored by the Brahmanical texts, till the time when all-out efforts were made to dislodge Buddhism and to win over all sections of society. This was perhaps necessary not only for combating Buddhism but also for bringing back to their fold the rich clientele that the traders provided to priests. Many sophisticated legal notions found in later smriti may owe their origin to the non-Aryan culture of Paṇis. The commercial usages and conventions which till now were ignored by the Aryan lawgivers found a place in the smriti.

Manusmṛiti is the first regular law book. The legal system introduced by Manu was further elaborated by Yajñavalkya, Bṛhaspati, Nārada, and Kātyāyana. Principles have been laid down by Manu and others which have bearing on Varna and caste, family, marriage, status of woman, kingship, administration, law and legal procedure. *Bṛhaspati, Nārada* and *Kātyāyana Smriti*s embody the most sophisticated stage of the development of traditional Indian jurisprudence and judicial procedure. The titles of law mentioned by Kautilya are systematized by Manu under 18 heads. These have received even more sophisticated treatment in later times in the smritis of Yajñavalkya, Bṛhaspati, Nārada, and Kātyāyana. All these lawgivers declare the king to be the guardian of law rather than the fountain of law. The court of justice, which consists of learned Brahmans, chiefs of guilds, etc., should assist the king in the administration of justice.

Custom has been recognized as an important component of law. Even those customs which do not have the full approval of smriti are nevertheless accorded recognition by them. We may mention for instance the Āsura, Rākṣasa and Paiśacha forms of marriage and the permission given rather reluctantly for marriage between cross-cousins. Yajñavalkya, Bṛhaspati, Nārada, and Kātyāyana mention some lower courts other than those headed by the king himself. These are: (i) one that is headed by the judge who has been appointed by the king, (ii) *Gaṇa* or assemblies of Brahmans, (iii) *Śreṇi* or corporation of traders or artisans, and (iv) *Kulani* or family gatherings, groups of agnatic and cognatic relatives, or village councils. Among these *Kula* is the lowest court and *Gaṇa* is the highest court.

Manusmṛti does not deal with judicial procedure in meticulous detail. Documents, which were later recognized as important means of proof in the treatises of Yajñavalkya, Bṛhaspati, Nārada, and Kātyāyana do not find mention in *Manusmṛti*. Elaborate definitions of various legal terms are also not found. A sonless widow is not recognized as an heir by Manu.

Yajñavalkya, Bṛhaspati, Nārada, and Kātyāyana treated judicial procedure more systematically than Manu. Documents are given due importance. Ordeals are prescribed by these lawgivers, in case of major crimes or on failure of documents, witness, or circumstantial evidence. Thus ordeals are to be relied upon only as a last resort. A number of legal terms together with their definitions can be found in these smriti, especially in *Nārada* and *Kātyāyana*.

Broad outlines of the evolution of legal procedure are discernible. From almost no material except the mention of *sabhā* and *samiti* in Vedas, in Brahmans we find the first mention of a judge, *praśmaviv"aka* or one who puts questions. The epithets used in relation to *sabhā* 'trouble' and 'vehemence' indicate that it was a place of hard discussion and controversy. *Dharmasūtras*, which can perhaps be designated as the first law books, clearly lay down the composition of court of law and the basic principles of dispensation of justice. Judicial procedure is given more attention in the *Manusmṛti*; and it becomes more concise and systematic in the *Yajña-valkyasmṛti*. But discussion on legal mechanisms and procedure reach the zenith of elaboration, refinement, and sophistication only in the later smritis of Nārada, Bṛhaspati, and Kātyāyana. The distinction made by Bṛhaspati and Kātyāyana between disputes arising out of wealth or injuries seems quite close to the current classification of civil and criminal law.

It has been clearly laid down that the court should be held in open. Bṛhaspati and Kātyāyana provide that the chief judge must not hold any conversation in private while the case is undecided. If they do so, they are liable to punishment.

Elaborate rules of procedure for receiving the facts of the dispute, categorization of the title of law to which the dispute belongs, pleadings and examination of the evidence, and pronouncement of judgment are given by the later smriti. Rules for the summoning of the defendant, exemption from appearance before the court, and appointment of someone else to represent one's case, are also laid down. Provisions governing adjournment of hearings became complex in course of time. While Gautama simply mentions such adjournment, Kātyāyana discusses a number of different conditions and accordingly prescribes varying periods of adjournment. Types of replies by the defendant and their possible defects are dealt with elaborately in later smriti.

Similarly defects in plaints have been analysed in great detail. The validity of various means of proof such as witnesses, documents, and possession is closely examined and these are divided and sub-divided into numerous categories. Forgery of documents finds mention in texts as ancient as the *Vishnu Dharmasūtra* and the smriti of Manu and Yajñavalkya. It finds elaborate discussion in the later smriti.

Though provisions regarding various kinds of commercial transactions appear in a rudimentary form in earlier works, these acquire a high degree of sophistication in later smritis. In these law books we find intricate provisions regarding debts, surety, deposits, unauthorized sales, partnership, resumption of gifts, non-payment of wages, breach of contract of services, transgression of contract or conventions of guilds, and rescission of purchase or sale. The period (around, second to sixth centuries AD) of the composition of the later Smritis must have been marked by a rich growth of commerce and industry; otherwise there would not have been any need of such sophisticated legal provisions and procedures. The way some of the later Smritis welcome divisions of family property among brothers even when the father was alive, indicate the rise of individualistic values regarding property. The merchant class seems to have acquired great importance in society during the period. The *Kātyāyanasmriti* lays down that some merchants should be included In the court and they should listen to the causes and look to the administration of justice. With the decline of Indian maritime trade in later centuries, sophisticated legal provisions governing commerce and industry seem to have fallen into disuse. But the tradition of law did not lose all vigour. Legal commentaries and digests continued to be written at least up to the nineteenth century. And traditional judicial notions, such as those put forward by the *Mitaksara* and the *Dayābhāga* (both of which are based on different interpretations of the concept of *Sapinda* in *Yajñavalkyasmriti*) have continued to guide the life of Indian people till contemporary times.

NOTES

1. *Rgveda*, X. 8.
2. There is only one reference to all the four *varnas* in *Rigveda* (*Purushasukta* X. 33) and this too is of a comparatively late origin.
3. *Parasharasmrti*, VI. 16.
4. *Gautama Dharmasutra*, XII. 1; *Baudhayāna Dharmasutra*, II. 10.27.14.
5. *Gautama Dharmasutra*, XII, 8–14.
6. *Manusmrti*, VIII. 267–270; *Yajñavalkyasmrti*, II. 207, 302.

7. *Gautama Dharmasutra,* XIII. 1; *Manusmṛti,* VIII. 279–280; *Bṛhaspatismṛti,* XXI.22. *Nāradasmṛti,* XVIII. 22.
8. *Gautama Dharmasutra,* XXIII. 14–15.
9. *Gautama Dharmasutra,* XII. 2–3.
10. *Rigveda, Vasistha,* VII. XXI. 5.
11. *Taittiriya Samhita,* VII. 1.1.6
12. *Satapatha Brahmana,* 141.1.1.31.
13. *Aitareya Brahmana,* 35.3.
14. *Rigveda, Gauriviti Sakti-putra,* X. 73.9.
15. *Rigveda,* VIII. 19.36.37.
16. *Parashara Gṛhyasutra,* I. 4. 8–11.
17. *Parashara Gṛhyasutra,* I. 3.27.
18. *Parashara Gṛhyasutra,* I. 19.7–11.
19. *Sankhayana Gṛhyasutra,* I. 11.5.
20. *Parashara Gṛhyasutra,* I. 11.2–4.
21. *Parashara Gṛhyasutra,* III. 8.3.
22. *Hiranyakeshin Gṛhyasutra,* I. 4.15.6.
23. *Baudhayāna Dharmasutra,* I. 1.1.12.
24. *Apastamba Dharmasutra,* II. 5.11.5–6.
25. *Gautama Dharmasutra,* X. 56–62.
26. *Vasishtha Dharmasutra,* XVIII. 13–14.
27. *Baudhayāna Dharmasutra,* 1.11.20.13–15.
28. *Baudhayāna Dharmasutra,* I. 4.7. 1–2.
29. *Baudhayāna Dharmasutra,* I. 11.21–2.
30. *Baudhayāna Dharmasutra,* II. 2.4. 7–9; *Vasishtha Dharmasutra,* XVII. 55–56.
31. *Vasishtha Dharmasutra,* III. 17.
32. *Apastamba Dharmasutra,* 1.9. 6–25; *Baudhayāna Dharmasutra,* II. 1.2. 18–23.
33. *Baudhayāna Dharmasutra,* II. 6.11.27; *Gautama Dharmasutra,* II. 36.
34. *Baudhayāna Dharmasutra,* II.6.11.27–34; *Apastamba Dharmasutra,* II.9.24.8.
35. *Majjhim Nikaya,* 2, 147 ff.
36. *Digha Nikaya,* 3.28. ff.
37. *Digha Nikaya,* 3.180. ff.
38. We find such localization of craft in prehistoric remains of Mohenjodaro as well as in modern India.
39. *Mugapakkha Jataka,* IV. 411.

20

Law and Social Change in India*

YOGENDRA SINGH

The interaction between law and society can be seen at several levels: the legal system, its profession and subculture, the judicial process and its sociocultural linkages, law as an indicator of the nature of societal complexity with its attendant problems of integration and finally as an agent of modernization and social change. A sociology of law would have to deal with all the above levels of interaction between law and society. In our analysis however, we shall focus mainly on the relationship that law may bear with the processes of social change and modernization in the context of the Indian society. Our perspective being sociological, we shall treat law in its institutional and historical context, and analyse its dialectics with society in its broader social structural setting.

EMERGING DIALECTIC OF LAW AND SOCIETY: THE GLOBAL PERSPECTIVE

The dialectic of law and society in India has been determined by historical experiences of passage from colonialism to nationalism in course of which both the paradigms of society and legal systems have evolved. The process bears acute imprint of historicity and yet in the light of our observation of similar interactions between law and society in the industrially advanced Western countries, some convergence of experiences at a universalistic level cannot be denied. So, today the processes of law and social change in India, being in large measure unique, do share some commonalities of crisis and contradiction of pradigms of law and society with industrially advanced nations.

*Excerpted from Yogendra Singh, 'Law and Social Change in India: A Sociological Perspective', *Relevant Sociology*, vol. III, nos 1–2, 1986, pp. 1–17.

The chief components of both legal system and paradigms of modernization in the industrially advanced countries were based on the ideology of rational utilitarianism; the *Gesellschaft* model of society implied movement away from status to contract, from community to individual, from participation to administration, from guild to state, and from empathy to objectivity. It was the product of the laisse-faire ethos of market-oriented non-personaliszed legal system. Bentham, Max Weber, and Schumpeter, the mentors of this 'rational legal order' were bridges between the legal system and social structure. The crisis of the late 1960s and early 1970s in the industrial societies, the reawakening of the interests in the Frankfurt school of sociology, neo-Marxism, and phenomenological existentialism tended to swing the pendulum, at least in ideological if not structural terms, towards search for alternative models of both modernization and legal system. Largely, this development is a product of the structural contradictions of the post-industrial society and it surpasses the ideological confines of the capitalist and socialist states.

This new perception of the legal system and its paradigm obviously inheres the contradictions of industrial society with its increasing uni-dimensionality, its failure in the liberation of human personality, its dehumanizing abstractness resulting in the alienation of man. This process represents a legal order which, in course of structural and normative changes that it brought about, also introduced seeds of disenchantment and mystification. This challenge necessarily brings sociological jurisprudence into full play as the social dialectic tends to influence the legal system deeply. It spurs shift from

> private law, concerned with the security of the individual, to public law, concerned with welfare and social utility. Even in the heart of the private law, in the law of tort or torts, and in contract, they have discerned similar developments. In torts there is the movement from the legal-individualistic principle of fault liability to the social, actual cost-benefit analysis that leads to the principle of loss distribution; in contract, the concept of a bargain struck between ideally equal and freely contracting parties is increasingly infringed upon by the court recognition of social and economic inequalities and of the one-sided restriction of the power to bargain by the existence of standard contract.

In addition to the above, new areas of law in the fields of industry, environment, consumer protection, and social services come into being which are beyond the nineteenth-century conception of the common law and its judicial processes. The deeper implications of the changes in the industrial society are responsible for these legal innovations as also for the demand for basic alteration of the paradigm of industrial society. Thus the crisis of the legal system is also simultaneously a crisis of the industrial society. The transition from the industrial to post-industrial stage of development ushers in social demands on the one hand and, on the other, structural changes in the society, especially in its modes of production and leisure time and its patterns. All this necessitates redefinition of the legal order of society at the interpersonal, inter-group, and inter-societal or international levels. What emerges more sharply is a new meaning of 'responsibility' and 'freedom', 'civic culture' and 'rationality'. The structural changes which ensured at the post-industrial stage of development tend to contribute not only to formal 'differentiation' in roles and relationships but also to their 'de-differentiation', 'personalization', and possible revitalization of the principle of 'status' in 'contract'. This may be possible by new leaps in both technology and culture, somewhat already in evidence in the electronic and computer revolution.

We have so far discussed the challenges faced by the industrial societies at a higher stage of development. The dialectic of law and society in the industrially developed nations has, however, an evolutionary endogenous character. The new challenges and contradictions that legal system is faced with in these societies are historically different from the one faced by the developing society such as India, where colonial interlude fundamentally transformed the indigenous evolution of the legal system. The legal system in India unlike in the West started with dualism of the indigenous hierarchical and colonial utilitarian traditions. The universalistic element in the contradictions of the Indian legal system is confined mainly to the utilitarian–Benthamite legal administration and philosophy which the British imposed on India, and which too at one level is faced with similar contradictions as in the industrial societies in the face of waning impact of utilitarian liberalism and the increasing demands of welfarism and socialism.

The dialectic of legal system in India thus tends to be more complex, entrenched as this system is in the 'multiplex of social structures' and roles on the one hand and, on the other, in its inherent multiplicity of traditions—indegenous, colonial, and developmental. The significant element in the interaction between law and society in India is that it bears a heavy burden of these multiple traditions and the social concerns and orientations of each. The convergence between the dialectic of legal system of the industrialized nations and that of India would refer more to the developmental phase of the legal system in India following independence. The contradictions of choices in the administration of justice, such as between abstract individual rights to property, pursuit of occupation and profit on the one hand of the social justice, protection of weaker sections and socially and vulnerable categories on the other, represent a similar crisis of paradigms of both society and the legal system in India as in the industrially developed West. Only the dimensions of this process in India are far more complex.

LAW AND SOCIETY IN INDIA

The relationship between law and society in India could generally be studied in three phases: the traditional or indigenous, the colonial, and the developmental. The indegenous legal system did not have a homogeneous character. It reflected the basic feature of the Indian social organization which was based on the principle of 'inter-structural autonomy'. The polity, the system of stratification and cultural norms, the three basic components of the social system in India were relatively autonomous, a feature rare in other societies. Under this system, the king or his administrative and judicial authorities constituted the top of the hierarchy, and centres of redressal of appeal and intervention were there only in a few cases. The system even prohibited the king to intervene in many disputes related to local customs, norms, and practices of castes, sub-castes, or tribes, which had their own judicial processes through panchayats, community leadership of elders or the intervention by the chief of local dominant castes.

In the studies of many scholars who have commented upon the indegenous legal system in India (*see* Cohn 1961, 1965; Galanter 1968, 1972; Kane 1950) one finds the focus on the diversity rather than on the linkages which provided integrative principle of the system. It may well be as Bernard S. Cohn suggests that in eighteenth-century India, social relations operated in a 'multiplex' manner, 'a relationship in which a person tends to occupy same position relative to the same set of other persons in all networks of purposive ties—economic, political, procreative, religious, educational' (Cohn 1961: 617) but the unit of interaction being caste or sub-caste, fluctuations of fortunes within each such unit by individual families would always cut across such matrix of multiplex relationships. This is the phenomenon which still obtains in India. The important feature in the indigenous legal system therefore, was its subsystemic autonomy which rendered the same highly enduring and innovative despite the ups and downs in the polity in traditional India.

The main attributes of this legal system and its 'judicial processes' were: wider participation, paternalism, flexibility and innovativeness, emphasis on compromise, and hierarchy. Since community living in the *Biradari* or kin-group was an essential social matrix within which justice was sought and imparted, orientation was more on 'adjustment' rather the 'judgement' as such. This judicial process was as informal as it was inexpensive. It went in harmony with the cultural ethos of hierarchy and continuity and community ties. No doubt in this system too, the role of dominant castes, families and kin-groups did occasionally vitiate the process of justice, but this was more frequent in matters of property, land, and hereditary obligations. In the big towns, where the *Mahajana* supervised over the justice of contractual obligations, trade, and commerce, there was more catholicity in commitment to norms.

The British who introduced the colonial legal system could never have a fuller appreciation of the traditional legal system and its judicial process. It could not be understood in dissonance with the traditional Indian polity, economy, and social structure. Their colonial interests were basically at variance with these institutions and their linkages. They overemphasized the elements of discontinuity, lack of system, and normative multiplicity because it went well with their objective of colonical appropriation and profit. The interest both of the East India Company and of the British government coincided in this respect. The need for 'order', nevertheless, led to the imposition of a new legal system, and the only legal system upon which the British administrators could think of improvisation was that of the Benthamite–utilitarian tradition. There was for a while the debate between the models of Cornwallis and Munro, the former opting for an embodiment of the commands of the government in formal legislative acts, and entrusting them to independent judicial administration both to secure private property and to control the abuse of executive power. Munro, on the other hand, based his model on 'paternalistic ideology', assuming the role of personal authority to be supreme in Indian culture; hence his emphasis on evolving a judicial system anchored upon village panchayats, local customary tribunals of elders, and native judges which complete the separation between the judicial and executive functions. This debate continued for some time, and Munro also experimented with some elements of it in Madras. But finally, it was the Cornwallis model of legal system and judicial administration, patterned after the British Constitution and common law, which triumphed (*see* Stokes 1959).

Cornwallis imparted a formal basis for judicial administration to India which has come to stay. Its main features were: establishment of a court in every district (under British control) for administration of law and order; administration of personal law in accordance with the customs of

each religious group and of revenue matters based on usage or pre-existing
Muslim law; modelling of judicial or court procedure after British practice; appointment of covenanted judges or British civil servants at the
district court and provision for appointment of Indians at the lower levels;
assistance in the district courts in personal matters by Hindu and Muslim priests; establishment of a legal profession; fixation of revenue on a
permanent basis and recognition of individuals or corporate groups as
owners of land for revenue payment; separation of revenue and judicial
functions of the administration; settlement of ownership rights in civil
courts and; establishment of court of appeal from decisions of the district
courts (*see* Cohn 1961: 614). Along with this structure of legal administration also came codification. For this, Macaulay played a crucial role.
As president of the First Law Commission set up in 1834 he produced the
draft of the Indian Penal Code which became law in 1860.The Law Commission between 1853 and 1870 contributed to the enactment of Codes
of Procedure—civil and criminal in 1859 and 1861 respectively. About
this time the supreme and sadar courts were unified into high courts
giving a uniform judicial structure. The Law Commission's efforts also
led to the enactment of the Succession Act (1865), the Limitations Act
(1871), and the Evidence Act and the Contract Act (both 1872); under
the direction of the Government of India there came the Specific Relief
Act (1877), the Negotiable Instrument Act (1882), and the Easement Act
(1882), the Trust Act (1882), the Transfer of Property Act (1882) (*see*
Singh 1973: 98).

This spurt of legislation implied emergence of a radically different
legal order impinging directly and deeply upon the normative and cultural system of Indian society. It was not only a measure of formalization
but also essentially a mode of modernization through westernization.The
social legislations which followed in its wake carried this process further
forward. The Native Marriages Act was legislated in 1872; this was to accommodate the marriage custom of the Brahmos, who claimed to be
neither Hindus nor Muslims, but its inadvertant implication was that of
a civil marriage law, the first secular legislation of its kind. In 1891, the
Age of Consent Act was passed. Similarly, the Press Act came in 1878, the
Newspapers Act in 1908, and Factory Act in 1881 revised many times
later. The Bengal Tenancy Act was legislated in 1885 setting a pattern for
tenurial reform in land and in 1904 the Cooperatives Act was passed.
Hence, both formal administrative and social legislations were brought
on the statute books laying down the foundation of a modern civil society
and state in India modelled on British lines.

As we have mentioned above, behind these legislations there was initially a great philosophic debate or; the merits of indigenization and westernization. The model which finally emerged, however, bore the deep imprint of the utilitarian–Benthamite tradition. It is this element in the colonial legal system, which even today prevails almost intact, which introduced significant sociological dimensions in terms of social change and modernization. Both in terms of the normative structure and judicial procedure the British legal system in India marked a fundamental departure from the principles of hierarchy, holism, and participation, characteristic of the indigenous system of legal administration. O'Malley writes:

> Two results of the judicial system could be briefly noted, viz., the establishment of the principle of equality and the creation of the consciousness of positive rights. The last was a plant of slow growth owing to the abject submissiveness of the lower classes, which prevented them from taking advantage of the system of equal law and vindicating their right by legal action. A change was gradually effected. In 1841, for example, it was noticed that the Chamars, despised untouchables of northern India, were not afraid to bring suits against their landlords, and it was added, 'nothing vexes or annoys the zamindars in our whole system so much as this' (O'Malley quoted in Singh 1973: 100).

The significance for social change of the colonial legal system is indeed great. It brought slowly into being a new professional class of legal experts, lawyers, judges, court administrators and bureaucracy, the basic component of a civic society. It led to an arousal of aspirations and demands for positive rights not only in and by the deprived classes and communities but in course of time along with other educated classes it also created the substructure of a new middle class of capitalists, entrepreneurs, civil servants, professional categories of various sorts, who led the movement of national independence. It is needless to emphasize the role of legal profession in the leadership of India's independence movement. It is this movement which led to the drafting of the Constitution of India after independence in order to provide the legal boundaries for social change. The important feature of social change which the colonial process of modernization brought forth is its substructural and subcultural character.

The inter-structural autonomy of which we have made a mention above rendered it possible for the new middle classes in the legal profession to emerge from specific castes, communities, and groups which already enjoyed a privileged position in society. This made it possible for social and cultural innovations to be introduced in society, without however, coming into conflict with the core of the structural and cultural foundations of society—its caste structure and its cultural ethos.The new forces of change thus could be absorbed and filtered through the middle classes to the rest of society in stages. The rise of the national movement throughout the three decades of the twentieth century in India served also to forge these forces and aspirations for change into a national ideology. The contradictions which the independent India face today in the legal framework of social change is anchored in the levels of misfits between this ideology (which has egalitarian, secular, and civic features) and the structure of the legal profession and its ideology, which is class-oriented, mystifying, and which posits rights for the individual in the abstract, unconcerned of social responsibility.

The colonial legal system thus introduced new challenges and possibilities for social change in India, but it also created legal institution which in terms of pedagogy and procedure were alien to common means, experience, and reach. It did away with the traditional participant mode of justice through the panchayats chiefs' and kings' courts. It introduced systematic codification in law rooted into an alien cultural and philosophical soil in place of familiar codes and rules of religious traditions—the *dharmashastras*, the *Koran* and the *Hadith*—the customs and conventions. It also rendered justice expensive and remote, a matter of mystification and suspicion. It is this element which led to the emergence of two cultures in the legal profession and its organization in India, called 'lawyers' law' and 'local law ways' by Marc Galanter and B.S. Cohn. The cultural hiatus that this dualism creates in the realm of law and legal profession is not specific but a general problem in the modernization of a traditional society of India's level of historical and cultural depth. The crisis in cultural terms is of reconciliation between traditionalization and modernization.

Law and Society after Independence

The nationalist movement in India which culminated in the independence of the country failed to evolve an indigenous legal system fully. Mahatma Gandhi did voice his suspicion of the British-sponsored courts and the lawyers in his many exhortations of civil disobedience movements, but when India gained freedom, and framing of the Constitution began, the Gandhian emphasis on an indigenous legal system and judicial administration was not acceptable to most members of the Constituent Assembly. The Constitution as it emerged contained elements of the Gandhian ideology—village panchayats and democratic decentralization in the directive principles of state policy. The entire juridical structure was otherwise kept intact. Indeed, the Gandhian ideologues who wanted a complete decentralization and autonomy for village panchayat system, even as late as the Ashok Mehta Committee on Panchayati Raj established in late 1970s, did not find support. The Law Commission of 1958 while evaluating the need for indigenization of legal system did not see any major contradiction between the present legal system and the 'genius' of the people (Government of India, Ministry of Law 1958). It noted that:

> It is true that in the opinion of the Law Commission the Indian legal system no doubt has deep imprint of alien system but in course of its functioning it has undergone modification suitable to Indian conditions. Moreover, had the indegenous system been allowed to evolve free from colonial intervention, it would also have tended to grow normally on similar lines as the present legal system did.

This analysis of the Commission puts into perspective the dilemma of the Indian middle classes in dealing with the challenges of modern nation building on the one hand and the rhetorics of indigenization on the other. Studies done on this problem, however, show that the dualism of the two traditions has been functionally adapted well in the Indian legal system (*see* Khare 1972; Marc Galanter 1972).

An important innovation since independence is that of the Panchayati Raj system in villages which together with activities of community development also incorporated the system of *nyaya* panchayats for lower-level local judicial administration. Two national committees since independence went into the nature of its administration and functions, and finally it was decided to accord to these panchayats judicial power relevant to day-to-day administration of justice based mainly on the ideology of village community, participation, and relatively informal judicial procedure free from the role of lawyers. This innovation was to render some levels of justice freely available to rural folk at low cost and free from the legal subculture of abstract rules and impersonal procedures. The system has had uneven success in different states. The evaluative studies by study teams and state committees have found these *nyaya* panchayats to be largely non-functioning, ridden with factious interests and politicized due to the electoral procedure of election of the *pancha*s or court members. The states of Maharashtra and Rajasthan whose committees reviewed the functioning of these village courts have received recommendation for disbanding them. This also coincides with the views of the Law Commission studies which recommend that judicial and electoral processes need to be kept separate which has not been done in case of the *nyaya* panchayats. This has led to their enmeshing into the structural contradictions of rural politics and alienation from the masses. As Upendra Baxi rightly suggests this institution of otherwise great significance has not made an impact due to ambiguity of ideology and marginality of the institutional linkages that has come as another constraint in their functioning (*see* Baxi 1982: 323–7).

LAW AND SOCIAL CHANGE IN INDIA

The ideology of social change which India has adopted after independence is enshrined in the Constitution. It incorporates both the elements of the liberal democratic and the Gandhian values on social change ideology. This can be discerned in the dualism that one would find in the fundamental rights and the directive principles of the state policy. The former is rational, liberal, and individualistic in ethos, whereas the latter lays down the principle of communal welfare, decentralization of power, amelioration of the condition of the weaker sections and backward classes, and commitment to abolition of practices considered unhealthy in the Gandhian tradition, for example, liquor consumption. Whereas, Constitution recognizes individuals only as units of legal rights for voting purposes and in all manners of relationship with the state, it also acknowledges the legitimacy of specific castes, communities, groups for favoured treatment, for example, the scheduled castes and the scheduled tribes, the religious minorities and backward classes. The instrument of social change in this model is social legislation. Social justice, equality, secularism, and democracy are its fundamental normative goals.

The Constitution thus brings out two apparently opposite principle-those of universalism and of particularism—in the same ideological package of social change. Is this a product of ad hocism of quirk of history or colonial legacy? Or, is this an eclectic effort to synthesize modern with traditional values in the ideology of change? Sociologically, the answer to these questions lies in the fundamental commitment that the nation has made through the Constitution to introduce changes in a peaceful manner (a Gandhian and later on, a Congress ideology) so that India could become a modern secular, democratic, and socialist state. Values of egalitarianism on the one hand and that of freedom on the other are indeed difficult to reconcile in the statecraft of a nascent democracy just liberated from colonial exploitation. It presents several conditions which logically call for judicious and selective use of legislation for social changes commensurate with the objectives of the Constitution.

The civic model of change which is derived from the Constitution could not logically recognize primordiality, caste, religion, and ethnicity; but it also could not leave the most exploited, vulnerable, and weaker sections at the mercy of the market forces of social change which structurally always tend to go in favour of the rich and the strong. Hence, reservations, protective discriminations, and special favour to religious minorities and weaker categories! The strategy of change implicit in this model is that of pressure of social justice through structural changes in the social, economic, and cultural systems with the aid of legislative reforms. The Constitution for this purpose enjoins special responsibilities upon the executive, the legislature, and the judiciary.

The contradictions of the relationship between law and social change in India rest not so much in the inadequacy of the model, as in the processes of implementation and execution of these models as such. During the three-and-a-half decades of functioning as a democratic nation with planned developmental strategy India has succeeded on many frontiers of social change: the landed aristocracy stands abolished as a class; the power structure in the villages has passed almost completely from the traditional rural elites to a new rural middle class, the former tenantry of landlords; a new class structure has emerged in the villages—a peasant middle class, which is aggressively entrepreneurial, adopts scientific methods and techniques of agriculture fast, and is the leader of the green revolution; the monopoly in higher education, so far a privilege of the upper caste and classes, has now slowly started percolating to the middle classes in the villages. This resulted from agrarian legislation and reform measures. The reservations which the Constitution accorded in the legislatures, government services, schools, and colleges to the scheduled castes and tribes has now successfully brought up a new generation of middle classes and educated youth in this category of people that adds new voice to their demands, and contributes to ever-new mobilizations in the social structure. This has rendered its demonstration effect so acute that in some pockets of the country it has led to retroactive protests. In the field of land reform legislation, the ceiling level on landholdings has been lowered to half between the 1950s and 1960s in most states in India—an indicator of the consciousness for reconciliation. The impact of land reforms though uneven from state to state, has spurred agricultural growth and green revolution in several parts of India. This in turn has brought into being a new phenomenon of labour mobility from poorer states, such as Bihar and eastern Uttar Pradesh to the states of Haryana and Punjab. It has far-reaching social consequences. It liberates the working classes in the home state from the clutches of dominant classes or castes, it brings new capital and savings for investment in land, house, and cattle; it opens up possibilities for social mobilization, and independent political functioning as a group by the working classes, the Harijans and Girijans, and other low castes. The recent increase in inter-caste tensions in rural areas are indeed a result of these mobility processes in the rural social structure.

Another important area where 'civic revolution' seems to have made a successful impact in India is that of the electoral behaviour. The electoral awareness has been introduced all over the country from village and towns to cities through a series of election procedure: the village panchayats, the *nyaya* panchayats, the assembly, and the parliamentary elections. All these situations involve direct elections. In addition, there are electoral procedures for several bodies of voluntary association, cooperatives, etc. The electoral politics and its consciousness has created a new sense of power and self-esteem in various sections of rural and urban population. No doubt, it has also activated factional politics and kindled casteism and ethnicity of a narrow kind. Also sometimes, these identities emerge into communal principles in voting. But if we go by the voting participation of both the rural and the urban population, it is significant and comparable to some developed democracies. The electoral politics and participation has indirectly also reinforced legal consciousness as a vital component of the civic culture.

Another positive social change which has taken place since independence is in the field of industrialization and growth of entrepreneurial classes and its subculture. No doubt, the commanding height of economic power continued to vest with the public sector industries almost till recently, but during the past five decades or so a sizeable middle class of small entrepreneurs, commercial classes, and professional groups has emerged in the urban centres, which together with the rural middle classes comprises one-fifth of the population roughly. The rise of this middle class is stablizing and at the same time a critical element in India's process of social change today. On the one hand it adds stability to the system, contributes to economic growth and mobility, offers employment opportunities, and makes use of public and private resources for development. On the other, this class also suffers from the cultural gauchery of the new rich, is less scrupulous about conformity to legal norms and established middle class values, and its demonstration effect on the social structure is acute and yet deviant. Its approach to the weaker sections is cynical and indifferent rather than cosmopolitan; it has therefore, the tendency to flout increasingly the norm of 'reconciliation' and 'consensus' as we analysed above. It is indicative of what is known as 'underdevelopment of development' process in India.

A positive direction of social changes has also been ushered in the field of science and technology and in technical manpower. The scientific manpower in the country is said to be the third largest in the world. Managerial skill and innovation and credibility in science and scientific ways have taken deep roots even in remote villages: But the hold of tradition and traditional thought has not declined. There is a precarious and often dialectical coexistence of the two in Indian society. The same holds for the nature of the legal profession. Studies in this area by sociologists show persistence of a large segment of traditional ties and non rational practices both in the structure of the profession as well as in its functioning and organization (*see* Gandhi 1982; Sharma 1982; Oommen 1983). The problem that the legal system now confronts is the product of the process of underdevelopment of certain sections of society in the wake of overall development and social change.

CONTRADICTIONS OF SOCIAL CHANGE AND THE LEGAL SYSTEM

The positive aspects of social changes in India discussed above have also generated substantial contradictions in the social system. The rise of the middle classes in villages and cities has led to hostile attitude of these towards the weaker sections and the poor. In villages the tensions between the Harijans and caste Hindus have increased, necessitating the passage of Civil Rights and Disabilities Act which makes derogatory reference to the scheduled caste status a cognizable offence. Exploitation of the labourers by rich peasants held under bondage through extension of loans has been held legally void, but there are evidences to its perpetuation. The Minimum Wages Act for labourers in the unorganized sector such as agriculture, small scale enterprises, and shops, etc., has been introduced but is not uniformly implemented. Similarly, the legal norms in respect of the vulnerable sections of society, the children, the prisoners, the undertrials, the women, inmates of rescue homes, the prostitutes, the slum dwellers and pavement dwellers, etc., either do not exist or where they exist their enforcement is rendered impossible by vested interests which are influential, resourceful, and powerful.

The developmental aspects of social change in India has given birth also to a new awakening among the scheduled castes and tribes, the poor working classes, and other weaker sections. Evaluation studies show that measures of social reform, economic and social upliftment of these groups taken by the state, mostly do not reach them. The places where such groups are sizeable or organized, it culminates into protest movements which are often an effective recourse for redressal of grievances. But wherever these sections are isolated and scattered, only voluntary social workers could come to their help, which quite often is inadequate or even rare.

The basic contradiction that legal system has to deal within India in the wake of the increasing social awareness of asymmetry of the developmental process, the gap between the rich and the poor, between the agricultural labourers and the rich peasants and similar other segments, is that of rendering it possible that instruments of legal protection, legal redressal, and legal bargain are made available to them. During the past quarter-century or so much awareness in this field has been created in India. A movement for 'legal aid' to the poor and the destitute undertrials has picked up. A government-appointed committee has given report on its modalities and implications. There has in addition been a significant response from the bar and the bench in this direction. The Supreme Court in India has allowed third-party petitions on matters of social concern by voluntary social workers and associations, and instituted investigations on this basis on several matters of legal aid and legal rights as a citizen. Until some years ago this would not have been possible. Nandita Haksar writes:

> Now a public spirited citizen, concerned lawyer or journalist or a democratic rights organisation can move the court on behalf of an oppressed or exploited person or group of persons. The court will recognise their *locus standi* (legal standing). This right was first recognised in the famous transfer of judges case and later elaborated in the Asiad case. This was in conformity with the trend in other parts of the world (the *Hindustan Times*, New Delhi, 22 May 1983).

Supreme Court judgments are binding for all courts of the land and the initiative of the Court in matters of social justice and social concern tends to set a new democratization process of justice in the country. It is reported that hundreds of letters now pour in courts for legal aid; these letters are addressed directly to the judges of the Supreme Court. The cases of the bonded workers in Haryana, of prisoners (undertrials) in Bihar, of inmates of womens rescue home in Delhi, of children in juvenile institutions, of the torture of ordinary Naga citizens by the army provide a wide spectrum of this new movement for legal aid. A new area of what is called public interest litigation has come into being in India today. It is run by public-spirited lawyers, professors of law, social workers, journalists, and public men. Several organizations for the protection of democratic rights have come into being. Considering the vastness of the country and the magnitude of the population needy for such legal protection this new development still touches only the fringe of the problem, but by undertaking selectively most critical issues of legal aid, this movement has already made a very significant impact.

The impediments that have been observed in the way of this movement is the indifference or sometimes even hostility of the executive and the political functionaries. There are many feudal elements in politics and the civil services, and it is necessary that some aspect of the legal aid movement is institutionalized by government support. As we mentioned, the democratic development in India is bound to throw up an upsurge of the rural and urban poor, and their protest movements are bound to grow (*see* Desai 1983). The 'civic revolution' as a model of social transformation would render it a logical necessity that law as an instrument of social change is held under continual review. More important than this, in the judicial processes and legal administration, the role of executives in proper implementation of the legal norms should not only be rendered more effective, but government efforts in this area should be linked with that of public efforts and enterprises.

REFERENCES

Daxi, Upendra, *The Crisis of the Indian Legal System*, New Delhi; Vikas Publishing House, 1982.

Cohn, B.S., 'From Indian Status to British Contract', *Journal of Economic History*, 21-613-618, 1961. 'Anthropological Notes on Disputes and Law in India', *American Anthropologist*, vol. 67, no. 6, 1965.

Desai, A.R., Sociology of the under-privileged, Inaugural address, 5th Sociological Conference, U.P., Kanpur, University Kanpur, 1983.

Haksar, Nandita, 'Justice For the Common Man', The *Hindustan Times*, New Delhi May 22, 1983.

Stokes, Eric, *The English Utilitarians and India*, Oxford: Oxford University Press, 1959.

21
Constitutions and Revolutions*

PETER G. SACK

The text of the Indian Constitution leaves not a single doubt: it constitutes, and constitutes only, the Indian State (as a Union of states)—and not Indian society or any other body of people. Indeed, it proclaims with unusual vigour in Article 1 that India is, first and foremost, a *territorial* state and gives throughout the issue of territorial integrity (and national unity) special prominence. The people of India—and the nation to be formed by them—play second fiddle and are, by and large, relegated to the Preamble. The body of the Constitution speaks instead of 'citizens', who are contrasted with 'persons' (who may or may not be citizens).

While this emphasis on the territorial rather than on the population aspect of the state is understandable in the light of India's historical position at the time the Constitution was drafted, its lasting consequences must be recognized clearly, since they make the Indian state constitutionally virtually independent of the Indian people. There is no constitutional recognition of the fact, which many would regard as essential for a democracy, that the powers of the state are originally the collective powers of the people which the state merely exercises on their behalf. Instead the Indian state is constituted primarily as a *government*; and although this government is arranged in accordance with the conventional doctrine of separation of powers, the executive is given pride of place. Like the God of the Old Testament, the Indian Constitution pronounces in Article 52: 'There shall be a President of India', and Article 53 vest the executive power of 'the Union'—not of the people of India—in this single person.

There is no need to detail the system or government the Indian Constitution establishes, but it is worth emphasizing its marked hierarchical

*Excerpted from Peter G. Sack, 'Constitutions and Revolutions', Thiruvananthapuram: The Academy of Legal Publications, 1990, pp. 17–35.

character which is all the more remarkable since the hierarchical character of Indian *society* is, as we shall see, the main target of the envisaged social revolution.

This may lead a cynic to observe that the underlying aim of the Constitution is not equality but the replacement of the old social hierarchy with a new political hierarchy. At any rate, it is now understandable why the principle or 'general adult suffrage'—the democratic electoral process—plays a crucial role in the Indian constitutional scheme, for it provides, intentionally or otherwise, the legitimation for the new hierarchical political order. It also heightens the suspicion that the Indian Constitution regards a hierarchical order as necessary for stable and effective government. Thus it becomes at least a welcome by-product of an anti-hierarchical social revolution that destroys the power base of an alternative social leadership structure which could challenge the monopoly which the Constitution confers on the state system.

Let me illustrate what I mean by the hierarchical structure of the system of Indian government. It begins, as we have seen, with the non-recognition of the Indian people as the source of state power. As far as the Constitution is concerned, the Indian state is born fully armed and its powers, at least its executive powers, are initially vested in a single head, in the president of India and not, for example, collectively in a national executive council of equals. Rather, the council of ministers which holds office 'during the pleasure of the president' (Article 75 [2]) and which is formally limited to an advisory role before the president is bound to heed its advice, is in turn to be *headed* by a prime minister (Article 74). The authority of the latter is further strengthened by making the council of ministers only *collectively* responsible to the House of the People (Article 75 [3])— since this merely removes the individual responsibility of ministers—and by making it the exclusive duty of the prime minister to advise the president of the decisions of the council of ministers (Article 78) which the latter appoints on the former's (binding) advice (Article 75 [1]).

In addition, while adopting the doctrine of separation of powers structurally—Chapter I of Part V dealing with the executive, Chapter II with Parliament, and Chapter IV with the judiciary of the Union—the Indian Constitution does not entrench this separation. On the contrary, the president becomes an integral part of Parliament (Article 79) and the vice-president the *ex officio* chairman of the Council of States (Article 89). Moreover, the president is given not only extensive powers of control over the two Houses of Parliament (Article 85) but also legislative powers of his own (Article 123)—whereas the legislative powers of the two Houses are rather taken for granted (*see* Article 107), although Article 73 defines the extent of the executive powers of the Union initially by reference to the legislative power of Parliament. Even the separation of the judiciary from the executive ranks in the Constitution only as a 'Directive Principle of State Policy' (*see* Article 50).

Furthermore, each segment of this executive-dominated structure is hierarchically organized: each state of the Union is headed by a governor (Article 153); the judicial system is headed by the Chief Justice of the Supreme Court (Article 124); and the Attorney General (Article 76) as well as the Comptroller and Auditor General (Article 148) are single persons whose military designation indicates that they are generals commanding armies of underlings rather than being personally charged with carrying out a 'generality' of functions.

How does the Indian Constitution approach Indian society and its revolution? Understandably, it does not guarantee the existing social structure—and this includes the family which many other Constitutions protect as the basic unit of society. But neither does the Constitution abolish this structure nor does it say with what kind of structure it is to be replaced.

This lack of determination has, I suggest, two main reasons: firstly, because we are moving into an extremely sensitive area, and, secondly, because Indian society became a conveniently blank spot in the vision of India enshrined in the Constitution. Indian society is so overshadowed by the Indian state on the one hand and the individual Indian citizen on the other, that it remained a frightening shadow. Instead of being seen as a vital source of India's strength, the Constitution regards it as an enemy who needs to be disarmed and dismantled—despite the knowledge that India's future depends on its well-being. Thus the Indian Constitution does not provide a positive charter for a fundamental social revolution, which replaces one social structure with another, better one, but embarks on a hesitant social clear-felling exercise which, if carried through to its logical conclusion, would bring about the total destruction of Indian society in any form.

What evidence do I have for this outrageous and, some may say, sacrilegious claim?

Let us first consider the Preamble of the Constitution. At a first glance it appears to be essentially a restatement of the three central goals of the French Revolution: liberty, equality, and fraternity. However, to these a fourth overarching goal—'Justice, social, economic and political'—is added, moving the state, as the provider and guarantor of justice, into the centre of the stage. Furthermore, fraternity, the only truly 'social' of the three conventional revolutionary goals, is separated from the other two and given a different, subordinate role to play.

While justice, liberty, and equality are to be *secured* to all Indian citizens *individually*—obviously by the state—fraternity is merely to be *promoted* (again by the state) *among* them. Even here the purpose is no longer *social*, for fraternity is to be promoted to assure 'the dignity of the individual and the unity and integrity of the Nation'. This implies not only that the Constitution is concerned with the nation state and its relations with its individual citizens, rather than with society, but also that the constitution makers saw the existing social system as decidedly 'unbrotherly', in the sense of being contrary to the dignity of the individual and politically divisive, hence the stress on the need for *social* justice and the equality of *status* which, in the context, can only mean *social* status.

The picture of Indian society conveyed by the Preamble is therefore negative indeed. 'Traditional' society is presented as a millstone weighing down the neck of the new nation state. But although it is the task of the state to secure henceforth social justice and equality—and, of course, to defend national unity and integrity—it can, unfortunately, do no more than to promote the essential feeling of brotherhood among its citizens; and we should take particular note of the implied acknowledgement that the creation of fraternity, in contrast to liberty and equality, is, in principle, beyond the capacity of the state.

It is, under these circumstances, not surprising that the Indian Constitution, unlike other constitutions of former colonies on attainment of independent, does not link the new nation state with its pre-colonial past. Independent India was not to be built on its own historical foundations, although it was made the duty of the state to protect physical remains of artistic or historic interest, provided that they had been declared by the state to be of national importance (Article 49). The Indian Constitution does not consider independence as a long-fought-for opportunity to sweep away unwelcome colonial impositions, but as a chance to liberate India, more radically than its former colonial masters chose or dared to do, from its own surviving traditions.

This was expressed with admirable frankness at the time. Santhanam, for example, wrote in 1946 that a social revolution was required to get India 'out of the medievalism based on birth, religion, custom, and community and reconstruct her social structure on modern foundations of law, individual merit, and secular education' (quoted in Austin 1966: 26). In other words the desired social revolution demanded nothing less than the *total* destruction and reconstruction of Indian society. But how was this to be achieved, and what shape was the new social structure to take

quite apart from the question as to how Santhanam's dynamic meritocracy can be reconciled with the apparently also imported ideas of equality
and fraternity?

There is no question that the central value system which the Indian
Constitution embodies is to be individualistic and rationalistic. The Individual was to be liberated from superstition as well as from 'community'.

What need or room was there, in this struggle, for a new social structure? From now on all Indians were going to become brothers rather than
fathers and mothers, parents and children, husbands and wives, brothers and sisters, younger and older brothers, daughters-in-law and uncles,
members of different villages, castes, tribes, religions, language groups,
professional groups, political parties, unions, sports clubs, youth organizations and so forth.

It is a tragedy that brotherhood, this most of lovable and elusive of all
human ideals, is once more used by the Indian Constitution as an alibi
for shirking away from the crucial task of all constitution makers: to work
pragmatically but committedly for a newer ideal but improved human
society. Fraternity is no surrogate for social structure and cohesion but,
seen in splendid isolation, it creates the dangerous but serviceable illusion
of a social vacuum which must be filled by an increasingly powerful state
machinery charged with the performance of impossible tasks.

This, I am sad to say, is not a cautionary tale but a direct reflection of
Article 38 of the Indian Constitution, the first Directive Principle of State
Policy. Instead of an Indian society there is to be a social *order* defined and
maintained by the state. Social institutions give way to institutions of
national life (that is governmental bodies) which are to *eliminate* social
inequalities and to promote the welfare of the people as individuals.

However, the Constitution, as a product of political accommodation
and consensus could not advocate or engage in full-scale social slaughter.
But before turning to the patchwork quilt of elimination and conservation it offers, we need to consider another aspect of Article 38: its reference
to 'justice, social, economic and political'. This reference, linking Article
38 directly with the Preamble, strongly suggests that the Constitution
perceived the social revolution as part of a revolutionary package deal
which encompassed the political sector and the economy as much as
society and for which the political and economic revolutions provided the
positive impetus that the social revolution by itself was lacking.

Yet, the constitution makers were collectively convinced that even
these economic revolutions could not be given first priority. As Austin
summed up the attitude of the Constituent Assembly:

. . . any thought of social betterment for the nation would be mere romantic nonsense if the requisite conditions did not exist in the country. If the country were not united, if the government were not stable, if the government lacked the cooperation or the acquiescence [!] of the people, there could be no economic progress and no government initiative [!] for social change.

Despite this neat reversal of the priorities later expressed in the Constitution, Austin insists that the Constituent Assembly was basically concerned to decide whether it should turn to the European or Indian political tradition in order best to arrive at the goal of social revolution. Moreover, Austin concludes that the Assembly not only settled for a democratic, centralized, parliamentary constitution in the European tradition to achieve the objective of social revolution, but also that 'the ideal of reformed village life would be central to the programme for the modernization of Indian society'. He ends his laudation of Indians and their Constitution by stressing again that it was inter alia a sense of 'their rich cultural heritage' which permitted Indians to muster the national maturity for the creation and working of government, thus not defaulting 'their tryst with destiny'.

Austin is hard put when it comes to identifying concretely the original *Indian* contribution to the Constitution and its making. He settles for the related, procedural factors of 'consensus' and 'accommodation', just as sympathetic Western observers have pointed to 'consensus' and to the 'willingness to compromise' when trying to show the significant contribution of, for example, Melanesian culture to the independence constitutions in that part of the world, thus demonstrating that a consensual approach to politics, insofar as it exists anywhere, is no more typically Indian—or Melanesian—than, for instance, individualism or the concern for justice is a prerogative of the West. Besides, Austin casually balances these positive cliches with a far more telling negative one.

According to him it has been the greatest success of the Indian Constitution that it

> has provided a framework for social and political development, a rational, institutional basis for political behaviour. It establishes not only the national ideals, more importantly it lays down the rational, institutional manner by which they are to be pursued—a gigantic step for a people previously committed largely to irrational means of achieving other-worldly goals.

So much for the genius of the Indian people. So much also for the Indian Constitution as a charter for a fundamental revolution, social or otherwise. Leaving the red herring of rationality and irrationality aside, the

Indian Constitution is, according to Austin's praise at best the end and not the beginning for any kind of fundamental revolution. It replaces whatever revolutionary change may have previously occurred with a firm institutional framework within which social and political *development* are henceforth to be pursued in a prescribed manner. It makes—and quite legitimately so—a social revolution unconstitutional and therefore illegal. Liberty means from then on, as proclaimed in the Preamble, only the liberty 'of thought, expression, belief, faith and worship' and not freedom of social, much less political action. In addition to establishing the national ideals and providing an institutional basis for government action the Constitution establishes a *normative* order which the state is committed to defend against its own citizens.

Let us return to the part the social revolution was to play within this scheme of things. According to Austin, the starting point of the Constituent Assembly was almost as extreme and negative as that of Santhanam: the task was to free 'the mass of Indians from centuries of mental and psychological stagnation and passivity' and this required a 'fundamental alteration in the structure of Indian society'. Nonetheless, the route by which this goal had to be pursued looked very different. It was not seen as a process of total demolition and reconstruction—which apparently involved, for Santhanam, 'religion' and 'community' as well as 'birth' and 'custom'. Instead, the social revolution was submerged in the economic and political revolutions. Economic progress [says Austin apodictically]—making available to the masses better food, clothing and shelter—was itself, of course, an objective of the social revolution. Moreover, as a 'prerequisite' it was also a 'means' for carrying through the social revolution; but it was by itself not sufficient, not even combined with 'national unity' and 'governmental stability'. What was required was not *social* but rather *political* reform. The introduction of democratic government on the basis of adult suffrage was to become 'the pillar of the social revolution' because it would bring 'enlightenment and will promote the standard of life, the comfort, and the decent living of the common man'. K.M. Panikkar claimed, the whole Constitution was 'a solemn promise to the people of India that the legislature will do everything possible to renovate and rebuild society on new principles'.

This seems to place the responsibility for the social revolution squarely on the shoulders of India's parliamentarians—but they were to be elected by the common man. On the other hand, it was the Constitution which turned the social revolution into a *legislative* exercise and which therefore had to lay down the 'new principles' which were to guide the legislators.

We all know that these new principles are to be found in Part IV of the Constitution (the 'Directive Principles of State Policy'), but that Part IV needs to be considered together with Part III (the 'Fundamental Rights') and Part IVA (the 'Fundamental Duties').

Before examining the content of these provisions in relation to the envisaged social revolution, we need to appreciate their legal design.

Part IV constructs the Directive Principles as duties of the state which are non-justiciable, that is to say not enforceable by any court of law, and it charges the state in particular, to apply these principles in making laws (Article 38).

Similarly, the Fundamental Duties which Article 51A lays down for every citizen of India are by themselves non-justiciable.

The construction of Part III is more complex. It is, as its heading indicates, primarily concerned with the fundamental *rights* of individuals, in particular Indian citizens, but it also protects the rights of certain groups or bodies, especially minorities, and it also establishes *duties* not only for the state but also for the public in general. In addition, it includes straightforward prohibitions and abolitions.

I shall later return to this 'legalistic' rights/duties terminology. In this overview it is sufficient to say that the Indian Constitution is strongly committed to it. How is it applied as far as the social revolution is concerned?

We have already discussed the central Article 38 which, I suggested, expresses a basically negative attitude towards the existing social structures—and understandably so—since otherwise there would be no need for a fundamental social revolution. Article 51A, inserted in the Constitution in 1976, confirms this negativity by reviving the fraternity theme and making it the duty of every Indian citizen 'to promote harmony and the spirit of common brotherhood amongst all the people of India transcending religious, linguistic and regional or sectional diversities . . .' which is, somewhat incongruously, followed by the duty to value and preserve the rich heritage of our composite culture.

Here the stress is on the divisive nature of Indian society rather than on its hierarchical character as in Article 38. But while the Constitution exhorts Indian citizens to transcend these divisions in a spirit of brotherhood, it stops again short of abolishing their root causes. On the contrary, it guarantees, for example, in Articles 25 and 26, the individual right 'freely to profess, practice and propagate religion' and the collective right of 'every religious denomination and any section thereof' freely to manage its religious affairs.

Similarly, Article 29 guarantees 'any section' of Indian citizens having a distinct language, script, or culture the right to conserve the same. Furthermore, Article 30 gives religious and linguistic minorities the right to establish and administer educational institutions of their choice. On the other hand it must be emphasized that Article 25 (2) (b) distinguishes between protected *religious* practices and unprotected *secular* activities associated with them and that it declares specifically, and independently from that distinction, that the right to freedom of religion did not prevent the state from enacting, inter alia, social reform legislation.

The attitude of the Constitution to the hierarchical divisions of Indian society is different. There was no need and certainly, no desire to protect, for example, the caste system, its most pronounced expression, but nor was it abolished—although 'untouchability' is 'outlawed' in Article 17. Instead the Constitution uses the 'discrimination device'. Article 15 (1) makes it a duty of the state not to discriminate against any citizen 'on the grounds only of religion, race, caste, sex, place of birth or any of them'. Subsection (2) extends the discrimination prohibition, broadly speaking, to the public domain as a whole, whereas Subsections (3) and (4) grant the state the right to discriminate positively in favour of women, children, socially and educationally backward classes, or scheduled castes and scheduled tribes.

The details of these provisions need not detain us, but we must appreciate the general scheme which ranges from the abolition of 'untouchability' over the general discrimination prohibition—and the possibility of selective positive discrimination in favour of disadvantaged groups—to the protection of religious freedom and the rights of cultural minorities, permitting the state in the former case to limit the rights in the interests of social reform.

Despite this wide scope the Constitution appears to leave the basic social structures of Indian society virtually untouched, although it could be argued—at least theoretically—that by virtue of Article 13 (1) and (3) all law, including all customs and usages having the force of law, did become automatically void insofar as they contravened the discrimination prohibition in Subsection (2).

This does not mean that paper tigers cannot be given teeth or that a great deal more could have been achieved by using the existing constitutional weapons more effectively, but it seems to me essential for Indians today to appreciate that the Constitution does not provide a charter for any kind of constructive social revolution and that it may—in the light of this precedent—be unrealistic and misguided to expect any Constitution to provide such a charter or to expect any form of state government to put it into effect. In other words, if Indians, are as serious now about a fundamental social revolution as the constitution makers were forty years ago, it simply will not do to blame either the Constitution or their current political leaders: they have, just as they had forty years ago, without realizing it, no choice but to bring it about themselves, individually and collectively.

This involves, of course, a revolutionary change of approach from that adopted by the Constitution but this, I submit, would be perfectly in accord with its spirit. It also does not imply a dismissal of the efforts of the constitution makers; it simply recognizes that the position in the late 1940s, in India and elsewhere, was vastly different, intellectually and materially, from that of the 1980s. India's Constitution has now been in operation for over five decades, the Indian experience can now be compared with that of many other former Western colonies, and we all have, or should have, learned a great deal about the persistence of social structures, about the relations between law and social change, about the dangers of technological progress, about the limits of economic growth and many other pertinent issues.

It is inconceivable that if it was being drafted today, the Indian Constitution would incorporate as pathetic a provision as Article 40 which directs the state to 'take steps to organise village panchayats and endow them with such powers and authority as may be necessary to enable them to function as units of self-government — in the genuine belief that this would set in train a development leading to a realization of the ideal of reformed village life which was, according to Austin, central to the programme for the modernization of Indian society; just as it is inconceivable that Austin could have written his study 20 years later, or that Upendra Baxi would have reviewed it as he did in 1967.

Tempora mutantur et nos mutamur in ilis—the times change and we change with them—the question is to what extent we can influence the direction, the speed, and the breadth and depth of this change.

Contributors

Upendra Baxi is Professor, School of Law, University of Warwick and former Vice Chancellor, University of Delhi.

J. Duncan Derret is Emeritus Professor of Oriental Law, University of London.

V.R. Krishna Iyer is retired Judge of the Supreme Court of India.

Krishna Kumar is the Director of National Council of Educational Research and Training.

J.S. Gandhi is Former Professor, Centre for the Study of Social Systems, Jawaharlal Nehru University.

Samuel Schmitthener served as a missionary in India.

K.L. Sharma is Professor, Centre for the Study of Social Systems, Jawaharlal Nehru University.

Charles Morrison is former Professor of Anthropology, Michigan State University.

Donald Eugene Smith is Emeritus Professor, Department of South Asia Studies, University of Pennsylvania.

John H. Mansfield is John H. Watson, Jr Professor of Law, Harvard Law School.

Dieter Conrad (1932–2001).

Kavita Khory is Associate Professor of Politics, Mount Holyoke College, MA.

Marc Galanter is John and Rylla Bosshard Professor of Law and Professor of South Asian Studies. University of Wisconsin Law School.

M.P. Singh is Professor, Faculty of Law, University of Delhi.

Ram Jethmalani is Senior Advocate at the Supreme Court of India.

S.P. Sathe is Professor and Honorary Director, Institute of Advanced Legal Studies, Pune.

Mahabaleswar N. Morje is Advocate, Mumbai High Court and Former Professor of Law, University of Mumbai.

Indra Deva is Professor Emeritus, Department of Sociology, Pt. Ravishankar Shukla University, Raipur, Chattisgarh.

Shrirama (1938–2005).

Yogendra Singh is Former Professor of Sociology, Centre for the Study of Social Systems, Jawaharlal Nehru University.

Peter G. Sack is Former Senior Fellow, Research School of Social Sciences, Australian National University, Canberra.

Index